FUTURE 4

English for Work, Life, and Academic Success

Second Edition

Series Consultants
Sarah Lynn
Ronna Magy
Federico Salas-Isnardi

Authors
Jane Curtis
with Ingrid Greenberg,
Hilary Hodge,
Julie Schmidt,
and Geneva Tesh

Pearson

Future 4
English for Work, Life, and Academic Success

Pearson Education, 221 River Street, Hoboken, NJ 07030 USA

Staff credits: The people who made up the ***Future*** team, representing content development, design, manufacturing, marketing, multimedia, project management, publishing, rights management, and testing, are Pietro Alongi, Jennifer Castro, Dave Dickey, Gina DiLillo, Warren Fischbach, Pamela Fishman, Gosia Jaros-White, Joanna Konieczna, Michael Mone, Mary Perrotta Rich, Katarzyna Starzyńska-Kościuszko, Claire Van Poperin, Joseph Vella, Gabby Wu

Text composition: ElectraGraphics, Inc.
Cover Design: EMC Design Ltd
Illustration credits: See Credits page 286.
Photo credits: See Credits page 286.
Audio: CityVox
Development: Blue Crab Editorial Services

Library of Congress Cataloging-in-Publication Data
A catalog record for the print edition is available from the Library of Congress.

ISBN-13: 9780135278345 (Student Book with App and MyEnglish Lab)
ISBN-10: 0135278341(Student Book with App and MyEnglish Lab)

ISBN-13: 9780134858500 (Student Book with App)
ISBN-10: 0134858506 (Student Book with App)

www.pearsoneltusa.com/future2e

CONTENTS

TO THE TEACHER

Welcome to *Future: English for Work, Life, and Academic Success*

Future is a six-level, standards-based English language course for adult and young adult students. *Future* provides students with the contextualized academic language, strategies, and critical thinking skills needed for success in workplace, life, and academic settings. *Future* is aligned with the requirements of the Workforce Innovation and Opportunity Act (WIOA), the English Language Proficiency (ELP) and College and Career Readiness (CCR) standards, and the National Reporting System (NRS) level descriptors. The 21st-century curriculum in *Future*'s second edition helps students acquire the basic literacy, language, and employability skills needed to meet the requirements set by the standards.

Future develops students' academic and critical thinking skills, digital literacy and numeracy, and workplace and civic skills, and it prepares students for taking standardized tests. Competency and skills incorporating standards are in the curriculum at every level, providing a foundation for academic rigor, research-based teaching strategies, corpus-informed language, and the best of digital tools.

In revising the course, we listened to hundreds of *Future* teachers and learners and studied the standards for guidance. *Future* continues to be the most comprehensive English communication course for adults, with its signature scaffolded lessons and multiple practice activities throughout. *Future's* second edition provides enhanced content, rigorous academic language practice, and cooperative learning through individual and collaborative practice. Every lesson teaches the interpretive, interactive, and productive skills highlighted in the standards.

Future's Instructional Design

Learner Centered and Outcome Oriented

The student is at the center of *Future.* Lessons start by connecting to student experience and knowledge, and then present targeted skills in meaningful contexts. Varied and dynamic skill practice progresses from controlled to independent in a meticulously scaffolded sequence.

Headers highlighting Depth of Knowledge (DOK) terms are used throughout *Future* to illuminate the skills being practiced. Every lesson culminates in an activity in which students apply their learning, demonstrate their knowledge, and express themselves orally or in writing. A DOK glossary for teachers includes specific suggestions on how to help students activate these cognitive skills.

Varied Practice

Cognitive science has proven what *Future* always knew: Students learn new skills through varied practice over time. Content-rich units that contextualize academic and employability skills naturally recycle concepts, language, and targeted skills. Individual and collaborative practice activities engage learners and lead to lasting outcomes. Lessons support both student collaboration and individual self-mastery. Students develop the interpretative, productive, and interactive skills identified in the NRS guidelines, while using the four language skills of reading, writing, listening, and speaking.

Goal Setting and Learning Assessment

For optimal learning to take place, students need to be involved in setting goals and in monitoring their own progress. *Future* addresses goal setting in numerous ways. In the Student Book, Unit Goals are identified on the unit opener page. Checkboxes at the end of lessons invite students to evaluate their mastery of the material, and suggest additional online practice.

High-quality assessment aligned to the standards checks student progress and helps students prepare to take standardized tests. The course-based assessment program is available in print and digital formats and includes a bank of customizable test items. Digital tests are assigned by the teacher and reported back in the LMS online gradebook. All levels include a midterm and final test. Test items are aligned with unit learning objectives and standards. The course Placement Test is available in print and digital formats. Test-prep materials are also provided for specific standardized tests.

One Integrated Program

Future provides everything adult English language learners need in one integrated program using the latest digital tools and time-tested print resources.

Integrated Skills Contextualized with Rich Content

Future contextualizes grammar, listening, speaking, pronunciation, reading, writing, and vocabulary in meaningful activities that simulate real workplace, educational, and community settings. A special lesson at the end of each unit highlights soft skills at work. While providing relevant content, *Future* helps build learner knowledge and equips adults for their many roles.

Meeting Work, Life, and Education Goals

Future recognizes that every adult learner brings a unique set of work, life, and academic experiences, as well as a distinct skill set. With its diverse array of print and digital resources, *Future* provides learners with multiple opportunities to practice with contextualized materials to build skill mastery. Specialized lessons for academic and workplace skill development are part of *Future*'s broad array of print and digital resources.

In addition to two units on employment in each level, every unit contains a Workplace, Life, and Community Skills lesson as well as a Soft Skills at Work lesson.

Workplace, Life, and Community Skills Lessons

In the second edition, the Life Skills lesson has been revised to focus on workplace, life, and community skills and to develop the real-life language and civic literacy skills required today. Lessons integrate and contextualize workplace content. In addition, every lesson includes practice with digital skills on a mobile device.

Soft Skills at Work Lessons

Future has further enhanced its development of workplace skills by adding a Soft Skills at Work lesson to each unit. Soft skills are the critical interpersonal communication skills needed to succeed in any workplace. Students begin each lesson by discussing a common challenge in the workplace. Then, while applying the lesson-focused soft skill, they work collaboratively to find socially appropriate solutions to the problem. The log at the back of the Student Book encourages students to track their own application of the soft skill, which they can use in job interviews.

Academic Rigor

Rigor and respect for the ability and experiences of the adult learner have always been central to *Future.* The standards provide the foundation for academic rigor. The reading, writing, listening, and speaking practice require learners to analyze, use context clues, interpret, cite evidence, build knowledge, support a claim, and summarize from a variety of text formats. Regular practice with complex and content-rich materials develops academic language and builds knowledge. Interactive activities allow for collaboration and exchange of ideas in workplace and in academic contexts. *Future* emphasizes rigor by highlighting the critical-thinking and problem-solving skills required in each activity.

Writing Lessons

In addition to the increased focus on writing in Show What You Know! activities, *Future* has added a cumulative writing lesson to every unit, a lesson that requires students to synthesize and apply their learning in a written outcome. Through a highly scaffolded approach, students begin by analyzing writing models before planning and finally producing written work of their own. Writing frameworks, Writing Skills, and a checklist help guide students through the writing process.

Reading lessons

All reading lessons have new, information-rich texts and a revised pedagogical approach in line with the CCR and ELP standards and the NRS descriptors. These informational texts are level appropriate, use high-frequency vocabulary, and focus on interpretation of graphic information. The readings build students' knowledge and develop their higher-order reading skills by teaching citation of evidence, summarizing, and interpretation of complex information from a variety of text formats.

Future Grows with Your Student

Future takes learners from absolute beginner level through low-advanced English proficiency, addressing students' abilities and learning priorities at each level. As the levels progress, the curricular content and unit structure change accordingly, with the upper levels incorporating more advanced academic language and skills in the text and in the readings.

Future Intro	Future Level 1	Future Level 2	Future Level 3	Future Level 4	Future Advanced
NRS Beginning ESL Literacy	NRS Low Beginning ESL	NRS High Beginning ESL	NRS Low Intermediate ESL	NRS High Intermediate ESL	NRS Advanced ESL
ELPS Level 1	**ELPS** Level 1	**ELPS** Level 2	**ELPS** Level 3	**ELPS** Level 4	**ELPS** Level 5
CCRS Level A	**CCRS** Level A	**CCRS** Level A	**CCRS** Level B	**CCRS** Level C	**CCRS** Level D
CASAS 180 and below	**CASAS** 181–190	**CASAS** 191–200	**CASAS** 201–210	**CASAS** 211–220	**CASAS** 221–235

TO THE TEACHER

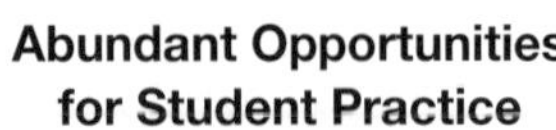

Abundant Opportunities for Student Practice

Student

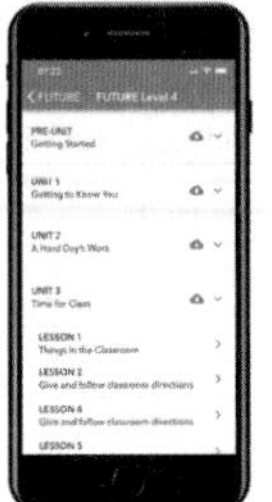

The **Pearson Practice English App** provides easy mobile access to all of the audio files, plus Grammar Coach videos and activities. Listen and study on the go—anywhere, any time!

Student books are a complete student resource, including lessons in grammar, listening and speaking, pronunciation, reading, writing, vocabulary, and Soft Skills at Work, taught and practiced in contextual activities.

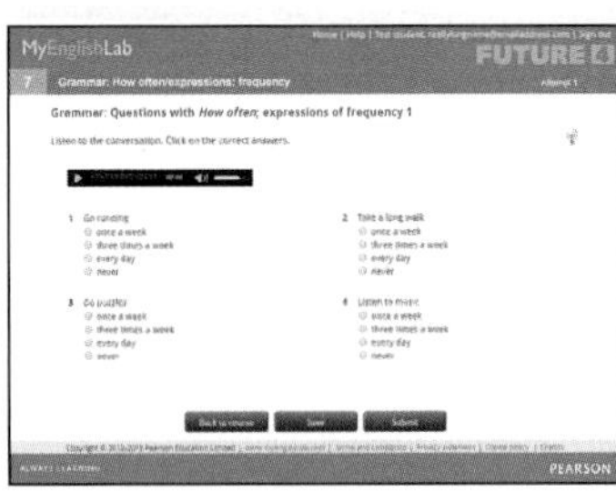

MyEnglishLab allows online independent self study and interactive practice in pronunciation, grammar, vocabulary, reading, writing, and listening. The MEL includes the popular Grammar Coach videos and new Pronunciation Coach videos and activities.

Workbook—with audio—provides additional practice for each lesson in the student book, with new readings and practice in writing, grammar, listening and speaking, plus activities for new Soft Skills at Work lessons.

Outstanding Teacher Resources

Teacher

Teacher Edition and Lesson Planner includes culture notes, teaching tips, and numerous optional and extension activities, with lesson-by-lesson correlations to CCR and ELP standards. Rubrics are provided for evaluation of students, written and oral communication.

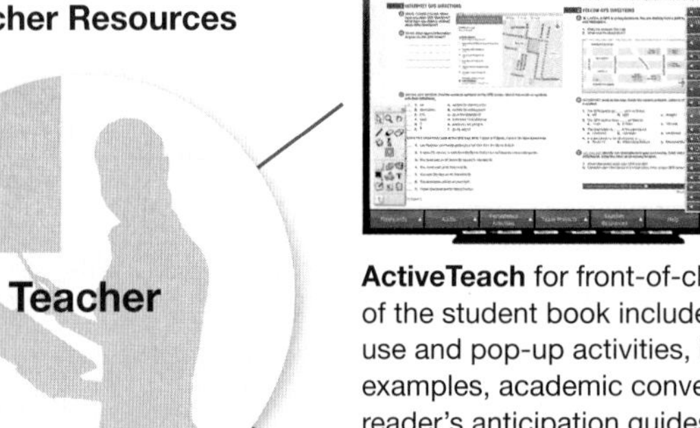

ActiveTeach for front-of-classroom projection of the student book includes audio at point of use and pop-up activities, including grammar examples, academic conversation stems, and reader's anticipation guides.

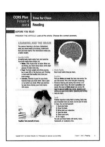

College and Career Readiness Plus Lessons supplement the student book with challenging reading and writing lessons for every level above Intro.

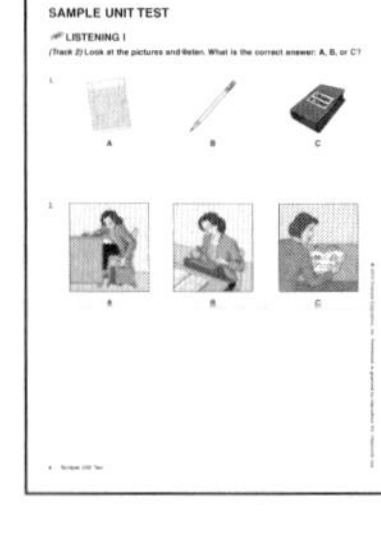

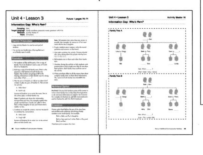

The **Assessment Program**, accessed online with interactive and printable tests and rubrics, includes a Placement Test; unit, midterm, and final exams; and computer-based ExamView with additional ready-to-use and customizable tests. In addition, sample high-stakes test practice is included with CASAS test prep for listening and reading.

Multilevel Communicative Activities provide an array of reproducible communication activities and games that engage students through different modalities. Teachers' notes provide multilevel options for pre-level and above-level students, as well as extension activities for additional speaking and writing practice.

Go to the Teacher website for easy reference, correlations to federal and state standards, and course updates. www.pearsonelt.com/future2e

Preview questions activate student background knowledge and help the teacher assess how much students know about the unit theme.

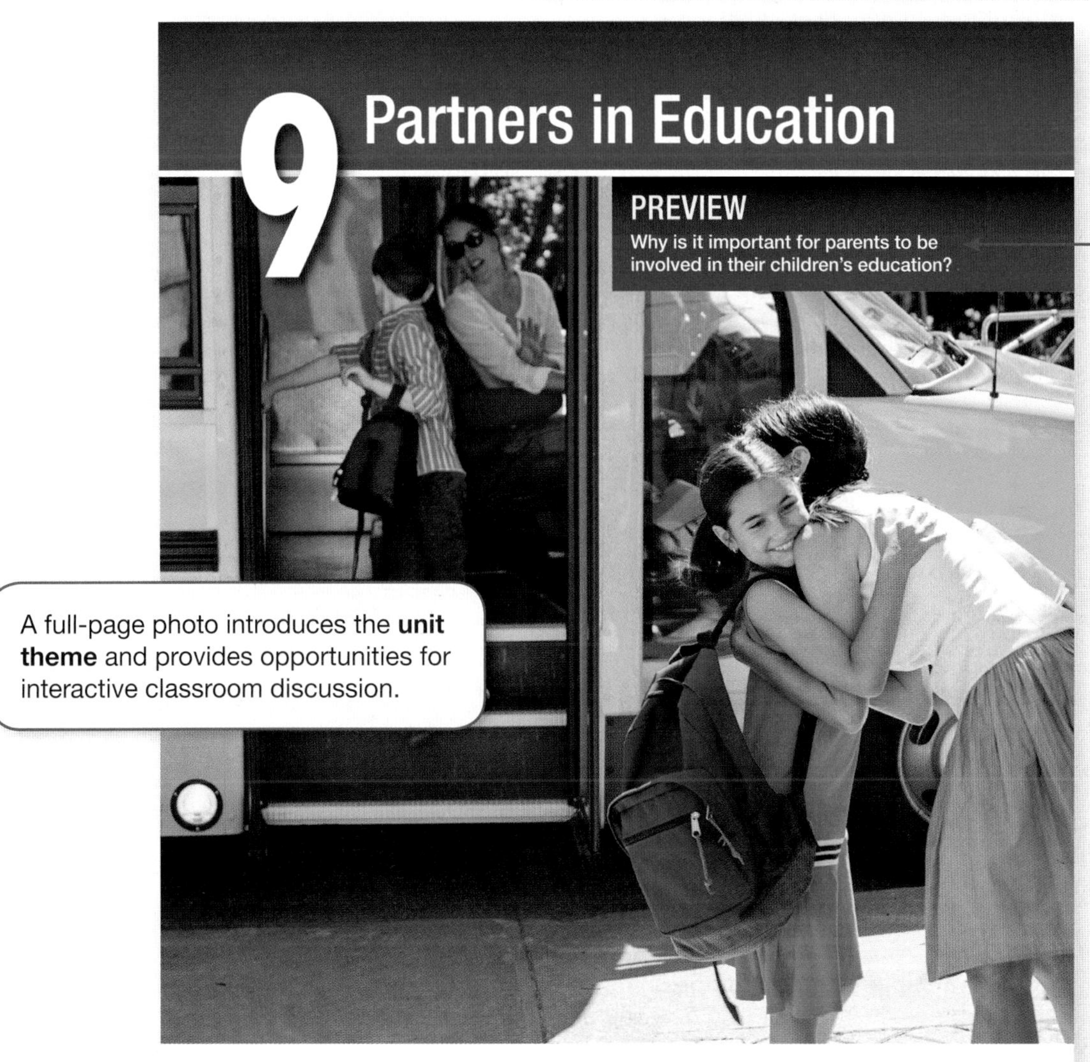

9 Partners in Education
PREVIEW
Why is it important for parents to be involved in their children's education?

A full-page photo introduces the **unit theme** and provides opportunities for interactive classroom discussion.

UNIT GOALS

- ☐ Discuss a student's progress
- ☐ Interpret and respond to a report card
- ☐ Talk with school personnel
- ☐ Discuss school safety
- ☐ Write a letter to the editor
- ☐ **Academic skill:** Distinguish fact from opinion
- ☐ **Writing skill:** Use paragraph structure
- ☐ **Workplace soft skill:** Manage time well

165

Unit goals introduce the competencies taught in the unit and allow students to track and reflect on their progress.

UNIT TOUR

Three **Listening and Speaking** lessons provide students opportunities for realistic conversations in work, community, and educational settings.

Pronunciation activities help students learn, practice, and internalize the patterns of spoken English and relate them to their own lives.

Listening and Speaking

Discuss a student's progress

1 BEFORE YOU LISTEN

A **INTERPRET. The word *grade* has two meanings. What does it mean in each of these sentences?**

1. My daughter is in the second **grade**.
2. Her **grade** on the spelling test was an A.

B **MAKE CONNECTIONS. In many places in the U.S., the school system has three levels: elementary school, middle school, and high school. How are the schools organized where you live?**

2 LISTEN

Mrs. Patel is talking to the guidance counselor at her children's school.

A **LISTEN FOR MAIN IDEA. Listen to the first part of the conversation. What is the purpose of the appointment? Circle the answer.**

The guidance counselor made the appointment with Mrs. Patel because _______________.

a. her son is having some problems with his grades
b. her son will start high school this fall
c. he wants her daughter to be a better student
d. he wants to help her daughter go to college

B **PREDICT. Why does the guidance counselor think Monika should start thinking about college before starting high school?**

C **LISTEN FOR DETAILS. Listen to the whole conversation. Write *T* (true) or *F* (false). Correct the false statements.**

__F__ 1. Monika is ~~already~~ not making plans to go to college.
____ 2. Monika might be able to get a scholarship to go to college.
____ 3. Mrs. Patel doesn't want her daughter to go to college.
____ 4. There are special classes to help students prepare for college.
____ 5. Mrs. Patel will bring her husband on her next visit to the guidance office.

D **ANALYZE. Was your prediction about the guidance counselor's reason for starting to think about college correct? What did the counselor mean when he said, "Yes and no" to the statement that college was a long way off?**

166 Unit 9, Lesson 1

Listening and Speaking

3 PRONUNCIATION

A **PRACTICE. Listen. Then listen again and repeat.**

A: Her daughter has problems with her **grades**.
B: No, her son has problems with his grades.

A: Her daughter is sixteen years **old**.
B: No, her daughter is thirteen years old.

Highlighting information

Use stress to highlight information that is new or different. This information is often the last important word in a clause or sentence. To correct or disagree with something, highlight the information that is different.

B **APPLY. Listen. Put a dot (•) over the stressed words in each pair of sentences.**

1. A: John's science teacher assigns too much homework.
   B: No, his math teacher assigns too much homework.
2. A: The elementary school is having an open house.
   B: No, the middle school is having an open house.
3. A: The school nurse left us a message.
   B: No, the school counselor left a message.

4 CONVERSATION

Mrs. Patel is now talking to one of her son's teachers.

A **LISTEN AND READ. Then practice the conversation with a partner.**

Teacher: I'm so glad you could come to talk about your son. I'm Mr. Manning, Robert's math teacher.
Mrs. Patel: It's nice to meet you. Robert says he's having some problems with math.
Teacher: Well, Robert is a great kid, and he seems to enjoy the class. But, yes, I think he needs a little help.
Mrs. Patel: I saw his last test. He got a 70. I think it was because he didn't study enough.
Teacher: That's possible. Since he's having some trouble, it would be good for Robert to have a tutor.
Mrs. Patel: That sounds like a good idea. Will it be expensive?
Teacher: No! We have a free after-school program. Students help each other. It's peer tutoring.

B **DEFINE. What is a parent-teacher conference? What is Parent-Teacher Night?**

____

____

C **PRESENT. Describe an experience you have had talking to teachers or other school personnel—either for your child or for yourself.**

I can discuss a student's progress. ☐ I need more practice. ☐

For more practice, go to MyEnglishLab.

Unit 9, Lesson 1 167

Conversations carefully scaffold student learning and build language fluency.

Multiple listening opportunities progress from listening for general understanding, to listening for details, to listening to an extended version of the conversation.

Checkpoints at the end of lessons provide students an opportunity to reflect on their progress and identify further resources for more practice.

Before You Listen activities let students make connections between the topic and their own experience.

Each unit presents three **Grammar** lessons in a systematic grammar progression. Every Grammar lesson focuses on language introduced in the preceding Listening and Speaking lesson. Additional grammar practice is available in the Grammar Review and online.

Real-life examples provide context for meaningful grammar practice.

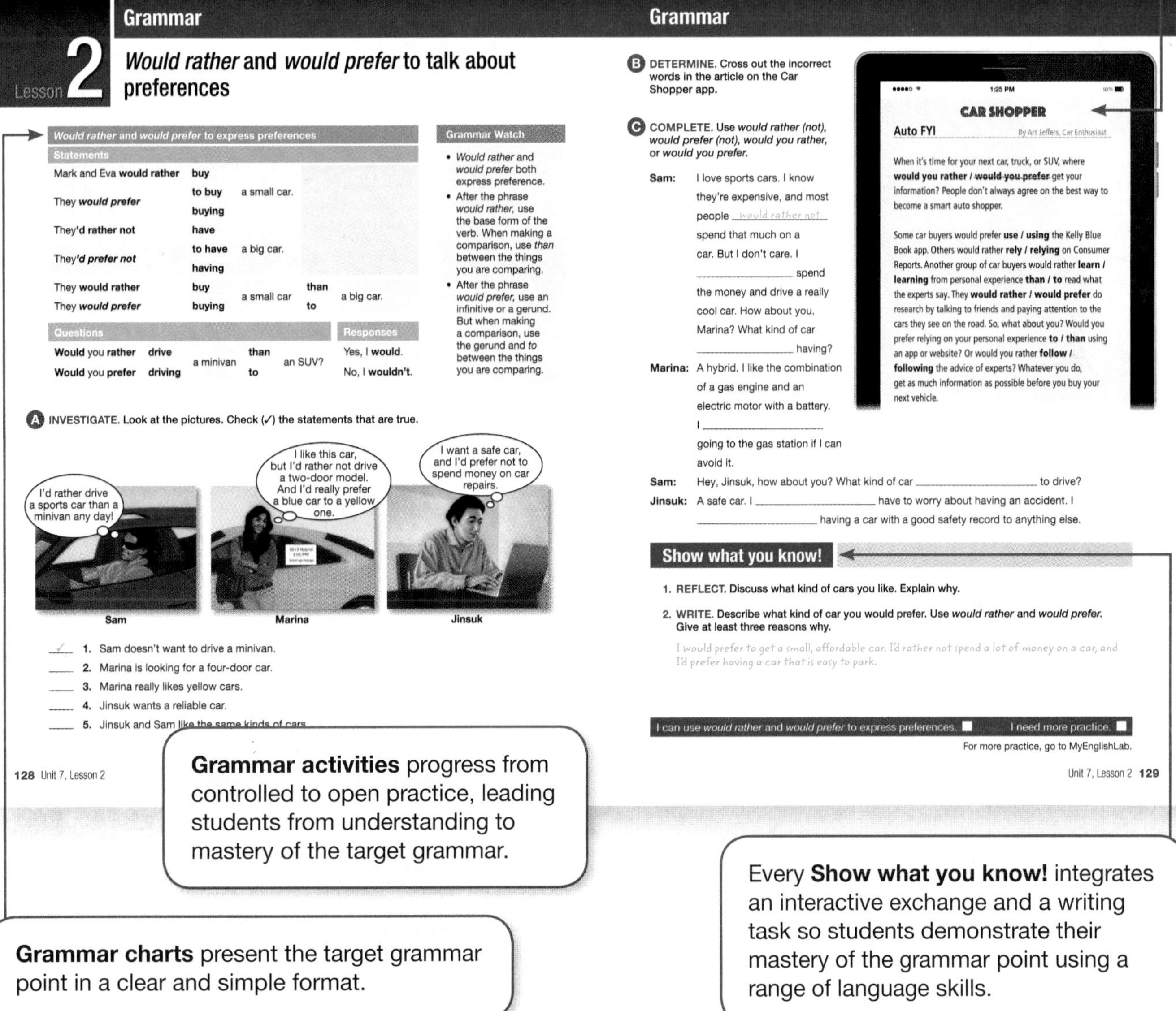

Lesson 2

Grammar

Would rather and *would prefer* to talk about preferences

Would rather and *would prefer* to express preferences				
Statements				
Mark and Eva **would rather**	**buy**			
They ***would prefer***	**to buy** / **buying**	a small car.		
They**'d rather not**	**have**			
They**'d *prefer not***	**to have** / **having**	a big car.		
They **would rather**	**buy**	a small car	**than**	a big car.
They ***would prefer***	**buying**		**to**	

Questions					**Responses**
Would you **rather**	**drive**	a minivan	**than**	an SUV?	Yes, I **would**.
Would you **prefer**	**driving**		**to**		No, I **wouldn't**.

Grammar Watch

- *Would rather* and *would prefer* both express preference.
- After the phrase *would rather,* use the base form of the verb. When making a comparison, use *than* between the things you are comparing.
- After the phrase *would prefer,* use an infinitive or a gerund. But when making a comparison, use the gerund and *to* between the things you are comparing.

A INVESTIGATE. Look at the pictures. Check (✓) the statements that are true.

I'd rather drive a sports car than a minivan any day!
I like this car, but I'd rather not drive a two-door model. And I'd really prefer a blue car to a yellow one.
I want a safe car, and I'd prefer not to spend money on car repairs.
Sam
Marina
Jinsuk

__✓__ 1. Sam doesn't want to drive a minivan.
____ 2. Marina is looking for a four-door car.
____ 3. Marina really likes yellow cars.
____ 4. Jinsuk wants a reliable car.
____ 5. Jinsuk and Sam like the same kinds of cars.

128 Unit 7, Lesson 2

Grammar

B DETERMINE. Cross out the incorrect words in the article on the Car Shopper app.

C COMPLETE. Use *would rather (not), would prefer (not), would you rather,* or *would you prefer.*

Sam: I love sports cars. I know they're expensive, and most people __would rather not__ spend that much on a car. But I don't care. I ________ spend the money and drive a really cool car. How about you, Marina? What kind of car ________ having?

Marina: A hybrid. I like the combination of a gas engine and an electric motor with a battery. I ________ going to the gas station if I can avoid it.

Sam: Hey, Jinsuk, how about you? What kind of car ________ to drive?

Jinsuk: A safe car. I ________ have to worry about having an accident. I ________ having a car with a good safety record to anything else.

CAR SHOPPER

Auto FYI By Art Jeffers, Car Enthusiast

When it's time for your next car, truck, or SUV, where **would you rather / ~~would you prefer~~** get your information? People don't always agree on the best way to become a smart auto shopper.

Some car buyers would prefer **use / using** the Kelly Blue Book app. Others would rather **rely / relying** on Consumer Reports. Another group of car buyers would rather **learn / learning** from personal experience **than / to** read what the experts say. They **would rather / would prefer** do research by talking to friends and paying attention to the cars they see on the road. So, what about you? Would you prefer relying on your personal experience **to / than** using an app or website? Or would you rather **follow / following** the advice of experts? Whatever you do, get as much information as possible before you buy your next vehicle.

Show what you know!

1. REFLECT. Discuss what kind of cars you like. Explain why.
2. WRITE. Describe what kind of car you would prefer. Use *would rather* and *would prefer.* Give at least three reasons why.

I would prefer to get a small, affordable car. I'd rather not spend a lot of money on a car, and I'd prefer having a car that is easy to park.

I can use *would rather* and *would prefer* to express preferences. ☐ I need more practice. ☐

For more practice, go to MyEnglishLab.

Unit 7, Lesson 2 129

Grammar activities progress from controlled to open practice, leading students from understanding to mastery of the target grammar.

Every **Show what you know!** integrates an interactive exchange and a writing task so students demonstrate their mastery of the grammar point using a range of language skills.

Grammar charts present the target grammar point in a clear and simple format.

Workplace, Life, and Community Skills lessons develop real-life language and civic literacy, prepare students for the workplace, and encourage community participation.

In **Go Online activities,** students use their devices to practice concrete online tasks, such as researching information or inputting data.

Lesson 3

Workplace, Life, and Community Skills

Interpret and respond to a report card

1 INTERPRET A REPORT CARD

A MAKE CONNECTIONS. How often do children receive report cards? What kind of information normally appears on a report card? What type of grading systems can be used?

B SCAN. THEN READ. What information is in the *Academic Subjects* section of the report card? In the *Habits and Attitudes* section? In the *Social Habits section*? After scanning, read the entire report card.

http://www.westapollomiddleschool.org/reportcards

School Year:	2019–2020	Period:	1	Date: 11/15/19
Student Name:	Manuel Medina	Days Absent:	3	
Teacher Name:	Ms. Arlene Brown	Days Late:	1	

Academic Subjects	**Grade and Comments**
English Language Arts	**78** Needs to improve writing—Needs to read more
Mathematics	**98** Excels in all aspects of math
Science	**72** Has trouble with science vocabulary
Social Studies	**70** Difficulty with reading affects ability to perform well on tests
Computer Lab	**95** Has done an excellent job on all computer assignments

Habits and Attitudes		
Work Habits		
Follows directions		
Completes all class and homework assignments	X	Needs to turn in homework regularly and on time
Social Habits		
Works well in groups	X	Needs to participate in group activities
Shows respect for others	✓	Is very polite to all individuals
Is responsible and reliable		

Key
90–100 = A (Excellent)
80–89 = B (Good)
70–79 = C (Average)
60–69 = D (Poor)
Below 60 = F (Failing)
X = Needs improvement
✓ = Exceptional

C DEFINE KEY WORDS. Find the words on the left in the report card. Match the words with their definitions.

____ 1. academic
____ 2. grade
____ 3. A
____ 4. comments
____ 5. key
____ 6. work habits

a. the highest score
b. notes that a teacher writes about a student
c. relating to schoolwork
d. an explanation of the grades and symbols on a report card
e. score given for an assignment or course
f. the typical way a student completes assignments

170 Unit 9, Lesson 3

Workplace, Life, and Community Skills

D LOCATE DETAILS. Write *T* (true) or *F* (false). Correct the false statements.

__T__ 1. Manuel was absent more often than he was late.
____ 2. The lowest grade on Manuel's report card is in social studies.
____ 3. Manuel has a C in two classes.
____ 4. Manuel has done well on all computer assignments.
____ 5. Manuel's grade in science is a 70.

E DISCUSS. What should a parent do if a child receives a low or failing grade on a report card?

2 RESPOND TO A REPORT CARD

Manuel's mother, Bertha Medina, has written to Ms. Brown, the teacher. And Ms. Brown has answered.

A EXPLAIN.

1. Why did Bertha Medina write the note?
2. How does Ms. Brown respond?

B DETERMINE.

1. What does Ms. Medina need to do now to arrange a meeting with Ms. Brown?
2. Are Ms. Medina and Ms. Brown going to meet in the morning, afternoon, or evening? Why?
3. What are Ms. Medina and Ms. Brown going to discuss?

C WRITE. Write a note to your child's teacher about something you would like to discuss. If you don't have children, write a note to your English teacher about your own learning. Use Ms. Medina's email as a model.

D GO ONLINE.

1. SEARCH. Find the website for a Parent-Teacher Association (PTA) for a neighborhood school. What is the website? ____________
2. LIST. List some activities that the PTA has already completed. List the activities that the PTA is planning to do in the future.

E ANALYZE. Why are the activities planned by the PTA important for the students? for the teachers? for the community?

To: Ms. Brown
From: Bertha Medina
Subject: Manuel's report card

Dear Ms. Brown,

My husband and I looked at Manuel's report card yesterday. We are concerned about his grades in social studies, science, and English. We have been trying to get him to read more, but it is difficult.

Could we have a conference to talk about how to help him? I would prefer to meet in the early evening after work, but I can be available almost anytime.

Thank you for your help.

Sincerely,

Bertha Medina

To: Bertha Medina
From: Ms. Brown
Subject: Re: Manuel's report card

Dear Ms. Medina,

Thank you for contacting me about Manuel's grades.

I would be happy to meet to discuss ways to help Manuel read more. I can be at the school in the evening so you don't have to miss work. Please call me at 310-555-9904 to set up a day and time for our conference.

Sincerely,

Arlene Brown

I can interpret and respond to a report card. ☐ I need more practice. ☐

For more practice, go to MyEnglishLab.

Unit 9, Lesson 3 171

Interactive activities develop real-life communication and collaboration skills.

All-new informational **Reading** lessons develop academic language and build content knowledge to meet the rigorous requirements of the CCRS.

Informational readings containing level-appropriate complex text introduce academic language and build content knowledge.

Students develop **numeracy** skills by interpreting numeric information in charts and graphs.

Lesson 6

Reading

Read about life expectancy

1 BEFORE YOU READ

A DISCUSS. Look at the graph in the article below. Discuss. What information does it show?

B PREDICT. Skim the article. What is it about?

2 READ

Listen and read.

Academic Skill: Scan information for details

Scan information quickly to look for specific details such as facts or numbers.

Be Healthy and Live Long

People in the U.S. have been living longer and longer. In 1900, the average American lived to the age of 47. In 1950, the average life span was 68. In 2017, mean life expectancy reached 78.6. So, what would it take for the average American to live to the age of 100? Some experts believe that we can increase longevity if we look at the leading causes of death.

What the Numbers Say

The chart below shows that heart disease and cancer are the top causes of death in the United States. For every 100,000 people, 166 people died from heart disease. 156 died from cancer. Fortunately, deaths from these causes have been going down recently. Chances are good that they will continue to decline. Why? Modern medicine is constantly improving. Doctors are getting better at diagnosing and curing diseases.

The Top Five Causes of Death in the United States in 2016 (Deaths per 100,000 people)

Heart disease	166
Cancer	156
Unintentional injuries	47
Chronic lower respiratory diseases	41
Stroke	37

Source: NCHS, National Vital Statistics System, Mortality

What We Should Do

Doctors are also getting better at disease prevention. They know which conditions are responsible for deaths in the United States. They are working hard to stop these conditions from developing in their patients. For example, experts have concluded that smoking and obesity are risk factors that can lead to the two top causes of death, heart disease and cancer. Smoking rates have declined substantially in the United States in recent years. However, according to the Centers for Disease Control and Prevention, obesity rates still remain high. 36.5 percent of American adults are obese. Reducing the percentage of obese Americans could be one important way to help Americans live longer. Losing weight gives people a better chance of avoiding heart disease, cancer, and other potential causes of death.

A Weighty Issue

- Body Mass Index, or BMI, is used as a screening tool for determining healthy weights. A BMI of 25 to 30 means you are overweight. If your BMI is 30 or higher, you are obese.
- If you are overweight, losing a small amount of weight (even 10 percent of your weight) will help decrease your chances of having health problems.
- It is not just adults who have weight problems. One in three U.S. children are overweight or obese.

The research is clear. Life expectancy rates in the United States should continue to rise if we keep working to prevent the diseases that most often cause our deaths.

3 CLOSE READING

A IDENTIFY. What is the main idea?

a. Heart disease and cancer kill many people in the United States.
b. Experts think that smoking and obesity can lead to heart disease and cancer.
c. People will live longer in the United States if we can prevent the deadliest diseases.

156 Unit 8, Lesson 6

Reading

B CITE EVIDENCE. Complete the sentences. Where is the information located? **Lines**

1. The average life expectancy of Americans in 1950 was ____. ______
   a. 47 **b.** 68 **c.** 78.6
2. In recent years, ____ rates have fallen. ______
   a. smoking **b.** obesity **c.** accident
3. If your BMI is ____, you are obese. ______
   a. under 25 **b.** 25 to 30 **c.** over 30
4. ____ the children in the United States are overweight or obese. ______
   a. One third of **b.** Half of **c.** One quarter of

C INTERPRET GRAPHICS. Complete the sentences about the bar graph.

1. In 2016, for every 100,000 people, ____ people died from cancer.
   a. 166 **b.** 156 **c.** 47
2. In 2016, more people died from chronic lower respiratory diseases than from ____.
   a. stroke **b.** cancer **c.** unintentional injuries
3. The leading causes of death in the United States in 2016 were ____.
   a. injuries **b.** fatal accidents **c.** illnesses
4. For every 100,000 people, 37 died from stroke and 47 died from ____.
   a. tumor **b.** accidental harm **c.** cancer

D INTERPRET VOCABULARY. Complete the sentences.

1. In the context of line 2, the word *average* means ____.
   a. typical **b.** not too good or too bad
2. In the context of lines 3–4, the phrase *life expectancy* means ____.
   a. length of a person's life **b.** quality of a person's life
3. In the context of line 26, the word *substantially* means ____.
   a. in many ways **b.** a lot
4. In the context of line 20, the phrase *responsible for* means ____.
   a. the main cause of **b.** supposed to take care of
5. In the context of the infographic, the word *stroke* means ____.
   a. a type of brain illness **b.** a petting movement

E SUMMARIZE. What are the most important ideas in the article?

Show what you know!

1. COLLABORATE. What major factors that lead to disease are mentioned in the article? What other factors do you think contribute to disease in America?
2. WRITE. Describe four risk factors that cause diseases. Which factor do you think is the most dangerous? What should people do to try to reduce that factor?

Smoking, obesity, not exercising, and eating unhealthy foods cause diseases in the United States . . .

I can scan information for details. ☐ I need more practice. ☐

To read more, go to MyEnglishLab.

Unit 8, Lesson 6 **157**

Close-reading activities require that students return to the reading to find textual evidence of detail, to summarize for general understanding, and to make inferences.

Graphs and charts introduce students to information in a variety of formats, developing their visual literacy.

Academic tasks, such as summarizing, help students develop academic skills.

Writing lessons follow a robust and scaffolded writing-process approach, engaging students in analyzing writing models, planning, and producing a final product.

A **Writing Skill** explains and models appropriate writing. Later in the lesson, students apply the skill to their own writing.

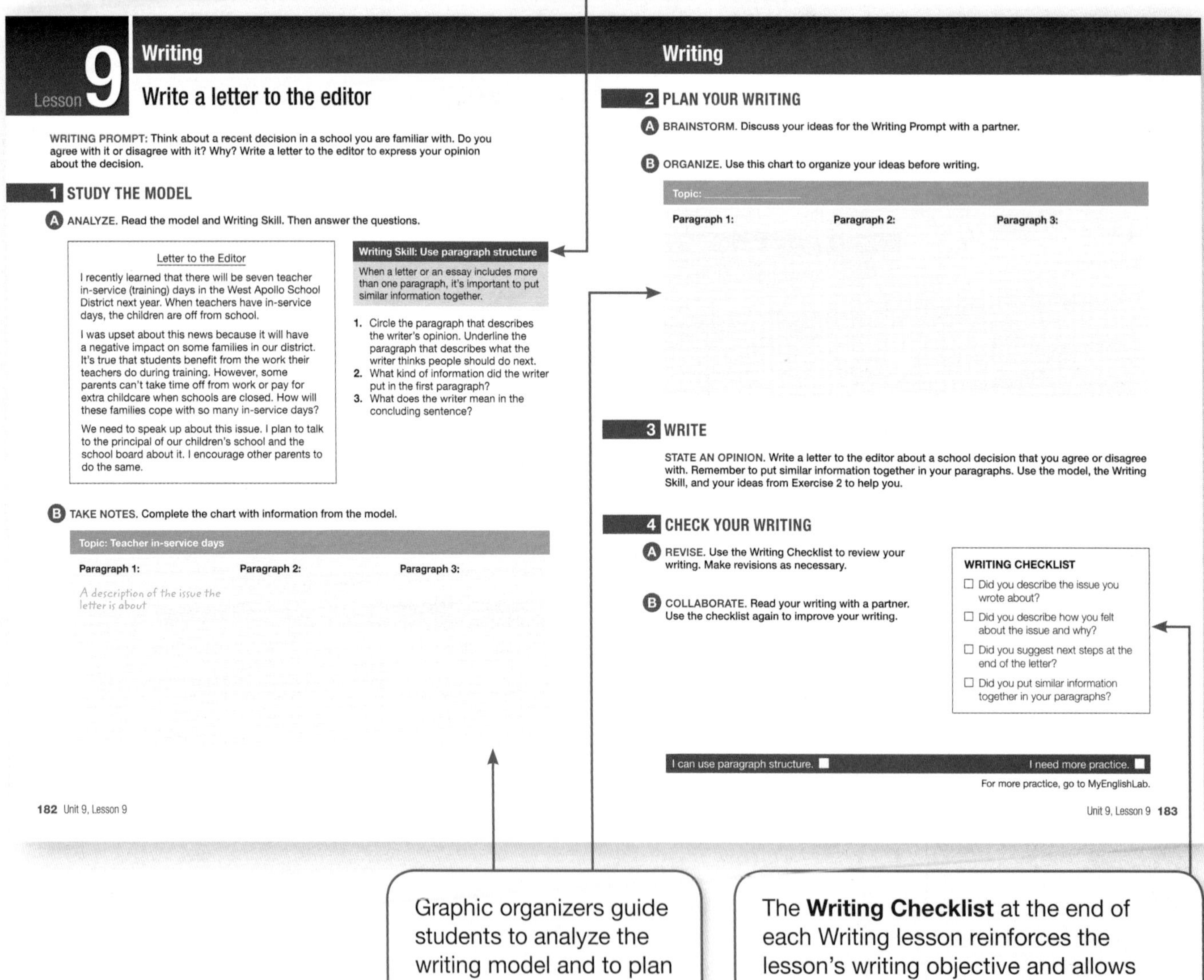

Lesson 9

Writing

Write a letter to the editor

WRITING PROMPT: Think about a recent decision in a school you are familiar with. Do you agree with it or disagree with it? Why? Write a letter to the editor to express your opinion about the decision.

1 STUDY THE MODEL

A ANALYZE. Read the model and Writing Skill. Then answer the questions.

Letter to the Editor

I recently learned that there will be seven teacher in-service (training) days in the West Apollo School District next year. When teachers have in-service days, the children are off from school.

I was upset about this news because it will have a negative impact on some families in our district. It's true that students benefit from the work their teachers do during training. However, some parents can't take time off from work or pay for extra childcare when schools are closed. How will these families cope with so many in-service days?

We need to speak up about this issue. I plan to talk to the principal of our children's school and the school board about it. I encourage other parents to do the same.

Writing Skill: Use paragraph structure

When a letter or an essay includes more than one paragraph, it's important to put similar information together.

1. Circle the paragraph that describes the writer's opinion. Underline the paragraph that describes what the writer thinks people should do next.
2. What kind of information did the writer put in the first paragraph?
3. What does the writer mean in the concluding sentence?

B TAKE NOTES. Complete the chart with information from the model.

Topic: Teacher in-service days		
Paragraph 1:	Paragraph 2:	Paragraph 3:
A description of the issue the letter is about		

182 Unit 9, Lesson 9

Writing

2 PLAN YOUR WRITING

A BRAINSTORM. Discuss your ideas for the Writing Prompt with a partner.

B ORGANIZE. Use this chart to organize your ideas before writing.

Topic:		
Paragraph 1:	Paragraph 2:	Paragraph 3:

3 WRITE

STATE AN OPINION. Write a letter to the editor about a school decision that you agree or disagree with. Remember to put similar information together in your paragraphs. Use the model, the Writing Skill, and your ideas from Exercise 2 to help you.

4 CHECK YOUR WRITING

A REVISE. Use the Writing Checklist to review your writing. Make revisions as necessary.

B COLLABORATE. Read your writing with a partner. Use the checklist again to improve your writing.

WRITING CHECKLIST

- ☐ Did you describe the issue you wrote about?
- ☐ Did you describe how you felt about the issue and why?
- ☐ Did you suggest next steps at the end of the letter?
- ☐ Did you put similar information together in your paragraphs?

I can use paragraph structure. ☐ I need more practice. ☐

For more practice, go to MyEnglishLab.

Unit 9, Lesson 9 183

Graphic organizers guide students to analyze the writing model and to plan their own writing.

The **Writing Checklist** at the end of each Writing lesson reinforces the lesson's writing objective and allows students to review and revise their work.

New **Soft Skills at Work** lessons engage students in real-life situations that develop the personal, social, and cultural skills critical for career success and help students meet the WIOA requirements.

A brief scenario introduces a common workplace problem that can be solved using **critical thinking** and **soft skills**.

Comprehension activity ensures student understanding of the workplace problem situation.

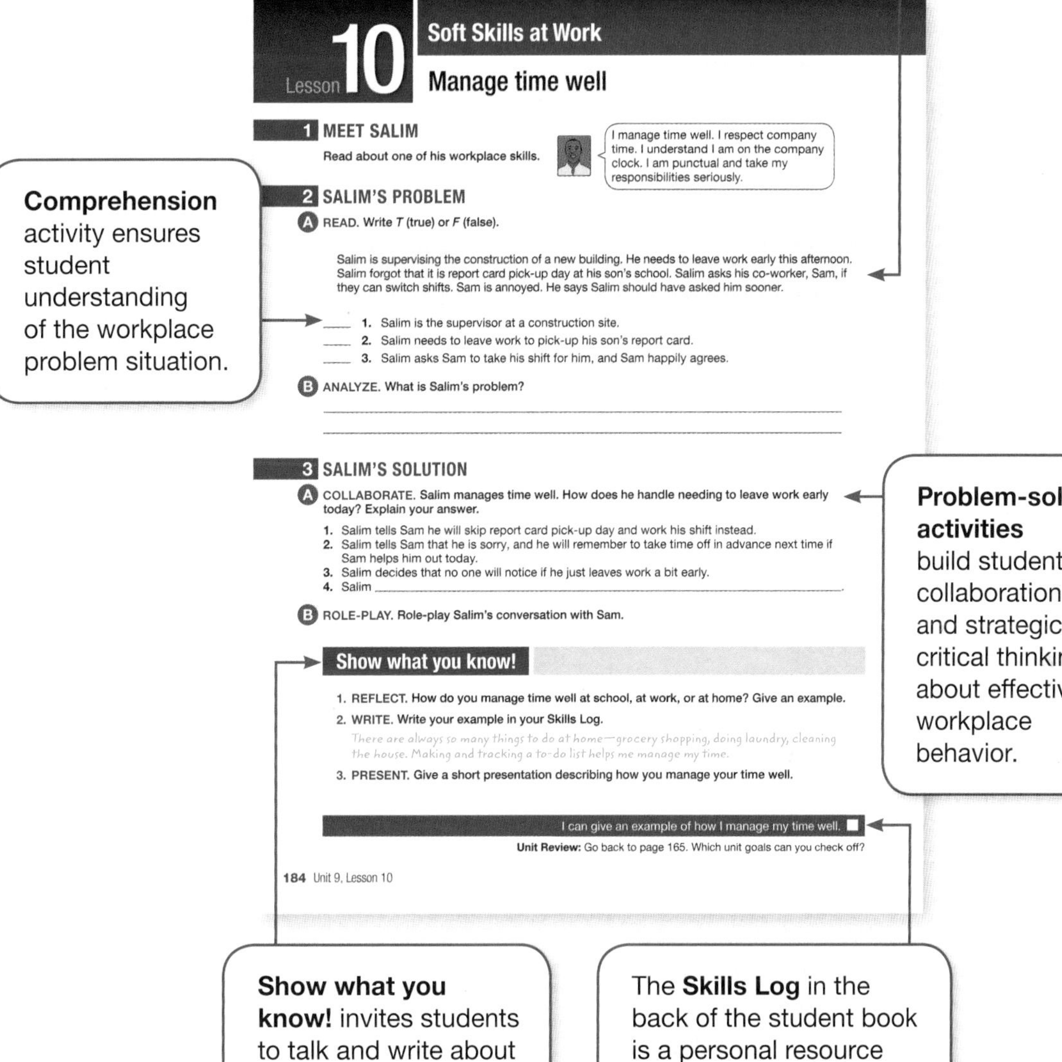

Lesson 10

Soft Skills at Work

Manage time well

1 MEET SALIM

Read about one of his workplace skills.

I manage time well. I respect company time. I understand I am on the company clock. I am punctual and take my responsibilities seriously.

2 SALIM'S PROBLEM

A READ. Write *T* (true) or *F* (false).

Salim is supervising the construction of a new building. He needs to leave work early this afternoon. Salim forgot that it is report card pick-up day at his son's school. Salim asks his co-worker, Sam, if they can switch shifts. Sam is annoyed. He says Salim should have asked him sooner.

_____ 1. Salim is the supervisor at a construction site.
_____ 2. Salim needs to leave work to pick-up his son's report card.
_____ 3. Salim asks Sam to take his shift for him, and Sam happily agrees.

B ANALYZE. What is Salim's problem?

3 SALIM'S SOLUTION

A COLLABORATE. Salim manages time well. How does he handle needing to leave work early today? Explain your answer.

1. Salim tells Sam he will skip report card pick-up day and work his shift instead.
2. Salim tells Sam that he is sorry, and he will remember to take time off in advance next time if Sam helps him out today.
3. Salim decides that no one will notice if he just leaves work a bit early.
4. Salim _______________________________.

B ROLE-PLAY. Role-play Salim's conversation with Sam.

Show what you know!

1. REFLECT. How do you manage time well at school, at work, or at home? Give an example.
2. WRITE. Write your example in your Skills Log.
   There are always so many things to do at home—grocery shopping, doing laundry, cleaning the house. Making and tracking a to-do list helps me manage my time.
3. PRESENT. Give a short presentation describing how you manage your time well.

I can give an example of how I manage my time well. ☐

Unit Review: Go back to page 165. Which unit goals can you check off?

184 Unit 9, Lesson 10

Problem-solving activities build student collaboration and strategic critical thinking about effective workplace behavior.

Show what you know! invites students to talk and write about the soft skills they bring to the job.

The **Skills Log** in the back of the student book is a personal resource for students as they apply for jobs or undergo performance reviews.

SCOPE AND SEQUENCE

Unit	Listening and Speaking	Reading	Grammar
Pre-Unit **Getting Started** *page 2*	• Meet your classmates • Listen for and give personal information	• Locate information in your book	• Verb tenses review
1 **Catching Up** *page 5*	• Talk about yourself and your family • Discuss goals • Discuss ways to succeed **Pronunciation skills:** • Stressed words • Speech chunks and pauses	• Read an article about an American success story **Academic skill:** • Skim for the general idea, scan for specific information	• Simple present and present continuous • Future with the present continuous, *be going to,* and *will* • Noun clauses
2 **Tell Me about Yourself** *page 25*	• Talk about work-related goals • Discuss job-information resources • Respond to common interview questions **Pronunciation skills:** • Reduced syllables • Stressed syllables	• Read an article about preparing for a job interview **Academic skill:** • Identify supporting details	• Infinitives and gerunds • Gerunds as objects of prepositions • Simple past and present perfect
3 **Community Life** *page 45*	• Talk about cultural diversity in neighborhoods • Describe community issues • Discuss ways to improve a community **Pronunciation skills:** • Pronouncing consonants • Pronouncing *to*	• Read an article about community gardens **Academic skill:** • Make inferences	• Participial adjectives • *Wish* in the present and future
4 **On the Job** *page 65*	• Communicate with supervisors and co-workers • Check your understanding of a situation at work • Ask and answer performance review questions **Pronunciation skills:** • Phrasal verbs • Auxiliary verbs	• Read about infection prevention in the workplace **Academic skill:** • Recognize restatements	• Phrasal verbs • Negative *yes/no* questions • Indirect instructions, commands, and requests

Writing	Document Literacy and Numeracy	Workplace, Life, and Community Skills	Soft Skills at Work
	• Take a survey and interpret the results • Use unit and page numbers	• Take a survey to learn about your learning style	
• Describe a person you admire **Writing skill:** • Use chronological order	• Understand a school application form • Calculate the length of time between two dates • Create a timeline	• Interpret a school application • Complete a school application **Digital skill:** • Go online and find an application for a school in your area	• Take responsibility for professional growth
• Write a cover letter **Writing skill:** • Keep cover letters brief	• Use a graphic organizer to sort information • Understand different sections of a résumé • Understand the format and structure of an email	• Interpret a résumé • Write a résumé **Digital skill:** • Go online and search for a job posting that you would like to apply for	• Have integrity
• Describe a neighborhood **Writing skill:** • Use examples to clarify details	• Use a graphic organizer to categorize information • Understand and follow GPS directions • Use a chart to take notes and organize ideas	• Interpret GPS directions • Follow GPS directions **Digital skill:** • Use a GPS device to get directions between two places in your community	• Respect others
• Write an email to a supervisor **Writing skill:** • Use the subject line to state the email topic	• Interpret an employee benefits plan • Use dates to calculate time span • Understand an employee performance review sheet	• Interpret employee benefits **Digital skill:** • Go online and find an employee benefits website	• Be adaptable

SCOPE AND SEQUENCE

Unit	Listening and Speaking	Reading	Grammar
5 **Safe and Sound** *page 85*	• Identify ways to prevent fires • Talk about dangerous weather • Communicate in a 911 emergency **Pronunciation skills:** • Clauses • Pronouncing vowel sounds /i/ and /ɪ/	• Read an article about earthquakes **Academic skill:** • Identify an author's purpose	• Present real conditionals • Adverb clauses of time • Past continuous for interrupted action
6 **Moving In** *page 105*	• Identify tenant responsibilities • Talk about landlord responsibilities • Discuss problems with neighbors **Pronunciation skills:** • Tag questions • Strong emotion	• Read an article about why people move **Academic skill:** • Distinguish main ideas from details	• Expressing obligation, expectation, and permission • Tag questions • Reported speech
7 **Behind the Wheel** *page 125*	• Talk about buying a car • Discuss car maintenance and repairs • Describe a car accident **Pronunciation skills:** • Important words • Pronouncing *had* and *would*	• Read an article about consumer-protection laws **Academic skill:** • Interpret infographics	• *Would rather* and *would prefer* to talk about preferences • Embedded questions • Past perfect
8 **How Are You Feeling?** *page 145*	• Communicate with medical personnel • Report a medical emergency • Identify healthcare services within the community **Pronunciation skills:** • Consonant clusters • Stress patterns	• Read an article about life expectancy **Academic skill:** • Scan a list for details	• Present perfect continuous • *Such . . . that* and *so . . . that* • *Should, ought to, had better,* and *must*

Writing	Document Literacy and Numeracy	Workplace, Life, and Community Skills	Soft Skills at Work
• Explain the process to take in an emergency situation **Writing skill:** • Use numbered steps to show order	• Interpret representational graphics • Understand an evacuation map • Use a graphic organizer to sequence a process into steps	• Interpret an evacuation map **Digital skill:** • Go online and search for an evacuation map for a city, country, or state	• Locate information
• Write about a housing problem **Writing skill:** • Clearly state a problem and solution	• Interpret signs • Understand a lease agreement • Interpret information in a map • Understand and compare percentages • Use graphic organizers to take notes and organize ideas	• Interpret a lease **Digital skill:** • Go online and find a sample rental lease	• Find creative solutions
• Explain the process used to make a major purchase **Writing skill:** • Use time words to show sequence	• Compare prices • Understand car insurance identification cards • Understand car insurance renewal notices • Interpret a pie chart • Interpret a labeled diagram • Use a graphic organizer to sequence steps in a process	• Interpret car insurance documents • Talk about buying car insurance **Digital skill:** • Go online and find a car insurance website	• Respond well to feedback
• Describe a health problem **Writing skill:** • Include sensory details	• Interpret a medical history questionnaire • Understand a health insurance enrollment form • Use birthdates to calculate age • Interpret a bar graph • Use a graphic organizer to categorize information	• Interpret a health insurance enrollment form **Digital skill:** • Go online and find a health insurance plan	• Be professional

SCOPE AND SEQUENCE

Unit	Listening and Speaking	Reading	Grammar
9 **Partners in Education** *page 165*	• Discuss a student's progress • Talk with school personnel • Discuss school safety **Pronunciation skills:** • Highlighting information • Past modals	• Read about after-school programs **Academic skill:** • Distinguish fact from opinion	• Adverb clauses and infinitives to express reason and purpose • Adjective clauses • Past modals
10 **Safety First** *page 185*	• Give a progress report • Talk about preventing accidents at work • Recognize requirements for promotion **Pronunciation skills:** • Sentence flow • Vowel sound for *o*	• Read an online article about workplace safety **Academic skill:** • Identify time words	• *Make/have/let/get* + object + verb • Reflexive pronouns • *Could you/I . . .? / Would you mind . . .? / Why don't you/I . . .?* to make polite requests
11 **Know the Law!** *page 205*	• Identify misdemeanors • Describe what happens in a courtroom • Discuss traffic laws **Pronunciation skills:** • Pronouncing *is, are, was, were* • Short unstressed words	• Read an article about DNA evidence **Academic skill:** • Break down long sentences	• Gerunds as subjects; *It* + infinitive • Passives: simple present and simple past • Adverb clauses of condition and contrast
12 **Saving and Spending** *page 225*	• Describe banking services • Prepare a monthly budget • Talk about dreams for the future **Pronunciation skills:** • Compound words • Pronouncing *would you*	• Read an article about financing a business **Academic skill:** • Summarize	• Articles: *a, an, the,* no article (Ø) • Future real conditionals • Present and future unreal conditionals

Writing	Document Literacy and Numeracy	Workplace, Life, and Community Skills	Soft Skills at Work
• Write a letter to the editor **Writing skill:** • Use paragraph structure	• Understand a report card • Understand the American grading system • Use a chart to take notes and organize ideas	• Interpret a report card • Respond to a report card **Digital skill:** • Go online and find a Parent-Teacher Association (PTA) website	• Manage time well
• Explain a problem and suggest a solution to improve workplace safety **Writing skill:** • State problem, causes, and solutions	• Understand social media postings • Understand an employee accident report • Calculate end date given start date and time span	• Interpret an employee accident report • Complete an employee accident report **Digital skill:** • Go online and find an accident report form	• Take responsibility
• Compare and contrast different legal systems **Writing skill:** • Use signal words to compare and contrast	• Interpret signs • Interpret traffic laws • Use a graphic organizer to categorize information	• Understand the Miranda warning and know your rights in a home search **Digital skill:** • Go online and find information on what to do if you are stopped by the police in your car	• Be accountable
• Describe a worthwhile charity **Writing skill:** • State main ideas and supporting details	• Understand banking fee structures • Understand and compare percentages • Interpret a monthly budget • Calculate projected savings • Understand a W-2 form	• Learn about tax forms • Interpret a W-2 form **Digital skill:** • Go online to the Internal Revenue Service website: www.irs.gov to find information about free tax preparation services	• Take initiative

CORRELATIONS

Unit	CASAS Reading Standards (correlated to CASAS Reading Standards 2016)	CASAS Listening Standards (correlated to CASAS Listening Basic Skills Content Standards)
1	**L3:** RDG 2.3, 2.8, 3.2, 3.9, 3.11, 4.2; **L6:** RDG 2.3, 2.8, 3.9, 3.11; **L7:** RDG 3.2; **L8:** RDG 3.2; **L9:** RDG 2.3, 4.5; **L10:** RDG 3.2, 4.3	**L1:** 1.4, 2.1, 2.3, 4.1, 4.2; **L2:** 2.1, 2.3, 3.1, 3.9, 4.1, 4.2; **L3:** 2.1, 2.3; **L4:** 2.1, 2.3, 4.1, 4.2; **L5:** 2.3, 3.9, 4.1, 4.2; **L6:** 2.3, 4.1, 4.2; **L7:** 2.1, 2.3, 4.2, 6.1; **L8:** 3.9; **L10:** 2.1, 4.6, 5.9
2	**L3:** RDG 2.3, 2.8, 3.2, 3.9, 3.11; **L4:** RDG 2.3; **L6:** RDG 2.3, 2.8, 3.11, 3.12, 4.2, 4.3; **L7:** RDG 3.2; **L8:** RDG 3.2; **L9:** RDG 2.3, 4.5; **L10:** RDG 3.2, 4.3	**L1:** 1.4, 2.1, 2.3, 4.1, 4.2, 6.1; **L2:** 2.1, 2.3, 3.1, 3.9, 4.1, 4.2; **L3:** 2.1, 2.3; **L4:** 2.1, 2.3, 4.1, 4.2; **L5:** 2.3, 3.9, 4.1, 4.2; **L6:** 2.3, 4.1, 4.2; **L7:** 2.1, 2.3, 4.2, 4.6, 6.1; **L8:** 3.9; **L10:** 2.1, 4.6, 5.9
3	**L1:** RDG 3.2, 4.3; **L3:** RDG 2.3, 2.8, 3.2, 3.4; **L4:** RDG 2.3; **L6:** RDG 2.3, 2.8, 3.11, 3.12, 4.2, 4.3; **L7:** RDG 3.2; **L8:** RDG 3.2; **L9:** RDG 2.3, 4.5; **L10:** RDG 3.2, 4.3	**L1:** 2.1, 2.3, 4.1, 4.2, 6.1; **L2:** 2.1, 3.9, 4.1, 4.2; **L3:** 2.1, 2.3; **L4:** 2.1, 2.3, 4.1, 4.2, 4.6; **L5:** 2.3, 3.9, 4.1, 4.2; **L6:** 2.3, 4.1, 4.2, 6.1, 6.3; **L7:** 2.1, 2.3, 4.2, 4.6, 6.1, 6.3; **L8:** 3.9; **L10:** 2.1, 4.6, 5.9
4	**L1:** RDG 3.2, 4.3; **L3:** RDG 2.3, 2.8, 3.2, 3.9; **L4:** RDG 2.3; **L6:** RDG 2.3, 2.8, 3.11, 3.12, 4.2, 4.3; **L7:** RDG 3.2; **L8:** RDG 3.2; **L9:** RDG 2.3, 4.5; **L10:** RDG 3.2, 4.3	**L1:** 2.1, 2.3, 2.4, 4.1, 4.2, 6.1; **L2:** 2.1, 3.9, 4.1, 4.2; **L3:** 2.1, 2.3; **L4:** 2.1, 2.3, 4.1, 4.2, 4.6; **L5:** 2.3, 3.6, 4.1, 4.2; **L6:** 2.3, 4.1, 4.2, 5.6, 6.1; **L7:** 2.1, 2.3, 4.2, 4.6, 6.1; **L8:** 3.4, 3.9, 5.6; **L10:** 2.1, 4.6, 5.9
5	**L1:** RDG 3.2, 4.3; **L3:** RDG 2.3, 2.8, 3.2, 3.11, 3.12, 3.14, 4.3, 4.6; **L4:** RDG 2.3, 3.10; **L6:** RDG 2.3, 2.8, 3.4; **L7:** RDG 3.2; **L9:** RDG 2.3, 4.5; **L10:** RDG 3.2, 4.3	**L1:** 1.4, 2.1, 2.3, 2.4, 4.1, 4.2, 6.1; **L2:** 2.1, 3.13, 4.1, 4.2; **L3:** 2.1, 2.3; **L4:** 2.1, 2.3, 4.1, 4.2; 4.6, 5.9, 6.1; **L5:** 2.3, 4.10, 5.8, 5.10; **L7:** 2.1, 2.3, 4.2, 4.6, 5.10, 6.1; **L8:** 3.9, 5.8, 5.9; **L10:** 2.1, 5.9
6	**L1:** RDG 3.2, 4.3; **L3:** RDG 2.3, 2.8, 3.2, 3.9, 3.12; **L4:** RDG 2.3; **L6:** RDG 2.3, 2.8, 3.9, 3.11, 3.12, 4.2, 4.3, 4.9; **L7:** RDG 3.2; **L8:** RDG 3.2; **L9:** RDG 2.3, 4.5; **L10:** RDG 3.2, 4.3	**L1:** 2.1, 2.3, 2.4, 4.1, 4.2, 5.8, 6.1; **L2:** 2.1, 3.4, 3.9, 4.1, 4.2; **L3:** 2.1, 2.3; **L4:** 2.1, 4.1, 4.2, 4.6, 4.11, 6.1; **L5:** 2.3, 3.14, 4.1, 4.2; **L6:** 2.3, 4.1, 4.2, 6.1; **L7:** 2.1, 2.3, 4.2, 4.6, 6.1; **L8:** 2.1, 2.3, 3.13, 4.2; **L10:** 2.1, 4.6, 5.9
7	**L1:** RDG 3.2, 4.3; **L3:** RDG 2.3, 2.8, 3.2, 3.9, 3.12; **L4:** RDG 2.3, 3.10; **L6:** RDG 2.3, 2.8, 3.4, 3.9, 3.11, 3.12, 4.2, 4.3, 4.9; **L7:** RDG 3.2; **L8:** RDG 3.2; **L9:** RDG 2.3, 2.4, 4.5; **L10:** RDG 3.2, 4.3	**L1:** 2.1, 2.3, 2.4, 4.1, 4.2, 6.1; **L2:** 2.1, 3.9; **L3:** 2.1, 2.3, 6.5; **L4:** 1.4, 2.1, 4.1, 4.2, 4.6, 4.11, 6.1; **L5:** 2.3, 3.14; **L6:** 2.3, 4.1, 4.2, 6.1; **L7:** 2.1, 2.3, 4.2, 4.6, 6.1; **L8:** 2.1, 2.3, 3.9, 4.2; **L10:** 2.1, 4.6, 5.9
8	**L1:** RDG 3.2, 4.3; **L3:** RDG 2.3, 2.8, 3.2, 3.9, 3.12; **L4:** RDG 2.3, 4.3; **L6:** RDG 2.3, 2.8, 3.4, 3.9, 3.11, 3.12, 4.2, 4.3, 4.9; **L7:** RDG 3.2; **L8:** RDG 3.2; **L9:** RDG 2.3, 4.5; **L10:** RDG 3.2, 4.3	**L1:** 2.1, 2.3, 2.4, 4.1, 4.2, 4.6, 6.1, 6.5; **L2:** 2.1, 3.9; **L3:** 2.1, 2.3; **L4:** 2.1, 4.1, 4.2, 4.6, 6.3, 4.11, 6.1; **L5:** 2.3, 3.9; **L6:** 2.3, 4.1, 4.2, 6.1; **L7:** 2.1, 2.3, 4.2, 4.6, 6.1; **L8:** 3.9, 4.2; **L10:** 2.1, 4.6, 5.9
9	**L1:** RDG 3.2; **L3:** RDG 2.3, 2.8, 3.2, 3.9, 3.12; **L4:** RDG 2.3; **L6:** RDG 2.3, 2.8, 3.9, 3.11, 3.12, 4.2, 4.3; **L7:** RDG 3.2; **L8:** RDG 3.2; **L9:** RDG 2.3, 4.5; **L10:** RDG 3.2, 4.3	**L1:** 2.1, 2.3, 2.4, 4.1, 4.2, 4.6, 6.1, 6.5; **L2:** 2.1, 3.13; **L3:** 2.1, 2.3; **L4:** 2.1, 4.1, 4.2, 4.6, 4.11, 6.1; **L5:** 2.3, 3.9; **L6:** 2.3, 4.1, 4.2, 6.1; **L7:** 2.1, 2.3, 4.2, 4.6, 6.1; **L8:** 3.9, 4.2; **L10:** 2.1, 4.6, 5.9
10	**L1:** RDG 3.2; **L3:** RDG 2.3, 2.4, 2.8, 3.2, 3.9, 3.11, 3.12, 4.2; **L4:** RDG 2.3; **L6:** RDG 2.3, 2.8, 3.9, 4.3; **L7:** RDG 3.2; **L8:** RDG 3.2; **L9:** RDG 2.3, 4.5; **L10:** RDG 3.2, 4.3	**L1:** 2.1, 2.3, 2.4, 4.1, 4.2, 4.6, 6.1; **L2:** 2.1, 3.9; **L3:** 2.1, 2.3, 5.8, 6.1; **L4:** 2.1, 4.1, 4.2, 4.6, 4,11, 6.1; **L5:** 2.1, 2.3, 3.2, 4.1, 4.2; **L6:** 2.3, 4.1, 4.2, 6.1; **L7:** 2.1, 2.3, 4.2, 4.6, 6.1; **L8:** 3.9, 4.2; **L10:** 2.1, 4.6, 5.9
11	**L1:** RDG 3.2, 3.6; **L3:** RDG 2.3, 2.8, 3.2, 3.9, 3.11, 3.12; **L4:** RDG 2.3; **L6:** RDG 2.3, 2.8, 3.9, 3.11, 4.2, 4.3; **L7:** RDG 3.2; **L9:** RDG 2.3, 4.5; **L10:** RDG 3.2, 4.3	**L1:** 2.1, 2.3, 2.4, 4.1, 4.2, 4.6, 6.1; **L2:** 2.1, 3.9; **L3:** 2.1, 2.3, 5.8, 6.1; **L4:** 2.1, 4.1, 4.2, 4.6, 4.11, 6.1; **L5:** 2.1, 2.3, 3.9, 4.1, 4.2; **L6:** 2.3, 4.1, 4.2, 4.6, 6.1; **L7:** 2.1, 2.3, 4.2, 6.1; **L8:** 3.13, 4.2; **L10:** 2.1, 4.6, 5.9
12	**L1:** RDG 3.2; **L3:** RDG 2.3, 2.8, 3.2, 3.8, 3.9, 3.11, 3.12, 4.2; **L4:** RDG 2.3; **L6:** RDG 2.3, 2.8, 3.9, 4.3; **L7:** RDG 3.2; **L8:** RDG 3.13, 4.2; **L9:** RDG 2.3, 4.5; **L10:** RDG 3.2, 4.3	**L1:** 2.1, 2.3, 2.4, 4.1, 4.2, 4.6, 6.1; **L2:** 2.1, 3.1; **L3:** 2.1, 2.3, 5.8, 6.1; **L4:** 2.1, 4.1, 4.2, 4.6, 4.11, 6.1; **L5:** 2.1, 2.3, 3.13, 4.1, 4.2; **L6:** 2.3, 4.1, 4.2; **L7:** 1.5, 2.1, 2.3, 4.2, 4.6, 6.1; **L10:** 2.1, 4.6, 5.9

CASAS: Comprehensive Adult Student Assessment System
CCRS: College and Career Readiness Standards (R=Reading; W=Writing; SL=Speaking/Listening; L=Language)
ELPS: English Language Proficiency Standards

CASAS Competencies (correlated to CASAS Competencies: Essential Life and Work skills for Youth and Adults)	CCRS Correlations, Level C	ELPS Correlations, Level 4
L1: 0.1.2, 0.1.5, 0.2.1; **L2:** 0.1.2, 0.1.4, 0.1.5, 0.1.6, 0.2.1; **L3:** 0.1.2, 0.1.5; **L4:** 0.1.2, 0.1.5, 0.2.1, 7.1.1, 7.1.2, 8.3.1; **L5:** 0.1.2, 0.1.4, 0.1.5, 0.2.1, 7.1.1, 7.1.2, 8.3.1; **L6:** 0.1.2, 0.1.4, 0.1.5, 2.8.5, 7.4.4, 7.7.3; **L7:** 0.1.2, 0.1.4, 0.1.5; **L8:** 0.1.2, 0.1.5, 7.1.1, 7.1.2; **L9:** 0.1.5; **L10:** 0.1.2, 0.1.5, 7.1.1, 7.1.2, 8.3.2	**L2:** SL.5.1a, SL.5.1b, SL.5.1c, SL.5.1d, L.4.1/L.5.1c, L.4.1/L.5.1f; **L3:** RI/RL.4.1, RI/RL.5.1, RI.4.2, RI.4.3, RI.5.4, SL.5.1a, SL.5.1b, SL.5.1c, SL.5.1d, SL.5.2, L.4.4/L.5.4a, L.4.6/L.5.6; **L5:** SL.5.1a, SL.5.1b, SL.5.1c, SL.5.1d, L.4.1/L.5.1c, L.4.1/L.5.1f; **L6:** RI/RL.4.1, RI/RL.5.1, RI.5.4, W.5.7, W.5.8, L.4.6/L.5.6; **L8:** SL.5.1a, SL.5.1b, SL.5.1c, SL.5.1d; **L9:** RI.4.5, W.4.2a, W.4.2b, W.4.2d, W.4.2e, W.5.4, W.5.5, L.4.2/L.5.2a, L.4.2/L.5.2h, L.4.3/L.5.3a, L.4.6/L.5.6; **L10:** RI/RL.4.1, RI/RL.5.1, SL.5.4	ELPS 1–3, 5, 7–9
L1: 0.1.2, 0.1.5, 0.2.1,7.1.1, 7.1.2; **L2:** 0.1.2, 0.1.4, 0.1.5, 0.1.6, 0.2.1, 7.1.2; **L3:** 0.1.2, 0.1.5, 4.1.2, 4.1.3, 7.4.4, 7.7.3; **L4:** 0.1.2, 0.1.3, 0.1.5, 0.2.1, 4.1.2, 4.1.3, 7.4.4, 7.7.3; **L5:** 0.1.2, 0.1.4, 0.1.5, 0.2.1, 4.1.8; **L6:** 0.1.2, 0.1.4, 0.1.5, 4.1.5; **L7:** 0.1.2, 0.1.5, 4.1.5; **L8:** 0.1.2, 0.1.5, 4.4.4; **L9:** 0.1.5; **L10:** 0.1.2, 0.1.5, 4.1.5, 7.5.2	**L1:** SL.5.1a, SL.5.1b, SL.5.1c, SL.5.1d; **L2:** L.4.1/L.5.1k; **L3:** RI/RL.4.1, RI/RL.5.1, RI.5.4, W.5.7, W.5.8, L.4.6/L.5.6; **L4:** SL.5.1a, SL.5.1b, SL.5.1c, SL.5.1d; **L5:** L.4.1/L.5.1a; **L6:** RI/RL.4.1, RI/RL.5.1, RI.4.2, RI.5.4, SL.5.1a, SL.5.1b, SL.5.1c, SL.5.1d, , SL.5.2, L.4.6/L.5.6; **L8:** L.4.1/L.5.1e, L.4.1/L.5.1f; **L9:** W.5.1a, W.5.1b, W.5.1c, W.5.1d, W.5.4; **L10:** RI/RL.4.1, RI/RL.5.1, W.5.4, W.5.5, SL.5.1a, SL.5.1b, SL.5.1c, SL.5.1d, SL.5.4	ELPS 1–5, 7, 9–10
L1: 0.1.2, 0.1.5, 0.2.1, 2.7.2, 2.7.9; **L2:** 0.1.2, 0.1.5, 2.7.2, 2.7.9; **L3:** 0.1.2, 0.1.5, 7.4.4, 7.7.3; **L4:** 0.1.2, 0.1.3, 0.1.5, 0.2.1, 2.5.8; **L5:** 0.1.2, 0.1.5, 0.2.1; **L6:** 0.1.2, 0.1.4, 0.1.5; **L7:** 0.1.2, 0.1.5, 5.6.1, 7.3.1, 7.3.2; **L8:** 0.1.2, 0.1.5, 7.3.1, 7.3.2; **L9:** 0.1.5, 5.6.1; **L10:** 0.1.2, 0.1.5, 4.8.1, 4.8.3, 4.8.5	**L1:** SL.5.1a, SL.5.1b, SL.5.1c, SL.5.1d; **L3:** RI.5.4, RI.4.7, RI.5.7, W.5.7, W.5.8, L.4.6/L.5.6; **L4:** L.4.6/L.5.6; **L5:** L.4.1/L.5.1d, L.4.1/L.5.1f; **L6:** RI/RL.4.1, RI/RL.5.1, RI.4.2, RI.5.4, W.5.4, SL.5.1a, SL.5.1b, SL.5.1c, SL.5.1d, SL.5.2, L.4.6/L.5.6; **L8:** W.5.4; **L9:** RI.4.5, RI.5.8, W.4.2a, W.4.2b, W.4.2c, W.4.2d, W.4.2e, W.5.4, W.5.5, L.4.2/L.5.2a, L.4.2/L.5.2h, L.4.3/L.5.3a; **L10:** SL.5.1a, SL.5.1b, SL.5.1c, SL.5.1d, SL.5.4	ELPS 1–3, 5–9
L1: 0.1.2, 0.1.5, 0.2.1, 4.8.1, 4.8.2, 4.8.3; **L2:** 0.1.2, 0.1.5, 4.8.1, 4.8.2, 4.8.3; **L3:** 0.1.2, 0.1.5, 3.1.6, 4.2.5, 7.4.4, 7.7.3; **L4:** 0.1.2, 0.1.5, 4.4.4, 7.3.1, 7.3.2; **L5:** 0.1.2, 0.1.5, 0.2.1, 4.8.1, 4.8.2, 4.8.3; **L6:** 0.1.2, 0.1.5, 3.4.2; **L7:** 0.1.2, 0.1.5, 4.4.4; **L8:** 0.1.2, 0.1.5, 4.6.1; L.4.2/L.5.2b; **L9:** 0.1.5, 4.5.2, 4.5.4, 4.5.5, 4.6.2, 4.8.1, 4.8.3, 5.6.1, 7.7.4; **L10:** 0.1.2, 0.1.5, 7.5.7	**L1:** RL.5.4, L.5.5, L.4.6/L.5.6; **L2:** SL.5.1a, SL.5.1b, SL.5.1c, SL.5.1d, L.4.1/L.5.1k, L.4.3/L.5.3d; **L3:** RI/RL.4.1, RI/RL.5.1, RI.5.4, W.5.7, W.5.8, L.4.6/L.5.6; **L5:** L.4.1/L.5.1k, L.4.2/L.5.2e; **L6:** RI/RL.4.1, RI/RL.5.1, RI.4.2, RI.4.3, RI.5.4, SL.5.1a, SL.5.1b, SL.5.1c, SL.5.1d, SL.5.2, L.4.6/L.5.6; **L9:** W.5.1a, W.5.1b, W.5.1c, W.5.1d, W.5.4, W.5.5, L.4.2/L.5.2a, L.4.2/L.5.2h, L.4.3/L.5.3a, L.4.6/L.5.6; **L10:** SL.5.1a, SL.5.1b, SL.5.1c, SL.5.1d, SL.5.4	ELPS 1–5, 7–10
L1: 0.1.2, 0.1.5, 1.4.8, 3.4.2; **L2:** 0.1.2, 0.1.5, 3.4.2; **L3:** 0.1.2, 0.1.5, 3.4.8; **L4:** 0.1.2, 0.1.5, 2.3.3; **L5:** 0.1.2, 0.1.5, 2.3.3; **L6:** 0.1.2, 0.1.5, 2.2.5, 3.4.8, 7.7.3, 7.4.4; **L7:** 0.1.2, 0.1.5, 2.1.2, 2.5.1; **L8:** 0.1.2, 0.1.5; **L9:** 0.1.5, 3.4.8; **L10:** 0.1.2, 0.1.5, 3.4.8, 7.7.3, 7.4.4	**L2:** L.4.1/L.5.1f, L.4.2/L.5.2d; **L3:** RI/RL.4.1, RI/RL.5.1, RI.4.2, RI.5.4, SL.5.1a, SL.5.1b, SL.5.1c, SL.5.1d, SL.5.2, L.4.6/L.5.6; **L5:** W.5.4, L.4.1/L.5.1b, L.4.1/L.5.1k, L.4.3/L.5.3d; **L6:** RI.5.4, RI.4.7, RI.5.7, W.5.7, W.5.8, L.4.6/L.5.6; **L8:** W.5.4, L.4.1/L.5.1f, L.4.2/L.5.2d; **L9:** RI.4.5, W.4.2a, W.4.2b, W.4.2c, W.4.2d, W.4.2e, W.5.4, W.5.5, W.5.7, W.5.8, W.5.9b, L.4.2/L.5.2a, L.4.2/L.5.2h; **L10:** SL.5.1a, SL.5.1b, SL.5.1c, SL.5.1d, SL.5.4	ELPS 1–3, 5, 7–10
L1: 0.1.2, 0.1.5, 1.4.5; **L2:** 0.1.2, 0.1.5, 1.4.5; **L3:** 0.1.2, 0.1.5, 1.4.3, 1.4.5, 7.7.3, 7.4.4; **L4:** 0.1.2, 0.1.5, 1.4.5, 1.4.7; **L5:** 0.1.2, 0.1.5, 0.2.1, 1.4.2, 1.4.5; **L6:** 0.1.2, 0.1.5; **L7:** 0.1.2, 0.1.5, 1.4.7, 5.6.1, 7.3.1, 7.3.2; **L8:** 0.1.2, 0.1.5, 1.4.7, 5.6.1, 7.3.1, 7.3.2; **L9:** 0.1.5, 1.4.5, 1.4.7, 7.3.1, 7.3.2; **L10:** 0.1.2, 0.1.5, 7.3.1, 7.3.2	**L1:** SL.5.2; **L2:** SL.4.6, L.4.3/L.5.3c; **L3:** RI/RL.4.1, RI.5.4, W.5.7, W.5.8, L.4.6/L.5.6; **L5:** W.5.4, SL.5.1a, SL.5.1b, SL.5.1c, SL.5.1d, L.4.2/L.5.2e; **L6:** RI/RL.4.1, RI/RL.5.1, RI.4.2, RI.4.7, RI.5.7, SL.5.1a, SL.5.1b, SL.5.1c, SL.5.1d, SL.5.2, L.4.6/L.5.6; **L8:** SL.4.6, L.4.2/L.5.2b, L.4.3/L.5.3c; **L9:** RI.4.5, W.5.1a, W.5.1b, W.5.1c, W.5.1d, W.5.4, W.5.5, L.4.2/L.5.2a, L.4.2/L.5.2h; **L10:** SL.5.4	ELPS 1–5, 7–9
L1: 0.1.2, 0.1.5, 1.9.5; **L2:** 0.1.2, 0.1.5, 1.9.5; **L3:** 0.1.2, 0.1.5, 1.9.8, 7.7.3, 7.4.4; **L4:** 0.1.2, 0.1.4, 0.1.5, 1.9.6; **L5:** 0.1.2, 0.1.5, 1.9.6; **L6:** 0.1.2, 0.1.5, 1.2.5, 1.6.3, 7.4.4, 7.7.3; **L7:** 0.1.2, 0.1.5, 1.9.7; **L8:** 0.1.2, 0.1.5, 1.9.7; **L9:** 0.1.5, 1.9.5; **L10:** 0.1.2, 0.1.5, 4.6.1, 7.5.3	**L2:** W.5.4; **L3:** RI/RL.4.1, RI/RL.5.1, RI.5.4, W.5.7, W.5.8, L.4.6/L.5.6; **L6:** RI/RL.4.1, RI/RL.5.1, RI.4.2, RI.4.3, RI.5.4, RI.4.7, RI.5.7, W.5.4, W.5.5, SL.5.1a, SL.5.1b, SL.5.1c, SL.5.1d, SL.5.2, L.4.6/L.5.6; **L8:** W.5.4, L.4.1/L.5.1e, L.4.1/L.5.1f; **L9:** RI.4.5, W.4.2a, W.4.2b, W.4.2c, W.4.2d, W.4.2e, W.5.4, W.5.5, L.4.2/L.5.2a, L.4.2/L.5.2h, L.4.3/L.5.3a; **L10:** SL.5.1a, SL.5.1b, SL.5.1c, SL.5.1d, SL.5.4	ELPS 1–3, 5, 7–9
L1: 0.1.2, 0.1.5, 3.2.1, 3.3.1, 3.3.4, 3.6.3; **L2:** 0.1.2, 0.1.5, 7.5.4; **L3:** 0.1.2, 0.1.5, 3.2.3, 7.4.4, 7.7.3; **L4:** 0.1.2, 0.1.5, 2.1.2, 2.5.1; **L5:** 0.1.2, 0.1.5, 3.5.9; **L6:** 0.1.2, 0.1.5, 3.5.9; **L7:** 0.1.2, 0.1.5, 3.1.3, 3.4.6; **L8:** 0.1.2, 0.1.5, 3.5.9; **L9:** 0.1.5, 3.6.3; **L10:** 0.1.2, 0.1.5, 4.8.3, 7.5.4	**L1:** L.4.4/L.5.4c; **L2:** L.4.1/L.5.1e, L.4.1/L.5.1f; **L3:** RI/RL.4.1, RI/RL.5.1, RI.5.4, W.5.7, W.5.8, L.4.6/L.5.6; **L4:** RI/RL.4.1, RI/RL.5.1; **L5:** SL.5.1a, SL.5.1b, SL.5.1c, SL.5.1d, L.4.1/L.5.1k, L.4.3/L.5.3d; **L6:** RI/RL.4.1, RI/RL.5.1, RI.4.2, RI.4.3, RI.5.4, RI.4.7, RI.5.7, SL.5.1a, SL.5.1b, SL.5.1c, SL.5.1d, SL.5.2, L.4.6/L.5.6; **L8:** L.4.1/L.5.1d, L.4.1/L.5.1k; **L9:** W.4.2a, W.4.2b, W.4.2d, W.4.2e, W.5.4, W.5.5, L.4.2/L.5.2a, L.4.2/L.5.2h, L.4.3/L.5.3a, L.4.6/L.5.6; **L10:** W.5.4, SL.5.4	ELPS 1–3, 5, 7, 9–10
L1: 0.1.2, 0.1.5, 2.8.6, 2.8.8; **L2:** 0.1.2, 0.1.5, 2.8.6, 2.8.8; **L3:** 0.1.2, 0.1.5, 2.8.6, 2.8.8, 7.4.4, 7.7.3; **L4:** 0.1.2, 0.1.5, 2.8.3, 2.8.6; **L5:** 0.1.2, 0.1.5, 2.8.6, 2.8.8; **L6:** 0.1.2, 0.1.5, 2.8.3; **L7:** 0.1.2, 0.1.5, 2.8.6, 2.8.8; **L8:** 0.1.2, 0.1.5, 3.5.9; **L9:** 0.1.5, 2.8.6; **L10:** 0.1.2, 0.1.5, 4.8.1, 4.8.3, 7.5.5, 7.5.6	**L1:** L.5.5; **L2:** SL.5.1a, SL.5.1b, SL.5.1c, SL.5.1d, L.4.3/L.5.3d; **L3:** RI/RL.4.1, RI/RL.5.1, RI.5.4, W.5.4, W.5.7, W.5.8, L.4.6/L.5.6; **L5:** L.4.1/L.5.1b; **L6:** RI/RL.4.1, RI/RL.5.1, RI.4.2, RI.5.4, SL.5.1a, SL.5.1b, SL.5.1c, SL.5.1d, SL.5.2, L.4.6/L.5.6; **L7:** L.4.1/L.5.1d; **L8:** SL.5.1a, SL.5.1b, SL.5.1c, SL.5.1d, L.4.1/L.5.1d; **L9:** RI.4.5, W.5.1a, W.5.1b, W.5.1c, W.5.1d, W.5.4, W.5.5; **L10:** SL.5.4	ELPS 1–5, 7–10
L1: 0.1.2, 0.1.5, 4.6.4; **L2:** 0.1.2, 0.1.5, 4.8.3, 4.8.5; **L3:** 0.1.2, 0.1.5, 4.3.2; **L4:** 0.1.2, 0.1.5, 3.4.2; **L5:** 0.1.2, 0.1.5, 3.4.2; **L6:** 0.1.2, 0.1.5, 4.3.4, 7.4.4, 7.7.3; **L7:** 0.1.2, 0.1.5, 4.4.2; **L8:** 0.1.2, 0.1.5, 4.6.2, 4.6.5, 4.8.3; **L9:** 0.1.5, 4.9.4; **L10:** 0.1.2, 0.1.5, 4.8.1, 4.8.3, 7.5.5, 7.5.6	**L2:** SL.5.1a, SL.5.1b, SL.5.1c, SL.5.1d; **L3:** RI/RL.4.1, RI/RL.5.1, RI.4.2, RI.5.4, SL.5.2, L.4.6/L.5.6; **L5:** W.5.4, SL.5.1a, SL.5.1b, SL.5.1c, SL.5.1d; **L6:** RI/RL.4.1, RI/RL.5.1, RI.5.4, W.5.4, W.5.7, W.5.8, L.4.6/L.5.6; **L8:** SL.5.1a, SL.5.1b, SL.5.1c, SL.5.1d, L.4.1/L.5.1d; **L9:** RI.4.5, W.5.1a, W.5.1b, W.5.1c, W.5.1d, W.5.4, W.5.5, L.4.2/L.5.2a, L.4.2/L.5.2h; **L10:** SL.5.4	ELPS 1–5, 7–9
L1: 0.1.2, 0.1.5, 5.3.7; **L2:** 0.1.2, 0.1.5, 5.3.1; **L3:** 0.1.2, 0.1.5, 5.3.2, 7.4.4, 7.7.4; **L4:** 0.1.2, 0.1.5, 5.3.3; **L5:** 0.1.2, 0.1.5, 5.3.3; **L6:** 0.1.2, 0.1.5; **L7:** 0.1.2, 0.1.5, 1.9.1, 1.9.2, 5.3.1; **L8:** 0.1.2, 0.1.5, 1.9.2; **L9:** 0.1.5, 1.9.2; **L10:** 0.1.2, 0.1.5, 4.8.1, 4.8.3, 4.8.5, 7.5.6	**L2:** SL.5.1a, SL.5.1b, SL.5.1c, SL.5.1d; **L3:** RI/RL.4.1, RI/RL.5.1, RI.5.4, W.5.7, W.5.8, L.4.6/L.5.6; **L5:** W.5.4, SL.5.1a, SL.5.1b, SL.5.1c, SL.5.1d, L.4.1/L.5.1f; **L6:** RI/RL.4.1, RI/RL.5.1, RI.4.2, RI.4.3, RI.5.4, SL.5.2, L.4.6/L.5.6; **L7:** RI.5.4, L.4.6/L.5.6; **L8:** W.5.4; **L9:** RI.4.5, W.4.2a, W.4.2b, W.4.2c, W.4.2d, W.4.2e, W.5.4, W.5.5, L.4.2/L.5.2a, L.4.2/L.5.2h; **L10:** SL.5.4	ELPS 1–3, 5, 7–9
L1: 0.1.2, 0.1.5, 1.8.3; **L2:** 0.1.2, 0.1.5, 1.8.1, 1.8.3; **L3:** 0.1.2, 0.1.5, 1.8.4, 1.8.5; **L4:** 0.1.2, 0.1.5, 1.5.1, 1.5.2; **L5:** 0.1.2, 0.1.5, 1.5.1, 1.5.2; **L6:** 0.1.2, 0.1.5, 5.4.1, 7.4.4, 7.7.4; **L7:** 0.1.2, 0.1.5; **L8:** 0.1.2, 0.1.5; **L9:** 0.1.5, 2.5.8; **L10:** 0.1.2, 0.1.5, 4.8.4, 7.1.3	**L2:** W.5.4; **L3:** RI/RL.4.1, RI/RL.5.1, RI.4.2, SL.5.1a, SL.5.1b, SL.5.1c, SL.5.1d, SL.5.2; **L5:** W.5.4, L.4.1/L.5.1f, L.4.2/L.5.2d; **L6:** RI.5.4, W.5.7, W.5.8, L.4.6/L.5.6; **L8:** SL.5.1a, SL.5.1b, SL.5.1c, SL.5.1d, L.4.1/L.5.1f; **L9:** RI.5.8, W.5.1a, W.5.1b, W.5.1c, W.5.1d, W.5.4, W.5.5, L.4.2/L.5.2a, L.4.2/L.5.2h; **L10:** SL.5.4	ELPS 1–7, 9

All units of *Future* meet most of the **EFF Content Standards**. For details, as well as for correlations to other state standards, go to www.pearsoneltusa.com/future 2e.

ABOUT THE SERIES CONSULTANTS AND AUTHOR

AUTHOR, SERIES CONSULTANT, AND LEARNING EXPERT

Sarah Lynn is an ESOL teacher trainer, author, and curriculum design specialist. She has taught adult learners in the U.S. and abroad for decades, most recently at Harvard University's Center for Workforce Development. As a teacher-trainer and frequent conference presenter throughout the United States and Latin America, Ms. Lynn has led sessions and workshops on topics such as fostering student agency and resilience, brain-based teaching techniques, literacy and learning, and teaching in a multilevel classroom. Collaborating with program leaders, teachers, and students, she has developed numerous curricula for college and career readiness, reading and writing skill development, and contextualized content for adult English language learners. Ms. Lynn has co-authored several Pearson ELT publications, including *Business Across Cultures, Future, Future U.S. Citizens,* and *Project Success.* She holds a master's degree in TESOL from Teachers College, Columbia University.

SERIES CONSULTANTS

Ronna Magy has worked as an ESOL classroom teacher, author, teacher-trainer, and curriculum development specialist. She served as the ESL Teacher Adviser in charge of professional development for the Division of Adult and Career Education of the Los Angeles Unified School District. She is a frequent conference presenter on the College and Career Readiness Standards (CCRS), the English Language Proficiency Standards (ELPS), and the language, literacy, and soft skills needed for academic and workplace success. Ms. Magy has authored/co-authored and trained teachers on modules for CALPRO, the California Adult Literacy Professional Development Project, including modules on integrating and contextualizing workforce skills in the ESOL classroom and evidence-based writing instruction. She is the author of adult ESL publications on English for the workplace, reading and writing, citizenship, and life skills and test preparation. Ms. Magy holds a master's degree in social welfare from the University of California at Berkeley.

Federico Salas-Isnardi has worked in adult education as a teacher, administrator, professional developer, materials writer, and consultant. He contributed to a number of state projects in Texas including the adoption of adult education content standards and the design of statewide professional development and accountability systems.

Over nearly 30 years he has conducted professional development seminars for thousands of teachers, law enforcement officers, social workers, and business people in the United States and abroad. His areas of concentration have been educational leadership, communicative competence, literacy, intercultural communication, citizenship, and diversity education. He has taught customized workplace ESOL and Spanish programs as well as high-school equivalence classes, citizenship and civics, labor market information seminars, and middle-school mathematics. Mr. Salas-Isnardi has been a contributing writer or series consultant for a number of ESL publications, and he has co-authored curriculum for site-based workforce ESL and Spanish classes.

Mr. Salas-Isnardi is a certified diversity trainer. He has a master's degree in applied linguistics and doctoral-level coursework in adult education.

AUTHOR

Jane Curtis began teaching ESOL in Barcelona, Spain. She has been a classroom teacher, materials writer, and teacher trainer for more than 30 years. Ms. Curtis currently teaches in the English Language Program at Roosevelt University, where she also serves as special programs coordinator.

ACKNOWLEDGMENTS

The Publisher would like to acknowledge the teachers, students, and survey and focus-group participants for their valuable input. Thank you to the following reviewers and consultants who made suggestions, contributed to this *Future* revision, and helped make *Future: English for Work, Life, and Academic Success* even better in this second edition. There are many more who also shared their comments and experiences using *Future*—a big thank you to all.

Fuad Al-Daraweesh The University of Toledo, Toledo, OH
Denise Alexander Bucks County Community College, Newtown, PA
Isabel Alonso Bergen Community College, Hackensack, NJ
Veronica Avitia LeBarron Park, El Paso, TX
Maria Bazan-Myrick Houston Community College, Houston, TX
Sara M. Bulnes Miami Dade College, Miami, FL
Alexander Chakshiri Santa Maria High School, Santa Maria, CA
Scott C. Cohen, M.A.Ed. Bergen Community College, Paramus, NJ
Judit Criado Fiuza Mercy Center, Bronx, NY
Megan Ernst Glendale Community College, Glendale, CA
Rebecca Feit-Klein Essex County College Adult Learning Center, West Caldwell, NJ
Caitlin Floyd Nationalities Service Center, Philadelphia, PA
Becky Gould International Community High School, Bronx, NY
Ingrid Greenberg San Diego Continuing Education, San Diego Community College District, San Diego, CA
Steve Gwynne San Diego Continuing Education, San Diego, CA
Robin Hatfield, M.Ed. Learning Institute of Texas, Houston,TX
Coral Horton Miami Dade College, Kendall Campus, Miami, FL
Roxana Hurtado Miami-Dade County Public Schools, Miami, FL
Lisa Johnson City College of San Francisco, San Francisco, CA
Kristine R. Kelly ATLAS @ Hamline University, St. Paul, MN
Jennifer King Austin Community College, Austin, TX
Lia Lerner, Ed.D. Burbank Adult School, Burbank, CA
Ting Li The University of Toledo, Ottawa Hills, OH
Nichole M. Lucas University of Dayton, Dayton, OH
Ruth Luman Modesto Junior College, Modesto, CA
Josephine Majul El Monte-Rosemead Adult School, El Monte, CA
Dr. June Ohrnberger Suffolk County Community College, Selden, NY
Sue Park The Learning Institute of Texas, Houston, TX
Dr. Sergei Paromchik Adult Education Department, Hillsborough County Public Schools, Tampa, FL
Patricia Patton Uniontown ESL, Uniontown, PA
Matthew Piech Amarillo College, Amarillo, TX
Guillermo Rocha Essex County College, NJ
Audrene Rowe Essex County School, Newark, NJ
Naomi Sato Glendale Community College, Glendale, CA
Alejandra Solis Lone Star College, Houston, TX
Geneva Tesh Houston Community College, Houston, TX
Karyna Tytar Lake Washington Institute of Technology, Kirkland, WA
Miguel Veloso Miami Springs Adult, Miami, FL
Minah Woo Howard Community College, Columbia, MD

Pre-Unit

Getting Started

1 MEET YOUR CLASSMATES

A Read and listen to the conversation.

Ivan: Hi. My name is Ivan.

Ruth: Hi. My name is Ruth. Nice to meet you.

Ivan: Nice to meet you, too. Where are you from, Ruth?

Ruth: Colombia. What about you?

Ivan: I'm from Ukraine.

Ruth: Oh! How long have you been here?

Ivan: Three years. I came here when I finished school.

Ruth: Wow! You speak English very well.

Ivan: Thank you, but I need to study more.

Ruth: Well, I've been a student here for a year now. It's an excellent school. You'll learn a lot here.

Ivan: Great! I think you speak well, too. Why are you studying English?

Ruth: I'm planning to go to college. I'm going to apply next year.

Ivan: That's terrific. I'm hoping to get a better job.

B **WORK TOGETHER.** Practice the conversation.

C Make similar conversations. Use your own names and information.

2 LEARN ABOUT YOURSELF

A Take the Learning Styles survey on page 3.

B Count the number of *a, b,* and *c* answers. Write the numbers.

7 a answers　　2 b answers　　1 c answers

C **WORK TOGETHER.** Discuss your learning styles.

- If you scored mostly a's, you may have a visual learning style. You learn by seeing and looking.
- If you scored mostly b's, you may have an auditory learning style. You learn by hearing and listening.
- If you scored mostly c's, you may have a kinesthetic learning style. You learn by touching and doing.

Knowing your learning style can help you understand why some things are easier for you than other things. Knowing your learning style also helps you recognize what ways to study may be most useful for you.

1. Are you surprised by the results you got? Explain.
2. Do you think knowing your learning style will help you in your class? In what ways?

What's Your Learning Style?

Choose the first answer that you think of.
Circle a, b, or c.

1 When I study, I like to ______.
a. read notes or read diagrams and illustrations
b. repeat information silently to myself
c. write notes on cards or make diagrams

2 When I listen to music, I ______.
a. picture things that go with the music
b. sing along
c. tap my feet

3 When I solve a problem, I ______.
a. make a list of things to do and check them off as I do them
b. talk about the problem with experts or friends
c. make a diagram of the problem

4 When I read for pleasure, I prefer ______.
a. a travel book with a lot of pictures
b. a novel with a lot of conversation
c. a crime story where you have to solve a mystery

5 When I'm learning to use a new app or computer program, I prefer ______.
a. watching a video about it
b. listening to someone explain it
c. using the app or program and figuring it out for myself

6 When I'm at a party, the next day I will remember ______.
a. the faces of the people I met there, but not their names
b. the names of the people there, but not their faces
c. what I did and said there

7 When I tell a story, I'd rather ______.
a. write it
b. tell it out loud
c. act it out

8 When I'm trying to concentrate, the thing I find most distracting is ______.
a. things I see, like people moving around
b. things I hear, like other people's conversations
c. things I feel, like hunger, worry, or neck pain

9 When I don't know how to spell a word, I will usually ______.
a. write it out to see if it looks right
b. sound it out
c. write it out to see if it feels right

10 When I'm standing in a long line, I'll usually ______.
a. read on my phone
b. talk to the person in line in front of me
c. tap my foot and move around

3 LEARN ABOUT *FUTURE*

A CLASS. Turn to page iii. Answer the questions.

1. What information is on this page? 1
2. How many units are in this book? 12
3. Which unit is about health? 8
4. Which unit is about money? 12
5. Which unit is about the legal system? 11
6. Which unit is about driving? 7

B Look inside the front cover. How will you get the audio?

C There is additional information for you at the back of the book. Find each section. Write the page number.

Grammar Review p 247 Audio Script p 266 Index 278

4 REVIEW VERB TENSES

Look at the conversation between Ivan and Ruth. Find one example of each of the following verb tenses and write the sentence on the line. There may be more than one correct answer.

Simple present: My name is Juventina

Simple past: I came here when I finish school.

Future: I hope to get a newer job.

Present perfect: You will Learn a lot here.

Present continuous: I'm plannig to go to College.

1 Catching Up

PREVIEW

Who are the people? What do you think they are saying to each other?

UNIT GOALS

- ☐ Talk about yourself and your family
- ☐ Discuss goals
- ☐ Interpret and complete a school application
- ☐ Discuss ways to succeed
- ☐ Write about a person you admire
- ☐ **Academic skill:** Skim for the general idea or scan for specific information
- ☐ **Writing skill:** Use chronological order
- ☐ **Workplace soft skill:** Take responsibility for professional growth

Lesson **1**

Listening and Speaking

Talk about yourself and your family

1 BEFORE YOU LISTEN

PREDICT. Look at the picture. Victor and Brenda work at the Café Royale, a restaurant in a large hotel. What do you think they're talking about?

2 LISTEN

A **LISTEN FOR MAIN IDEA.** Listen to the first part of the conversation. Then complete the sentences.

1. Brenda is ordering garden salad ______ for a customer.
2. Victor is surprised at the customer's order because Only for Lunch ______.

B **LISTEN FOR DETAILS.** Listen to the whole conversation. Circle the answers.

1. How do Victor and Brenda know each other?
   - **a.** Their families lived in the same neighborhood.
   - **b.** They dated in high school.
   - **c.** They worked together at another restaurant.
2. When did Victor begin working at the Café Royale?
   - **a.** a week ago
   - **b.** a month ago
   - **c.** sometime last year
3. What time of day does Victor usually work?
   - **a.** in the morning
   - **b.** in the afternoon
   - **c.** at night
4. What is the regular cook doing today?
   - **a.** looking for a new job
   - **b.** handling personal affairs
   - **c.** enjoying his vacation
5. Why was Victor surprised by the customer's order?
   - **a.** The customer ordered a burger and a steak.
   - **b.** The customer ordered a burger for breakfast.
   - **c.** Manny usually cooks breakfast.

C **INFER.** What do you think Victor and Brenda are going to talk about during their break?

______

______

Listening and Speaking

3 PRONUNCIATION

A **PRACTICE.** Listen. Then listen again and repeat.

Where are you **living**?

We **have** an **apartment** on **Fifth** Street.

It's a **little noisy**, but we **like** it.

Stressed words

The important words in a sentence are stressed. They sound louder and longer than grammar words, such as articles, helping verbs, and prepositions.

B **APPLY.** Listen. Put a dot (•) over the stressed words. Then listen again to check your answers.

1. How's your family?
2. My wife is working at a restaurant.
3. She usually works at night.
4. She's planning to go to school.
5. What does she want to study?
6. She wants to study nursing or nutrition.

4 CONVERSATION

Victor and Brenda are talking during their break.

A **LISTEN AND READ.** Then practice the conversation with a partner.

Brenda: So how's everything going? Where are you living now?
Victor: We have an apartment on Fifth Street. It's a little noisy, but we like it.
Brenda: We? So tell me about your family!
Victor: We have three beautiful kids. Isabel is eight. Michelle is five. And Victor Jr. is two.
Brenda: How wonderful! And your wife?
Victor: My wife is great. She's working in a law office. She's a receptionist now, but she's planning to go to school to be a paralegal. What's new with you?
Brenda: I live over on Jackson Street now. My apartment isn't too far from the old neighborhood.

B **ROLE-PLAY.** Make a similar conversation between two acquaintances. Both of you worked at the same company five years ago, but you haven't seen each other since then.

Student A: You're shopping at a supermarket near your home. You see Student B, an old work acquaintance. Tell about your life.

Student B: You're shopping at a supermarket near your job. You see Student A, an old work acquaintance. Tell about your life.

C **PRESENT.** Tell about a time you met someone you hadn't seen in a long time.

I can talk about myself and my family. ☐ I need more practice. ☐

For more practice, go to MyEnglishLab.

Lesson 2

Grammar

Simple present and present continuous

Simple present and present continuous	
Simple present	**Present continuous**
I always **work** later in the day.	**I'm working** in the morning this week.
He **doesn't** usually **work** at night.	He **isn't working** today.
Do you **work** mornings or evenings?	**Are** you **working** today?
How often **do** they **work** together?	Where **are** they **working** these days?

Grammar Watch

- Use the simple present to talk about usual activities or general statements of fact.
- Use the present continuous to talk about things that are happening now (today, this week, this month) or things that are happening temporarily.
- Stative (non-action) verbs such as *know* and *have* are commonly used in the simple present, not the present continuous: *I **have** a small apartment on Fifth Street now.*

(See page 260 for a list of stative verbs.)

A **INVESTIGATE.** **Underline the simple present verbs. Circle the present continuous verbs.**

Brenda: Hi, Victor. Why are you cooking breakfast again today?

Victor: I'm helping Manny out. He needs some more time off this week.

Brenda: I don't understand. Why is Manny missing work? Is he sick?

Victor: No, he's fine. He and his fiancée are preparing for their wedding this week. His family is visiting from Mexico, so it's a good time to discuss the plans.

B **DETERMINE.** **Cross out the incorrect verbs.**

Victor and Brenda **catch up / are catching up** during their break. They **have / are having** the same schedule because Manny **takes / is taking** some time off this week. They **talk / are talking** about Brenda's older brother, Edward. When Edward was young, he wanted to travel around the world, but he **doesn't care / isn't caring** about a life of adventure anymore. Instead, he **takes / is taking** a short two-week vacation every year and **works / is working** as a computer programmer the other fifty weeks of the year. He **thinks / is thinking** his life is wonderful.

Grammar

C **APPLY.** Use the simple present or the present continuous.

Victor: I *'m trying* _______ (try) to remember the name of your old friend from the neighborhood.

Oh, I _______ (know). Her name was Teresa, right?

Brenda: Right. You _______ (have) a great memory.

Victor: How _______ she _______ (do) these days? _______ you _______ (see) her anymore?

Brenda: Teresa and I _______ (be) both really busy, so we _______ (not talk) very often. But she and my sister usually _______ (hang out) together. They _______ (study) at the community college this semester. They both _______ (want) to be accountants.

D **EVALUATE.** Find and correct the mistakes in each conversation.

1. **Victor:** Are you always work during the day?

   Brenda: Yes. I am preferring a daytime schedule. I always feel tired when I'm working at night.

2. **Victor:** How you spend your evenings?

   Brenda: I usually watch TV, but sometimes my sister and I are going to a movie.

3. **Victor:** Are you having a pet to keep you company?

   Brenda: Yes, I have a dog named Lucky. But at the moment, he stays at doggie daycare. I will pick him up after work. I'm really missing him!

Show what you know!

1. **DISCUSS.** Think of three things you're doing this month. How are they different from what you usually do? Explain the differences.
2. **WRITE.** Describe how this month is different from your usual routine. Use simple present and present continuous verbs.

This month I'm working at night, but I usually work in the morning.

I can use the simple present and present continuous. ☐ I need more practice. ☐

For more practice, go to MyEnglishLab.

Lesson 3

Reading

Read about an American success story

1 BEFORE YOU READ

A **DISCUSS.** What is the "American dream"?

B **PREDICT.** Skim the article. What is it about?

Academic Skill: Skim for the general idea or scan for specific information

Before you read a text for complete understanding, skim it to get the general idea. Look at the title, the headings, and the photos or illustrations.

When you are looking for specific information, you can scan. Run your eyes quickly over the text looking for that information.

2 READ

Listen and read.

AN AMERICAN SUCCESS STORY

Moawia Eldeeb is an American success story. After years of poverty and a lot of hard work, he achieved the "American dream" and founded his own company. How did he do it?

Childhood Struggles

Moawia lived on a small farm in Egypt until he was nine years old. Then his brother was born with a terrible genetic condition. The baby couldn't sweat, and his parents knew that he wouldn't live long in Egypt's hot climate. So, they took part in the U.S. visa lottery. Luckily, they won, and they moved to New York City.

The family couldn't make ends meet in New York. Moawia had to drop out of school to earn money. He worked 12-hour shifts at a pizza restaurant for only $20 a day.

A Disaster Changes Things

Then, one day, the Eldeebs' apartment building burned down. "That was the scariest day, but … it was the best thing because it changed the course of our whole lives," Moawia said. The family moved to a homeless shelter where they didn't have to pay for food or rent. Moawia could stop working and go back to school.

Moawia worried that he would be behind his classmates, but a librarian told him about the Khan Academy's free online classes. "I basically did every single lesson on the website," he said. Moawia's hard work paid off when a local high school gave him a full scholarship. Next, he studied math at Queens College, and then transferred to Columbia University.

At first, Moawia thought Columbia University was intimidating. But he got over feeling scared when he realized that he was just as talented as the other students. Moawia did well in his classes, and he made the most of his time at the university.

Start-up Success

At Columbia, Moawia made extra money by working in a gym as a personal trainer. He was shocked that personal trainers cost so much. So, he and a classmate invented a "smart mirror." Instead of having a trainer show the correct position, the mirror shows the correct position and records all the information about the workout.

Moawia showed his invention to investors. They gave him $1.5 million to start his own company. He named his start-up SmartSpot. SmartSpot mirrors can now be found in many gyms.

In 2016, Moawia was named a Robin Hood Foundation Hero in honor of his incredible journey from extreme poverty to success. He is proud of his achievements. "America has given me everything that I've dreamed of."

3 CLOSE READING

A **IDENTIFY.** What is the main idea?

a. Moawia Eldeeb was born in Egypt and was very poor when he was a child.
b. Moawia Eldeeb invented a "smart mirror" to help people exercise more economically.
c. Because he went from poverty to owning his own company, Moawia Eldeeb is an American success story.

B CITE EVIDENCE. Complete the sentences. Where is the information located? **Lines**

1. Moawia Eldeeb and his family left Egypt because _____. _____
   - **a.** they couldn't make enough money on their farm to survive
   - **b.** Moawia's brother was born with a dangerous disease
   - **c.** they wanted to move from the countryside to a big city
2. As a child, Moawia worked in a pizza restaurant _____. _____
   - **a.** after school on weekdays
   - **b.** on weekends
   - **c.** for 12 hours a day
3. The fire in the Eldeebs' apartment building was _____. _____
   - **a.** a terrible disaster for Moawia because his family's apartment was destroyed
   - **b.** a good thing for Moawia because his family could move to a nicer apartment
   - **c.** a good thing for Moawia because he could stop working and go to school
4. To catch up with his classmates, Moawia _____. _____
   - **a.** studied by himself by taking online classes
   - **b.** studied by himself by reading books in the library
   - **c.** took a few classes at a local high school
5. Moawia and a classmate invented a mirror that _____. _____
   - **a.** can replace a personal trainer in a gym
   - **b.** helps students study at Columbia University
   - **c.** he sold to a big company for millions of dollars
6. Moawia achieved the "American dream" because _____. _____
   - **a.** he got a full scholarship to go to Columbia University
   - **b.** he worked his way up from poverty to go to college and own his own business
   - **c.** he moved to New York City and became an American citizen

C INTERPRET VOCABULARY. Complete the sentences.

1. In the context of line 12, the phrase *make ends meet* means _____.
   - **a.** save enough money
   - **b.** pay all their bills
2. In the context of line 31, the word *intimidating* means _____.
   - **a.** making him feel unsure about his or her abilities
   - **b.** making him feel physically weaker
3. In the context of lines 33–34, the phrase *made the most of* means _____.
   - **a.** improved as much as possible
   - **b.** earned a lot of extra money
4. In the context of line 53, the word *start-up* means _____.
   - **a.** set in motion
   - **b.** new, small company

D SUMMARIZE. What are the most important ideas in the article?

Show what you know!

1. **COLLABORATE.** In what ways is Moawia's story an American success story? Do you know other American success stories? How are they similar to or different from Moawia's story?
2. **WRITE.** Describe an American success story. Explain why it is a success story.

   My grandfather, Carlos Sánchez, is an American success story. He was born in a big city in Guatemala . . .

I can skim for the general idea or scan for specific information. ☐ I need more practice. ☐

To read more, go to MyEnglishLab.

Lesson 4

Listening and Speaking

Discuss goals

1 BEFORE YOU LISTEN

MAKE CONNECTIONS. Victor Pérez is an ambitious person. What does the word *ambitious* mean? Are you ambitious? Explain.

2 LISTEN

Victor is looking at this list of positions at the Palm Café. Brenda starts a conversation with him.

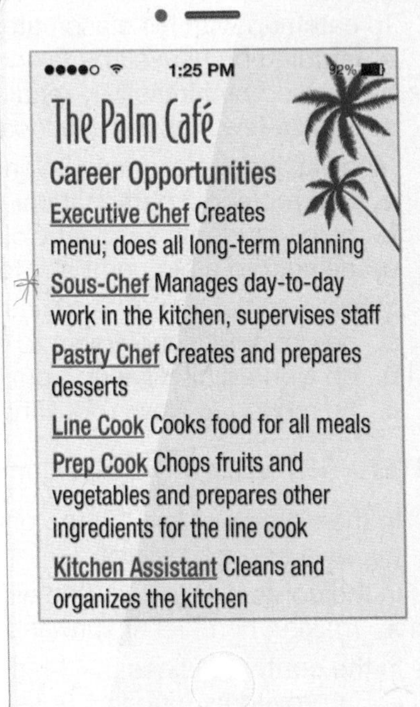

1:25 PM
The Palm Café
Career Opportunities
Executive Chef Creates menu; does all long-term planning
Sous-Chef Manages day-to-day work in the kitchen, supervises staff
Pastry Chef Creates and prepares desserts
Line Cook Cooks food for all meals
Prep Cook Chops fruits and vegetables and prepares other ingredients for the line cook
Kitchen Assistant Cleans and organizes the kitchen

A **LISTEN FOR MAIN IDEA.** Listen to the first part of the conversation. Then look at the screen to the right. Check (✓) the job that Victor has now. Circle the job he wants next.

B **LISTEN FOR DETAILS.** Listen to the whole conversation. Circle the answers.

1. What is Victor going to do next month?
   a. become a sous-chef
   b. start cooking classes
   c. own a restaurant
2. What is Victor's long-term goal? (What does he want to do ten years from now?)
   a. be a line cook
   b. be a sous-chef
   c. own a restaurant
3. What will Victor do after he finishes the program?
   a. be a line cook
   b. become a sous-chef
   c. start cooking classes
4. What is Brenda's long-term goal?
   a. be a manager
   b. own a restaurant
   c. get an Associate's degree

C **EXPLAIN.** Victor's short-term goals are to go to school and then become a sous-chef. His long-term goal is to own his own restaurant. What is the difference between a short-term goal and a long-term goal?

Now short term Long Term
Line cook Tak clases and became sous Chef own a restaurant

D **EVALUATE.** What do you think of Victor's plans? Does he need to set any more short-term goals in order to reach his long term-goal? If yes, what addtional goals does he need to set?

3 CONVERSATION

A ▶ **LISTEN AND READ.** Then practice the conversation with a partner.

A: I don't want to be a cashier my whole life. Eventually, I want to be a manager. I think it's time for me to go to school.
B: Have you decided where to study?
A: Not yet. First, I need to do more research. I'm looking at different business programs online.
B: Are you going to visit any schools?
A: Yes, a few. I'll send in my applications by the end of the month.
B: It sounds like you have a plan.

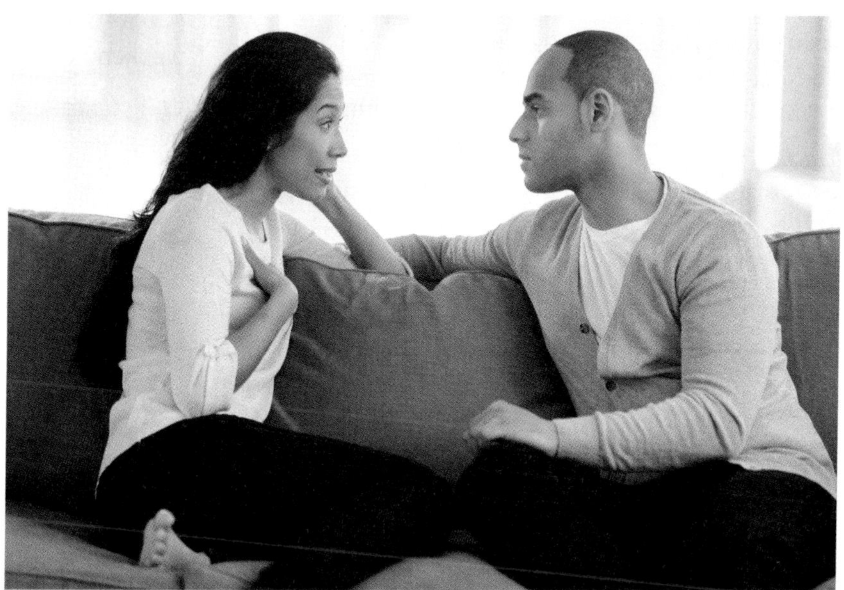

A young woman is describing her goals to a friend.

B **ANALYZE.** What is the young woman's long-term goal? What are her short-term goals? What else could she do to reach her long-term goal?

C **PROBLEM SOLVE.** What is a long-term goal you have at school, work, or home? What short-term goals will help you reach your long-term goal?

My short-term goals are to:		My long-term goal is to:
• ______________________	→	______________________
• ______________________		______________________
• ______________________		______________________

I can discuss my goals. ☐ I need more practice. ☐

For more practice, go to MyEnglishLab.

Lesson 5 Grammar

Future with the present continuous, *be going to,* and *will*

Future plans with the present continuous, *be going to,* and *will*		
Present continuous	***Be going to***	***Will***
I'**m starting** classes there next month.	I'**m going to go** to the Helman Culinary School.	I'**ll take** daytime classes and **work** in the evening.
I'**m not waiting** until next year.	I'**m not going to start** in July.	I **won't take** classes on weekends.
Are you **taking** a lot of classes next month?	**Are** you **going to finish** your classes soon?	**Will** you **take** classes in the evenings?
How many classes **are** you **taking**?	How soon **are** you **going to finish**?	When **will** you **take** classes?

Grammar Watch

- Use the present continuous to talk about definite plans in the future.
- Use *be going to* to talk about plans that are somewhat less certain.
- Also use *will* to talk about less certain plans or unplanned events.

A **INVESTIGATE.** Read the messages between two sisters. Underline the examples of future with the present continuous, *be going to,* or *will.*

Kayla

Can we talk later this afternoon, or are you working?

Sandy

I'm not working, but I'm going to meet with my manager this afternoon.

Really? What are you going to talk about?

I need to talk about where I'll be five years from now. I don't know whether to apply for a promotion at work or go back to school. The Davis College is having an open house tomorrow.

Are you going to go to it?

Yes. It will give me a chance to visit the campus and find out about classes. I'm also going to talk to a counselor at the career center.

That sounds exciting!

B **APPLY.** Complete the sentences with the correct future form.

1. My friend ___is starting___ a new job next week.
   (*present continuous*/start)
2. Do you have any idea where you ___will be___ in twenty years?
   (will/be)
3. I ___going to___ a late shift tomorrow.
   (be going to/work)
4. I ___won't have___ time to finish my homework tonight. I ___am working___ until midnight.
   (will/not/have) (*present continuous*/work)
5. He ___is going to Tell.___ his manager that he wants a promotion.
   (be going to/tell)

Grammar

C **COMPLETE.** Use the verbs in the box with the correct future form.

go have start

I recently saw my friend Mike from high school. He's doing well, but he's thinking about becoming a medical assistant. He *is going to go* (be going to) back to school, and he will start (will) in September. Canyon College is having (*present continuous*) an information session next week, and Mike is going to go (be going to) to it. The college will have (will) some counselors there to talk about the program—and Mike hopes they will have (will) refreshments!

D **APPLY.** Look at Marta's short-term goals and activities for next month. Write three sentences with *be going to* and two sentences with *will.*

Goals for Next Month
1. Plan for next semester's classes
   - register for classes
   - apply for financial aid
2. Research possible jobs for after graduation
   - attend job fair
   - search for jobs online
   - continue volunteer work at community center

Show what you know!

1. **DISCUSS.** What are two short-term goals you would like to achieve in the coming year? What small steps can you take to achieve those goals?

Get my driver's license.
1. *Get the driver's manual.*
2. *Study the manual.*
3. *Get a driver's learner permit.*
4. *Practice driving.*
5. *Pass the driving test.*

Get a better job.
1. *Finish my English courses.*
2. *Enroll in college.*

2. **WRITE.** Choose one short-term goal. Explain what you will do to achieve that goal.

I am working to become a teacher's assistant. First, I'm going to finish this class to improve my English . . .

I can use the present continuous, *be going to,* and *will* to express the future. ☐ I need more practice. ☐

For more practice, go to MyEnglishLab.

Lesson 6

Workplace, Life, and Community Skills

Interpret and complete a school application

1 INTERPRET A SCHOOL APPLICATION

A MAKE CONNECTIONS. What kinds of application forms have you completed? What information do most applications ask for?

B SCAN. THEN READ. What types of information does the application on page 17 ask for? After scanning, read the entire application.

C DEFINE KEY WORDS. Find the words on the left in the application. Match the words with their definitions.

e 1. credit
f 2. fee
d 3. GED
b 4. non-refundable
c 5. optional
a 6. transcript

a. document that shows student classes and grades
b. money that cannot be returned to you after you pay it
c. not required, but something you can choose to do
d. diploma that says you have the skills needed to graduate high school
e. unit used to measure college or university work
f. money you pay to do something

D LOCATE DETAILS. Read the statements about Victor. Write *T* (true) or *F* (false). Correct the false statements.

F 1. He wants to start classes in ~~Fall~~ Spring 2020.
f 2. His phone number at home is 858-555-1492.
T 3. He is a U.S. citizen.
f 4. He completed his GED in August 2007.
T 5. He was a prep cook before he became a line cook.
f 6. He worked as a prep cook for just under a year.

E DISCUSS. Answer the questions.

1. Why does the school want to know the applicant's work history?
2. Does the applicant need to answer the optional ethnicity question? Why does a school ask for that information?

F STATE AN OPINION. Do you think the applicant is ready for culinary school? Why? Why not?

____

____

Helman Culinary School www.helman.edu | 619-555-4000 | Office of Admissions | 1075 First Avenue, San Diego, CA 92101

Submit the following:
1. Application
2. $25 non-refundable application fee
3. Official transcripts of high school and college
4. Personal Statement

Applying for:
- ◯ Fall
- ● Spring 2020
- ◯ Summer

Specializing in:
- ● Cooking
- ◯ Event Planning
- ◯ Management

Contact Information

Last Name:	First Name:	Middle Name:	Street Address	City	State	Zip
Pérez	Victor	Antonio	2492 Jefferson St.	San Diego	CA	92110

Phone: 858-555-1452
Email: Victor1989@gotmail.com

Personal

Date of Birth: (mm/dd/yy): 06/27/75
Student Identification Number: 123-89-0000
◯ No Student Identification Number

Gender: ● Male ◯ Female
Citizenship: ● United States ◯ Other
Native Language: ◯ English ● Other bilingual in Spanish and English

Optional: *Helman Culinary School is an equal opportunity institution. This information is requested to comply with federal law and will not affect consideration of your application.*

Ethnicity:
◯ African American, Black ◯ American Indian/Alaskan ◯ Asian or Pacific Islander ● Hispanic or Latino ◯ White, Non-Hispanic ◯ Other ◯ Prefer not to answer

Education

Last High School Attended: Delgado H.S., San Diego, CA
◯ High School Graduate: (mm/yy)
● Passed GED Test: 08/17 (mm/yy)

Colleges Attended: Central College, San Diego, CA

Most Credits or Highest Degree Earned
◯ Associate's Degree ● Some Credits: 4
◯ Bachelor's Degree ◯ Certificate:

Work History (Begin with most recent employer.)

Employer:	Job Title:	City and State:	Dates Employed:		
Café Royale	Line Cook	San Diego, CA	08/17	to	present
Café Royale	Prep Cook	San Diego, CA	09/15	to	08/17
Mi Comida	Kitchen Assistant	San Diego, CA	03/14	to	09/15

Electronic signature: Please type your first and last name. Victor Pérez
Date: 12/01/19

● I understand that checking this box represents a legal signature confirming that I warrant the truthfulness of the information provided in this application.

SUBMIT

2 COMPLETE A SCHOOL APPLICATION

A GO ONLINE.

1. **SEARCH.** Find an application for a school in your area. What website is it on? ____________________
2. **COMPARE.** How is the application you found similar to the application found by another classmate? How is it different?

B **WRITE.** What types of information did the application you found ask for? Write your own information for those categories.

I can interpret and complete a school application. ☐ I need more practice. ☐

For more practice, go to MyEnglishLab.

Lesson 7

Listening and Speaking

Discuss ways to succeed

1 BEFORE YOU LISTEN

DECIDE. Entrepreneurs start new businesses. The first step in starting a new business is to create a business plan. Look at the list of questions an entrepreneur should consider. Check (✓) the three questions that you think are the most important for an entrepreneur.

- ☐ How much money do I need to start the business?
- ☐ How can I get a loan?
- ☐ What products will I sell?
- ☐ Where will I open the business?
- ☐ Who are my potential customers?
- ☐ Who are my competitors?
- ☐ Who will manage the business?
- ☐ How many employees will I need?

2 LISTEN

This is from a weekly podcast "Real-Life Entrepreneurs."

A ▶ **LISTEN FOR MAIN IDEA.** Listen to the first part of the podcast. What is the topic of this episode? Who is the guest?

Topic: ______________________

Guest: ______________________

B ▶ **LISTEN FOR DETAILS.** Listen to the entire podcast. Then read the statements. Write *T* (true) or *F* (false). Correct the false statements.

____ **1.** Susie opened a restaurant last week.

____ **2.** The prices at Asian Cottage will be very expensive.

____ **3.** The host thinks Susie's business plan is good.

____ **4.** Susie is worried about starting her business.

____ **5.** About fifteen percent of small businesses fail in the first five years.

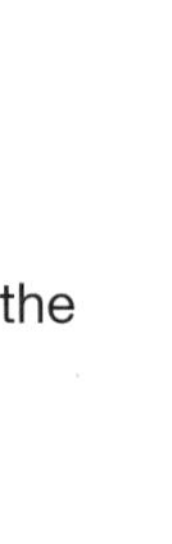

3 PRONUNCIATION

A **PRACTICE.** Listen. Then listen again and repeat.

I'm worried | that I'll miss the deadline.

Do you think | I should take a fourth class?

I'm glad | that I could help.

Speech chunks and pauses

Speakers divide speech into small chunks, or groups of words, to make it easier for listeners to understand. Speech chunks are separated by a short pause.

B **APPLY.** Listen. Mark a | to indicate a pause between speech chunks. Then listen again to check your answers.

1. I know that you're busy.
2. Are you sure we have time?
3. I'm worried we'll be late.
4. She's excited she found a new job.
5. I hope that she likes it.
6. He's afraid he won't finish.

4 CONVERSATION

Victor is meeting with his counselor at Helman Culinary School and sharing his plans.

A **LISTEN AND READ.** Then practice the conversation with a partner.

A: Hi, Victor. What can I do for you today?
B: I believe the deadline for registration is next week, so I need to select my classes. I'm worried that I'll miss the deadline.
A: Don't worry. You still have time. Let's see. This is your first semester, right?
B: That's right. I'm going to work in the evenings, so I feel that I should take only three classes.
A: That's a good plan. Let's start with your general requirements. You need to take Basic Food Preparation and Kitchen Safety. For the third class, do you want to take Knife Skills or Introduction to Baking?
B: I guess I prefer Knife Skills. These classes sound easy. Do you think I should take a fourth class?
A: If you want to graduate in two years, you'll need to take four classes every semester.
B: I'm certain that I want to finish in two years. I'll take both Knife Skills and Intro to Baking.
A: OK. Then you're all set. Do you know how to register online?
B: Yes, I do. Thank you.
A: I'm glad that I could help.

B **ROLE-PLAY.** Make a similar conversation. Then change roles.

Student A: You are a counselor at a community college. Ask the student about his or her goals and plans.

Student B: You are a student enrolling in a community college. Ask your counselor about course options.

C **PRESENT.** Think of a long-term goal you have for your life. Describe your goal. Make sure you tell how you feel about accomplishing that goal.

I can discuss ways to succeed. ☐ I need more practice. ☐

For more practice, go to MyEnglishLab.

Lesson 8

Grammar

Noun clauses

Noun clauses

I **know**

We **understand** **(that)** **it's not easy to open a new business.**

I'm **afraid**

Grammar Watch

- Noun clauses can begin with *that.* We often leave out *that* when speaking.
- Noun clauses often follow verbs that describe beliefs.
- Noun clauses also often follow adjectives that describe feelings.

(See page 260 for a list of verbs and adjectives that introduce noun clauses.)

A **INVESTIGATE. Read the paragraph. Underline the noun clauses.**

Mina wants to open a restaurant someday, but she knows she isn't ready yet. She has decided that she will start with a food truck first. She feels certain that she can get a small business loan. She heard that she also needs a permit to own a food truck. She still needs to do a lot of research. Mina is afraid that she won't be successful, but she also knows she has to take some risks.

B **IDENTIFY. Insert the word *that* at the beginning of the noun clause to show that it can be added.**

1. Eric realizes his business plan is not complete.
2. I hope I can start my own business next year.
3. Have you noticed there are a lot of new businesses downtown?
4. Linda learned she needs to apply for a permit.
5. Are you surprised your business has been so successful?
6. I'm certain I will be able to get a loan to start my business.

Grammar

C CHOOSE. **Use a verb or adjective from the box +** ***that*** **to complete the sentences. More than one answer may be possible.**

happy	know	sad	surprised	think	worried

1. She is ___happy that___ her business is doing well.
2. I __________ I can get a loan, but I'm not sure.
3. Banks __________ business loans are a risk, but they still offer them to entrepreneurs.
4. We were __________ Jenny started her own business.
5. He was __________ he couldn't get a loan from the bank.
6. They are __________ their business will not be successful.

D APPLY. **Use the sentences to answer the questions with noun clauses.**

1. What did the bank say?
   Every new business needs a business plan.
   The bank said that every new business needs a business plan.
2. What did you forget?
   The bank is closed on Saturday.
   ____
3. What does she understand?
   It's not easy to start a business.
   ____
4. Why is he worried?
   He might not get a loan.
   ____
5. Why was she surprised?
   Her interest rate was so low.
   ____

Show what you know!

1. **BRAINSTORM.** Discuss a future career goal. How certain or uncertain are you about reaching that goal?
2. **WRITE.** Write about your future career goals. Use noun clauses to talk about what you are certain or uncertain about.

   My goal is to be a nurse. I think it will be the perfect career for me because I love helping people. I know that it's not easy to become a nurse. I'm certain that I can work hard and get good grades. I'm uncertain that I have enough money to go to nursing school. I think that I'll have to take out a student loan.

I can use noun clauses. ☐ I need more practice. ☐

For more practice, go to MyEnglishLab.

Lesson 9

Writing

Write about a person you admire

WRITING PROMPT: Who is a person you admire? Why? What are some important events in that person's life? When did they happen? Write a biographical paragraph about that person.

1 STUDY THE MODEL

A ANALYZE. Read the model and Writing Skill. Then answer the questions.

Lifelong Learner

Anna Popa is my next-door neighbor. I admire her because she is a lifelong learner. Anna came to the U.S. from Moldova in 2010. Her first goal was to learn English, so she took classes at the local community college. Her next goal was to get a bachelor's degree in sociology. She began her studies in 2013 and graduated in 2017. Then she decided to become a social worker, so she enrolled in a master's degree program in social work in 2018. I want to be a lifelong learner just like Anna.

Writing Skill: Use chronological order

When you write a biographical paragraph, put information about the person's life in chronological (time) order.

1. Find the dates in the model. Then underline the events the dates refer to.
2. When did Anna Popa leave Moldova?
3. What did Anna do after she got her bachelor's degree in sociology?

B TAKE NOTES. Complete the time line with information from the model.

Date	Event
2010	• She moved to a United States.
	• studied English
2013–2017	• Get her a bachelor's degree in sociology.
2018	• She enrolled in a master's degree.
The Present	• taking classes to get a master's degree in social work

Writing

2 PLAN YOUR WRITING

A **BRAINSTORM.** Discuss your ideas for the Writing Prompt with a partner.

B **PUT IN ORDER.** Use this time line to organize your ideas before writing.

Date	Event
________–________	• ______________________________
________–________	• ______________________________
________–________	• ______________________________
________–________	• ______________________________
The Present	• ______________________________

3 WRITE

DESCRIBE. Write a biographical paragraph about a person you admire. Remember to put information about the person's life in chronological (time) order. Use the model, the Writing Skill, and your ideas from Exercise 2 to help you.

4 CHECK YOUR WRITING

A **REVISE.** Use the Writing Checklist to review your writing. Make revisions as necessary.

B **COLLABORATE.** Read your writing with a partner. Use the checklist again to improve your writing.

WRITING CHECKLIST

- ☐ Did you explain why you admire the person in your paragraph?
- ☐ Did you include important events in this person's life?
- ☐ Did you put the events in chronological order?
- ☐ Did you use correct capitalization, punctuation, and spelling?

I can put events in chronological order. ☐ I need more practice. ☐

For more practice, go to MyEnglishLab.

Lesson 10

Soft Skills at Work

Take responsibility for professional growth

1 MEET REHAN

Read about one of his workplace skills.

I take responsibility for my own professional growth. I let my supervisor know I want to advance in my career. I try to learn new skills that will help me at my job.

2 REHAN'S PROBLEM

A READ. Write *T* (true) or *F* (false).

Rehan is interested in becoming a manager at the restaurant where he works. He asks his supervisor what he needs to do to become a manager. His supervisor says she is very happy Rehan is interested in getting promoted. However, she says that all managers need experience working with budgets. Rehan has never worked with budgets before.

____ **1.** Rehan is a restaurant manager.

____ **2.** His supervisor says that managers need to work with a budget.

____ **3.** Rehan is very experienced with budgets.

B ANALYZE. What is Rehan's problem?

____

3 REHAN'S SOLUTION

A COLLABORATE. Rehan takes responsibility for his professional growth. What does Rehan do? Explain your answer.

1. Rehan tells his supervisor that managers need to be good with people not with numbers.
2. Rehan tells his supervisor that he will sign up for a class in budgeting.
3. Rehan asks his supervisor if she can teach him how to work with budgets.
4. Rehan ______________________________.

B ROLE-PLAY. Role-play Rehan's conversation with his supervisor.

Show what you know!

1. **REFLECT.** How do you take responsibility for your professional growth at school, at work, or at home? Give an example.
2. **WRITE.** Write your example in your Skills Log.

   I am interested in learning more about our company's computer networking system. I asked my manager how I can develop those skills.
3. **PRESENT.** Give a short presentation describing how you take responsibility for your professional growth.

I can give an example of how I take responsibility for my professional growth. ☐

Unit Review: Go back to page 5. Which unit goals can you check off?

2 Tell Me about Yourself

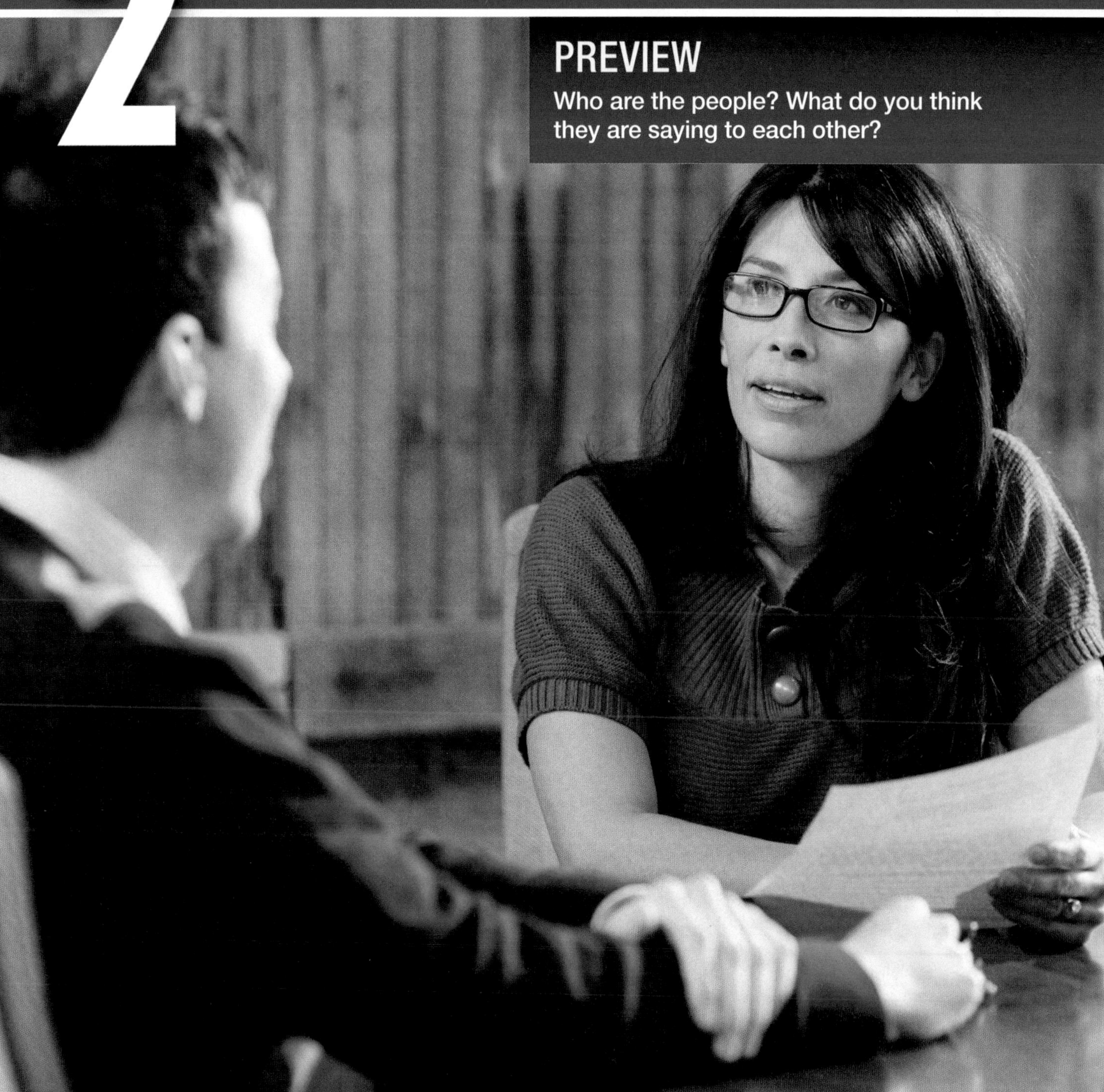

PREVIEW

Who are the people? What do you think they are saying to each other?

UNIT GOALS

- ☐ Talk about work-related goals
- ☐ Interpret and write a résumé
- ☐ Discuss job-information resources
- ☐ Respond to common interview questions
- ☐ Write a cover letter
- ☐ **Academic skill:** Identify supporting details
- ☐ **Writing skill:** Keep cover letters brief
- ☐ **Workplace soft skill:** Have integrity

Lesson 1

Listening and Speaking

Talk about work-related goals

1 BEFORE YOU LISTEN

A **EXPLAIN.** Why do people go to career centers? What can employment specialists do for their clients?

B **MAKE CONNECTIONS.** When you are *motivated,* you really want to be successful at doing something. What are you motivated to do?

2 LISTEN

An employment specialist is meeting with her client.

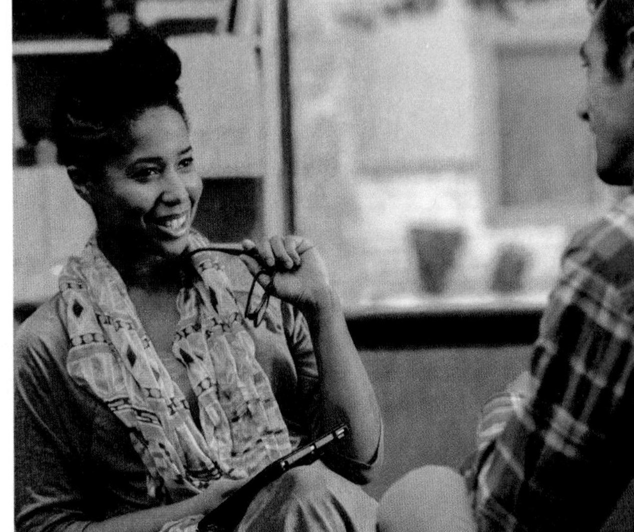

A ▶ **LISTEN FOR MAIN IDEA.** Listen to the first part of the conversation. Then answer the questions.

1. What are two reasons that clients come to Sun County Career Center?
   a. ______________________
   b. ______________________
2. What does Nedim want to do?

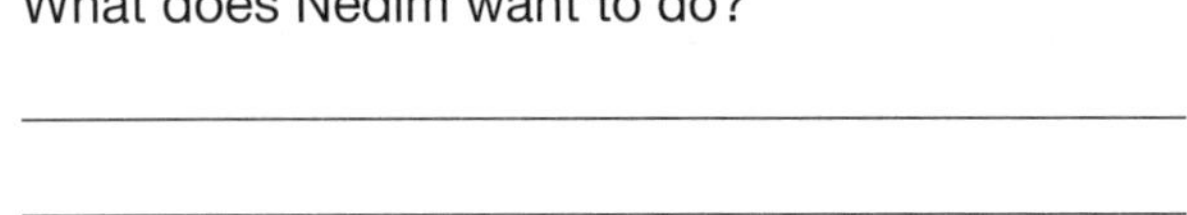

B ▶ **LISTEN FOR DETAILS.** Listen to the whole conversation. Write *T* (true) or *F* (false). Correct the false statements.

_____ 1. Today is Nedim's second meeting with the employment specialist.

_____ 2. Nedim has a job but is looking for a new one.

_____ 3. Nedim has good computer skills.

_____ 4. Nedim pays attention to details.

_____ 5. Nedim graduated from a university in Bosnia.

_____ 6. The employment specialist has already found a job for Nedim.

C **DETERMINE.** The employment specialist discussed the client's work experience, skills, and education. What other things do employment specialists ask clients about?

3 PRONUNCIATION

Reduced syllables

Some words have a syllable that is not usually pronounced.

A ▶ **PRACTICE.** **Listen. Then listen again and repeat.**

camera (2 syllables) | interested (3 syllables)
family (2 syllables) | different (2 syllables)

B ▶ **APPLY.** **Listen. Cross out the syllable that is not pronounced. Then listen again to check your answers.**

1. Good evening!
2. I'm looking for a job at a restaurant.
3. I'm applying for several jobs.
4. I look online every day.
5. There's a new business downtown.
6. I'm interested in applying there.

4 CONVERSATION

A ▶ **LISTEN AND READ.** **Then practice the conversation with a partner.**

A: What are you interested in?
B: I'm interested in technology.
A: What skills do you have?
B: Well, I have some basic programming skills, but I need to learn more. And I'm good at fixing things. I like to fix broken computers, tablets, and phones.
A: How would you describe yourself?
B: I'm quiet and serious. I like to solve problems. I'm a very hard worker.

B **MAKE CONNECTIONS.** **Think about your work-related goals.**

1. Fill in the chart with your ideas.
2. Then ask and answer these questions with a partner.
   What job do you want? What are your interests? What skills do you have? How would you describe yourself? What steps can you take to reach your goal?

Goal: I want to work as a(n) ________________________________.

Interests: what I am most interested in	**Skills:** what I know how to do	**Personal Qualities:** kind of person I am	**Steps:** ways to get the job I want

I can talk about my work-related goals. ☐ I need more practice. ☐

For more practice, go to MyEnglishLab.

Lesson 2

Grammar

Infinitives and gerunds

Infinitives and Gerunds	
Verb + Infinitive	**Verb + Gerund**
I **want** ***to find*** a job.	They **discussed** ***finding*** a job.
I **decided** ***to apply*** for a new job.	She **recommended** ***applying*** for a new job.
We can **start** ***to look*** at available positions.	We can **start** ***looking*** at available positions.
She **decided** ***not to apply*** for that job.	I **enjoy** ***not working*** on weekends.

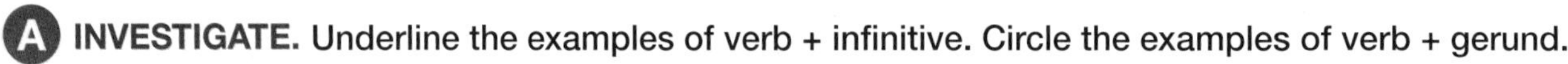

Grammar Watch

- Use an infinitive after verbs such as *agree, decide, need, wait, want,* and *would like.*
- Use a gerund after verbs such as *enjoy, discuss, finish,* and *recommend.*
- Use either an infinitive or a gerund after verbs such as *begin, continue, like, prefer,* and *start.*
- Add *not* before an infinitive or a gerund to make it negative.

(See page 261 for a list of verbs.)

A INVESTIGATE. Underline the examples of verb + infinitive. Circle the examples of verb + gerund.

Sun County Career Center

Sun County Career Center (SCCC) first began helping jobseekers more than thirty years ago. The founders of the organization wanted to help new immigrants in the community. From 1998 till 2018, SCCC provided English and work-skills classes to immigrants who needed to find employment. In 2018, the organization decided not to limit its services to immigrants only. Now SCCC is open to anyone who wants to look for a job. The organization has continued offering ESL classes and job training. It plans to offer even more classes soon. SCCC suggests visiting their website for additional information.

B DETERMINE. Complete the conversation between two co-workers at SCCC. Cross out the incorrect words.

Catherine: I met with an interesting client earlier today. When he came in, he wanted **to look / looking** at the job listings immediately. He couldn't wait **to find / finding** a job.

Co-worker: Once you recommended **to discuss / discussing** his abilities first, did he agree **to consider / considering** the kind of work that might be good for him?

Catherine: Yes. I explained why we needed **to talk / talking** about his personal qualities and his skills. Then he finally understood how important it is to look for a job that he can enjoy **to do / doing**.

Grammar

C DETERMINE. Complete the conversation with infinitives and gerunds. Where appropriate, write two answers.

A: Yesterday we discussed *setting* **(set)** long-term and short-term goals. Let's continue *to talk / talking* **(talk)** about that today.

B: I finished ________ **(read)** the information you gave me about goal-setting, and I'd really like ________ **(take)** the time to think about my goals. But I need ________ **(earn)** some money right now.

A: OK. Then you should consider ________ **(take)** a job that might lead to a better position later.

B: That's a good idea. I can start ________ **(make)** money while I'm planning for the future. As I think you know, I prefer ________ **(work)** in an office.

A: Yes. Let's see . . . You like ________ **(do)** research, don't you?

B: Definitely. That's what I liked most about my last job. The only reason I quit ________ **(work)** there was that I moved.

Show what you know!

1. **BRAINSTORM.** Complete these sentences to describe your interests and skills. What type of job would you like to have that uses your interests and skills?
   1. I really enjoy ________.
   2. My friends think I should try ________.
   3. My supervisor recommended ________.
   4. Someday, I would like to learn ________.
2. **WRITE.** Describe the job you would like to have in five years. Use infinitives and gerunds.

   I really enjoy working with children. In five years from now, I hope to have a job at an elementary school. I want to teach Spanish or art. My college advisor recommended getting a teaching certificate. I plan to enroll in classes next fall.

I can use infinitives and gerunds. ☐ I need more practice. ☐

For more practice, go to MyEnglishLab.

Lesson 3

Workplace, Life, and Community Skills

Interpret and write a résumé

1 INTERPRET A RÉSUMÉ

A **MAKE CONNECTIONS.** Have you used a résumé to apply for a job? Do people usually give a résumé to an employer before or after a job interview?

B **SCAN. THEN READ.** What kind of information is in the *Qualifications* section of the résumé? In the *Related Experience* section? After scanning, read the entire résumé.

Aki Kim
2038 Crabtree Court, Barrington, IL 60010
847-555-1054 • AkiKim@mymail.com

OBJECTIVE: To work as a software developer

QUALIFICATIONS

- Designer of new computer software
- Skilled at analyzing and solving problems
- Strong interpersonal skills: Highly dependable at meeting client's needs
- Strong communication skills: Effective at writing technical reports

RELATED EXPERIENCE

Technology Specialist Started *RescueMe Computing* to provide at-home visits for computer set-up and repair. Helped clients with business and personal computer needs. Designed database for doctors and dentists to collect and store critical information.
2016–present
RescueMe Computing
Barrington, IL

Sales Associate Answered customer questions and assisted in purchase of computers, televisions, and other equipment. Received an award for most sales in December 2015.
2012–2015
Ted's Electronics
Lake Zurich, IL

Volunteer Taught an after-school program: Computer Skills for the Classroom
2010–2012
District 10 Middle School

EDUCATION
Cutter College, B.S., Computer Science, June 2018
Chicago, IL

References available upon request.

Workplace, Life, and Community Skills

C DEFINE KEY WORDS. Find the words on the left in the résumé. Match the words with their definitions.

c 1. objective — a. list of skills and abilities needed for a job
a 2. qualifications — b. individuals who can describe a person's abilities
d 3. related experience — c. description of a goal or an ideal job
b 4. references — d. list of previous jobs held that shows relevant work history

D LOCATE DETAILS. Record your answers.

1. What type of contact information did the applicant include?
2. What two jobs has the applicant had? What volunteer position has the applicant had?
3. What educational degree does the applicant have? When did she get it?

E DISCUSS. Answer the questions.

1. What kinds of people can provide references?
2. Who would you use as a reference? Why?
3. Why can a résumé include a volunteer position along with paid jobs?

2 WRITE A RÉSUMÉ

A GO ONLINE. Search for a job posting that you would like to apply for. What website is it on? ____________________

B DESCRIBE. Write an objective that matches the job that you would like.

____

C BRAINSTORM. Think about your education, experience, and skills. Record your information.

Personal Information	
Objective	
Qualifications	
Related Experience	
Education	

D WRITE. Use your information from Exercise 2C to write your own résumé to apply for the job. Use the résumé on page 30 as a model.

I can interpret and write a résumé. ☐ I need more practice. ☐

For more practice, go to MyEnglishLab.

Lesson **4**

Listening and Speaking

Discuss job-information resources

1 BEFORE YOU LISTEN

MAKE CONNECTIONS. Have you tried any of the tips below? Check the boxes. What are some other ways to look for a job?

Job-Search Tips

- ☐ Go to job fairs.
- ☐ Download a job-search app.
- ☐ Look for job advertisements on social media sites.
- ☐ Take advantage of the services of a job-placement agency.
- ☐ Visit a school or community career-counseling center.
- ☐ Get information about possible jobs by networking (talking with people you already know and trying to meet new people).
- ☐ Look for "Help Wanted" signs in your neighborhood.

2 LISTEN

Lisa is giving her friend advice about finding a job.

A ▶ **LISTEN FOR MAIN IDEA.** What are some ways Lisa tells her friend to look for a job?

B ▶ **LISTEN FOR DETAILS.** Listen again. Then write the correct words to complete each sentence.

1. Lisa got her first job in the U.S. 20 years ago.
2. Lisa's first job was in Flower job.
3. Lisa found her first job by reading Help wanted sing.
4. Before she was hired, Lisa talked to The manager.

C **IDENTIFY.** Read the Job-Search Tips again. According to Lisa, what is the best way to find a job? Circle your answer.

D **STATE AN OPINION.** What do you think is the best way to find a job? online

I think the best way to find a job is, friends. Because → They now if that work is good and my friend can talk about me. recommend

Listening and Speaking

3 CONVERSATION

A **ANALYZE.** What kinds of information do you need to know about a job before you apply? Where can you get information about a job before you apply?

B **LISTEN AND READ.** Then practice the conversation with a partner.

A: How's your job-hunt going?
B: It's going OK. I've been sending my résumé out online, but I haven't heard back from anyone yet.
A: Have you thought about going to an employment agency?
B: Yeah, but I don't want to pay to get a job.
A: But you don't pay! The employer usually pays!
B: Really? That's great. I'll definitely try that then!
A: Also, what about getting help at the library? I think they give job-search workshops. Maybe they can give you some ideas.
B: That would be a big help. I'll check it out.

Two neighbors are talking about job hunting.

C **ROLE-PLAY.** Make a similar conversation. Then change roles.

Student A: You are talking to a friend about your job search. Talk about where you have already looked for jobs.

Student B: Look at the Job-Search Tips on page 32. Give your friend some advice.

D **DISCUSS.** Think about your experiences job-hunting.

1. Write lists.
   a. What resources did you use to find a job?

   ______________ ______________ ______________

   b. What other resources might you use if you were looking for a job today?

   ______________ ______________ ______________

2. Share your lists with a partner. What ideas can you add to your lists?

E **PRESENT.** Describe one of your past experiences in job hunting.

I can discuss job-information resources. ☐ I need more practice. ☐

For more practice, go to MyEnglishLab.

Lesson **5**

Grammar

Gerunds as objects of prepositions

Gerunds as objects of prepositions	
I **plan** **on** ***getting*** a better job soon.	
I'm **thinking** **about** ***applying*** for a position at a hair salon.	
I was **nervous** **about** ***not having*** enough money to live on.	

Verb + Preposition	Adjective + Preposition
believe in	capable of
choose between	good at
plan on	interested in
think about	nervous about

Grammar Watch

- Use a gerund (verb + *-ing*) after a preposition.

(See page 261 for a list of verbs + prepositions and for a list of adjectives + prepositions.)

A **INVESTIGATE.** Read the messages between two friends. Underline the prepositions. Circle the gerunds.

What's the matter? You seem worried lately. Are you still concerned about getting a job?

Yes. I didn't plan on looking for work for so long. I'm beginning to wonder if I'll ever find a job! And I'm getting tired of going on interviews.

I know. It's not much fun.

I'd be excited about taking any job, even a low-paying one, as long as it's something I'd enjoy doing. My friend Ben told me about a position as a customer service representative for a credit card company. I'm really interested in finding out more about it.

That would be a good job for you. You're good at helping people.

B **COMPLETE.** Use a preposition from the box and change the verb to a gerund.

about at for in of to with

A: I'm really not satisfied ________ **(work)** at a store. Thanks ________ **(let)** me know about the teacher assistant job.

B: I'm glad you're interested ________ **(apply)** for it. You've been talking ________ **(go)** back to school to become a teacher for a long time.

A: I'm not looking forward ________ **(call)** the school office to get more information about the job because I'm a little nervous. I'm terrible ________ **(talk)** to strangers.

B: You'll be fine. The first person that you'll talk to is the secretary, Mrs. Leshem. Don't be afraid ________ **(ask)** her anything you want. She's really nice.

Grammar

C **APPLY.** Complete each conversation. Use each phrase in the box once. Use gerunds.

answer questions about benefits	not have a certificate
~~apply for the teacher assistant job~~	send my application and résumé today
get your application materials	solve problems

1. **A:** Hello. I'm interested in applying for the teacher assistant job.
   B: OK. Please fill out the application online.
2. **A:** I want to apply for a job as an auto mechanic, but I'm worried about No having a certificate. Do I need to get a certificate?
   B: Yes. You need a Certificate of Completion from a vocational training program for a job with us.
3. **A:** If you're good at solving problems. and have a desire to learn, we'll give you on-the-job training.
   B: That's great. Thanks.
4. **A:** I'd like to discuss the benefits the company offers.
   B: I'm sorry. You'll have to talk to Jana Allen, but she's away from her desk. She's responsible for ansering cuestions.
5. **A:** You can go to our website and get the job application there.
   B: Thank you. I'm planning on sending my aplication.
   A: We look forward to quetting your aplication.

Show what you know!

1. **BRAINSTORM.** Choose a job. Complete the sentences about the job you chose.

A/An ____________
(name of job)

- must be good at curing her.
- is used to washing the hare.
- is responsible for Takere.
- is ready for attending people.

2. **WRITE.** Describe the job you chose. Use prepositions followed by gerunds.

I can use prepositions followed by gerunds. ☐ I need more practice. ☐

For more practice, go to MyEnglishLab.

Lesson 6 **Reading**

Read about preparing for a job interview

1 BEFORE YOU READ

A DISCUSS. Have you ever had a job interview? How did you prepare for the interview?

B PREDICT. Skim the article. What ways to prepare for an interview do you think the article will suggest?

2 READ

▶ Listen and read.

Academic Skill: Identify supporting details

Look for details to help you understand an author's main idea more completely.

Preparing for a Job Interview

You've updated your résumé. You've looked at countless job postings for open positions in your field. You've sent in applications for the positions that interest you. Now, you've finally gotten the response you've been waiting for. You've been called in for an interview! Congratulations! Your next step is to prepare as well as you can for the interview. The preparation will help you to feel relaxed and confident, and improve your chances of success.

What happens during the interview process? You, the candidate, will probably visit the company's office and meet with its employees. The first person you meet is often a representative from the Human Resources (HR) department. This department handles the general hiring process for the company. The HR representative may ask you general questions and give you basic information about the company. Then you will meet with the manager who needs to hire a new employee. This hiring manager will ask you specific questions to evaluate your qualifications for the job. He or she will decide whether or not to offer you the job. So, you want to make a great impression on this person.

How will you do that? Start by taking another look at the job posting you responded to when you sent in your application. Compare your skills to the job requirements listed there. Which of your skills match the requirements? During your interview, you want to emphasize those skills. You want to highlight any work experience that illustrates the skills. For example, if you are applying for a web developer job, talk about any experience you have working with websites. Try not to talk about skills or work experience that make you seem like a poor fit for the job.

Also, research the company you are applying to work for. Find out as much as you can about what it does and the challenges it is facing. Visit the company's website. Read news reports about it and its competitors. During the interview, ask detailed, knowledgeable questions about the company. This will show your interviewer that you really want to work there.

The Inside Scoop

You can learn a lot about a company by reading employee reviews on websites such as Glassdoor. Just don't mention any negative reviews during your interview!

Remember, the more you prepare for an interview, the more confident you will feel and the more likely it is that your interview will result in a job offer.

3 CLOSE READING

A IDENTIFY. What is the main idea?

a. During an interview, the candidate usually goes to a company's office and talks to managers there.
b. Candidates should always talk about any skills they have that match the job requirements.
c. If the candidate prepares well, he or she is more likely to have a successful interview and get the job.

Reading

B CITE EVIDENCE. **Answer the questions. Where is the information located?** **Lines**

10–11

1. Why should the candidate prepare well for a job interview? ________ 10-11
2. What is likely to happen during the interview process? ________ 14-15
3. What should the candidate do first when preparing for an interview? ________ 27-28
4. What should the candidate avoid talking about in an interview? ________ 33-34
5. How can doing research help a candidate in an interview? ________ 41-45
6. How can the candidate show that he or she wants to work at the company? ________ 41-45

C INTERPRET VOCABULARY. **Complete the sentences.**

1. In the context of line 13, the word *candidate* means __b__.
   a. person who wants to win an election **b.** person who is applying for a job
2. In the context of line 23, the phrase *make a great impression* means __b__.
   a. copy the way a person speaks and acts **b.** get someone to feel good about you
3. In the context of line 29, the word *emphasize* means __b__.
   a. speak loudly **b.** show that they are important
4. In the context of line 35, the word *research* means __b__.
   a. search again **b.** study it carefully
5. In the context of line 38, the word *challenges* means __a__.
   a. difficulties **b.** disabilities

D SUMMARIZE. **What are the most important ideas in the article?**

Show what you know!

1. **COLLABORATE. How does the article advise people to prepare for job interviews? Do you agree with the recommendations? What else can job candidates do to prepare?**
2. **WRITE. Explain several different ways that a job candidate can prepare for an interview.**

   Before the interview, the candidate can look at the job posting again and . . .

I can identify supporting details. ☐ I need more practice. ☐

To read more, go to MyEnglishLab.

Lesson 7

Listening and Speaking

Respond to common interview questions

1 BEFORE YOU LISTEN

GIVE EXAMPLES. What questions do employers ask applicants during a job interview? Have you ever been on a job interview? What questions were you asked?

2 LISTEN

Steve Santos is interviewing for a job at Capital Express Delivery Services.

A ▶ **LISTEN FOR MAIN IDEA.** What position would Steve like to have someday?

____

B ▶ **LISTEN FOR DETAILS.** Listen again. Then answer the questions.

1. What is Steve's job now?
   a. truck driver
   b. supermarket manager
   c. truck dispatcher
2. What kind of license does he have?
   a. chauffeur's license
   b. bus driver's license
   c. commercial driver's license
3. What is one reason that Steve wants to leave his job at Trends Supermarket?
   a. He wants a job closer to home.
   b. He wants different work hours.
   c. He wants more money.
4. What is one reason that Steve wants to be a dispatcher some day?
   a. He wants to work indoors.
   b. He enjoys solving problems.
   c. He is tired of his current job.

C **EVALUATE.** Do you think Steve made a good impression? Why or why not?

____

____

3 PRONUNCIATION

A **PRACTICE.** Listen. Then listen and repeat.

general   im**por**tant   de**liv**ery   **su**permarket

B **APPLY.** Listen. Put a dot (•) over the stressed syllable. Then listen again to check your answers.

1. control
2. interesting
3. experience
4. interview
5. responsible
6. absolutely

Stressed syllables

In words with more than one syllable, one syllable is stressed. The stressed syllable sounds louder than other syllables and has a strong, clear vowel sound.

4 CONVERSATION

Steve's job interview at Capital Express Delivery Services continues below.

A **LISTEN AND READ.** Then practice the conversation with a partner.

Interviewer: I have a general question. What's the most important thing you've learned from your work experience?

Steve: Oh, that's an interesting question! Let me think. I've learned a lot! Sometimes things happen that you don't expect; for example, when there's bad weather or something goes wrong with a delivery. I learned a long time ago that I can't control everything—especially not the weather—but I can control my response. There's no reason to get upset with things you can't control.

Interviewer: So, do you think you stay calm under pressure?

Steve: Yes. Absolutely. Everyone who knows me thinks I'm a really calm person.

B **ANALYZE.** Discuss the questions.

1. Do you think Steve gave a good answer to the interviewer's question about what he's learned from his work experience? Why or why not?
2. Imagine that you are being interviewed for a job. How would you answer that question?

C **ROLE-PLAY.** Make a similar conversation. Then change roles.

Student A: You are the interviewer. Ask, "What's the most important thing you've learned from your work experience?"

Student B: You are the job applicant. Use the answer you discussed in Exercise 4B.

D **PRESENT.** Describe the interview process that helped you get the job you have today. Or describe some other experience in which you answered questions about yourself.

I can respond to common interview questions. ☐   I need more practice. ☐

For more practice, go to MyEnglishLab.

Lesson **8**

Grammar

Simple past and present perfect

Simple past and present perfect	
Simple past	**Present perfect**
Steve **learned** a long time ago that he can't control everything.	Steve **has learned** a lot from his work experience.
Steve **worked** at Grand Supermarkets from 2010 to 2016.	Steve **has worked** for Trends Supermarkets since 2016.
When **did** you **start** working there?	How long **have** you **been** a driver?

Grammar Watch

- Use the simple past for actions, feelings, or situations that occurred at a specific time in the past.
- Use the present perfect for actions, feelings, or situations that occurred at an indefinite time in the past.
- Use the present perfect with *for* or *since* to show that an action, feeling, or situation started in the past and continues up to now.
- *Since* may introduce a time clause. Use the present perfect in the main clause and the simple past in the *since*-clause. The order of the clauses is not important.

  *She **has worked** for the same company **since** she **moved** to this city.*

  ***Since** she moved to this city, she **has worked** for the same company.*

A **INVESTIGATE.** Read the information about Li's work history. Underline six examples of the simple past. Circle five more examples of the present perfect.

I've lived in the U.S. since 2014, and I've been lucky with finding work. I've had a few different jobs at CDS Drugstores. My first job there was as a stock clerk. Next, I worked as a cashier. But then I got a job in the pharmacy department, and I really liked it. I've always liked working with people, and I was good in chemistry in school, so I decided to become a pharmacist. I have just enrolled in a program at the university. I haven't started my classes yet, but I hope to get a job as a pharmacist in the future.

B **COMPLETE.** Use the present perfect.

A: How long ___has Dan worked___ here?
(Dan / work)

B: Since 2016. He ___has been___ one of our best employees since he started here. He won
(be)
the Employee of the Month award three times in the last three years.

A: Is it true that he ___has had___ the highest sales in the company for the last two years?
(have)

B: Yes, and he's also very dependable. He ___has not missed___ a day of work in the last two
(not / miss)
years. And he's easygoing and calm. He ___has Never raise___ his voice.
(never / raise)

Grammar

C **PUT IN ORDER.** Write the sentences. Use the present perfect or the simple past.

Dan Miller

1. (five years ago / Dan / a job / at a restaurant)

   Dan got a job at a restaurant five years ago.

2. (for two years / a manager / He / be)

   ____

Alba Rivas

3. (not / Alba / talk a lot / at her last job)

   ____

4. (get / She / a job as a receptionist / a few months ago)

   ____

5. (improve / Her speaking skills / since she started her new job)

   ____

Michael Shen

6. (be / Michael / a security guard / for several years)

   ____

7. (like / He / when he first started it / his job)

   ____

8. (since he began working the late shift / He / be / not / happy)

   ____

Show what you know!

1. **DISCUSS.** Ask and answer the following questions.
   1. What is your current job? How long have you had the job? What are your job duties?
   2. What other jobs have you had? What were your job duties?
   3. Which job has been the best job for you? Why?

2. **WRITE.** Compare your current job to a previous one. Use simple past and present perfect.

   I have worked at a hotel for a year. In the past, I worked at a restaurant. My job at the hotel is different because I have more responsibilities. I am responsible for making and canceling hotel reservations. I also check guests in and out of their rooms. At the restaurant, I just cleared tables. I didn't like that job very much. But I have really enjoyed working in a hotel.

I can use simple past and present perfect. ☐ I need more practice. ☐

For more practice, go to MyEnglishLab.

Lesson 9

Writing

Write a cover letter

WRITING PROMPT: Think of a job you would like to apply for. What qualifications do you need to do the job? What qualifications do you have? Write a cover letter.

1 STUDY THE MODEL

A ANALYZE. Read the model and Writing Skill. Then answer the questions.

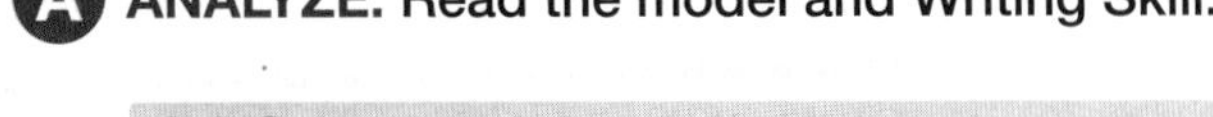

To: hiringmanager@striblinghotel.com
Subject: General manager position

Dear Hiring Manager,

I am writing to express interest in the general manager position listed on jobplacer.com. The qualifications you are seeking are a perfect fit with my skills, education, and experience.

I have excellent customer service and management skills. I have an associate's degree in Hotel Management and 15 years of work experience in the hospitality industry. I am currently an assistant hotel manager at Grantley Suites, where I supervise front desk and housekeeping staff. The attached résumé provides additional information on my background and qualifications.

I am ready to take the next step in my career, and it would be an honor to work for an industry leader like Stribling Hotel. Please contact me if you have any questions. I look forward to hearing from you to arrange a time for an interview.

Sincerely,
Frank Kouadio
frkouadio@tmail.com

Attachment: résumé
(Kouadio_resume.pdf)

Writing Skill: Keep cover letters brief

Do not add extra information to a cover letter. Employers have very little time to read these letters. Attach your résumé to give more details. End your cover letter by suggesting next steps.

1. Circle the job the person is applying for. Underline how the applicant found out about the job.
2. At what hotel is the applicant applying for a position?
3. How does the applicant close his cover letter?

B TAKE NOTES. Complete the outline with more information from the model.

Paragraph 1: Purpose of email:

____

Paragraph 2: Skills, Education, and Experience:

Excellent customer service and management skills, ______________________________

____

Paragraph 3: Next Steps:

Contact Frank if any questions, ______________________________

Writing

2 PLAN YOUR WRITING

A **BRAINSTORM.** Discuss your ideas for the Writing Prompt with a partner.

B **OUTLINE.** Use this outline to organize your ideas before writing.

Paragraph 1: Purpose of email:

TO aply for the job (General manager in the Hotel)

Paragraph 2: Skills, Education, and Experience:

asociate's the gree, an Hotel manager and 15 year of work

Paragraph 3: Next Steps:

arrange a time for an interwiw.

3 WRITE

PERSUADE. Write a cover letter email to apply for a job. Remember to avoid including extra information. Use the model, the Writing Skill, and your ideas from Exercise 2 to help you.

4 CHECK YOUR WRITING

A **REVISE.** Use the Writing Checklist to review your writing. Make revisions as necessary.

B **COLLABORATE.** Read your writing with a partner. Use the checklist again to improve your writing.

WRITING CHECKLIST

- ☐ Did you state the purpose of your cover letter?
- ☐ Did you describe your skills, education, and experience?
- ☐ Did you suggest next steps at the end of the letter?
- ☐ Did you avoid including any extra information?

I can write a brief cover letter. ☐ I need more practice. ☐

For more practice, go to MyEnglishLab.

Lesson 10 Soft Skills at Work

Have integrity

1 MEET HUA

Read about one of her workplace skills.

I have integrity. For example, in a job interview, I am honest about my work history. Even if I don't want to talk about a bad experience, I still tell the truth and focus on what I learned from the experience.

2 HUA'S PROBLEM

A READ. Write *T* (true) or *F* (false).

Hua has a job interview today. She is worried about how to talk about her last job. Her previous employer had financial problems and laid off several people, including Hua. Hua is nervous to tell the interviewer about her employment history. She's worried the interviewer will think it was her fault she was laid off.

f **1.** Hua has a job interview tomorrow.

T **2.** Hua was laid off from her last job.

f **3.** Hua is excited about the job interview.

B ANALYZE. What is Hua's problem?

She is worried for the interview

3 HUA'S SOLUTION

A COLLABORATE. Hua has integrity. What does Hua do in the interview? Explain your answer.

1. Hua explains that her previous employer was not good at handling money and blames the company for the layoffs.
2. Hua decides not to tell the interviewer that she lost her previous job.
3. Hua is truthful and says that she was laid off. She goes on to say that she has learned to keep positive even in hard times.
4. Hua ______________________________.

B ROLE-PLAY. Role-play Hua's conversation with the interviewer.

Show what you know!

1. **REFLECT.** How do you show you have integrity at school, at work, or at home? Give an example.
2. **WRITE.** Write your example in your Skills Log.

   I am honest with my employer. For example, if I am going to turn in a project late, I tell my supervisor as soon as possible.
3. **PRESENT.** Give a short presentation describing how you show your integrity.

I can give an example of my integrity. ☐

Unit Review: Go back to page 25. Which unit goals can you check off?

3 Community Life

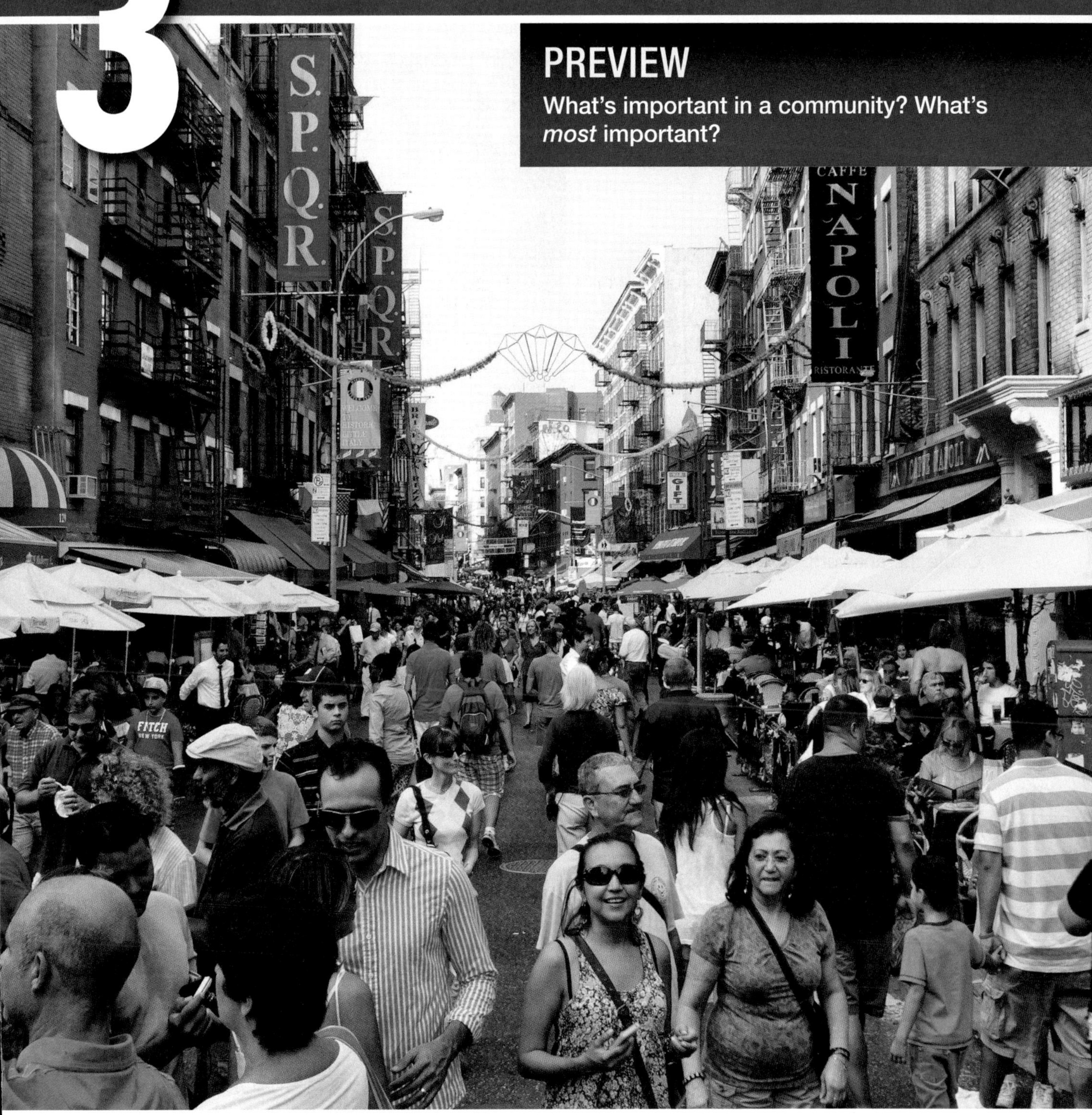

PREVIEW

What's important in a community? What's *most* important?

UNIT GOALS

- ☐ Talk about cultural diversity in neighborhoods
- ☐ Interpret and follow GPS directions
- ☐ Describe community issues
- ☐ Discuss ways to improve a community
- ☐ Write about a neighborhood
- ☐ **Academic skill:** Make inferences
- ☐ **Writing skill:** Use examples
- ☐ **Workplace soft skill:** Respect others

Lesson 1

Listening and Speaking

Talk about cultural diversity in neighborhoods

1 BEFORE YOU LISTEN

MAKE CONNECTIONS. Look at the picture. What kind of festival do you think this is? Do you have festivals like this in your community?

2 LISTEN

Two co-workers, Mali and Eric, are talking about a Thai festival in their neighborhood.

A ▶ **LISTEN FOR MAIN IDEA.** Who is going to the festival?

B ▶ **LISTEN FOR DETAILS.** Listen again. Circle the answers.

1. What does the festival celebrate?
   a. the first day of spring
   b. Thai Independence Day
   c. Thai New Year
2. When does the festival happen?
   a. the end of April
   b. the first week of April
   c. last Sunday of April
3. What do some children do at the festival?
   a. play games
   b. drink water
   c. throw water

C **COMPARE.** What things are common in your culture that are different in other cultures?

In Your Culture	Difference in Other Cultures

Listening and Speaking

3 PRONUNCIATION

Pronouncing consonants

The sounds /p/, /b/, /t/, /d/, /k/, and /g/ often have a short, quiet pronunciation at the end of a word.

A **PRACTICE.** Listen. Then listen again and repeat.

shop	great	at night	bored	think
cheap	best	food	back	perfect

B **APPLY.** Listen. Circle the words that you hear. Then listen again to check your answers.

1. Is this **grape / great** juice?
2. What do you **thing / think** about this?
3. Whose **back / bag** is this?
4. I work at **night / nine**.
5. Were you **born / bored** yesterday?

4 CONVERSATION

The two co-workers are talking after the festival.

A **LISTEN AND READ.** Then practice the conversation with a partner.

A: So what did you think of Thai Town?
B: It's pretty amazing. It has so many restaurants and shops. Is it always so crowded?
A: Mostly at night and on the weekends. A lot of people come to eat and shop.
B: The things in the stores looked really interesting. I'm usually bored by shopping, but I'd like to come back and check out the crafts.
A: Great. I'll tell you about the best restaurants where the food is cheap.
B: Perfect!

B **COMPARE.** Discuss the questions.

1. What kind of neighborhood do you live in? Is it a neighborhood like Thai Town where people share a common language and culture, or is it a diverse neighborhood?
2. Which kind of neighborhood do you prefer? Use this outline to organize your ideas.

Neighborhoods with a common culture		Culturally diverse neighborhoods	
Advantages	**Disadvantages**	**Advantages**	**Disadvantages**
communication customs.			

I can talk about cultural diversity in neighborhoods. ☐ I need more practice. ☐

For more practice, go to MyEnglishLab.

Lesson 2

Grammar

Participial adjectives

Participial adjectives	
The festival is pretty **amazing**.	I'm **amazed** at all the restaurants and shops.
Shopping is **boring**.	Eric is usually **bored** by shopping.

Grammar Watch

- Adjectives ending in *-ing* and *-ed* refer to feelings.
    - Use an *-ing* adjective to describe the thing that causes the feeling.
    - Use an *-ed* adjective to describe how the person feels.

  (See page 262 for a list of participial adjectives.)
- Prepositions often follow *-ed* adjectives: *Eric is bored by shopping.*
  (See page 262 for a list of -ed *adjectives + prepositions.)*
- Some adjectives, like *worried* and *relieved,* have only *-ed* forms.

A INVESTIGATE. Mark the boldfaced adjectives *F* (feeling experienced by a person) or *C* (cause of the feeling).

Because life in a new country is **exciting** but difficult, immigrants often live in neighborhoods with people from their homeland. That way, when they're **worried** about food, schools, or medical care, or when they feel **confused** about something that happens at work or school, they can find help. If it becomes too **frustrating** to speak English, there's always someone who can speak their native language. Besides, at the end of a long hard day, it's sometimes more **relaxing** to be in a place that seems like home.

B COMPLETE. Use the prepositions *about, at, by,* or *with.* Where appropriate, write more than one answer.

A: My husband and I moved to a new neighborhood about a month ago. At first, I was excited ___about___ having American neighbors. But that changed quickly. I'm surprised ___at or by___ how busy people are all the time.

B: I know what you mean. When I first moved to my neighborhood, I was worried ___about___ bothering the American family next door. I was embarrassed ___by___ my English, and the neighbors didn't seem very helpful. But then our kids started playing together, and everything changed. Now I'm thrilled ___by, with, about___ the great relationship I have with my neighbors.

Grammar

C **DETERMINE.** Cross out the incorrect words.

1. Sam is **disappointed / disappointing** with his new neighborhood.
2. One of Sam's neighbors always says, "Hello. How are you?" But the neighbor never waits for him to answer. Sam feels **confused / confusing**.
3. Sam asked one of his neighbors about her age. Later he found out that it's not OK to ask that question. It was an **embarrassed / embarrassing** experience.
4. Sam is **surprised / surprising** by how hard it is to make new friends in his neighborhood.
5. Sam learned about a soccer league in his neighborhood. It sounds **interested / interesting**.
6. He feels **encouraged / encouraging** that he will get to know some of his neighbors through the soccer league.

D **APPLY.** Complete the sentences with the *-ing* or *-ed* form of the verb in parentheses.

Sara attended a City Hall meeting last week because she is ___worried___ **(worry)** about crime in her neighborhood. Many people at the meeting agreed with Sara. The crime rate in their neighborhood is ___________ **(alarm)**. Residents are also ___________ **(disturb)** about the trash and litter problem. They are ___________ **(frustrate)** that the streets are so dirty. People are ___________ **(tire)** of complaining, and the situation is ___________ **(depress)**.

But the City Hall meeting was ___________ **(encourage)**. Sara and her neighbors feel ___________ **(satisfy)** that the city council will take steps to clean up the neighborhood. Everyone is ___________ **(excite)** about living in a safer, cleaner community.

Show what you know!

1. **REFLECT.** Check (✓) three adjectives to describe how you feel about your neighborhood. Then write statements about your feelings.

☐ worried	☐ frightened	☐ excited	☐ bored
☐ frustrated	☐ encouraged	☐ satisfied	☐ other: ___________

2. **DESCRIBE.** Write a paragraph about your neighborhood. Use participial adjectives.

I'm fascinated by the different backgrounds of my neighbors. My neighbors are interesting . . .

I can use participial adjectives. ☐ I need more practice. ☐

For more practice, go to MyEnglishLab.

Lesson 3

Workplace, Life, and Community Skills

Interpret and follow GPS directions

1 INTERPRET GPS DIRECTIONS

A MAKE CONNECTIONS. When have you used GPS directions? What have you liked or disliked about GPS directions?

B SCAN. What type of information is given on the GPS screen?

____

____

____

____

____

from Berks Station, 1900 N. Front St., Philadelphia, PA
to Las Parcelas, 2248 N. Palethorp St., Philadelphia, PA

6 min | 11 min | 4 min

11 min (0.5 mile)
via N. Howard St.

Berks Station
1900 N. Front St., Philadelphia, PA

Head west on W. Berks St. toward N. Howard St.
289 ft

Turn right onto N. Howard St.
0.2 mi

Turn left onto W. Diamond St.
500 ft

Turn right onto N. Hancock St.
0.1 mi

Turn left onto W. Susquehanna Ave.
550 ft

Turn right onto N. Palethorp St.
446 ft

Destination will be on the left.
Las Parcelas
2248 N. Palethorp St., Philadelphia, PA

Las Parcelas
W. Susquehanna Ave.
11 min
Diamond St.
N. Howard St.
N. Front St.
N
Similar ETA
N. 2nd St.
N. Palethorp St.
N. Hancock St.
W. Berks St.
Berks Station

C DEFINE KEY WORDS. Find the words or symbols on the GPS screen. Match the words or symbols with their definitions. Match the abbreviation with its meaning.

f	**1.** via	**a.**	symbol for starting point
e	**2.** destination	**b.**	symbol for ending point
d	**3.** ETA	**c.**	go in the direction of
c	**4.** head	**d.**	Estimated Time of Arrival
a	**5.** (light pin symbol)	**e.**	place you are going to
b	**6.** (dark pin symbol)	**f.**	go by way of

D INTERPRET GRAPHICS. Look at the GPS map. Write *T* (true) or *F* (false). Correct the false statements.

T **1.** Las Parcelas community garden, at 2248 N. Palethorp St., is a half mile from the Berks Station.

F **2.** It takes 20 minutes to walk from the Berks Station to Las Parcelas community garden.

F **3.** You head east on W. Berks St. toward N. Howard St.

T **4.** You make a left at W. Diamond St.

T **5.** You walk 500 feet on W. Diamond St.

F **6.** The destination will be on your right.

F **7.** These directions are for taking the bus.

E ▶ **LISTEN.** **Now listen to those GPS directions. How are the directions similar to other GPS directions you have used? How has the way you get directions changed in your lifetime?**

2 FOLLOW GPS DIRECTIONS

A ▶ **LISTEN.** **A GPS is giving directions. You are starting from a parking lot at the corner of Vine and Waterplace.**

1. Mark the route on the map.
2. What was the destination?

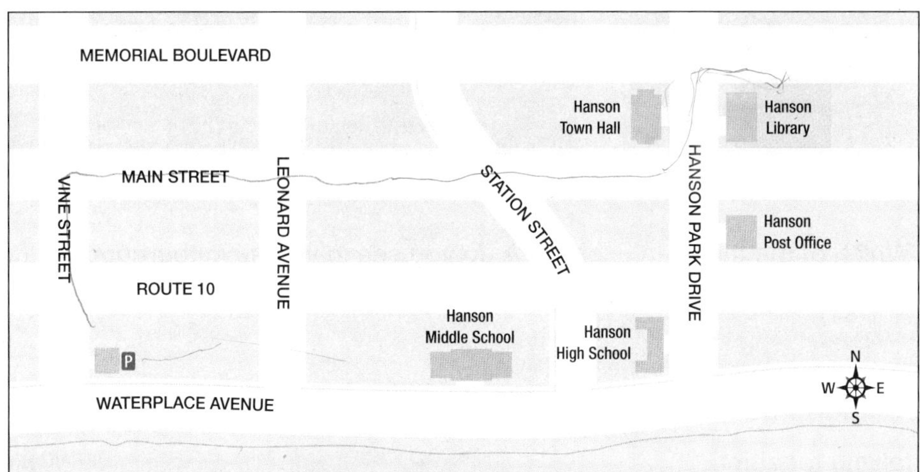

B **INTERPRET.** **Look at the map. Circle the correct answers. Listen to the directions again, if needed.**

1. The GPS said to go __b__ on Vine Street.
   a. left **b.** right **c.** straight
2. The GPS said to drive __a__ on Main St.
   a. 1 mile **b.** 2 miles **c.** 100 feet
3. The destination is __b__ of the parking lot.
   a. northwest **b.** northeast **c.** southwest
4. A cross-street by the destination is __c__.
   a. Route 10 **b.** Waterplace Avenue **c.** Memorial Boulevard

C GO ONLINE. **Identify two destinations in your community. Enter one as a starting location on a GPS device. Enter the other as an ending location.**

1. What information does your GPS provide?
2. Compare your information to a classmate's. How is your GPS screen similar? How is it different?

I can interpret and follow GPS directions. ☐ I need more practice. ☐

For more practice, go to MyEnglishLab.

Lesson 4

Listening and Speaking

Describe community issues

1 BEFORE YOU LISTEN

A DESCRIBE. Match the pictures with the words from the box. Write the numbers next to the words.

____ graffiti ____ a pothole ____ garbage ____ a vacant lot

1 2 3 4

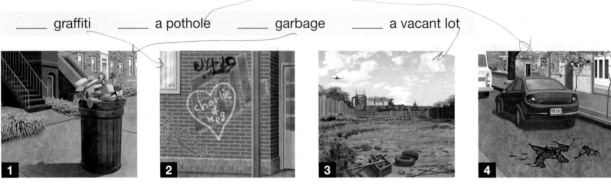

B MAKE CONNECTIONS. Which of the things in Exercise A do you see in your neighborhood? Where do you see them? Do you think they are problems? Why or why not?

2 LISTEN

A husband and wife are talking together.

A ▶ LISTEN FOR MAIN IDEA. What is the topic of the conversation?

B ▶ LISTEN FOR DETAILS. Listen again. Write *T* (true) or *F* (false). Correct the false statements.

____ **1.** Last week, the garbage truck came on schedule.

____ **2.** The wife called to complain about the garbage pick-up.

____ **3.** The fast food restaurants throw their garbage in the vacant lot.

____ **4.** The couple believes that teenagers should be in school.

____ **5.** The husband is upset because there aren't enough after-school programs.

C INTERPRET. The wife says that the trash in the vacant lot is a *health hazard.* What does she mean?

Listening and Speaking

3 CONVERSATION

The couple is talking again after work.

A ▶ **LISTEN AND READ.** **Then practice the conversation with a partner.**

A: I had lunch with Linlin at work today. We were complaining about problems in our neighborhoods. She has a problem with the garbage pick-up. They don't pick up the garbage at her house on schedule.

B: Oh, yeah? That's the same problem we have.

A: Yeah. And I told her about our problem with kids hanging out in the vacant lot near our house. Linlin also wishes there were more after-school programs in the community.

A: Yes, especially activities for young children.

B: That would be good, but we also need sports for teens.

A: Do you know what I wish?

B: What?

A: I wish we had a swimming pool in our neighborhood. It would be good for the whole community.

B **ROLE-PLAY.** **Make similar conversations with the wish lists below.**

Wish List 1	Wish List 2	Wish List 3
educational programs	services for senior citizens	concerts
homework help	health and fitness classes	movies and art shows
computer classes	free hot lunches for anyone over 65	a chess club

C **RANK.** **Think about community services.**

1. List six important community services.

   Education, Police department | Fire station.
   Green places | publick Transportation
   Swiming pool | publick garvix

2. Which community services are the most important? Number them from *1* (most important) to *6* (least important). Share your rankings with a partner.

D **PRESENT.** **Describe an issue in your community and what you would do to solve it.**

I can describe community issues. ☐ I need more practice. ☐

For more practice, go to MyEnglishLab.

Lesson 5

Grammar

Wish in the present and future

Wish in the present and future	
Present	**Future**
I **wish** (that) we **had** a swimming pool in our community.	I **wish** (that) our community **would get** a swimming pool.
She **wishes** (that) the garbage truck **came** on schedule.	She **wishes** (that) the garbage truck **would come** on schedule.
We **wish** (that) there **were** an after-school program.	We **wish** (that) the community center **could offer** an after-school program.

Grammar Watch

- Use *wish* + simple past to talk about things that you want to be true in the present, but that are not yet true.
- In the present, use *were,* instead of *was,* after *wish* to talk about those situations that are not yet true.
- Use *wish* + *could* or *would* (not *can* or *will*) + the base form of the verb to talk about things that you hope will be true in the future.

A **INVESTIGATE.** Circle *wish* and underline the verb in the statement of the wish.

A: I wish the library opened earlier in the morning.

B: I wish it didn't close at 4:00 P.M. on Fridays.

A: I wish the WiFi at the library were better. I have a hard time connecting to the Internet there.

B: I don't have a computer. I wish the library would get more computers.

A: Yes, that would be nice. And I wish we could check out computers from the library.

B **COMPLETE.** Use the correct form of the verbs.

1. The traffic is getting worse. I wish I ______ **(not need)** a car.
2. I just wish there ______ **(be)** more free parking downtown.
3. The streets are in bad condition. I wish the city ______ **(fix)** the potholes.
4. I wish that people ______ **(not drive)** so fast.
5. We need more stop signs. I wish we ______ **(have)** a stop sign on every corner.
6. I really like riding my bike. I wish the community ______ **(build)** a bike trail around the lake.

Grammar

C **DETERMINE.** Rewrite each person's opinion as a wish. More than one answer is sometimes possible.

Jack: I think we need a hospital in the neighborhood.

Fran: The streets are so noisy. What do you think, Jason?

Jason: I agree, but public transportation is the biggest problem for me. The buses should run more frequently—every ten minutes would be great.

Carol: Well, I'd just like to be able to go to the park more often!

Sarah: I want swings and slides in the playground.

Mark: I'd like a place to play baseball.

David: A baseball field is a good idea, Mark, but I don't know why this family complains so much.

1. Jack wishes there ___were___ a hospital nearby.
2. Fran wishes the streets ___were not___ so noisy.
3. Jason wishes the buses ___Ran___ every ten minutes.
4. Carol wishes she ___were able to go (could go)___ to the park more often.
5. Sarah wishes the playground ___had___ more equipment.
6. Mark wishes there ___Were___ a baseball field in the neighborhood.
7. David wishes his family ___wouldn't___ so much.

Show what you know!

1. **WRITE.** Write two sentences about your neighborhood.
   a. Describe something you wish were true now.
      I wish ______________________________.
   b. Describe something you hope will be true in the future.
      I wish ______________________________ in the future.
2. **COLLABORATE.** Describe your wishes to the class. Which three neighborhood changes were the most common?

I wish my neighborhood had more green space. I wish the city would build more parks in my neighborhood in the future.

I can use *wish* in the present and future. ☐ I need more practice. ☐

For more practice, go to MyEnglishLab.

Lesson 6

Reading

Read about community gardens

1 BEFORE YOU READ

A **DISCUSS.** Are there community gardens in the area where you live? Who plants these gardens?

B **PREDICT.** Skim the article. What does it say about community gardens?

2 READ

Academic Skill: Make inferences

If an author doesn't state information directly, use what the author does say to make a logical guess about what is probably true.

Listen and read.

Community Gardens

Communities around the United States are turning their neighborhoods green. They are planting community gardens. These gardens have made a significant impact on many neighborhoods in big American cities.

One Neighborhood's Story

The area of New York City located near John F. Kennedy Airport is called East New York. During the 1970s, East New York was in crisis. The bankrupt city government cut services. It stopped collecting garbage. Stores and other businesses left. Real estate values fell, and banks refused to loan homeowners money. Buildings deteriorated. So, the landlords abandoned them or burned them down. There were thousands of empty lots.

What did the residents of East New York do? They cleared out rubble and trash from the vacant lots. Then they planted gardens. There was little fresh food available in the area, so the residents grew their own fruits and vegetables. Nowadays, East New York is a gardener's paradise. Residents can eat the fresh food they cultivate. They can relax in beautiful natural surroundings.

Gardens Bring Benefits

Community gardening improves the appearance of a neighborhood. It also raises the value of the surrounding homes and businesses. Gardeners can sell the produce they grow. They earn much-needed income. Residents work together to maintain their plots. The physical activity improves their health. The residents get to know each other better. Local teenagers get involved in the gardens—this means they get into trouble less. Research has shown that city areas with more green have less crime.

The Future of Community Gardens

Clearly, community gardens make neighborhoods better in many different ways. However, these improvements also endanger their future. When neighborhoods become nicer places to live, wealthy people want to move in. This makes real estate prices go up. So, community gardens in East New York and other places face a serious challenge. The land they are situated on is becoming very expensive. Real estate developers are trying to take over the land. They want to build apartments and stores on it. But gardeners are finding ways to deal with this problem. They plant community gardens in schoolyards, churchyards, and public-housing blocks. They also plant them on pieces of land that are difficult to build on, such as steep slopes or very small areas. Hopefully, community gardens will continue to survive and thrive despite the challenges they face.

3 CLOSE READING

A **IDENTIFY.** What is the main idea?

a. Community gardens have improved many neighborhoods in American cities.
b. People in East New York took trash out of vacant lots and planted gardens.
c. Real estate developers want to build on community gardens' land.

Reading

B CITE EVIDENCE. Complete the sentences. Where is the information located?

Lines

1. During the 1970s, East New York was in crisis because ___. ___
   - **a.** real estate values went down quickly
   - **b.** real estate values went up
   - **c.** too many people moved there
2. It was hard to find fresh vegetables in East New York, so the residents ___. ___
   - **a.** went to other neighborhoods to buy them
   - **b.** grew their own
   - **c.** stopped eating them
3. Apartments near community gardens are more expensive because the gardens ___. ___
   - **a.** provide jobs for teenagers
   - **b.** are beautiful
   - **c.** are costly to maintain
4. Community gardeners are usually healthier than other residents because ___. ___
   - **a.** they eat only fruits and vegetables
   - **b.** they have to walk to the gardens
   - **c.** gardening is good exercise
5. When wealthy people move into a neighborhood, ___. ___
   - **a.** the number of community gardens increases
   - **b.** real estate values go up
   - **c.** real estate values fall
6. Community gardens help to create relationships because ___. ___
   - **a.** gardeners sell fresh fruits and vegetables to each other
   - **b.** teenagers have to work in the gardens
   - **c.** people work together to take care of the gardens

C INTERPRET VOCABULARY. Complete the sentences.

1. In the context of line 8, the word *crisis* means ___.
   - **a.** an unusual situation
   - **b.** a very bad situation
2. In the context of line 12, the word *deteriorated* means ___.
   - **a.** wore away
   - **b.** became worse
3. In the context of line 39, the word *endanger* means ___.
   - **a.** causes the death of
   - **b.** puts at risk
4. In the context of line 47, the word *developers* means ___.
   - **a.** people who buy land and build on it
   - **b.** people who think of new ideas or products

D SUMMARIZE. What are the most important ideas in the article?

Show what you know!

1. **COLLABORATE.** Are there community gardens in your area? What benefits does the article say that community gardens bring? Do you think the gardens provide those benefits? Why or why not?
2. **WRITE.** Describe a community garden that you have seen or read about. Summarize the benefits the garden provides, and predict what might happen to it in the future.

   The community garden in my neighborhood is very beautiful, and people grow lots of fruits and vegetables in it . . .

I can make inferences. ☐ I need more practice. ☐

To read more, go to MyEnglishLab.

Lesson 7

Listening and Speaking

Discuss ways to improve a community

1 BEFORE YOU LISTEN

DEFINE. Match the words with their definitions.

d	**1.** convince	**a.**	make the size or amount of something larger
c	**2.** urge	**b.**	say who someone is or what something is
b	**3.** identify	**c.**	try hard to persuade someone to do something
a	**4.** increase	**d.**	persuade; get someone to agree
f	**5.** investigate	**e.**	make the size or amount of something smaller
e	**6.** reduce	**f.**	try to find out the truth about something

2 LISTEN

Clara Ramos is a city council representative. She is answering a resident's questions.

A **LISTEN FOR MAIN IDEA.** What is the resident worried about?

B **LISTEN FOR DETAILS.** Listen again. Write the correct words to complete each sentence.

1. The resident was worried that the Police station was closing.
2. The residents want to reduce Crime in the area.
3. The Community-Policing Program encourages residents to work with the police.
4. The first meeting of the Community-Policing Program will take place N1xt week.

C **INFER.** Read this quote: "Safety is the responsibility of everyone in the community, not just the police." Who would probably make the statement, Clara Ramos or a resident? Explain.

Clara Ramos

3 PRONUNCIATION

A ▶ **PRACTICE.** Listen. Then listen again and repeat.

1. **to** come with me	I'd like you **to** come with me.
2. **to** make a difference	This is our chance **to** make a difference.
3. want **to** ("wanna") have	We want **to** ("wanna") have better services.
4. going **to** ("gonna") tell	Now you're going **to** ("gonna") tell me to go to the meeting.

Pronouncing *to*

The word *to* usually has a short, weak pronunciation when it is followed by a verb, instead of a noun or noun phrase. And in conversation, *want to* is often pronounced "wanna" and *going to* is often pronounced "gonna."

B ▶ **APPLY.** Listen. Does *to* have a weak or clear pronunciation? Check the box. Then listen again to check your answers.

	weak	clear
1	✓	
2		✓
3		✓
4	✓	
5		✓

4 CONVERSATION

A ▶ **LISTEN AND READ.** Then practice the conversation with a partner.

A: I'm worried about crime in our neighborhood.
B: If you really feel that way, I urge you to attend the next community policing meeting.
A: I didn't even know we had community policing. I'd like you to tell me more about it.
B: Well, it wasn't easy, but we finally convinced the city council to start a Community-Policing Program. Now we need residents to participate. There's a lot of information online. I'll send you the link.
A: Thanks! When is the next meeting?
B: It's next Friday. I'll call and remind you to come.

B **MAKE CONNECTIONS.** Would you like to participate in a community-policing meeting? Explain.

C **PROBLEM SOLVE.** Read about Hugo.

Hugo saw several young men in his neighborhood breaking windows and writing graffiti on the wall at the community center. They live in the Southland neighborhood, so he knows them and their families well.

1. What is Hugo's problem?
2. Discuss possible solutions to the problem. Make a list. Decide on the best solution.

I can discuss ways to improve a community. ☐ I need more practice. ☐

For more practice, go to MyEnglishLab.

Lesson 8

Grammar

Verb + object + infinitive

Verb + object + infinitive		
We **don't want**	**the city**	**to take away** services.
She **urged**	**us**	**not to believe** everything we hear.

Grammar Watch

- An infinitive is *to* + base form of the verb. To make a negative infinitive, use *not* + *to* + base form of the verb.
- With verb + object + infinitive, use object pronouns (*me, you, him, her, us, them*).

(See page 262 for a list of verbs followed by an object + infinitive.)

A INVESTIGATE. Circle the verb, draw a line under the object, and draw two lines under the infinitive.

Officer: My Name is Officer Brown. As part of our community-policing effort, I urge you to check on neighbors who might need help.

Resident: My neighbor, Mrs. Soto, is eighty years old. I always ask her to call if she needs anything, but she tells me not to worry. What should I do?

Officer: Continue what you're doing. And, please, if you notice any change in her daily routine, try to find out what's going on.

Resident: I've noticed that some senior citizens are too trusting. They open the door when strangers knock. I've told Mrs. Soto not to do that.

Officer: That can be a problem. We have a safety class for seniors at the community center. We teach them to ask for identification even when they've made a call for service. We remind them not to open their doors until they know it's safe.

B LOCATE. Cross out the object in each sentence. Then change the object to a pronoun.

1. The mayor doesn't want ~~the sanitation workers~~ *them* to go on strike.
2. The Community-Policing Program encourages the residents in our neighborhood to work with the police.
3. Community council members urge residents not to miss meetings.
4. The police expect my neighbors and me to report anything unusual.
5. Tell Mrs. Soto not to leave her door unlocked.
6. Please ask Mr. Lee to check on Mrs. Soto once or twice a week.

C **APPLY.** Pretend you are giving a class on street safety. Write the instructions with a pronoun and the correct form of the verb.

Prepare a list of *"Street-Smart Tips"* for your students. Teach

them to follow (to follow) the four basic rules. Tell

_______________ (stay away) from areas like parking lots and alleys

that are empty or poorly lit. Remind _______________ (not carry)

lots of cash. Advise _______________ (be) careful with their

phones and wallets. Just last week I saw a man who was a target for

crime. I warned _______________ (not keep) his wallet in his back

pocket.

Street-Smart Tips

- Be alert. Keep your eyes and ears open.
- Show that you're confident. If you're nervous, don't show it.
- Trust your instincts. If you think something is wrong, it probably is.
- Use your common sense. You know how to make the right decisions.

D **COMPLETE.** Use a pronoun + infinitive.

1. All city parks close at 11:00 P.M., but there are people in Southland Park all night. The police should tell them to go home.
2. Women who walk in the park are often easy targets. Why don't we organize special self-defense classes, like karate? The classes will teach _______________.
3. The vacant lot across from the park is full of litter. Let's talk to Ms. Hall, the owner of the lot. We can ask _______________.
4. Mr. Torres likes walking his dog in the park late at night. Someone should tell _______________.

Show what you know!

1. **PROBLEM SOLVE.** Describe a problem in the neighborhood where you live or work.
   - Who can you talk to in order to find a solution to the problem?
   - What will you say to get help?
2. **PERSUADE.** Write a letter to the City Council Members. Ask them to help fix the problem. Use verbs followed by pronoun + infinitive.

Dear City Council Members,

Every day, I see cars speed down King Street. A lot of children live on this street, and there is an elementary school nearby. I would like police officers to patrol this street. I want them to stop those speeders. I also urge you to add a speed bump and school zone signs on King Street.

Thank you,
Brenda Kent

I can use verbs followed by object + infinitive. ☐ I need more practice. ☐

For more practice, go to MyEnglishLab.

Lesson 9

Writing

Write about a neighborhood

WRITING PROMPT: What do you like about your neighborhood? What do you dislike? Write a paragraph to describe your neighborhood. Give examples of what you like and what you don't like.

1 STUDY THE MODEL

A ANALYZE. Read the model and Writing Skill. Then answer the questions.

My Neighborhood

I live in a neighborhood in the countryside, far away from the city. There are a lot of things I like about it. For example, it's very peaceful. I only have a few neighbors, and there is hardly any traffic. It's also beautiful. I live right next to a lovely forest, and there's a lake to swim in.

There are also some things I don't like about my neighborhood. For instance, shopping is hard. There aren't any supermarkets, so I have to drive a long way to buy food. Also, it's sometimes kind of boring. I wish there were concerts or classes I could go to nearby. But overall, I'm really happy in my neighborhood.

Writing Skill: Use examples

Examples are an excellent way to give details. They make your writing clearer.

1. Underline phrases the writer uses to introduce examples.
2. What does the writer like about her neighborhood? Give examples.
3. What does the writer dislike about her neighborhood? Give examples.

B TAKE NOTES. Complete the chart with information from the model.

Examples of things the writer likes	Examples of things the writer dislikes
1. *Very peaceful*	1. *Shopping is hard*
2. few neighbors.	2. no soper marker
3. hardly any traffic	3. Boring
4. beaulifful	4. no concerts or classes
5. by a Forest	
6. Next to a Lake.	

also, another in addition.

Writing

2 PLAN YOUR WRITING

A **BRAINSTORM.** Discuss your ideas for the Writing Prompt with a partner.

B **ORGANIZE.** Use this chart to organize your ideas before writing.

Examples of things you like	Examples of things you dislike
1.	1.
2.	2.
3.	3.
4.	4.

3 WRITE

EXPLAIN. Write a paragraph about things you like and dislike about your neighborhood. Remember to use examples to give details. Use the model, the Writing Skill, and your ideas from Exercise 2 to help you.

4 CHECK YOUR WRITING

A **REVISE.** Use the Writing Checklist to review your writing. Make revisions as necessary.

B **COLLABORATE.** Read your writing with a partner. Use the checklist again to improve your writing.

WRITING CHECKLIST

- ☐ Did you describe things you like in your neighborhood?
- ☐ Did you describe things you dislike in your neighborhood?
- ☐ Did you use examples to give details?
- ☐ Did you use correct capitalization, punctuation, and spelling?

I can use examples. ☐ I need more practice. ☐

For more practice, go to MyEnglishLab.

Lesson **10**

Soft Skills at Work

Respect others

1 MEET MARY

Read about one of her workplace skills.

I care about and respect my co-workers. I always try to be polite and pleasant. I avoid any negative talk about other people.

2 MARY'S PROBLEM

A **READ.** Write *T* (true) or *F* (false).

Mary works at a bank in her neighborhood. She gets along very well with most of her co-workers. However, one of her co-workers, Jan, gossips about everyone on the team. Mary doesn't like to gossip. She thinks it is disrespectful. At lunch today, Jan started talking about another co-worker's old-fashioned clothes.

T **1.** Mary tries to be polite and pleasant with her co-workers.
F **2.** Mary likes how her co-worker, Jan, behaves.
F **3.** Mary likes to gossip about other people on the team.

B **ANALYZE.** What is Mary's problem?

___

___

3 MARY'S SOLUTION

A **COLLABORATE.** Mary respects others. How does she handle Jan's gossiping at work? Explain your answer.

1. Mary changes the topic of the conversation.
2. Mary tells Jan to stop gossiping.
3. Mary tries to only gossip about people from other departments.
4. Mary 2___.

B **ROLE-PLAY.** Role-play Mary's conversation with Jan.

Show what you know!

1. **REFLECT.** How are you respectful of others at school, at work, or at home? Give an example.
2. **WRITE.** Now write an example in your Skills Log.
   I respect my co-workers. I try to value the different skills that each co-worker has.
3. **PRESENT.** Give a short presentation describing how you are respectful of others.

I can give an example from my life of being respectful. ☐

Unit Review: Go back to page 45. Which unit goals can you check off?

4 On the Job

PREVIEW

Where are the people? What job might each person have?

UNIT GOALS

- ☐ Communicate with supervisors and co-workers
- ☐ Interpret information about employee benefits
- ☐ Check your understanding of a situation at work
- ☐ Ask and answer performance review questions
- ☐ Write an email to a supervisor
- ☐ **Academic skill:** Recognize restatements
- ☐ **Writing skill:** Use email structure
- ☐ **Workplace soft skill:** Be adaptable

Lesson **1**

Listening and Speaking

Communicate with supervisors and co-workers

1 BEFORE YOU LISTEN

DEFINE. Match the words with their definitions.

c	**1.** automatically	**a.**	watch and take in
d	**2.** endorse	**b.**	a set way of doing something
e	**3.** firsthand	**c.**	done by a machine, without a person
a	**4.** observe	**d.**	sign your name
b	**5.** procedure	**e.**	experienced on your own

2 LISTEN

It is Sandra's first day of work at People's Bank. She is talking to her manager.

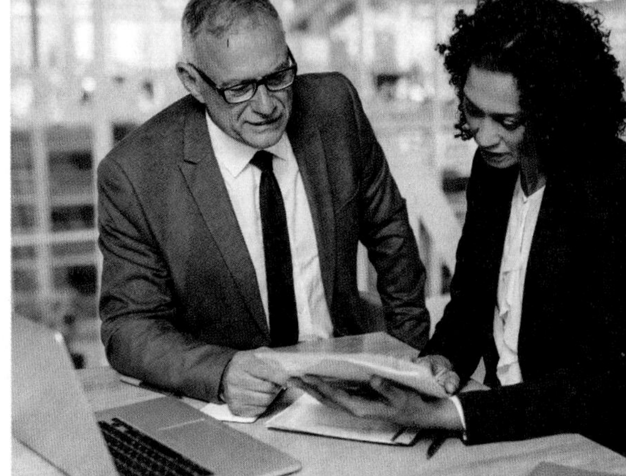

A **LISTEN FOR MAIN IDEA.** Listen to the first part of their conversation. How does Sandra feel about having to observe her manager? Why?

B **LISTEN FOR DETAILS.** Listen to the whole conversation. Write *T* (true) or *F* (false). Correct the false statements.

F **1.** Sandra is training to be a ~~manager~~ teller.

F **2.** Sandra will receive on-the-job training from Robert for ~~two~~ one weeks.

F **3.** Robert explains how to ~~cash~~ Deposit a check.

F **4.** The customer endorses the ~~front~~ back of the check.

F **5.** ~~All~~ many the bank's customers use mobile banking.

T **6.** The amount on the check and the deposit slip must be the same.

F **7.** The teller prints out a receipt for every deposit. or sen text/email

C **INTERPRET.** Sandra says, "I'm a little nervous, but I'll get over it." What does the phrase *get over it* mean? continue.

D **EVALUATE.** Sandra asked her manager a lot of questions. Is it a good idea to ask so many questions on the first day of a job? Explain. Yes

We need now everything.

3 PRONUNCIATION

A ▶ **PRACTICE.** Listen to the sentences. Notice the stressed words. Then listen again and repeat.

Fill out the **form**. **Fill** the **form** out. **Fill** it **out**.

B ▶ **APPLY.** Listen. Put a dot (•) over the words in the underlined sections that are stressed. Then listen again to check your answers.

1. Let me know if I can help you out.
2. I can help out the next customer.
3. Shut the computer down before you leave.
4. I already shut it down.
5. There's a lot to learn, but you're picking it up quickly.

Phrasal verbs

Phrasal verbs are verb phrases that have a verb followed by a word like *up, down, on, off, after, by, in,* or *out.* In most phrasal verbs, both words are stressed (*help out, set up*).

But if an object comes in the middle of the phrase, the object may be stressed instead of the second word of the phrase. However, if that object is a pronoun, then the pronoun is never stressed.

4 CONVERSATION

Sandra is talking to another bank teller.

A ▶ **LISTEN AND READ.** Then practice the conversation with a partner.

A: There sure is a lot to learn for this job.
B: There *is* a lot to learn, but you're picking it up quickly. Let me know if there's any way I can help you out.
A: Thanks, Jason. Right now, I need to find out about my health benefits.
B: You're in luck. There's a meeting tomorrow to discuss our health plan.
A: Oh, yeah. I forgot. What time is the meeting?
B: Two o'clock. But you should check with Robert.

B **MAKE CONNECTIONS.** What things would you expect someone to show you on the first day at a job? Make a list of four things.

1. How to sign in.
2. ______________________
3. ______________________
4. ______________________

I can communicate with supervisors and co-workers. ☐ I need more practice. ☐

For more practice, go to MyEnglishLab.

Lesson 2 Grammar

Phrasal verbs

Phrasal verbs	
Inseparable phrasal verbs	**Separable phrasal verbs**
I'll **get over** my nervousness.	**Fill out** the deposit slip.
I'll **get over** it.	**Fill** the deposit slip **out** completely.
I **get along** with Sarah.	**Fill** it **out** completely.

Grammar Watch

- A phrasal verb consists of a verb + a **particle**. Particles are words such as *up, down, on, off, after, by, in,* and *out.*
- In **inseparable phrasal verbs**, when the phrasal takes an object, the verb and the particle must stay together, and the object must go at the end.
- Some inseparable phrasal verbs have two particles that must stay together (*get along with, look forward to*).
- With **separable phrasal verbs**, the verb and the particle can stay together or be separated. When the object of a separable phrasal verb is a noun, the object can come before or after the particle. When the object is a pronoun, the object must come before the particle.

(See pages 263 for a list of phrasal verbs and their meanings.)

A INVESTIGATE. Underline the phrasal verbs. Then write each phrasal verb next to its definition.

Robert: When the bank closes, there's still quite a bit of work for the tellers. Most evenings, you'll work until 6:00. At the end of the day, don't shut down your computer until we've put together our final report for the day. It's important that we have an exact record of all transactions.

Sandra: What if there's a problem and I can't figure it out?

Robert: For now, you'll talk it over with me or another teller. If we see any problems, we'll point them out. But I'm not worried. You're doing an excellent job.

Sandra: Thanks. You can count on me to do my best.

1. ____________ = stop
2. ____________ = discuss
3. ____________ = depend on
4. ____________ = assemble
5. ____________ = solve a problem
6. ____________ = indicate, show

B **PUT IN ORDER.** Write the sentences. Where appropriate, write two answers.

1. filled / The customer / out / the form

   The customer filled the form out. / The customer filled out the form.

2. the new employee / out / We / with her first assignment / to help / offered

3. he'll / over / He's / about the new schedule, / it / get / but / upset

4. me / on time / count / the job / can / You / on / to do

5. talk / should / with your manager / over / it / You

C **DETERMINE.** Circle the object in each sentence. Then change the object to a pronoun and rewrite the sentence.

1. Be sure to shut down your computer before you leave.

   Be sure to shut it down before you leave.

2. Can you point out the new employees?

3. Their accountant figured out the problem.

4. The managers put this plan together.

5. She can count on her co-workers.

Show what you know!

1. **DISCUSS.** Think about your first day at a new job. What questions did you have? Who helped you out? What did you have to figure out on your own?

2. **WRITE.** Describe your first day at a new job or at a new school. What things did you do? Use phrasal verbs.

   My first job was at a grocery store. I was scared my first day, but I got over it. My manager was very kind and helped me out a lot. I messed up and made a lot of mistakes, but she didn't get angry. My new co-workers took me out to lunch that day. I ended up having a great day.

I can use phrasal verbs. ☐ I need more practice. ☐

For more practice, go to MyEnglishLab.

Lesson 3

Workplace, Life, and Community Skills

Interpret employee benefits

A **MAKE CONNECTIONS.** Employees are given certain days off by their employers. What kinds of days off do you or someone you know get?

B **SCAN. THEN READ.** What kind of information is in the *Overtime* section? What forms of *Paid Time Off* does this company offer? After scanning, read the entire benefit plan.

http://www.acecomputer.com

HOME | RESOURCES | POLICY | MISSION | CONTACT US 

ACE Computer Solutions. Human Resources

Employee Benefits Overview

Welcome to Ace! We are pleased to provide you with information about your employment here. (Note: This information applies only to full-time employees.)

PAYROLL: All employees are paid bi-weekly, that is, at the end of every 2 weeks.

HOURS: The normal workday is 8 hours with 30 minutes for lunch and 2 fifteen-minute breaks. You are expected to work Monday through Friday.

OVERTIME: Here at Ace, we work overtime only when necessary. Full-time employees are allowed to work a maximum of 10 hours of overtime per week. The company pays employees one and one-half times their hourly rate for overtime work. Supervisors must approve all overtime.

PAID TIME OFF (PTO): After 90 days of service, you are eligible for PTO:

Sick leave: 7 paid sick days per year. Please note that if you are out sick longer than 7 days, you must supply a doctor's note. The note must describe the type of illness and give a date when you can return to work.

Vacation: Vacation days are based on length of service (less than 5 years = 5 days per year; 5–10 years = 10 days per year; 11–19 years = 15 days per year; 20 or more years = 20 days per year.

Personal days: You are allowed 5 personal days per year. If possible, please get permission from your supervisor at least 10 business days in advance.

Holidays: Ace is closed on these holidays: New Year's Day, Martin Luther King, Jr. Day, President's Day, Memorial Day, Independence Day, Labor Day, Thanksgiving, and Christmas.

Workplace, Life, and Community Skills

C **DEFINE KEY WORDS.** Find the words on the left in the Employee Benefits Overview. Match the words with their definitions.

____ **1.** overtime	**a.** every two weeks
____ **2.** personal day	**b.** the department that handles hiring employees and employee benefits
____ **3.** bi-weekly	**c.** paid day off to handle appointments or other necessities
____ **4.** human resources	**d.** extra pay for working more than 40 hours per week
____ **5.** in advance	**e.** tell someone about something before it happens

D **LOCATE DETAILS.** Look at the Employee Benefits Overview. Circle the correct answers.

1. How many days do Ace employees need to work before getting a paid vacation?
   a. 10 **b.** 30 **c.** 90
2. An Ace employee was sick for over a week. What does the employee need to do?
   a. get permission from a supervisor **b.** see a doctor **c.** notify a co-worker
3. An Ace employee has been with the company for thirteen years. How many vacation days can the employee take?
   a. ten **b.** fifteen **c.** twenty
4. Another Ace employee wants to take a personal day on her birthday, June 30. What is the last day she can ask for permission from her supervisor?
   a. May 30 **b.** June 1 **c.** June 20
5. Which is NOT a paid holiday for Ace employees?
   a. Veterans Day **b.** Memorial Day **c.** Labor Day

E **DISCUSS.** Answer the questions.

1. Do you think that Ace has good employee benefits? Explain.
2. This page is only a small part of employee benefits. What other information do most employee benefits include?
3. Why do you think Ace doesn't want employees to work overtime for more than ten hours?

F GO ONLINE.

1. **SEARCH.** If you work, find the employee benefits website for your company. If you don't work, find the benefits website for a government employee, such as a city or county employee or a postal service worker. What website is the benefit information on? ____________________
2. **COMPARE.** How is the employee benefit plan you found similar to the plan found by a classmate? How is it different?

G **EVALUATE.** Would you prefer to work at a company with a higher salary or a better benefit plan? Why?

I can interpret employee benefits. ☐ I need more practice. ☐

For more practice, go to MyEnglishLab.

Lesson 4 Listening and Speaking

Check your understanding of a situation at work

1 BEFORE YOU LISTEN

DETERMINE. Look at the picture of the resident, who is training to be a doctor, and the nurse. What job duties do you think each person has?

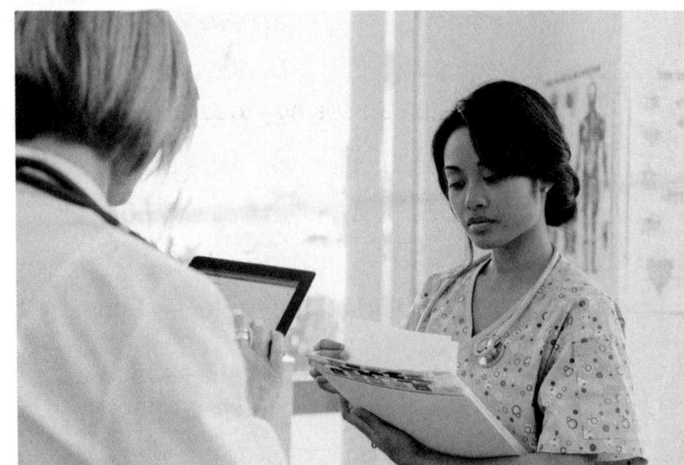

2 LISTEN

The resident and the nurse are talking about a patient.

A **LISTEN FOR MAIN IDEA.** What kind of nurse is Nina—responsible or irresponsible? Explain.

B **LISTEN FOR DETAILS.** Listen again to the conversation. Circle the answers.

1. The nurse doesn't see Mr. Peng's _____ listed in his record.
   a. medications **b.** vital signs
2. The nursing assistant _____ to record Mr. Peng's vital signs.
   a. forgot **b.** didn't forget
3. Nina _____ Mr. Peng's vital signs.
   a. remembers to write **b.** offers to take

C **LISTEN FOR DETAILS.** Listen to another conversation between the resident and Nina. Write *T* (true) or *F* (false). Correct the false statements.

T 1. Mrs. Worth had a gallbladder operation yesterday.

F 2. Mrs. Worth needs to wait for a while before she walks.

T 3. The nurses have helped Mrs. Worth walk.

F 4. There are a lot of nurses on duty on Nina's floor.

T 5. Nina will help Mrs. Worth later.

Listening and Speaking

3 PRONUNCIATION

A **PRACTICE.** **Listen to the sentences. Notice the strong or weak pronunciations. Then listen again and repeat.**

1. **Can't** she see Mr. Singer?
   Yes, she **can**. She can see him today.
2. **Couldn't** he wait?
   Yes, he **could**. He could wait until tomorrow.
3. **Haven't** they taken her out of bed?
   Yes, they **have**. Where have they taken her?

Auxilliary verbs

Auxiliary verbs (such as *have, can,* and *could*) usually have a strong pronunciation, with a clear vowel sound, in negative contractions and at the end of a sentence. They have a weak pronunciation, with a short, quiet vowel sound, when they don't come at the end of a sentence.

B **APPLY.** **Listen to the sentences. Circle the words you hear. Then listen again to check your answers.**

1. **Has / Hasn't** Mrs. Worth been out of bed?
2. **Did / Didn't** the nurse take her vital signs?
3. **Could / Couldn't** we look at her chart?
4. **Have / Haven't** any of the nurses walked with her?
5. I **can / can't** help her right now.

4 CONVERSATION

Two nurses are talking at the nurses' station.

A **LISTEN AND READ.** **Then practice the conversation with a partner.**

A: Mr. Singer would like to talk with Dr. Paige. Have you seen her?
B: I don't think she's on call today. Wasn't she on call last night?
A: I don't know. I was pretty sure she was on the schedule for today.
B: Let me check. See. She was here last night. Dr. Garcia is on duty today. Can't he see Mr. Singer?
A: He could, but Dr. Paige is his doctor. Mr. Singer really wants to talk to her. He wants to know the results of his recent tests.
B: Well, in that case, tell him that Dr. Paige will be in tomorrow. Couldn't Mr. Singer wait until then?
A: I think so. I'll explain that to him.

B **ROLE-PLAY.** **You are co-workers at Greenville General Hospital. Solve the problem.**

Student A: You're looking for some bandages in the supply closet. A co-worker told you that Student B had put them in there. Speak to Student B about the bandages.

Student B: You aren't in charge of the bandages. Another person stocks them in the supply closet.

I can check my understanding of a situation a work. ☐ I need more practice. ☐

For more practice, go to MyEnglishLab.

Lesson 5

Grammar

Negative *yes/no* questions

Negative *yes/no* questions	
Questions	**Responses**
Didn't the nurse **take** Mr. Peng's vital signs?	No, she didn't. They're not in his records.
Haven't they **tried** to take her down the hall?	Yes, they have. They walked with her last night.

Grammar Watch

- Negative *yes/no* questions begin with negative forms of *be* or negative forms of auxiliary verbs, like *do, did, have, can, will,* and *should.* Use contractions in negative questions.
- Use negative *yes/no* questions to check information that you think is true.
- Respond to negative questions with short answers. Answer with *yes* if the information is true and *no* if it is not true.

A **INVESTIGATE.** Underline the negative questions.

A: Didn't you train for the cashier job?

B: No, I didn't. I trained to take orders.

A: Do you like your job?

B: Yes, I like being a cashier, but I don't like the hours.

A: Didn't your manager give you the schedule you wanted?

B: No, he didn't. I'm working nights, but it's OK.

A: Haven't you gotten a paycheck yet?

B: No, I haven't. I think I get paid tomorrow.

B **PUT IN ORDER.** Write the questions.

1. they / about the schedule change? / you / tell / didn't
   Didn't they tell you about the schedule change?
2. yet? / arrived / hasn't / the cleaning crew
   ____
3. about that? / won't / complain / the customers
   ____
4. get / part-time employees / don't / health insurance?
   ____

Grammar

C **COMPLETE.** Use the correct form of the verb to write negative questions.

1. Didn't you clock in yet?
   (you / did clock in)
2. ______________________ the morning shift instead?
   (I / can work)
3. ______________________ your uniform?
   (you / did bring)
4. ______________________ soon?
   (we / should close up)
5. ______________________ your break yet?
   (you / have taken)
6. ______________________ the counters?
   (they / should clean)

D **APPLY.** Use the words to write negative questions.

1. **A:** ______________________? (you / finish the report / yet)
   B: No, I haven't. I'm still working on it.
2. **A:** ______________________? (he / about the problem / tell his supervisor)
   B: No, he didn't. He didn't want her to know.
3. **A:** ______________________? (we / prepare / for the meeting)
   B: Of course we should. The director will be there.
4. **A:** ______________________? (they / for the holiday season / hire more workers)
   B: No, they can't. They're already over budget.

Show what you know!

1. **ROLE-PLAY. Make a similar conversation. Then change roles.**

   Student A: You have a good job but you want to quit.
   Student B: You don't think your friend should quit. Ask negative questions, such as "Don't you like your job anymore?" to help change his or her mind.

2. **WRITE. Write your friend a message asking him or her to think more carefully about quitting. Use negative questions.**

   Hi John,

   I know you're tired of your job, but shouldn't you think about this more carefully? Don't you like your co-workers? Isn't the schedule perfect for you?

I can use negative *yes/no* questions. ☐ I need more practice. ☐

For more practice, go to MyEnglishLab.

Lesson 6 Reading

Read about infection prevention in the workplace

1 BEFORE YOU READ

A **DISCUSS.** What do you do to protect yourself from infection when people around you are sick?

B **PREDICT.** Skim the announcement. What is it about?

Academic Skill: Recognize restatements

When you read, look for information that the author repeats or explains again with different words.

2 READ ▶ Listen and read.

www.springdalehospital.org

Caring People, Caring for People

About Us Careers Billing News Giving Search

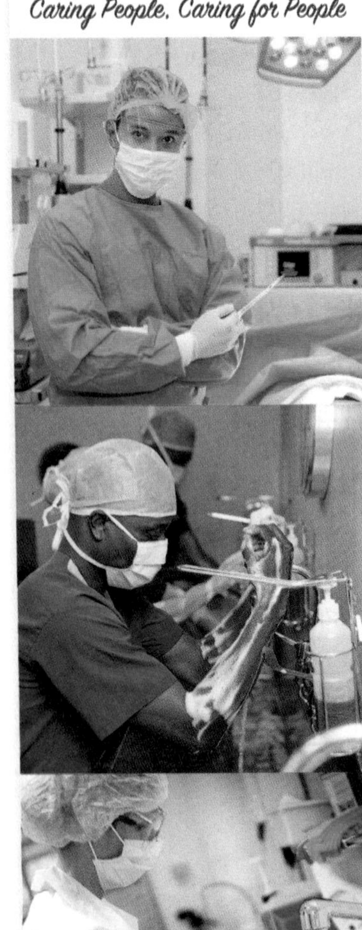

INFECTION PREVENTION GUIDELINES

In the hospital workplace, we constantly face the risk of infection. Every day, our employees are exposed to a wide variety of germs. These germs can cause life-threatening infections in both employees and patients. Therefore, all employees must follow the guidelines below to prevent the spread of infection.

Hand hygiene is the number one way to prevent infection. Do not wear jewelry or watches on your hands or arms at work. Always wash your hands with soap and water after you use the restroom. Also, do this before you eat or handle food.

Assume that every patient is potentially infected with germs. You can easily infect other patients with these germs. So, wear gowns and gloves every time you have physical contact with a patient. If patients are coughing, offer them surgical masks to wear over their mouths. If they can't wear a mask, you must wear one when you are close to them.

Clean your hands with alcohol both before and after treating a patient. Rub alcohol all over your hands and wrists. However, do not scrub your hands with a brush. This can injure your skin and make you vulnerable to infection.

Make sure that you sterilize any medical equipment used to treat the patient. Immediately after you use the equipment, rinse it in hot water and scrub it. Then put it in a plastic pouch and place it in an autoclave machine. Also, use disinfectant to clean any objects or surfaces where germs may have spread.

Medical procedures such as drawing blood can be especially risky. Avoid contact with a patient's blood or bodily fluids as you perform these procedures. If you are exposed to dangerous fluids, immediately call Employee Health (extension 4444). They will give you instructions on the appropriate steps to take to protect yourself.

If you feel ill, stay home. Never report to work if you have an infectious illness. Also, take the day off if you have a wound that cannot be covered. You should report all contagious illnesses to Employee Health.

It is every employee's responsibility to prevent infection. Following these guidelines will protect both you and our patients. If you have any questions or concerns, contact the Safety Committee (extension 2324).

Reading

3 CLOSE READING

A IDENTIFY. What is the main idea?

To prevent the spread of infection, hospital employees must _____.

a. scrub their hands **b.** follow infection prevention guidelines **c.** wear masks if they have an infectious illness

B CITE EVIDENCE. Circle the answer. Where is that restatement found in the article? Write the line number.

1. The author says, *In the hospital workplace, we constantly face the risk of infection.* Which sentence in the article restates that idea?
   a. Therefore, all employees must follow the guidelines below to prevent the spread of infection. _____
   b. Every day, our employees are exposed to a wide variety of germs. _____
2. The author says, *Clean your hands with alcohol both before and after treating a patient.* Which sentence in the article restates that idea?
   a. Rub alcohol all over your hands and wrists. _____
   b. However, do not scrub your hands with a brush. _____
3. The author says, *Make sure that you sterilize any medical equipment used to treat the patient.* Which sentence in the article restates that idea?
   a. Immediately after you use the equipment, rinse it in hot water and scrub it. _____
   b. Wear gowns and gloves every time you have physical contact with a patient. _____
4. The author says, *If you feel ill, stay home.* Which sentence in the article restates that idea?
   a. You should report all contagious illnesses to Employee Health. _____
   b. Never report to work if you have an infectious illness. _____

C INTERPRET VOCABULARY. Complete the sentences.

1. In the context of line 4, the word *infection* means _____.
   a. injury **b.** sickness caused by germs
2. In the context of line 5, the word *hygiene* means _____.
   a. cleaning **b.** any practice that supports health
3. In the context of line 14, the word *scrub* means _____.
   a. wash **b.** rub
4. In the context of line 15, the phrase *vulnerable to* means _____.
   a. weakened by **b.** unprotected from
5. In the context of line 23, the word *appropriate* means _____.
   a. correct **b.** possible

D SUMMARIZE. What are the most important ideas in the article?

Show what you know!

1. **COLLABORATE. What guidelines does the announcement tell hospital employees to follow to prevent infection? What types of safety guidelines do employees at other workplaces have to follow?**
2. **WRITE. Compare safety guidelines for hospital employees with safety guidelines for employees at another workplace.**

In hospitals, employees have to wear gloves and masks when they treat patients. In restaurant kitchens, employees have to . . .

I can recognize restatements. ☐ I need more practice. ☐

To read more, go to MyEnglishLab.

Lesson 7

Listening and Speaking

Ask and answer performance review questions

1 BEFORE YOU LISTEN

EXPLAIN. Why do companies give their employees performance reviews?

Premium Parts **Employee Performance Review**

Employee: Supervisor: Date:

1 = Unacceptable 2 = Needs Improvement 3 = Meets Job Requirements 4 = Exceeds Job Requirements

	1	2	3	4	Comments
Does quality work	○	○	●	○	
Meets quotas	○	○	●	○	
Follows instructions	○	○	●	○	
Has a positive attitude	○	○	○	○	
Works as a team member	○	○	○	●	
Follows safety procedures	○	●	○	○	
Is punctual	○	○	○	○	on time

2 LISTEN

A supervisor is giving a performance review to a new employee.

A **LISTEN FOR MAIN IDEA.** Look at the Employee Performance Review. In which category of job requirements does the employee need improvement?

B **LISTEN FOR DETAILS.** Listen again. Then circle the answers.

1. How does the manager feel about the employee's work in general?
   a. He's happy. **b.** He's upset. **c.** He's nervous.
2. In which two categories does the employee receive a "3"?
   a. meets quotas and is punctual **b.** follows instructions and meets quotas **c.** safety procedures and teamwork
3. How does the employee feel about being part of a team?
   a. She likes it. **b.** She doesn't like it. **c.** She isn't sure yet.
4. What items did the employee wear to work?
   a. a long dress **b.** earrings and rings **c.** sandals and a necklace

C **RANK.** Fill in the correct numbers in the performance review above based on what the manager said. Do not fill in the categories that he did not discuss.

3 CONVERSATION

A **LISTEN AND READ.** Listen to this part of Helena's performance review. Then practice the conversation with a partner.

A: First of all, I want you to know that we're happy in general with your work.
B: Oh, thank you!
A: Yes, the quality of your work is very good. And you're meeting your quotas, which is really important. I gave you a "3" in both categories.
B: Thank you. I understand how important it is to get all the packages out on time.
A: Exactly. And you're good at following instructions. I gave you a "3" there, too.
B: Sometimes, I have to ask for clarification.
A: That's great. You should always ask if you're not sure. It's better to ask than to do the wrong thing.
B: OK. Good.

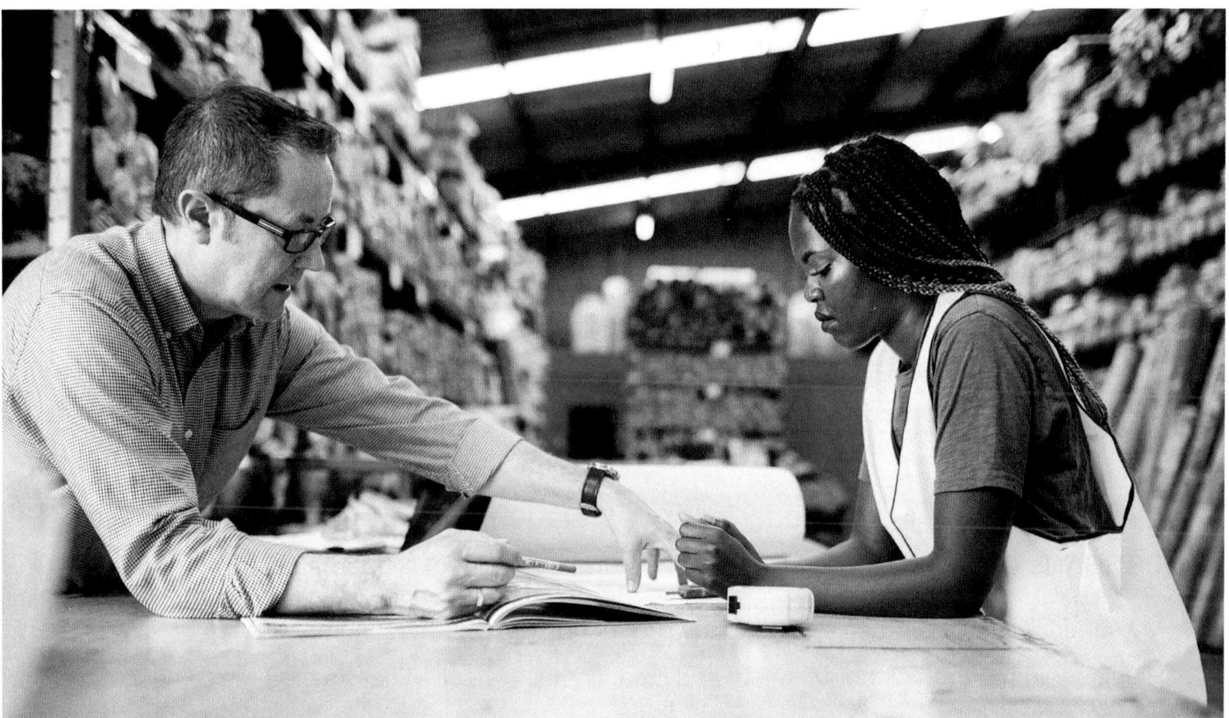

B **ROLE-PLAY.** Make a similar conversation. Then change roles.

Student A: You are a supervisor at Premium Parts. You are giving a performance review to one of your employees. Fill out the Employee Performance Review form before you begin. Make up the information.

Student B: You are an employee at Premium Parts. You are meeting with your supervisor to discuss your performance review. Respond to your supervisor's comments.

C **PRESENT.** How do performance reviews help an employee? How do performance reviews help the employer? How useful do you think performance reviews are? Support your opinion with examples.

I can ask and answer performance review questions. ☐ I need more practice. ☐

For more practice, go to MyEnglishLab.

Lesson 8

Grammar

Indirect instructions, commands, and requests

Direct speech	Indirect speech		
	Reporting verb	Object	Indirect request or command
"Ask a question if **you're** not sure.	He **said**		**to ask** a question if **we're** not sure.
"Leave **your** earrings and rings at home."	She **told**	us	**to leave our** earrings and rings at home.
"Please don't wear jewelry on the job."	She **asked**	them	**not to wear** jewelry on the job.
"Wear shoes that will protect **your** feet."	The company **requires**	us	**to wear** shoes that will protect **our** feet.

Grammar Watch

- When direct instructions, requests, and commands change to indirect speech, the verb changes to the infinitive form. Pronouns may also change to preserve the original meaning of the speaker.
- Use *not* before the infinitive for negative commands.
- Use reporting verbs, such as *advise, ask, instruct, order, say, tell,* and *warn,* to introduce indirect instructions, requests, and commands.
- Most verbs that report indirect instructions, requests, and commands have an object. However, the verb *say* does not.

A INVESTIGATE. Circle the reporting verbs. Underline the indirect requests and commands.

1. My supervisor asked me to speed up my production. I'm not meeting my quotas.
2. He also told me to think about safety and cleanliness. He specifically asked me to keep my work area cleaner.
3. My manager told me not to take such long breaks. She said to limit my breaks to twenty minutes.
4. She reminded me to wash my equipment at the end of my shift.
5. My boss warned me not to be late again or I might lose my job.
6. My supervisor asked me to check my work more carefully.
7. At the start of my review, my boss told me to relax.

Grammar

B **APPLY.** Change the direct commands into indirect instructions and requests.

http://www.acecomputer/humanresources.com

Search

Password procedures

1. Create a new password with at least 8 characters.
2. Use both numbers and letters.
3. Do not include your name or address in your password.
4. Do not use any special characters, such as question marks or pound signs.
5. Don't share your password with anyone.
6. Change your password every 30 days.

1. My manager told ___me to create___ a new password.
2. He told ____________ both letters and numbers.
3. He said ____________ my name or address in my password.
4. He instructed ____________ any special characters.
5. He warned ____________ my password with anyone.
6. He said ____________ my password every 30 days.

Show what you know!

1. **EXPLAIN.** Think of instructions for a simple procedure, such as how to use a copy machine or how to download a new app. Tell your instructions to another student.
2. **WRITE.** Listen to another student give instructions. Write down the instructions. Use indirect instructions.

Mary explained how to convert a file to a different format. She said to open the file. She told me to select save. Then she said to choose the file format . . .

I can use indirect instructions, commands, and requests. ☐ I need more practice. ☐

For more practice, go to MyEnglishLab.

Lesson 9

Writing

Write an email to a supervisor

WRITING PROMPT: Think about your workplace or a business you know. Could it work better in some way? What action would you like to suggest to the person in charge? Write an email to make your suggestion.

1 STUDY THE MODEL

A ANALYZE. Read the model and Writing Skill. Then answer the questions.

To: havalos@finestfurnishings.com
Subject: Warehouse reorganization Topic

Hi Henry,

I would like to make a suggestion. I think we should reorganize the warehouse. As you know, our most popular products, like the Pinestar sofa, are currently stored at the far end of the warehouse. Shouldn't we make these products easy to load? I think we should move them closer to the loading area. To make room for them, we can move the less popular products to the far end.

I think this change will really help our workers out. They'll be able to get the fastest-selling products on the trucks a lot more easily. I know this reorganization will take time and money. However, I think it will really make us more efficient and reduce our delivery times.

Best,

Lev

Writing Skill: Use email structure

Write the email topic in the subject line. The subject line is the first information the reader sees. Use the body of the email to make suggestions.

1. Circle the topic of the email. Underline the main suggestion that the writer makes.
2. What do you think might be the relationship between Henry and Lev?
3. What specific action(s) does the writer suggest? Why?

B TAKE NOTES. Complete the outline with information from the model.

Topic of email: ______________

What action does the writer suggest?

The writer suggests moving popular products closer to the Loading area.

Why does he think this is a good idea?

Because he thinks this will make the workers more efficient and reduce our delivery time.

2 PLAN YOUR WRITING

A **BRAINSTORM.** Discuss your ideas for the Writing Prompt with a partner.

B **ORGANIZE.** Use this outline to organize your ideas before writing.

Topic of email: ____________________

What action do you suggest?

____

____

Why?

____

____

3 WRITE

PROPOSE. Write an email to make a suggestion to a supervisor. Remember to write the email topic in the subject line. Use the model, the Writing Skill, and your ideas from Exercise 2 to help you.

4 CHECK YOUR WRITING

A **REVISE.** Use the Writing Checklist to review your writing. Make revisions as necessary.

B **COLLABORATE.** Read your writing with a partner. Use the checklist again to improve your writing.

WRITING CHECKLIST

- ☐ Did you put the topic of the email in the subject line?
- ☐ Did you clearly explain the action you are suggesting?
- ☐ Did you use correct capitalization, punctuation, and spelling?

I can use email structure. ☐ I need more practice. ☐

For more practice, go to MyEnglishLab.

Lesson **10**

Soft Skills at Work

Be adaptable

1 MEET WEI

Read about one of his workplace skills.

I am adaptable. I try to be flexible and adapt to changes or challenges. For example, I don't let disappointment interfere with my attitude at work.

2 WEI'S PROBLEM

A **READ.** Write *T* (true) or *F* (false).

Wei has been in the same job for two years. He applied for a position to become a team leader, but he just found out he is not going to be interviewed for the job. Wei is upset because he wants to be eligible for promotions in the future.

f 1. Wei has only been in his job for one year.
T 2. Wei has just applied for a new job.
f 3. Wei got the new position as a team leader.

B **REFLECT.** What is Wei's problem?

He wants a new posiction.

____

3 WEI'S SOLUTION

A **COLLABORATE.** Wei is adaptable. How does he respond to not getting an interview at work? Explain your answer.

1. Wei tells his supervisor he deserves the team leader role.
2. Wei tells his supervisor he will look for a job at another company.
3. Wei asks his supervisor how he can improve in his job so that he can advance.
4. Wei ______________________________.

B **ROLE-PLAY.** Role-play Wei's conversation with his supervisor.

Show what you know!

1. **REFLECT.** How are you adaptable at school, at work, or at home? Give an example.
2. **WRITE.** Write your example in your Skills Log.

   I am adaptable at school when I continue to study hard even when I miss a class.
3. **PRESENT.** Give a short presentation describing how you are adaptable.

I can give an example of how I am adaptable. ☐

Unit Review: Go back to page 65. Which unit goals can you check off?

5 Safe and Sound

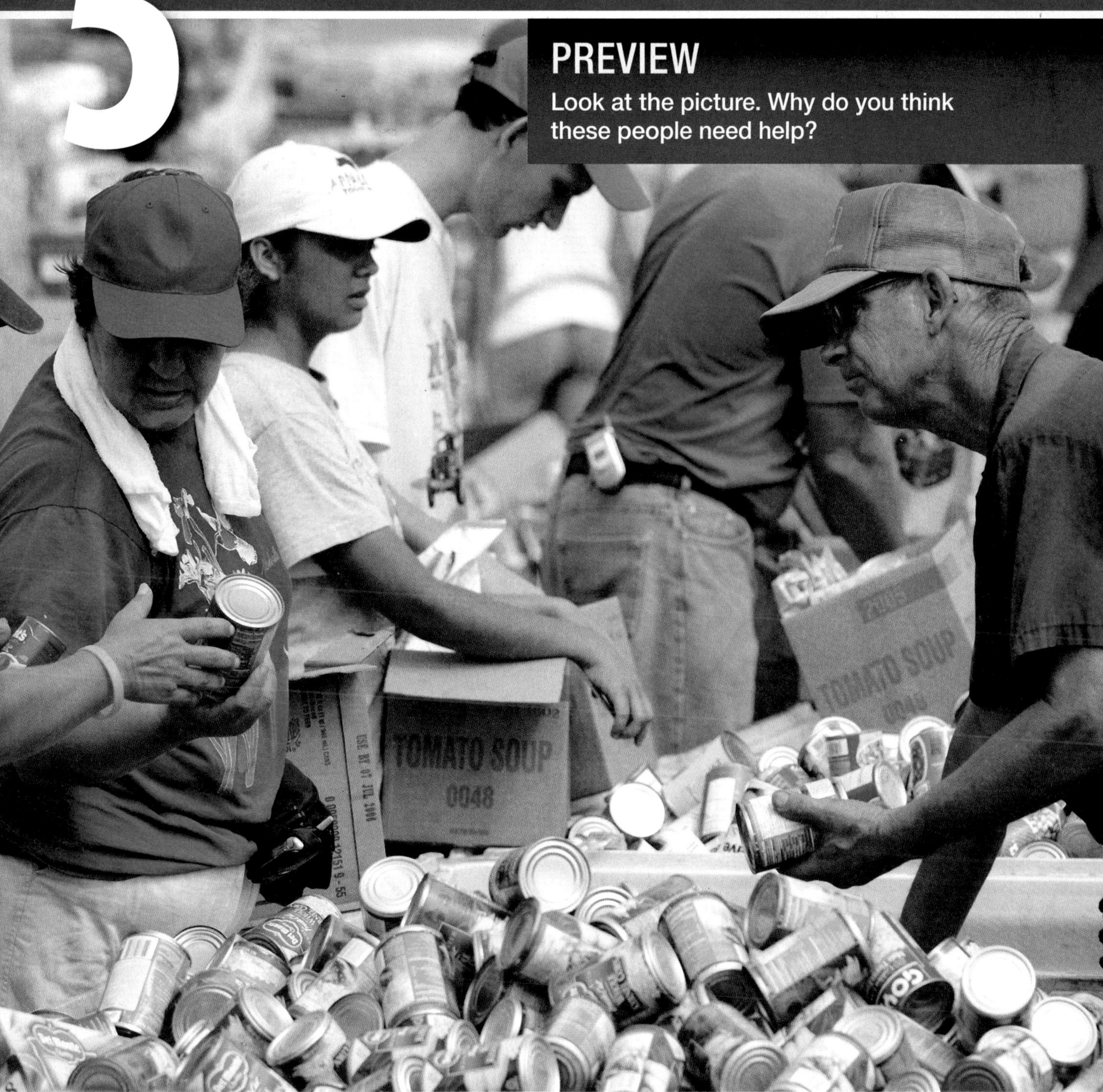

PREVIEW

Look at the picture. Why do you think these people need help?

UNIT GOALS

- ☐ Identify ways to prevent fires
- ☐ Talk about dangerous weather
- ☐ Interpret an evacuation map
- ☐ Communicate in a 911 emergency
- ☐ Write steps to take in an emergency situation
- ☐ **Academic skill:** Identify an author's purpose
- ☐ **Writing skill:** Use numbered steps to show order
- ☐ **Workplace soft skill:** Locate information

Lesson 1

Listening and Speaking

Identify ways to prevent fires

1 BEFORE YOU LISTEN

A **PREDICT.** What do you think the people in a fire-safety class want to learn?

B **DETERMINE.** How does each of these devices help with safety in a home?

- smoke alarm
- carbon monoxide detector
- fire extinguisher

2 LISTEN

The Fire Lieutenant is teaching the first class in a series of fire-safety classes.

A ▶ **LISTEN FOR MAIN IDEA.** What is the focus of tonight's class?

Prevention firee in home ____________________

____

B ▶ **LISTEN FOR DETAILS.** Listen again. Then write the correct words to complete each sentence.

1. The Fire Lieutenant will first talk about fire safety in Kitchen.
2. Coking is the main cause of fires in homes in the U.S.
3. If food catches fire, you should put a lid on it.
4. You should never leave the kitchen while The stove is on.
5. Teach your children don't touch anything on the stove.

C **RELATE.** What is one question that you would like to ask the Fire Lieutenant?

____

____

Listening and Speaking

3 PRONUNCIATION

A ▶ **PRACTICE.** **Listen. Then listen again and repeat.**

If we want to keep our home safe, what do you recommend?

When you're in the kitchen, pay attention to what you're doing.

B ▶ **APPLY.** **Listen. Add a comma where the voice should go up or down and pause. Then listen again to check your answers.**

1. When you are cooking, you should stay in the kitchen.
2. If you leave a towel or oven mitt near the stove, it can catch on fire.
3. If you have hot cooking oil, do not throw it in a trash can.
4. If a pan of food catches fire, put a lid over it.
5. When you finish cooking, remember to turn off the stove and oven.
6. If you have children, you should be extra careful in the kitchen.

Clauses

When there is more than one clause in a sentence, each clause usually has its own intonation. When you start a sentence with a clause that begins with *if* or *when,* let your voice go up or down a little and pause at the end of that clause.

4 CONVERSATION

The Fire Lieutenant is asking the class questions.

A ▶ **LISTEN AND READ.** **Then practice the conversation with a partner.**

A: Let's continue talking about how to prevent home fires. Does anyone know some causes of electrical fires?
B: Old appliances and cords, right?
A: That's right. Cords are especially dangerous if they are under rugs or near curtains.
B: A faulty electrical outlet can also cause a fire.
A: Right again. If you have old appliances or outlets, you should replace them.
B: What should we do if we have an electrical fire?
A: You should switch off the appliance and pull out the plug. Cover the fire with a blanket or use a fire extinguisher. Never use water because water conducts electricity. If you use water, you could get an electric shock.

B **DETERMINE.** **Talk about situations that can cause fires. Use the ideas in the pictures or your own ideas.**

C **PRESENT.** **What are some ways to improve fire safety in your own home?**

I can identify ways to prevent fires. ☐ I need more practice. ☐

For more practice, go to MyEnglishLab.

Lesson **2**

Grammar

Present real conditionals

Present real conditionals	
***If* clause**	**Result clause**
If a pan of food **catches** fire,	**put** a lid over it and turn the stove off.
If you **have** children,	you **should be** extra careful.
If you **don't have** a smoke detector,	your home **isn't** safe.
If we **want** to keep our home safe,	what **do** you **recommend**?

Grammar Watch

- Present real conditional sentences describe true situations that can occur under possible conditions. They are also used to give instructions or advice under these conditions.
- Conditional sentences can begin with either the *if* clause or the result clause. Use a comma between the clauses only when the *if* clause comes first:

  If you have children, you should be extra careful.

  BUT:

  You should be extra careful if you have children.

A INVESTIGATE. Read the poster that the Fire Lieutenant used during the class on fire safety. Draw one line under the *if* clause and two lines under the result clause.

What to Do in CASE of FIRE

- If you see smoke coming under the door, don't open the door! Don't open the door if it is very hot or warm! Go to another exit.
- If the door is cool, open it slowly.
- If there is smoke along your escape route, drop to the floor and crawl on your hands and knees below the smoke.
- If you are trapped, close the doors between you and the fire. If you can get to a phone, dial 911 and ask for the fire department. If you can't reach a phone, go to a window and signal for help with a sheet or a flashlight.

Grammar

B **APPLY.** Make conditional sentences about fire safety. Keep the clauses in the same order and add *if* to one clause. Include a comma if necessary.

1. (a fire occurs / leave your home immediately)
   If a fire occurs, leave your home immediately.
2. (you have small children / tell them not to hide under a bed in case of fire)
3. (family members can't escape by themselves / make plans to help them)
4. (don't open a door / it is hot to the touch)
5. (your clothes catch fire / drop to the floor and roll back and forth)

C **EVALUATE.** Correct the underlined clauses to make the statements true.

1. If you don't know where the fire exits in your building are, don't worry.
2. If you hear the fire alarm, don't leave your work area until firefighters arrive.
3. Get your personal belongings if you don't have them with you.
4. If you work on the 10th floor, take the elevator to exit the building.
5. Keep walking forward if you see smoke.

Show what you know!

1. **LIST.** Make a list stating what you should do in case of fire at home or at work.
2. **WRITE.** You are a manager at a restaurant. Write a message to your employees that explains how to prevent a fire and what to do in case of a fire. Use present real conditionals.

   Dear staff,
   Please be very careful in the kitchen. If you are wearing long sleeves, roll them up when you are cooking. If a fire starts on the stove, cover it with a lid . . .

I can use present real conditionals. ☐ I need more practice. ☐

For more practice, go to MyEnglishLab.

Lesson 3

Reading

Read about earthquakes

1 BEFORE YOU READ

A **DISCUSS.** What happens during an earthquake? What do you know about them?

B **PREDICT.** Skim the article. What is it about?

2 READ

LISTEN AND READ.

Academic Skill: Identify an author's purpose

Think about an author's objective or purpose. Is it to *entertain* you by telling a story? Is it to *inform* you by giving facts? Is it to *persuade* you to agree with a specific opinion?

EARTHQUAKES: BELIEFS VS FACTS

Many of us believe things about earthquakes that are simply not true. Unfortunately, our misconceptions may shape the way that we prepare for this very dangerous natural disaster. Here are a few common beliefs about earthquakes and the facts that disprove them.

BELIEF 1: In the United States, earthquakes happen only on the West Coast.

FACT: It's true that Alaska, on the West Coast, is the U.S. state with the most earthquakes per year. California also experiences many powerful quakes. However, one of the most active earthquake states is now Oklahoma, in the middle of the United States. Research shows that earthquakes can happen anytime, anywhere. That's why it's important to earthquake-proof your home wherever you live. Make sure that heavy or breakable objects won't fall during an earthquake.

BELIEF 2: The safest place to be during an earthquake is in a doorway.

FACT: This was once true, but experts nowadays generally disagree with this notion. In the past, the door frame was the strongest part of a home. It was sometimes the only thing left standing after an earthquake. However, in modern homes, doorways are no stronger than other parts of the house. Also, they can't protect you from flying or falling objects. So, people are now discouraged from standing in doorways during earthquakes. Instead, the best strategy is to get under a piece of furniture. Practice "Drop, Cover, and Hold On." Drop and crouch under a desk or table. Cover your head with one arm. Hold onto something solid with the other arm.

BELIEF 3: After the shaking of an earthquake stops, the danger is over.

FACT: It's a mistake to assume that you are safe immediately after the shaking has stopped. Aftershocks can occur minutes after the first quake ends. They are usually not as strong, but they can cause additional damage and injuries. It's safest to stay in the "Duck, Cover, and Hold" position for a few minutes after the shaking stops. Earthquakes can also cause serious damage to buildings. This damage may not be obvious right away. The buildings may collapse some time after the earthquake ends. As soon as you can do so safely, you should evacuate the area. It is best to plan your escape route in advance.

WHEN THE EARTH SHAKES: KNOW WHAT TO DO

Don't be misled by these or other common misconceptions. Plan, prepare, and practice so that you'll be ready when an earthquake occurs.

3 CLOSE READING

A **IDENTIFY.** What is the main idea?

a. If you are aware of common misconceptions about earthquakes, you will be able to prepare for them better.

b. Oklahoma is in the middle of the United States, and it has many earthquakes.

c. When an earthquake happens, you should duck under a desk or table and cover your head with one arm.

Reading

B **CITE EVIDENCE.** Complete the sentences. Where is the information located? **Lines**

1. In this reading, the author's purpose is __b__. 2-3
   - a. to entertain readers with stories about crazy things people believe about earthquakes
   - b. to inform readers that common beliefs about earthquakes are not true
   - c. to persuade readers that earthquakes are dangerous
2. Research shows that earthquakes happen __c__. 10-11
   - a. mostly on the West coast of the United States
   - b. in Alaska, California, and Oklahoma
   - c. anytime, anywhere
3. When you earthquake-proof your home, you __a__. 11-14
   - a. move heavy or breakable items to places where they won't fall
   - b. strengthen the doorways
   - c. move objects away from doorways
4. During an earthquake, you should __c__. 25-27
   - a. get under a doorway and stay there until the earthquake ends
   - b. get under a doorway, then crouch down and hold onto it
   - c. duck, cover yourself with a desk or table, and then hold onto it
5. You should evacuate the area __b__. 33-35
   - a. immediately after the shaking stops
   - b. several minutes after the shaking stops
   - c. several hours after the shaking stops
6. The author probably thinks that most people __c__. 36-40
   - a. live in areas where earthquakes are very common
   - b. are well prepared for earthquakes because they know a lot about them
   - c. are not well-informed about the dangers of earthquakes

C **INTERPRET VOCABULARY AND GRAPHICS.** Answer the questions.

1. In the context of line 8, what's another word for *experiences*?
   - a. has
   - b. feels
2. In the context of line 24, what's another word for *strategy*?
   - a. skill
   - b. plan
3. In the context of line 30, what's another way to say *assume*?
   - a. believe without proof
   - b. take over the duties of
4. In the context of line 37, what's another word for *collapse*?
   - a. fold up
   - b. fall
5. In the context of the graphic, what does the label *cover* mean?
   - a. cover your head
   - b. crawl under something and cover your head

D **SUMMARIZE.** What are the most important ideas in the article?

Show what you know!

1. **COLLABORATE.** Discuss. Which of the earthquake preparation tips described in the article can also help in other natural disasters, such as hurricanes or tornadoes?
2. **WRITE.** Describe two safety steps to take in the case of a hurricane or tornado.

   First of all, people should hurricane-proof their homes before a hurricane . . .

I can identify an author's purpose. ☐ I need more practice. ☐

To read more, go to MyEnglishLab.

Lesson 4

Listening and Speaking

Talk about dangerous weather

1 BEFORE YOU LISTEN

A **EXPLAIN.** What do you know about hurricanes? What do you know about tornadoes?

B **INTERPRET.** Read the hurricane warning. What do the boldfaced words mean?

"**Meteorologists** at the National Weather Service have issued a severe weather **warning**. People who live in **coastal areas** should be prepared to **evacuate** their homes and go to a safe inland location. **Tides** will be high, and rain will be extremely heavy. Residents in areas near rivers and lakes should be prepared for **floods**."

2 LISTEN

This is a podcast called *Know Your World.* The host is interviewing a meteorologist, Dr. Kay Wilkins.

A ▶ **LISTEN FOR MAIN IDEA.** Listen to the first part of the podcast. What makes a hurricane different from other tropical storms?

B ▶ **LISTEN FOR DETAILS.** Listen to the whole podcast. Write *T* (true) or *F* (false). Correct the false statements.

____ **1.** Hurricanes form over cool ocean water.

____ **2.** Hurricane season in the Atlantic Ocean is from July 1 through November 30.

____ **3.** A storm surge occurs when high winds push the water toward the shore and cause sea levels to rise.

____ **4.** A Category 1 storm cannot cause flooding.

____ **5.** A Category 3 storm has wind speeds of 96 to 110 miles per hour.

____ **6.** The strongest hurricane is a Category 5.

____ **7.** A hurricane warning is more serious than a hurricane watch.

C **DESCRIBE.** Discuss the following questions.

1. Which hurricanes have you either heard about or experienced personally?
2. How did the hurricane affect peoples' lives?

3 CONVERSATION

A ▶ **LISTEN AND READ. Then practice the conversation with a partner.**

A: Can you believe this weather?
B: It's been really bad lately. Now there's a flood watch.
A: I know. I heard it on the radio before I left home this morning.
B: The National Weather Service says there could be three more inches of rain. There's a severe weather watch that lasts until midnight.
A: Wow . . . this could be very dangerous.
B: Yeah. It's probably a good idea to keep checking the weather report for updates.
A: You're right. On days like today, it pays to be prepared.

B **PRESENT. Describe an experience that you have had in bad weather.**

I can talk about dangerous weather. ☐ I need more practice. ☐

For more practice, go to MyEnglishLab.

Lesson 5

Grammar

Adverb clauses of time

Adverb clauses of time	
Adverb clause (time)	**Main clause**
When there is the possibility of a hurricane in the next 36 hours,	the National Weather Service issues a hurricane watch.
As soon as you hear the warning,	make sure that your emergency preparations are complete.
Until the weather service cancels the storm watch,	you should check the weather report regularly.
After they hit land,	hurricanes lose strength.

Grammar Watch

- Adverb clauses of time use words like *when, before, after,* or *as soon as* to tell when one action happened in relation to another.
- Sentences can begin with the adverb clause or the main clause. Use a comma between the clauses only when the adverb clause comes first.
  After they hit land, hurricanes lose strength. BUT: *Hurricanes lose strength after they hit land.*

A **INVESTIGATE. Underline the adverb clauses.**

1. After lightning flashes in the sky, you hear the sound of thunder.
2. The sky usually turns dark before a thunderstorm begins.
3. When there's a thunderstorm, you should not stand under a tree.
4. Get inside a building or a car as soon as you see lightning.
5. You should stay inside until the thunderstorm ends.

B **COMPLETE.** Use *when, before, until,* or *after.*

___When___ scientists predict storms like tornadoes quickly and correctly, they save lives. ___before___ they had technology to help them do their job, meteorologists worked slowly. Their work became easier and faster ___when or after___ they began using computers.

Today, weather forecasters give up to thirty minutes' advance warning ___before___ a tornado actually arrives. As a result, people have time to find a safe place to stay ___until___ the storm is over. For example, ___when___ powerful tornadoes passed through Oklahoma in 1999, only 44 people died. However, 695 people lost their lives and 2,000 more were injured in 1925 because the tornadoes went through just a few minutes ___after___ people had received the tornado warning.

C **PUT IN ORDER.** Decide which of the events in brackets occurred first. Mark one event *1* (occurred earlier) and the other event *2* (occurred later).

1. [Tornadoes occur] [when cold, dry air from Canada meets warm, moist air from the Gulf of Mexico.]
2. [After the winds of a tornado begin to turn in a circular direction,] [they move faster and faster.]
3. [Before a tornado arrives in an area,] [you will usually hear a loud warning siren.]
4. [Until scientists learned some basic facts about tornadoes,] [they had trouble predicting them.]
5. [When the violent winds of a tornado hit buildings,] [serious structural damage often occurs.]
6. [Weather Service personnel use weather radar to confirm a potential tornado] [before they issue a tornado warning.]

D **APPLY.** Use the adverb to combine the two sentences. Keep the sentences in the same order. Include a comma if necessary.

1. The military used radar during World War II. / They wanted to know the location of planes and ships. (when)
   The military used radar during World War II when they wanted to know the location of planes and ships.
2. Radar worked very well. / There was bad weather. (until)
   ____
3. It began to rain or snow. / Radar operators noticed that something strange happened with their equipment. (as soon as)
   ____
4. The war ended. / Scientists were able to improve the radar technology to filter out the effects of rain or snow. (after)
   ____
5. The improvements to radar were made. / Finding the location of ships and planes became easier. (when)
   ____

Show what you know!

1. **PREPARE.** Watch a weather report on television or online. Take notes on the information.
2. **WRITE.** Summarize the weather report. Use adverb clauses of time.

I can use adverb clauses of time. ☐ I need more practice. ☐

For more practice, go to MyEnglishLab.

Lesson 6

Workplace, Life, and Community Skills

Interpret an evacuation map

A MAKE CONNECTIONS.

1. Describe an evacuation you know about. Where, when, and why did it happen?
2. Do you have an evacuation map at school, at work, or at home? Describe the map.

B SCAN.

1. How many storm surge zones are there?
2. What color is used for each level?
3. What color are the evacuation routes?

C DEFINE KEY WORDS. Find the words or symbols on the map. Match the words or symbols with their definitions.

b 1. evacuation
e 2. storm surge
a 3. route
d 4. zone
f 5. ——
c 6. N W E S (compass symbol)

a. planned way to travel
b. when people are asked to leave a building or region to get away from danger
c. symbol showing the four directions on a compass
d. a specific area that is different from some other area
e. extremely high and sudden rise in the level of the water
f. symbol for the evacuation routes

D INTERPRET GRAPHICS. Look at the evacuation map. Write *T* (true) or *F* (false). Correct the false statements.

F 1. The storm surge zone nearest the coast is usually yellow.
T 2. The zone with the highest chance of storm surge is Level A.
F 3. Most of the longer evacuation routes in Miami-Dade County run East-West.
F 4. The islands off the coast are in zones B and C.
T 5. The Atlantic Ocean would rise in a storm surge along this coast.
f 6. The zone furthest inland is zone C.

E GO ONLINE.

1. **SEARCH.** Find a map of the evacuation routes for your city, county, or state.
   What website is it on? ______________________________
2. **COMPARE.** Which routes would you and your family follow to evacuate? Which routes would another classmate take?

F PRIORITIZE. What supplies would you take with you in an evacuation? What supplies might you need to purchase to be ready for an evacuation?

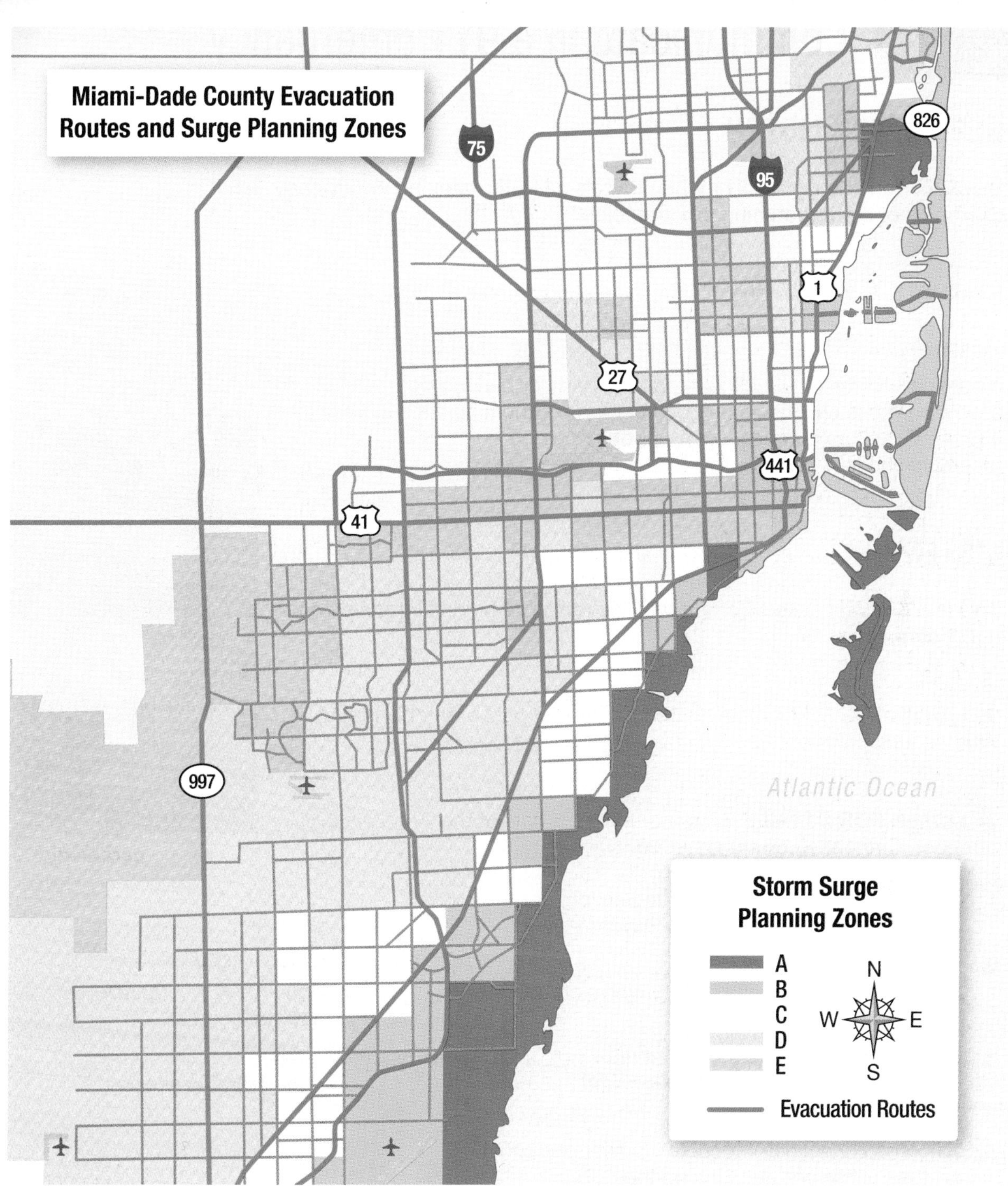

I can interpret an evacuation map. ☐ I need more practice. ☐

For more practice, go to MyEnglishLab.

Lesson 7 Listening and Speaking

Communicate in a 911 emergency

1 BEFORE YOU LISTEN

A **DECIDE.** You should call 911 when there's a life-threatening emergency. What are examples of life-threatening emergencies?

B **EVALUATE.** In which of these situations should you call 911?

You see . . .

a burning vehicle
a person who is unconscious
a person who has allergies
a person who is choking
a loud party or barking dog
a person waving a gun in a store
a power outage

paramedic

2 LISTEN

This is a podcast called *Community Matters.* The host is interviewing a 911 dispatcher.

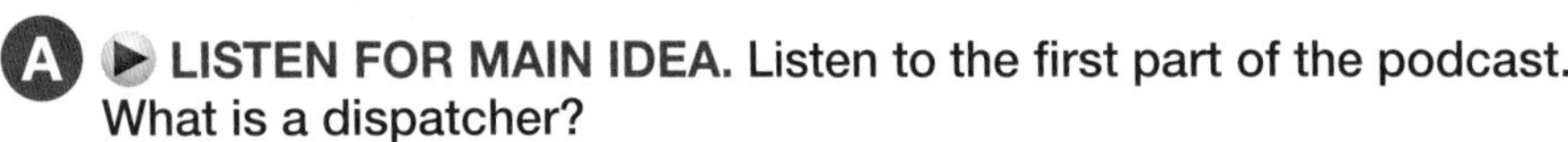

A **LISTEN FOR MAIN IDEA.** Listen to the first part of the podcast. What is a dispatcher?

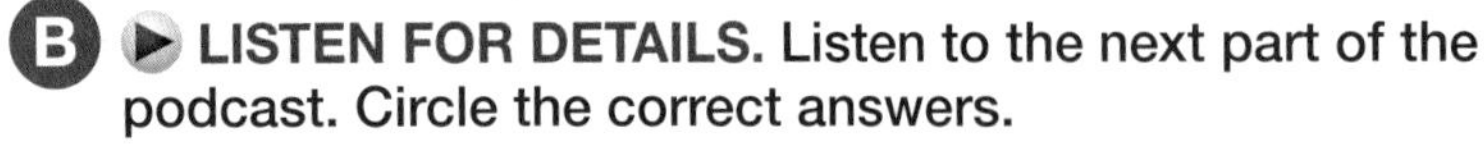

B **LISTEN FOR DETAILS.** Listen to the next part of the podcast. Circle the correct answers.

1. Many 911 dispatchers have a degree in ________________.
   a. biology **b.** psychology **c.** education
2. Many of the calls Mark takes ________________.
   a. require firefighters **b.** involve crimes **c.** don't need emergency assistance at all
3. What is an example of a call that does not require emergency assistance?
   a. a fire **b.** a crime that happened two days ago **c.** a major traffic accident
4. Who should you call if there is a power outage?
   a. the utilities company **b.** the police **c.** 911
5. What is the most important piece of information the dispatcher collects?
   a. the caller's name **b.** the caller's phone number **c.** the location of the emergency

C **INFER.** Why would a dispatcher need to be certified in CPR and first aid?

D **MAKE CONNECTIONS.** Describe a 911 call you have made or have heard about.

Listening and Speaking

3 PRONUNCIATION

A ▶ **PRACTICE.** Listen. Then listen again and repeat.

/i/	/ɪ/
eat	it
breathe	will
bleeding	minutes

Vowel sounds

The vowel sound /i/ (as in *eat*) is usually spelled with the letter *e*. The vowel sound /ɪ/ (as in *it*) is usually spelled with the letter *i*.

B ▶ **APPLY.** Listen. Circle the words you hear. Then listen again to check your answers.

1. eat / it **2.** feel / fill **3.** leave / live **4.** seat / sit **5.** steal / still

4 CONVERSATION

A ▶ **LISTEN AND READ.** Then practice the conversation with a partner.

Dispatcher: Ma'am, I have your address and phone number. The ambulance will be there in a few minutes.
Caller: OK . . . but what should we do until it arrives?
Dispatcher: Is your sister still having trouble breathing?
Caller: Yes, but my husband is helping her. He took a first-aid class last year, so he must know what to do.
Dispatcher: Your sister may be having an allergic reaction.
Caller: Well, she's allergic to nuts, but she was eating chocolate cake when the problem started. There weren't any nuts in the cake, so that couldn't be the problem.
Dispatcher: If the cake is from a bakery, there might be nuts in it. I'll tell the EMTs about your sister's allergy.

B **ROLE-PLAY.** Make a similar conversation. Then change roles.

Student A: You are at home. You just walked into the living room and found your grandfather on the floor. He is unconscious, but he's breathing. You know that your grandfather has a heart problem. You call 911. Answer the 911 operator's questions.

Student B: You are a 911 dispatcher. You just received an emergency medical call. Find out who the victim is and where he is. Ask if the person is unconscious or bleeding.

I can communicate in a 911 emergency. ☐ I need more practice. ☐

For more practice, go to MyEnglishLab.

Lesson 8

Grammar

Past continuous for interrupted action

Past continuous for interrupted action	
She **was eating** chocolate cake	when the problem **started**.
While he **was performing** CPR,	the ambulance **arrived**.

Questions	
Was she **eating** nuts when the problem **started**?	No, she **wasn't**. / Yes, she **was**.
What **were** you **eating** when you **began** to choke?	I **was eating** peanut butter.
Where **was** she **going** when the accident **happened**?	She **was going** home.

Grammar Watch

- The past continuous describes an activity that was in progress at the time another action happened. Use the past continuous for the action that was in progress. Use the simple past for the action that interrupted the action in progress.
- The verb in a *while* clause is often in the past continuous. The verb in a *when* clause is often in the simple past.
- Use a comma after the *while* clause or the *when* clause only when they come first in the sentence.

A **INVESTIGATE. Underline the past continuous verbs. Circle the simple past verbs.**

Alice is a 911 dispatcher. She (had) several emergency calls this afternoon. The first caller was cooking dinner when a fire started on his stove. Another caller was driving her car when she hit a man on a bicycle. A woman called because her sister had an allergic reaction while she was eating lunch. Someone else called because he was running downstairs when he tripped and fell. And another person was swimming when a jellyfish stung her. In each situation, Alice stayed calm while she was reporting the emergency.

Grammar

B **DETERMINE.** Cross out the incorrect words.

1. We **were working / worked** in the front office when the fire alarm went off.
2. While I **was cooking / cooked** dinner, I **was burning / burned** my hand.
3. When the nurse **was arriving / arrived**, several patients **were already sitting / already sat** in the waiting room.
4. She **was talking / talked** to the 911 dispatcher when the police **were arriving / arrived**.
5. He **was eating / ate** shrimp when he **was having / had** a serious allergic reaction.

C **COMPLETE.** Use the simple past or the past continuous.

A: Hello. 911. What's your emergency?

B: I need help! I hit a man on a bicycle. I think his leg is broken.

A: Can you tell me exactly what happened?

B: Yes. I ________________ **(drive)** down the road when a bicycle ________________ **(appear)** out of nowhere.

A: ________________ **(he, wear)** a helmet when your car ________________ **(strike)** him?

B: Yes.

A: OK, that's good. How fast ________________ **(you, go)** when you ________________ **(hit)** him?

B: Not very fast. I saw him a few seconds before the accident, so I ________________ **(slow down)** when the impact ________________ **(occur)**.

A: OK. An ambulance will be there any minute. Please stay on the line while you wait, and tell the victim not to move.

Show what you know!

1. **REPORT. Tell a partner about an emergency that you witnessed or heard about. What happened? Use the past continuous and the simple past.**
2. **SUMMARIZE.** Summarize the accident your partner told you about.

Malek was working at a restaurant when a fire started in the kitchen. A cook was frying hamburgers when the oil became too hot and caught on fire. While the cook was spraying the fire with the fire extinguisher, Malek called 911. Another restaurant worker helped all the customers get outside. Everyone was waiting outside the building when the fire fighters arrived. Luckily, no one was hurt.

I can use the past continuous for interrupted action. ☐ I need more practice. ☐

For more practice, go to MyEnglishLab.

Lesson 9

Writing

Write steps to take in an emergency situation

WRITING PROMPT: Find out what to do after an earthquake, tornado, blizzard, or wildfire. Do research online. Then write a list of steps to take.

1 STUDY THE MODEL

A ANALYZE. Read the model and Writing Skill. Then answer the questions.

After a Flood: First Steps

If your house seems safe to enter, follow these instructions:

☐ STEP 1: Put on waders and rubber gloves
Before you enter your home, you need to protect your body from the floodwaters. The water often contains sewage and chemicals, which can make you sick.

☐ STEP 2: Turn off the electricity
Find your fuse box and switch off the electricity as soon as you can. If the power comes back on and you are standing in water, you could be electrocuted.

☐ STEP 3: Take pictures
It can be difficult to get money from insurance companies to pay for flood damage. Before you remove any water or make repairs, photograph all the damage so you can show exactly what has happened.

☐ STEP 4: Call your insurance company
Tell your insurer about the flood and the damage it has caused. Ask if you need to wait for your property to be inspected before you start on repairs.

Writing Skill: Use numbered steps to show order

When you write about how to do something, organize the information into a series of numbered steps.

1. Circle the words that the writer used to organize the information.
2. What is the first step you should take before you enter your home?
3. What should you do after you take pictures of the damage to your home?

B TAKE NOTES. Complete the list with information from the model.

What to Do After a Flood

STEP 1: Put on waders and rubber gloves.

STEP 2: Turn of electricity

STEP 3: Teke pichure

STEP 4: call insurance. company.

2 PLAN YOUR WRITING

A **BRAINSTORM.** Discuss your ideas for the Writing Prompt with a partner.

B **ORGANIZE.** Use this list to organize your ideas before writing.

What to Do After a ______________

STEP 1:

STEP 2:

STEP 3:

STEP 4:

3 WRITE

ADVISE. Write about what to do after a natural disaster. Remember to organize the information into a series of numbered steps. Use the model, the Writing Skill, and your ideas from Exercise 2 to help you.

4 CHECK YOUR WRITING

A **REVISE.** Use the Writing Checklist to review your writing. Make revisions as necessary.

B **COLLABORATE.** Read your writing with a partner. Use the checklist again to improve your writing.

WRITING CHECKLIST

- ☐ Did you explain what to do after a natural disaster?
- ☐ Did you include several different steps?
- ☐ Did you list the steps in numbered order?
- ☐ Did you use correct capitalization, punctuation, and spelling?

I can ... ☐ I need more practice. ☐

For more practice, go to MyEnglishLab.

Lesson **10**

Soft Skills at Work

Locate information

1 MEET MARITZA

Read about one of her workplace skills.

I'm good at researching and locating information online. For example, I found a great website that had a list of all the items I should put in a first-aid kit. I'm going to make a similar kit to keep at my house.

2 MARITZA'S PROBLEM

A **READ.** Write *T* (true) or *F* (false).

Last week, there was a tornado just a few miles from Maritza's office. Maritza's manager has asked her to ensure the office is prepared for potential disasters in the future. He wants Maritza to hold a safety training for the staff, create an evacuation plan, and make a disaster kit for the office. Maritza doesn't know how to do any of those things. She has never thought about how to prepare for a weather disaster before.

F **1.** Maritza was injured in a tornado.
T **2.** Maritza's manager asked her to lead a safety training.
F **3.** Maritza knows all about how to prepare for disasters.

B **ANALYZE.** What is Maritza's problem?

____

____

3 MARITZA'S SOLUTION

COLLABORATE. Maritza is good at locating information. How does she find out how to prepare her office for potential disasters? Explain your answer.

1. Maritza uses government websites to get ideas for what to cover in the training, how to plan for evacuations, and what to include in the disaster kit.
2. Maritza asks her boss what he thinks she should cover in the training and put in the disaster kit.
3. Maritza goes online and picks out items that seem like they would be helpful to have in an emergency.
4. Maritza ____.

Show what you know!

1. **REFLECT.** How do you locate information at school, at work, or at home? Give an example.
2. **WRITE.** Write your example in your Skills Log.

   I can find information online about how to create emergency plans for my family. We need to agree on where we will meet if there is a disaster.
3. **PRESENT.** Give a short presentation describing how you locate information.

I can give an example of how I locate information. ☐

Unit Review: Go back to page 85. Which unit goals can you check off?

6 Moving In

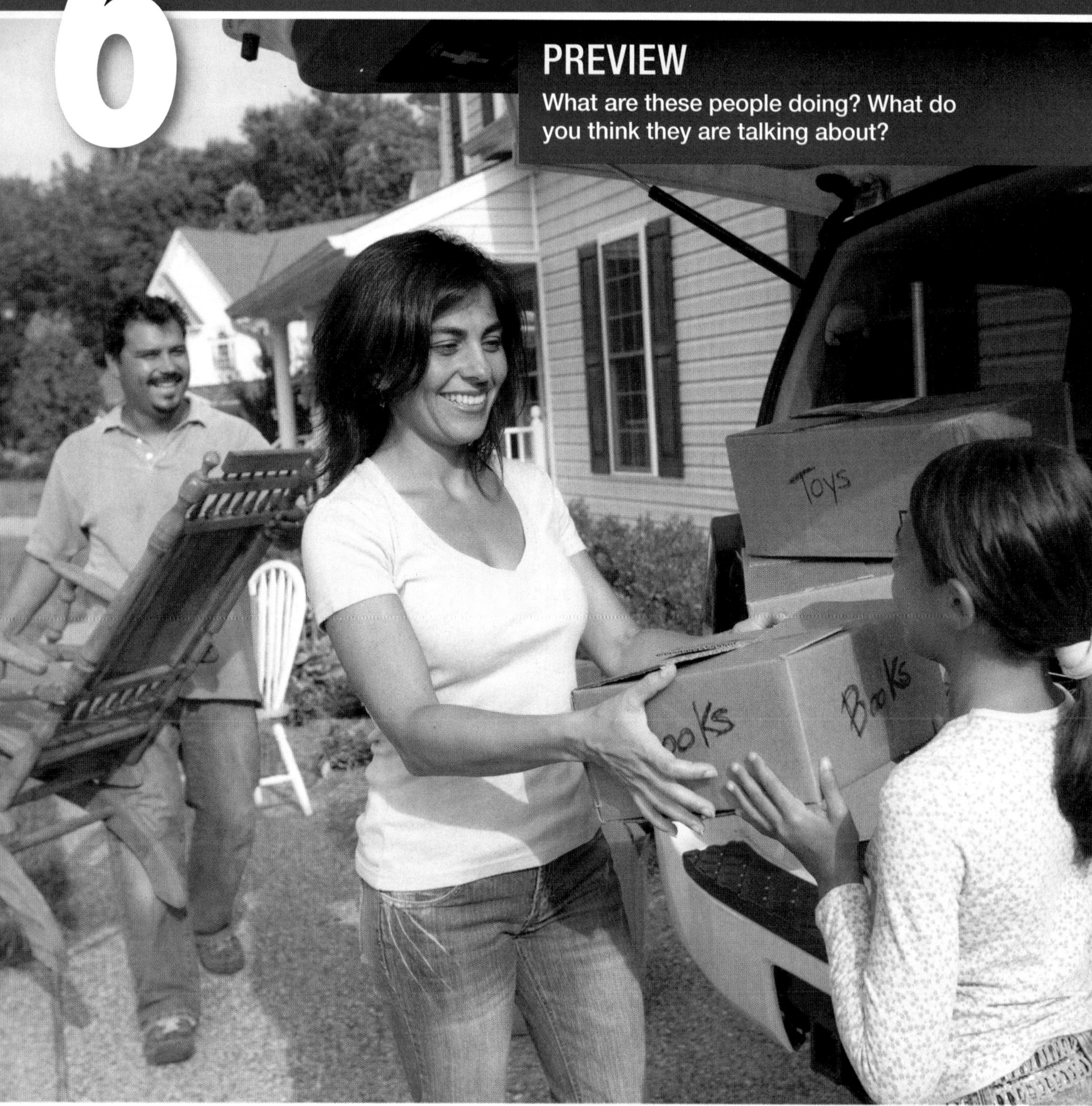

PREVIEW

What are these people doing? What do you think they are talking about?

UNIT GOALS

- ☐ Identify tenant responsibilities
- ☐ Interpret a lease
- ☐ Talk about landlord responsibilities
- ☐ Discuss problems with neighbors
- ☐ Write about a housing problem
- ☐ **Academic skill:** Distinguish main ideas from details
- ☐ **Writing skill:** Clearly state a problem and solution
- ☐ **Workplace soft skill:** Find creative solutions

Lesson **1**

Listening and Speaking

Identify tenant responsibilities

1 BEFORE YOU LISTEN

DETERMINE. When you rent a house or an apartment, you are called the tenant, and you are responsible for certain things. Tenants often have to give the landlord a *security deposit* when they move in. What is a security deposit for?

2 LISTEN

Jenn is calling about an apartment listing.

A ▶ **LISTEN FOR MAIN IDEA.** Listen to the first part of the conversation. What kind of apartment does Jenn want?

____

____

B ▶ **LISTEN FOR DETAILS.** Listen to the whole conversation. Write *T* (true) or *F* (false). Correct the false statements.

____ **1.** Jenn thinks the apartment is expensive.

____ **2.** The rent includes cable.

____ **3.** The apartment has a playground.

____ **4.** Covered parking is free.

____ **5.** The security deposit is $800 for tenants with pets.

____ **6.** Jenn can look at the apartment until 5:00 today.

C **SELECT.** Listen again. Check the items that are not included in the rent.

☐ water	☐ Internet
☐ electricity	☐ uncovered parking
☐ cable	☐ covered parking
☐ gas	☐ security deposit

3 CONVERSATION

Jenn and her family have rented the apartment. She is talking to the building manager.

A ▶ **LISTEN AND READ.** Then practice the conversation with a partner.

A: Where can I get my parking permit?
B: Right here. You're in spot number 11. You're supposed to keep this permit on your mirror.
A: OK, thanks. And where is the laundry room?
B: It's on the first floor of Building J. Please be sure the door is closed and locked when you leave.
A: No problem. How can I enter the laundry room?
B: Use this access card to get into the laundry room, gym, pool, and tennis courts. Do not give your card to anyone else. Guests are not allowed in those places without a tenant. And be careful not to lose this card. A replacement card is $100.

B **ROLE-PLAY.** Look at the three pictures. Make similar conversations.

Student A: You are a tenant.

Student B: You are the building manager. Tell the tenant each building rule.

1

2

3

I can identify tenant responsibilities. ☐ I need more practice. ☐

For more practice, go to MyEnglishLab.

Lesson 2

Grammar

Expressing obligation, expectation, and permission

Expressing obligation, expectation, and permission

Tenants	**are**	**required to** / **supposed to**	recycle glass, metal, and paper.
	are not	**allowed to** / **permitted to**	smoke in the building.

Questions about obligation, expectation, and permission

Why	**are**	we	**required**	to pay a security deposit?
	Am	I	**supposed**	to get a parking permit?
	Are	visitors	**allowed to**	park in this lot?
Where	**are**	visitors	**permitted to**	park?

Grammar Watch

- Use *be required to* when you talk about obligations, or things that people must do.
- Use *be supposed to* when you talk about expectations, or things that people should do.
- Use *be allowed / be permitted to* when you talk about permission, or things that people may do or may not do.
- *Be permitted to* means the same thing as *be allowed to,* but it is more formal.

A **INVESTIGATE.** Read the apartment building rules. Circle the tenant responsibilities that state obligations. Underline the expressions that merely describe an expectation. Use a double underline below the expressions that give or deny permission.

480 Cumberland Drive

- Tenants are required to pay their rent on the first of the month.
- Tenants who pay their rent late are required to pay a late fee of $50.
- Tenants are not supposed to make noise in their apartments after 10:00 P.M.
- Tenants are not allowed to keep bicycles or strollers in the hall. They are supposed to keep them in their apartments.
- Tenants are permitted to park only in their own parking spots.

Grammar

B **COMPLETE.** Use the correct form of one of the phrases in the box. More than one answer may be possible.

(not) be required to	(not) be supposed to	(not) be allowed to

1. Tenants are ___not supposed to___ make changes to the apartment.
2. No one ____________ smoke in the building.
3. If the rent is paid late, the tenant ____________ pay a late fee of $50.00.
4. Tenants ____________ entertain guests in the common areas of the apartment building. No one ____________ have parties after 10 P.M.
5. New tenants ____________ to keep their apartments clean and sanitary.
6. Tenants ____________ keep the front door of the building locked at all times.
7. Tenants ____________ give three months' notice if they plan to move out.
8. All tenants ____________ dispose of garbage in trash containers.
9. Tenants ____________ put glass, cans, and paper in the green recycling containers.
10. Tenants ____________ return all keys at the end of their lease term.

C **MAKE CONNECTIONS.** If you ever rented an apartment, which rules were true where you lived? If you haven't rented, which rules are important for visitors?

____

____

Show what you know!

1. **STATE AN OPINION.** Which of the rules in Exercises A and B do you think are reasonable? Are there any rules that you think are unreasonable? Explain.
2. **RANK.** Decide which five rules in Exercises A and B are the most important. Write those rules. Then number them from *1* (most important) to *5* (least important). Explain why.

I can express obligation, expectation, and permission. ☐ I need more practice. ☐

For more practice, go to MyEnglishLab.

Lesson 3

Workplace, Life, and Community Skills

Interpret a lease

A MAKE CONNECTIONS. When people rent an apartment or a house, they usually sign a *lease.* The lease describes the tenant's and the landlord's rights and responsibilities. What things do you think leases include?

B SCAN. THEN READ. What type of information is included in each of these sections of the lease: *Parties, Description of Premises, Term,* and *Rent*? After scanning, read the entire lease.

C DEFINE KEY WORDS. Find the words on the left in the lease. Match the words with their definitions.

____ **1.** landlord
____ **2.** tenant
____ **3.** premises
____ **4.** security deposit
____ **5.** wear and tear
____ **6.** term

a. apartment building and its facilities, such as parking spaces
b. breaking down of something from normal everyday usage
c. number of months for the lease
d. money paid by the tenant in advance, in case of damage to the apartment
e. owner of the apartment building
f. person who pays rent to live in the apartment

D LOCATE DETAILS. Write *T* (true) or *F* (false). Correct the false statements.

_F_ **1.** The landlord pays for ~~electricity and~~ water.

____ **2.** The landlord is required to make sure appliances work and fix them if they break.

____ **3.** Both the landlord and the tenant are required to keep certain areas clean and safe.

____ **4.** The tenant is not supposed to make changes to the apartment without permission.

____ **5.** The tenant is not allowed to smoke in the hallways, but is allowed to smoke in his or her apartment.

____ **6.** The tenant is not allowed to use the laundry room after 8:00 P.M.

E ANALYZE. Read the questions. What problem might occur if you didn't know the answer to the question?

1. How long is the lease for?
2. Can other family members or other roommates be added to the lease later?
3. Can you get out of the lease if you need to move early, for instance, because of a job change or a family emergency?

F GO ONLINE.

1. **SEARCH.** Find a sample rental lease. What website is it on? ____________________
2. **COMPARE.** How is the lease you found similar to the lease found by another classmate? How is it different?

G **LIST.** What are the typical responsibilities of the landlord? What are the typical responsibilities of the tenant? Make two lists.

Lease Agreement

1. **PARTIES.** Vaslav Novak, the landlord, agrees to rent to Anita Cruz, the tenant, the premises described in paragraph 2, below.
2. **DESCRIPTION OF PREMISES.** The premises are described as 1000 Center St., Apt. 32A, Mountain View, CA 94040 and include refrigerator, dishwasher, and laundry facilities and one parking space in the parking lot, but exclude garage space.
3. **TERM.** The lease shall begin on April 1, 2018 and shall end on March 31, 2019.
4. **RENT.** The total rent for the premises for the lease term is $21,600 payable each month at $1,800. Rent is payable in advance by the 5th day of each month, and will be delivered to Vaslav Novak, 1000 Center St., Apartment 40 B, Mountain View, CA 94040. If the rent is paid after the 5th day of the month, a late fee of $80 will be charged. The late fee is due by the end of the month.
5. **SECURITY DEPOSIT:** The landlord acknowledges receipt of $1,800 as a cleaning and security deposit. At the end of the lease, the landlord may keep all or any part of this deposit of this rental agreement for any of the following reasons:
   i) to cover unpaid rent owed to the landlord
   ii) to pay the cost of repairing any damage to the premises resulting from abuse, misuse, or neglect, not including normal wear and tear.
6. **UTILITIES:** The tenant agrees to pay for all utilities except water, which shall be paid by the landlord.
7. **PETS:** Tenants shall not keep a pet on the premises.
8. **LANDLORD RESPONSIBILITIES.** *The landlord shall:*
   i) keep the public areas in a clean and safe condition.
   ii) keep the appliances in the rental unit in good working order.
   iii) paint the rental unit every three years.
   iv) supply a smoke alarm and carbon monoxide detector in each bedroom.
9. **TENANT RESPONSIBILITIES.** *The tenant shall:*
   i) pay rent promptly when due.
   ii) keep the rental unit in a clean and safe condition.
   iii) place garbage and refuse in the containers provided.
   iv) park only in the parking spot provided in the tenants' parking lot.
10. **TENANT RESPONSIBILITIES.** *The tenant shall not:*
    i) alter the premises (for example, paint) without permission of the landlord.
    ii) smoke on the premises.
    iii) use the laundry facilities between the hours of 10 P.M. and 6 A.M.

I can interpret a lease. ☐ I need more practice. ☐

For more practice, go to MyEnglishLab.

Lesson 4

Listening and Speaking

Talk about landlord responsibilities

1 BEFORE YOU LISTEN

MAKE CONNECTIONS. Where can you go if you have a problem with your landlord? What agencies in your community might provide free assistance?

2 LISTEN

Manny López is a guest on the podcast *This Week.*

A ▶ **LISTEN FOR MAIN IDEA.** What kind of questions does Manny answer?

____

____

B ▶ **LISTEN FOR DETAILS.** Listen to the podcast again. Write *T* (true) or *F* (false). Correct the false statements.

__F__ **1.** Manny is a ~~tenant with a problem~~ tenant rights lawyer.

_____ **2.** Chris wants his landlord to install new smoke detectors in his apartment.

_____ **3.** Chris's smoke detectors aren't working.

_____ **4.** Chris hasn't called his landlord yet to complain about his problem.

_____ **5.** Manny tells Chris to replace the smoke detectors himself.

C ▶ **EXPAND.** Listen to the next part of the podcast. Circle the correct answers.

1. What does Eva's landlord want to do?
a. raise the rent **b.** end the lease **c.** renew the lease

2. When is Eva's lease up?
a. in a year **b.** last September **c.** in six months

3. How often does Eva pay her rent late?
a. sometimes **b.** every six months **c.** never

4. When can the landlord raise Eva's rent?
a. immediately **b.** when the lease is up **c.** next month

5. What does Eva have to do after September 1st?
a. write to Manny again **b.** pay her rent **c.** sign a new lease

Listening and Speaking

3 PRONUNCIATION

Tag questions

Add a short tag question like *aren't you?* or *doesn't he?* to check information. Use rising intonation to show that you are not sure the information is correct. Make your voice go up at the end of the tag question.

A **PRACTICE.** Listen. Then listen again and repeat.

aren't you?	You're going to stay there with him, **aren't** you?
is he?	The repairman isn't there yet, **is** he?
doesn't he?	He has to replace the smoke detectors, **doesn't** he?
does she?	Your landlord doesn't pay for water, **does** she?

B **APPLY.** Listen. Underline the tag question in each sentence. Then listen again and use an arrow to mark the intonation.

1. You paid the rent, didn't you?
2. The plumber isn't here yet, is he?
3. The landlord is taking care of this problem, isn't he?
4. We aren't going to have to pay for this, are we?

4 CONVERSATION

A **LISTEN AND READ.** Then practice the conversation with a partner.

A: Good afternoon, Garden Oaks Apartments.
B: Hi. This is Lisa Ming. Could I speak with the building manager, please?
A: Hi, Lisa. This is John Cove, the building manager. How can I help you?
B: We don't have any hot water in the bathroom. Could you send someone over?
A: Sure. I'll send a plumber to your place. Let's see. You live in 5F, don't you?
B: That's right.
A: And you're home now, aren't you?
B: Yes, but I'm leaving for work in a few minutes.
A: No problem. I can let the plumber in for you. That's OK with you, isn't it?
B: I guess so. You're going to stay here with him, aren't you?
A: Yes, I will.
B: I don't want any strangers in our apartment while we're out.
A: I completely understand. Don't worry. I'll be there while he does the work.
B: Thanks, Mr. Cove.

B **ROLE-PLAY.** Make a similar conversation. Then change roles.

Student A: You are a tenant. The lock on the door of your building is broken, and anyone can walk in. You ask the building manager to take care of the problem.
Student B: You are a building manager. You will send a locksmith to fix the door right away.

C **PRESENT.** Did you or someone you know ever have a problem with a building manager? What was the problem? What did you or that person do? What did the building manager do?

I can talk about landlord responsibilities. ☐ I need more practice. ☐

For more practice, go to MyEnglishLab.

Lesson 5

Grammar

Tag questions

Tag questions with *be*		Tag questions with *do* as an auxiliary verb	
Affirmative statement	**Negative tag**	**Affirmative statement**	**Negative tag**
The plumber **is** on his way,	**isn't** he?	You **called** the landlord,	**didn't** you?
You**'re going to stay** there,	**aren't** you?	He **has to fix** this,	**doesn't** he?
Negative statement	**Affirmative tag**	**Negative statement**	**Affirmative tag**
The plumber **isn't** here,	**is** he?	You **don't pay** for water,	**do** you?
He **wasn't** in the office,	**was** he?	He **didn't come** yet,	**did** he?

Grammar Watch

- Use tag questions to check that information is correct or when you are not sure the other person will agree.
- Use negative tags with affirmative statements. Use affirmative tags with negative statements.

A INVESTIGATE. Read the conversation. Circle the main verb in each sentence. Then draw one line under the tag question if it is affirmative and two lines under the tag question if it is negative.

1. You called the landlord, didn't you?
2. You didn't see mice in the apartment, did you?
3. The plumber fixed the sink, didn't he?
4. The landlord has to paint the lobby, doesn't he?
5. There isn't any lead paint in the apartment, is there?
6. The electrician isn't in the basement, is he?

B DETERMINE. Cross out the incorrect words.

1. You checked the lease, **did / didn't** you?
2. The landlord wasn't in the office, **was / wasn't** he?
3. You're going to sign the lease, **are / aren't** you?
4. The building manager takes care of all the repairs, **does / doesn't** she?
5. You sent a letter to the landlord, **did / didn't** you?
6. There isn't any damage in your apartment, **is / isn't** there?
7. The landlord is responsible for keeping the building safe, **is / isn't** she?
8. The landlord and the painter are finished with the work, **are / aren't** they?

Grammar

C **MATCH.** **Complete the statements with the correct tag questions.**

f	**1.** You paid the rent,	**a.**	doesn't he?
____	**2.** We don't have to pay a deposit,	**b.**	don't we?
____	**3.** The electrician is fixing the problem,	**c.**	is he?
____	**4.** We need new carpet,	**d.**	do we?
____	**5.** The landlord has a key to our apartment,	**e.**	isn't he?
____	**6.** The plumber isn't here yet,	**f.**	didn't you?

D ▶ **COMPLETE.** **Use tag questions. Then listen and check your answers.**

1. A: What's wrong, Li An?
B: The landlord kept our security deposit because the carpet has stains on it.
A: Oh . . . but we didn't stain the carpet, ________________?

2. A: The landlord charged us for damage to the living room wall.
B: But why? The living room wall isn't damaged, ________________?

3. A: You didn't like the apartment we saw this morning, ________________?
B: Yes, I did. I liked it very much!

4. A: That apartment would be perfect for us! What did you think?
B: I liked it, too. But it's kind of expensive, ________________?
A: The rent *is* a little high. But the landlord pays for gas and electricity, ________________?

Show what you know!

1. **DISCUSS.** **You found an apartment that you like. Describe what is surprising to you about the apartment. Use tag questions to express your surprise.**

2. **WRITE.** **You found an apartment that you like. You want to get your friend's opinions on the apartment. Write a message using tag questions.**

Hi Jan,

I found a two-bedroom apartment for $1,200 a month. That seems like a good price, doesn't it? The rent includes Internet and cable. That's unusual, isn't it?

I can use tag questions. ☐ I need more practice. ☐

For more practice, go to MyEnglishLab.

Lesson 6

Reading

Read about why people move

1 BEFORE YOU READ

A **DISCUSS.** What are some reasons that people choose to move to a new city or town?

B **PREDICT.** Skim the article. What is it about?

2 READ

Listen and read.

Academic Skill: Distinguish main ideas from details

Use the organization of a text to distinguish an author's main ideas from the details that explain or support those ideas.

Americans on the Move

Americans are famous for moving a lot. The United States is an immigrant nation. Moving to seek new opportunities has traditionally been part of what makes Americans American. In 2013, a Gallup survey found that 24% of U.S. adults had moved within the country in the past five years. The only other countries where people moved that often were New Zealand (26%), Finland (23%), and Norway (22%).

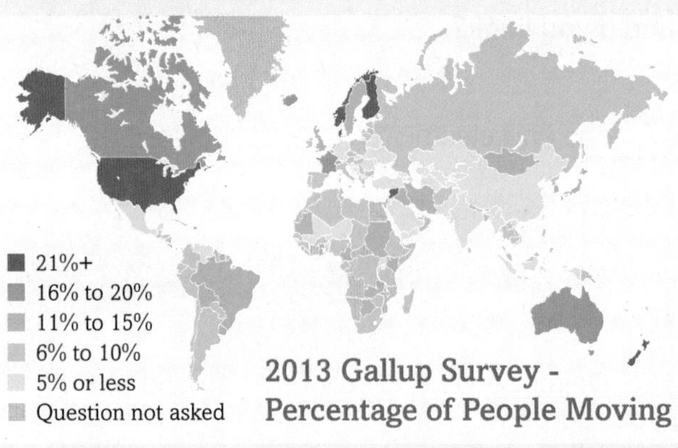

2013 Gallup Survey - Percentage of People Moving

Why do so many Americans move? Historically, the most common reason that people relocate has been to find jobs. When businesses close and jobs disappear in an area, people move away. When new jobs are created in an area, people move to that area. Americans also often move because their company asks them to relocate to a new place. People at the computer company IBM joked that it stood for I've Been Moved.

Many people also move for housing-related reasons. Rents and housing prices are becoming unaffordable for many residents. Some residents are forced to move to cheaper areas. Others choose to move so that they can buy better homes. And people move for personal reasons. They move to get married or to retire.

However, there has been an interesting recent development. Currently, Americans are not moving as much as they used to. In a survey from 2016, the percentage of Americans who moved over a one-year period fell to 11%. This is considerably lower than in previous years. Among those who moved, 42% moved because they wanted a new home. About 27% moved because of family. Only 20% moved for work.

Why are more people staying put in the United States? The answer may be that working conditions for Americans have recently changed. In many families, both parents now work. It's difficult for them both to move to a new place. In addition, workers now telecommute more often. They don't always have to move to a new location to take a new job. The most important factor is probably that the American workforce is aging. Older workers are less likely to move than younger workers.

People in the U.S. are still moving. However, moving is not as central to the American experience as it once was.

3 CLOSE READING

A **IDENTIFY.** What is the main idea?

a. Moving to seek new opportunities is part of what makes Americans American.
b. Many people move for housing-related reasons or for personal reasons.
c. Nowadays, workers don't always have to move to a new location to take a new job.

B **CITE EVIDENCE.** Answer the questions. Where is the information located? **Lines**

1. According to the article, what are Americans famous for around the world?

   ______________________________ ______

2. What information in the article supports the idea that Americans move a lot?

   ______________________________ ______

3. Historically, what has been the most common reason that Americans move?

   ______________________________ ______

4. For what two housing-related reasons might Americans move?

   ______________________________ ______

5. Why is the age of the American workforce a factor in Americans moving less often?

   ______________________________ ______

C **INTERPRET GRAPHICS.** Complete the sentences about the survey.

1. According to the 2013 survey, _____ of Americans moved within the U.S.
   a. less than 15% **b.** more than 20% **c.** between 15% and 20%
2. Only 5% or less of all citizens of _____ moved within their country.
   a. Australia and Brazil **b.** Mexico and Canada **c.** Mexico and China

D **INTERPRET VOCABULARY.** Complete the sentences.

1. In the context of line 4, the word *survey* means _____.
   a. map showing boundaries **b.** set of questions
2. In the context of line 19, the phrase *are forced to* means _____.
   a. have to **b.** prefer to
3. In the context of line 24, the word *development* means _____.
   a. improvement **b.** change
4. In the context of line 38, the word *factor* means _____.
   a. reason **b.** number

E **SUMMARIZE.** What are the most important ideas in the article?

Show what you know!

1. **COLLABORATE.** Have you ever moved? Why did you move? Were your reasons for moving described in the article? How likely are you to move again?
2. **WRITE.** Are you likely to move or stay in the place you live now? Explain.

   I am not likely to move soon. I like my home. And both my wife and I have good jobs in this city . . .

I can distinguish main ideas from details. ☐ I need more practice. ☐

To read more, go to MyEnglishLab.

Lesson 7

Listening and Speaking

Discuss problems with neighbors

1 BEFORE YOU LISTEN

GIVE EXAMPLES. Answer the questions.

1. What kinds of problems can people have with their neighbors?
2. If someone has a problem with a neighbor, what can he or she do about it?

2 LISTEN

Oscar and Marta live in an apartment building. They are talking about their neighbors.

A ▶ **LISTEN FOR MAIN IDEA.** What is the problem?

____

____

B ▶ **LISTEN FOR DETAILS.** Listen again. Then write the correct words to complete each sentence.

1. The TV in apartment _______________ was playing very loudly.
2. The couple is worried because _______________.
3. Marta wants to call _______________.
4. Oscar wants to _______________.
5. Residents are not allowed to make loud noise in the building after _______________.

C **ANALYZE.** What should Oscar and Marta do about their neighbors?

D **MAKE CONNECTIONS.** Describe a problem you have had with a neighbor or someone else you didn't know very well.

____

____

____

Listening and Speaking

3 PRONUNCIATION

A ▶ **PRACTICE.** Listen. Then listen again and repeat.

Oh, no!　　That's horrible!　　It's disgusting!

Strong emotion

To show strong feeling, make your voice go up very high and then fall.

B ▶ **APPLY.** Listen. Underline the words that show strong feelings. Then listen again to check your answers.

1. I can't believe it!
2. That noise is awful!
3. How terrible!
4. That's amazing!

4 CONVERSATION

A ▶ **LISTEN AND READ.** Then practice the conversation with a partner.

A: I saw a mouse in the laundry room last night!
B: Oh, no! That's horrible! Li Ping told me that she had mice in her building, too.
A: She did? It must be the construction next door. She said they were repairing the pipes.
B: Come to think of it, there's some construction here, too, in the basement near the laundry room. I bet that's why there are mice.
A: Ugh! I can't stand mice! I'm going to call the landlord. I'll ask him to call the exterminator.

B **ROLE-PLAY.** Make a similar conversation between two neighbors. Then change roles.

Student A: A neighbor has parked in your parking spot three times this week, and you have had to park your car in the street. Tell Student B about your problem.

Student B: Tell Student A to find out who has been parking in the spot. Then tell Student A to talk to that neighbor and ask him or her to stop parking there.

C **PROBLEM SOLVE.** Read the problem. What are a few possible solutions?

One of Pedro's neighbors, Leo, leaves for work very early in the morning. Leo's co-worker picks him up at 4:00 A.M. Many mornings, the co-worker honks his horn to let Leo know he's waiting. The horn wakes Pedro up, and he can never go back to sleep.

____

____

I can discuss problems with neighbors. ☐　　I need more practice. ☐

For more practice, go to MyEnglishLab.

Lesson 8

Grammar

Reported speech

Reported speech					
Direct speech	**Reported speech**				
Lena told her neighbor, "**Your** car **is** in **my** parking spot."	Lena	told	her neighbor		**his** car **was** in **her** parking spot.
The landlord said, "**I will** fix it tomorrow."	The landlord	said		(that)	**he would** fix it tomorrow.
Lena said, "**You are** too noisy."	Lena	said			**they were** too noisy.

Grammar Watch

- Use reported speech to tell what a speaker says without using the exact words.
- In both direct and reported speech, the verb *tell* takes an object. The verb *say* does not.
- In formal English, when the reporting verb is in the past, the verb in the reported speech is also in the past. In informal English, the verb in the reported speech does not change to the past, especially when speech is reported soon after it is spoken: *Lena said they're too noisy.*
- Pronouns and possessives in reported speech usually change to keep the speaker's original meaning.

(See page 264 for additional changes in verb tenses, pronouns, and possessives in reported speech.)

A **INVESTIGATE.** Read the tenant message board. Underline the reported speech.

Lost & Found
Neighborhood
For Sale
Pets
General
Browse

@HallieJ: One of my neighbors smokes all the time. I told him that smoking wasn't allowed in the building. I also told him that my children are getting sore throats. He said he would stop, but I can still smell smoke from his apartment. Does anyone have any advice?
2d ago 15 4

@Lin75: The ceiling in our bathroom leaks every time our upstairs neighbors take a shower. The building manager said he would send a plumber, but it's been three days. I told my neighbors that they should call, too. They said they did, but nothing has happened. Does anyone else have this problem?
3d ago 23 12

B **COMPLETE.** Use *said* or *told.*

My friend Inez called me last week. She was really upset. She ___told___ me that her neighbor had bought two big dogs. She __________ the dogs were always running in the halls. When they saw her, they jumped on her. She __________ she was terrified. I __________ her that she should complain to the landlord, but she __________ that she didn't like to complain. I __________ her I would call the landlord for her, but she __________ she would work it out.

Grammar

C **WRITE.** Read the tenants' problems. Rewrite them using *said* and informal English.

1. **Ivan:** "My neighbors' kids are very loud and wake me up early."
   Ivan said that his neighbors' kids are very loud and wake him up early.
2. **Victor:** "The hallway in our building always smells like fried food from the restaurant next door."
   ____
3. **Ada:** "My neighbors have visitors late at night, and they sometimes ring my doorbell by accident."
   ____
4. **Ming:** "We live close to a fire station, and the sirens wake our kids up all the time."
   ____
5. **Hamid:** "My neighbor parks her car in my space almost every weekend."
   ____

D **COMPLETE.** Use the correct form of the verbs. Use formal English.

Last week, I spoke to the building manager about two problems. The first is with the front door. I told him that it didn't close (**not close**) properly and that this __________ (**be**) a dangerous situation. He said he __________ (**know**) about the problem. I told him that he __________ (**need**) to install an automatic lock. He said he __________ (**look**) into it. The second problem is with the nightclub down the block. It closes late, and people make a lot of noise when they leave. The manager said he __________ (**be**) sorry but that he __________ (**not be able**) to do anything about it.

Show what you know!

1. **MAKE CONNECTIONS.** Talk about a problem you have had with a neighbor or someone else you don't know very well. Use reported speech.
2. **WRITE.** Describe the problem you had with your neighbor. What did you say? What did your neighbor say? How did you resolve the problem? Use reported speech.

   Last year, my neighbor let his kids play alone in the hallway. I told him that his kids were very loud. He said that he was sorry about the noise. After that, his kids didn't play in the hallways. I felt much better. I was worried that they weren't safe alone.

I can use reported speech. ☐ I need more practice. ☐

For more practice, go to MyEnglishLab.

Lesson 9

Writing

Write about a housing problem

WRITING PROMPT: Think of a problem in a home you are renting that you might complain to your landlord about. What is a possible solution to this problem? Write a letter of complaint to explain the problem and ask for a solution.

1 STUDY THE MODEL

A ANALYZE. Read the model and Writing Skill. Then answer the questions.

To: dblake22@yoohoo.com
Subject: Broken stove in Apt 3C

Dear Mr. Blake,

I am writing to let you know that the stove in my apartment is broken. Two of the burners don't work. The stove needs to be fixed or replaced.

I checked my lease (see attached), and it said that the landlord was responsible for making sure that all appliances are in good working order. Therefore, could you please send someone immediately to fix or replace the stove? You can call me at (605) 555-7932 to arrange a time.

Thank you. I look forward to hearing from you very soon.

Best,

Lidia Martínez
Buena Vista Apartments, Apt. 3C

Writing Skill: Clearly state a problem and a solution

When you write a letter of complaint, clearly state the problem and ask for, or suggest, a solution to the problem.

1. Underline the sentence that states the problem. Circle the sentence that states the solution.
2. What did the tenant do before she called the landlord?
3. What two steps does the tenant ask the landlord to take?

B TAKE NOTES. Complete the boxes with information from the model.

PROBLEM	→	SOLUTION

2 PLAN YOUR WRITING

A **BRAINSTORM.** Discuss your ideas for the Writing Prompt with a partner.

B **ORGANIZE.** Use these boxes to organize your ideas before writing.

PROBLEM		SOLUTION
	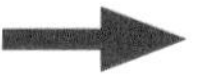	

3 WRITE

PROPOSE. Write a complaint email to a landlord about a housing problem. Remember to clearly state the problem and ask for a solution. Use the model, the Writing Skill, and your ideas from Exercise 2 to help you.

4 CHECK YOUR WRITING

A **REVISE.** Use the Writing Checklist to review your writing. Make revisions as necessary.

B **COLLABORATE.** Read your writing with a partner. Use the checklist again to improve your writing.

WRITING CHECKLIST

- ☐ Did you clearly explain the problem?
- ☐ Did you ask for a solution?
- ☐ Did you include your name, address, and telephone number?
- ☐ Did you use correct capitalization, punctuation, and spelling?

I can clearly state a problem and a solution. ☐ I need more practice. ☐

For more practice, go to MyEnglishLab.

Lesson 10 Find creative solutions

1 MEET AYO

Read about one of her workplace skills.

I like to find creative solutions to problems. For example, when something changes at work that impacts my life, I try to find a positive way to deal with the change.

2 AYO'S PROBLEM

A READ. Write *T* (true) or *F* (false).

Ayo's company is moving some employees to a new building. The new building is much bigger and nicer than the old building. There is free parking and a cafeteria in the basement. However, the new building is almost twice as far from Ayo's house as the old building. Ayo is worried the longer commute will mean she'll be late to pick up her daughter from daycare.

_____ **1.** Ayo's company is moving to a bigger building with free parking and a cafeteria.
_____ **2.** Ayo's company is moving to a building near her home.
_____ **3.** Ayo is worried that she will be late picking up her daughter from daycare.

B ANALYZE. What is Ayo's problem?

____

____

3 AYO'S SOLUTION

A COLLABORATE. Ayo finds creative solutions. What does Ayo do about her new commute? Explain your answer.

1. Ayo asks to be moved back to the old building.
2. Ayo asks her supervisor if she can change her schedule to come in and leave the office earlier each day.
3. Ayo tells her supervisor she needs to find a new job that is closer to her home.
4. Ayo ____.

B ROLE-PLAY. Role-play Ayo's conversation with her supervisor.

Show what you know!

1. **REFLECT.** How do you find creative solutions at school, at work, or at home? Give an example.
2. **WRITE.** Write your example in your Skills Log.

   Our new office only has one fire alarm. I suggested to my supervisor that we install more fire alarms.

3. **PRESENT.** Give a short presentation describing how you find creative solutions.

I can give an example of how I find creative solutions. ☐

Unit Review: Go back to page 105. Which unit goals can you check off?

7 Behind the Wheel

PREVIEW

How much does it cost to buy and own a car? What are some things that car owners have to spend money on?

UNIT GOALS

- ☐ Talk about buying a car
- ☐ Interpret car insurance documents and talk about buying insurance
- ☐ Discuss car maintenance and repairs
- ☐ Describe a car accident
- ☐ Write about how to make a major purchase
- ☐ **Academic skill:** Interpret infographics
- ☐ **Writing skill:** Use time words to show sequence
- ☐ **Workplace soft skill:** Respond well to feedback

Lesson 1

Listening and Speaking

Talk about buying a car

1 BEFORE YOU LISTEN

MATCH. When you buy a car, you need to consider a lot of factors. Match the factors on the left with the correct descriptions or examples.

1. vehicle type ____ **a.** miles per gallon (mpg) of gasoline

2. make and model ____ **b.** total distance a car has traveled

3. warranty ____ **c.** seat belts, air bags, antilock brakes, etc.

4. optional features ____ **d.** how well a car works; dependability

5. mileage ____ **e.** Ford Focus, Honda Civic, Toyota Corolla, etc.

6. gas mileage ____ **f.** sedan, convertible, SUV, minivan, pickup, etc.

7. reliability ____ **g.** GPS, entertainment system, sunroof, etc.

8. safety features ____ **h.** written promise to fix or replace a product that doesn't work

2 LISTEN

Eva and Mark are talking about buying a car.

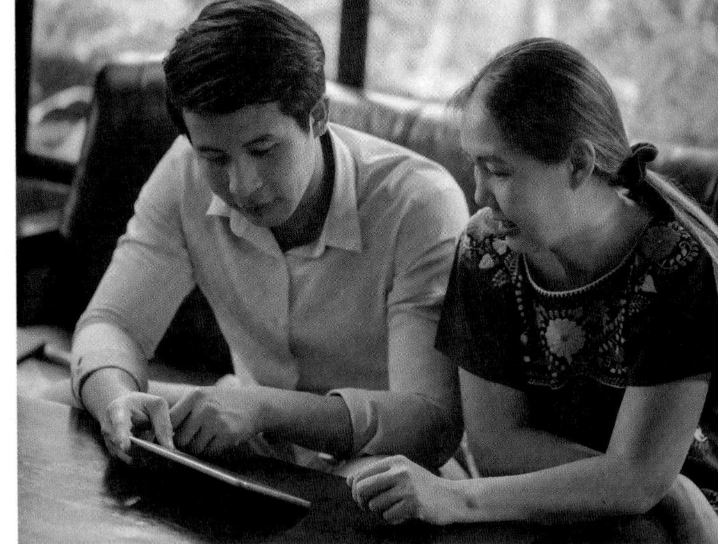

A ▶ **LISTEN FOR MAIN IDEA.** Listen to the first part of the conversation. Does the couple want to buy a car from a dealership or a private owner? Why?

____

____

B ▶ **LISTEN FOR DETAILS.** Listen to the whole conversation. Write *T* (true) or *F* (false). Correct the false statements.

____ **1.** Mark and Eva think it's important for a car to have a warranty.

____ **2.** They want to buy a car with a sunroof.

____ **3.** They don't care about a rearview camera.

____ **4.** They want a car that's three or four years old.

____ **5.** Mark and Eva have agreed they want a red car.

Listening and Speaking

3 CONVERSATION

Mark and Eva are talking to a salesperson at Tri-State Motors.

A ▶ **LISTEN AND READ.** Then practice the conversation with a partner.

Salesperson: So, you're looking at the red sedan. It's a great little car, isn't it? It's only three years old. I can let you have it for just under $15,000.
Mark: We've checked prices for this make and model. I think we can get the car for less.
Salesperson: I might be able to get you a lower price. I'll talk to my manager.
Eva: I see there are 38,000 miles on the car. How many previous owners have there been?
Salesperson: Just one. She drove it mostly for shopping. Our mechanics have inspected the car. It's in excellent condition. Would you like to take a test drive? I can go get the keys for you.
Mark: Thanks, but not right now. We'd rather look at some other cars first.

B **RANK.** Decide which are the three most important factors in buying a car. Number them *1* (most important), *2,* and *3.*

____ make and model ____ gas mileage ____ purchase price

____ safety ____ reliability ____ other: ______________

C **REFLECT.** Look at the pictures. Which car would you most like to have? Why?

D **MAKE CONNECTIONS.** How would you feel about going to a car dealership to buy a car? Would you be more excited or nervous? Explain your feelings.

____

____

E **PRESENT.** Describe the first time you bought a car or made some other major purchase. What additional responsibilities came with that purchase? What benefits came from that purchase?

I can talk about buying a car. ☐ I need more practice. ☐

For more practice, go to MyEnglishLab.

Lesson 2

Grammar

Would rather and *would prefer* to talk about preferences

Would rather and would prefer to express preferences

Statements

Mark and Eva **would rather**	**buy**	a small car.		
They ***would prefer***	**to buy** / **buying**	a small car.		
They**'d rather not**	**have**	a big car.		
They**'*d prefer not***	**to have** / **having**	a big car.		
They **would rather**	**buy**	a small car	**than**	a big car.
They ***would prefer***	**buying**	a small car	**to**	a big car.

Questions					Responses
Would you **rather**	**drive**	a minivan	**than**	an SUV?	Yes, I **would**.
Would you **prefer**	**driving**	a minivan	**to**	an SUV?	No, I **wouldn't**.

Grammar Watch

- *Would rather* and *would prefer* both express preference.
- After the phrase *would rather,* use the base form of the verb. When making a comparison, use *than* between the things you are comparing.
- After the phrase *would prefer,* use an infinitive or a gerund. But when making a comparison, use the gerund and *to* between the things you are comparing.

A **INVESTIGATE.** Look at the pictures. Check (✓) the statements that are true.

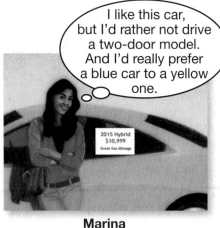

I'd rather drive a sports car than a minivan any day!
Sam

I like this car, but I'd rather not drive a two-door model. And I'd really prefer a blue car to a yellow one.
2015 Hybrid
$10,999
Great Gas Mileage
Marina

I want a safe car, and I'd prefer not to spend money on car repairs.
Jinsuk

__✓__ **1.** Sam doesn't want to drive a minivan.

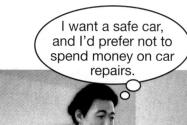

_____ **2.** Marina is looking for a four-door car.

_____ **3.** Marina really likes yellow cars.

_____ **4.** Jinsuk wants a reliable car.

_____ **5.** Jinsuk and Sam like the same kinds of cars.

B **DETERMINE.** Cross out the incorrect words in the article on the Car Shopper app.

C **COMPLETE.** Use *would rather (not), would prefer (not), would you rather,* or *would you prefer.*

Sam: I love sports cars. I know they're expensive, and most people would rather not spend that much on a car. But I don't care. I ________ spend the money and drive a really cool car. How about you, Marina? What kind of car ________ having?

Marina: A hybrid. I like the combination of a gas engine and an electric motor with a battery. I ________ going to the gas station if I can avoid it.

Sam: Hey, Jinsuk, how about you? What kind of car ________ to drive?

Jinsuk: A safe car. I ________ have to worry about having an accident. I ________ having a car with a good safety record to anything else.

●●●●○ 1:25 PM 92%

CAR SHOPPER

Auto FYI By Art Jeffers, Car Enthusiast

When it's time for your next car, truck, or SUV, where **would you rather** / ~~**would you prefer**~~ get your information? People don't always agree on the best way to become a smart auto shopper.

Some car buyers would prefer **use / using** the Kelly Blue Book app. Others would rather **rely / relying** on Consumer Reports. Another group of car buyers would rather **learn / learning** from personal experience **than / to** read what the experts say. They **would rather / would prefer** do research by talking to friends and paying attention to the cars they see on the road. So, what about you? Would you prefer relying on your personal experience **to / than** using an app or website? Or would you rather **follow / following** the advice of experts? Whatever you do, get as much information as possible before you buy your next vehicle.

Show what you know!

1. **REFLECT.** Discuss what kind of cars you like. Explain why.
2. **WRITE.** Describe what kind of car you would prefer. Use *would rather* and *would prefer.* Give at least three reasons why.

I would prefer to get a small, affordable car. I'd rather not spend a lot of money on a car, and I'd prefer having a car that is easy to park.

I can use *would rather* and *would prefer* to express preferences. ☐ I need more practice. ☐

For more practice, go to MyEnglishLab.

Workplace, Life, and Community Skills

Lesson **3**

Interpret car insurance documents and talk about buying car insurance

1 INTERPRET CAR INSURANCE DOCUMENTS

A ANALYZE. All drivers in the U.S. must have car insurance and must carry insurance identification cards in their vehicles. All drivers must renew their insurance once or twice a year. Why do you think car insurance is so important?

B SCAN. THEN READ. What two types of documents are shown? What is the difference between them? When do you get each one? After scanning, read both documents.

C DEFINE KEY WORDS. Find the words on the left in the documents. Match the words with their definitions.

b 1. agent
f 2. issuer
d 3. make
e 4. model
a 5. premium
c 6. renewal

a. amount of money you pay for insurance
b. person who sells insurance and handles claims
c. making active for additional time
d. the car company
e. the type of car
f. the insurance company

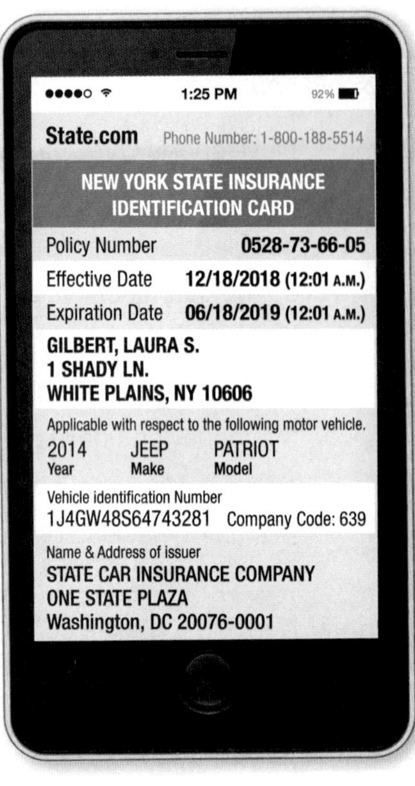

State.com Phone Number: 1-800-188-5514

NEW YORK STATE INSURANCE IDENTIFICATION CARD

Policy Number **0528-73-66-05**
Effective Date **12/18/2018 (12:01 A.M.)**
Expiration Date **06/18/2019 (12:01 A.M.)**

GILBERT, LAURA S.
1 SHADY LN.
WHITE PLAINS, NY 10606

Applicable with respect to the following motor vehicle.

2014	JEEP	PATRIOT
Year	Make	Model

Vehicle identification Number
1J4GW48S64743281 Company Code: 639

Name & Address of issuer
STATE CAR INSURANCE COMPANY
ONE STATE PLAZA
Washington, DC 20076-0001

D LOCATE DETAILS. Circle the correct answers.

1. Who is Tom Russo?
   a. insurance agent (b.) car owner c. owner of the insurance company
2. How long is the policy for?
   a. a month (b.) a year c. six months
3. How much does the policy cost a year?
   a. $126.00 (b.) $1,512.00 c. $1,260.00
4. How much does the owner pay before the insurance company begins to cover any expenses?
   (a.) $500.00 b. $100.00 c. $126.00
5. What make of car is being insured?
   (a.) Ford b. Jeep c. Honda
6. When you are driving, which document do you need to keep with you?
   a. the renewal notice b. insurance estimate (c.) insurance identification card

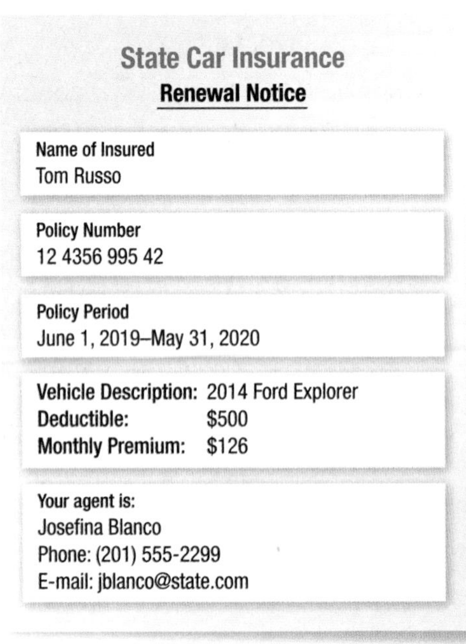
State Car Insurance

Renewal Notice

Name of Insured
Tom Russo

Policy Number
12 4356 995 42

Policy Period
June 1, 2019–May 31, 2020

Vehicle Description: 2014 Ford Explorer
Deductible: $500
Monthly Premium: $126

Your agent is:
Josefina Blanco
Phone: (201) 555-2299
E-mail: jblanco@state.com

2 TALK ABOUT BUYING CAR INSURANCE

A **MAKE CONNECTIONS.** How would you find out about car insurance? What types of questions would you ask?

B **PREDICT.** What are some things that insurance companies ask when you want to get a quote, or price estimate, for car insurance? Check (✓) the information companies probably ask about.

- [ ] annual salary
- [x] age
- [x] marital status
- [ ] checking account number
- [x] type of car (year, make, and model, etc.)
- [x] safety features
- [ ] when you bought the car
- [x] estimated number of miles you drive each year

C **LISTEN TO CHECK PREDICTIONS.** Amy and Tom are talking about getting a quote. Were your predictions in Exercise B correct? Change your answers if necessary.

D **LISTEN FOR DETAILS.** Tom mentions several things that affect a person's car insurance. List three things that can raise insurance premiums.

1. What tipe of car.
2. How many Mail.
3. Marital status, age.

E GO ONLINE.

1. **SEARCH.** Find a car insurance website. What is the website? ______________________
2. **ESTIMATE.** Fill in the car insurance form on the Internet to get an estimated quote for your car or for the car described on page 130. How much was the quote? Was the quote higher or lower than you anticipated?

F **STATE AN OPINION.** Insurance companies adjust your premiums based on certain things about you, like your age. Do you think it is fair that some drivers have to pay higher premiums than other drivers? Why or why not?

I can interpret car insurance documents and talk about buying car insurance. ☐ I need more practice. ☐

For more practice, go to MyEnglishLab.

Lesson 4

Listening and Speaking

Discuss car maintenance and repairs

1 BEFORE YOU LISTEN

INTERPRET. Read the tips from a website about car maintenance and repair. What do the boldfaced words in the tips mean?

Car Maintenance Tips

A tire's **tread** becomes worn either because it has been used for a long time, or because it doesn't have enough air. You should check your tires' tread regularly, especially before a long trip.

In addition to gas, don't forget the other things that you must put into your car. **Oil** keeps your car's engine running well. **Engine coolant** keeps the engine from getting too hot. Other **fluids** that you should check and add to your car when necessary are **transmission fluid** and **brake fluid**. And then there's the **washer fluid**. After all, you need to see out your windows. Finally, remember that the **air pressure**, or amount of air in your tires, is important. And keep in mind that what goes in sometimes comes out, so be on the lookout for **leaks**.

2 LISTEN

Jake is the host of a podcast about car maintenance called *All Things Auto.*

A **LISTEN FOR MAIN IDEA.** In Jake's opinion, what is the number one car-care tip?

____

____

B **LISTEN FOR DETAILS.** Listen again. Then circle the correct answers.

1. How often should you change the oil in your car?
   a. once a week b. once a month c. once every three months
2. How often should you check your car's tires?
   a. once a week b. once a month c. once every three months
3. Where can you find out how much air to put in your tires?
   a. under the hood b. under the car c. in your owner's manual
4. What color is transmission fluid?
   a. red b. yellow c. brown
5. What color is engine coolant?
   a. green or brown b. green or yellow c. red or black
6. What happens when you do regular car maintenance?
   a. You save money. b. You spend more. c. You drive more.

Listening and Speaking

3 PRONUNCIATION

A ▶ **PRACTICE.** Listen. Then listen again and repeat.

Can you tell me what the **prob**lem is?

When I looked under the **car** this morning, I noticed a dark **stain**.

You might have an **oil** leak.

I'll see you to**mo**rrow, then.

Important words

Use stress and intonation to show which word in a clause or sentence is the most important. Make your voice go up on the accented syllable of that word and make the vowel sound longer.

B ▶ **APPLY.** Listen. Put a dot (•) over the stressed word in each sentence. Then listen again to check your answers.

1. Something's wrong with my car.
2. I hear a funny noise when I start it.
3. The brakes aren't working well.
4. Do you know a good mechanic?

4 CONVERSATION

A mechanic at an auto repair shop is talking to a customer.

A ▶ **LISTEN AND READ.** Then practice the conversation with a partner.

Mechanic: Osman's Auto Repair. How can I help you?
Customer: I want to know if I can bring my car in tomorrow.
Mechanic: Sure. Can you tell me what the problem is?
Customer: When I looked under the car this morning, I noticed a dark stain.
Mechanic: You might have an oil leak. Bring the car in tomorrow morning, and we'll take a look at it. We open at 7:00 A.M.
Customer: Thanks. I'll see you tomorrow, then.

B **LIST.** Which car maintenance tips are most important? List three important tips. Discuss your lists.

______________________ ______________________ ______________________

I can discuss car maintenance and repairs. ☐ I need more practice. ☐

For more practice, go to MyEnglishLab.

Lesson **5**

Grammar

Embedded questions

Direct question	Embedded *wh-* question		
What is the problem?	Can you tell me	**what**	**the problem is?**
Why does the "Check Engine" light go on?	Could you explain	**why**	**the "Check Engine" light goes on?**
When did the noises start?	I don't know	**when**	**the noises started.**
What time will my car be ready?	I wonder	**what**	**time my car will be ready.**
How much will the repairs cost?	I want to know	**how much**	**the repairs will cost.**

Direct question	Embedded *Yes/No* question		
Does my car need an oil change?	Can you tell me	**if** / **whether**	**my car needs an oil change?**
Can I bring my car in tomorrow?	I want to know		**I can bring my car in tomorrow?**
Did they fix the problem?	Do you know		**they fixed the problem?**

Grammar Watch

- Use embedded questions to ask for information politely, or to express information about which you are uncertain.
- Put embedded questions inside questions such as *Can you tell me . . . ?*
- Put embedded questions inside of statements such as *I don't know. . . .*
- Use statement word order (subject + verb) for embedded questions.

A **INVESTIGATE.** Underline the embedded *wh-* questions and circle the embedded *yes/no* questions.

A: Do you know whether the car will be ready tomorrow?
B: Yes, it will. I'm a little worried. I don't know how much the repairs are going to cost.
A: I can't believe you didn't get a written estimate from the mechanic! He should tell you what it's going to cost before he begins work on your car.
B: Of course, you're right. I don't know why I didn't think of that. I wonder if it's too late to ask for an estimate.

B **PUT IN ORDER.** Write the embedded questions to complete the sentences.

Katy: Do you know ___where the receipt from the mechanic is___?
(is / the / receipt / where / the / from / mechanic)

Doug: I don't remember ______________________ when I came home.
(it / with / what / did / I)

Katy: We need to know ______________________.
(is / where / receipt / that)

Doug: It's probably in my wallet. Can you tell me ______________________________?
(so / why / it / is / important)

Katy: I want to know ______________________________ in the radiator.
(coolant / how much / the / put / mechanic)

Doug: ______________________________?
(do / need / you / know / to / why / that)

Katy: There's steam coming from the hood. I want to find out ______________________________.
(the / is / what / problem)

Maybe he put in too much coolant, or not enough.

C **COMPLETE.** Change the direct questions to embedded questions. Include a period or a question mark.

Customer: *Can you tell me if you have windshield wipers for a 2016 Honda Accord?*
(Do you have windshield wipers for a 2016 Honda Accord?)

Salesperson: Yes, we do. They're in Aisle 6.

Customer: Do you know ______________________________
(Are they on sale?)

Salesperson: I'm not sure ______________________________ I'll find out.
(Did the sale end yesterday?)

Customer: My turn signal isn't working. Could you also find out

____
(Will I need a special bulb?)

Salesperson: Yes, you will. I'll see ______________________________.
(Where are they located?)

D **EVALUATE.** Correct the mistakes in the embedded questions.

1. He wants to know ~~does~~ *if* the car ~~need~~ *needs* new brakes.
2. They asked whether was it safe to drive with a damaged tire.
3. Can you tell me does the engine need more coolant?
4. Do you know how late is the mechanic open.
5. We wonder that the leak is coming from the radiator.
6. I want to know how can I change the oil.
7. The mechanic wasn't sure did they have the parts he needed to repair my car.

Show what you know!

1. **BRAINSTORM.** What other things do you want to know about car maintenance and repairs?
2. **WRITE.** Make a list of things you want to learn about car maintenance. Use embedded questions.
   - *I want to learn where I should go to check the brakes.*
   - *I'd like to find out how often I'm supposed to change the tires.*

I can use embedded questions. ☐ I need more practice. ☐

For more practice, go to MyEnglishLab.

Lesson 6

Reading

Read about consumer-protection laws

1 BEFORE YOU READ

A **DISCUSS.** Have you ever had problems with a car or another product you owned? What did you do about them?

B **PREDICT.** Skim the article. What is it about?

2 READ

Listen and read.

Academic Skill: Interpret infographics

Use charts, graphs, and other visuals to learn important facts.

Complaints about Cars

Shawn Chastain bought the car of his dreams at an auto dealership a few months ago. But his dream car is turning out to be a nightmare. It's constantly breaking down. He's followed the procedures described in the car's warranty. He's taken the car back to the dealership, and they've tried to fix it...several times. But they've failed. Shawn is frustrated. What options does he have?

Since the auto dealership hasn't been able to fix the car, Shawn's next step should be to send a complaint letter to the car's manufacturer. In this letter, he should describe all the problems his car has had and the repair work that has been done. He should ask the manufacturer to replace his car or give him a refund.

If the manufacturer refuses to help Shawn, he can take advantage of his state's "lemon laws." These laws require manufacturers to repair, replace, or buy back "lemons," or cars that are defective and beyond repair. Shawn will have to prove the following: His car is new. It has a major defect. He has tried multiple times to have it repaired, and it's spent at least 30 days in an auto repair shop.

Luckily, Shawn has the paperwork he needs to prove that his car is a "lemon." So, he can use the lemon laws to file a complaint with a government agency like the Better Business Bureau or the Department of Motor Vehicles. To find out how to proceed, Shawn should go online and look up how to file a consumer complaint in his state. Then he should visit the appropriate agency's website and fill out a consumer complaint form. The agency will then negotiate with the manufacturer on Shawn's behalf. Hopefully, the negotiations will be successful, and Shawn will either get a new car or a refund.

One drawback of filing a consumer complaint is that Shawn may have to wait a long time for the agency to act. If Shawn has tried all the options above and his problem still hasn't been solved, there is one last resort. He can always hire a lawyer and sue the auto dealership or the manufacturer.

Shawn's "lemon" problem may cause him a lot more aggravation before it is solved. But if he keeps complaining and asking for justice, in the end, he may still get the new car of his dreams.

Which industry or practice received the most consumer complaints in 2015?
Many consumers complain about cars, but other industries and practices receive far more complaints.

3 CLOSE READING

A **IDENTIFY.** What is the main idea?

a. Shawn Chastain's new car breaks down all the time, and he is angry because the dealership can't fix it.
b. When people buy defective cars, they should keep complaining to different organizations because they may be able to get a new car or a refund.
c. Lemon laws allow Shawn Chastain to complain to government agencies about his defective car.

Reading

B **CITE EVIDENCE.** **Complete the sentences. Where is the information located?** **Lines**

1. Shawn Chastain's new car still has a lot of problems because _____. _______
   a. the dealership refused to repair it
   b. the dealership couldn't repair it
   c. he couldn't get it repaired because he doesn't have a warranty
2. After contacting the dealership, Shawn's next step should be to _____. _______
   a. sue the dealership and the manufacturer
   b. send a complaint letter to the manufacturer
   c. file a consumer complaint with a government agency
3. To prove that his car is a "lemon," Shawn needs to show _____. _______
   a. he recently bought his car
   b. the auto manufacturer makes many defective cars
   c. his car has been in an auto repair shop 30 times

C **INTERPRET GRAPHICS.** **Complete the sentences about the pie chart.**

1. According to the chart, 4% of consumer complaints are about _____.
   a. television b. imposter scams c. banks and lenders
2. Shopping at home, _____ received the same percentage of complaints in 2015.
   a. catalog sales, and banks b. automotive, and catalog sales c. catalog sales, and lotteries
3. The collection of debts is a practice which _____ of consumers complained about in 2015.
   a. almost 1/3 b. less than 1/4 c. half

D **INTERPRET VOCABULARY.** **Answer the questions.**

1. In the title of the infographic, what's another word for *consumers*?
   a. sellers b. buyers
2. In the context of line 10, what's another word for *frustrated*?
   a. angry b. depressed
3. In the context of line 15, what's another word for *manufacturer*?
   a. seller b. maker
4. In the context of line 26, what's another way to say *defective*?
   a. not working b. poor quality
5. In the context of line 45, what's another way to say *negotiate*?
   a. bargain on the price b. make a deal

E **SUMMARIZE.** **What are the most important ideas in the article?**

Show what you know!

1. **COLLABORATE.** **Search online to find out how car owners can complain about new cars in your state. Discuss how those rules are the same as, or different from, those described in the article.**
2. **WRITE.** **Explain the correct steps to take to complain about a "lemon" in order to get a new car or a refund in your state.**

   This is what you should do in our state if you buy a "lemon." First, you should go to the dealership and . . .

I can interpret infographics. ☐ I need more practice. ☐

To read more, go to MyEnglishLab.

Lesson 7 Listening and Speaking

Describe a car accident

1 BEFORE YOU LISTEN

DEFINE. What is a *fender bender?* What are some causes of fender benders?

2 LISTEN

Nora and Frank were involved in a fender bender.

A ▶ **LISTEN FOR MAIN IDEA.** Why did the accident happen? Check (✓) the cause.

☐ **a.** Nora was talking on her phone.
☐ **b.** Frank didn't put on his turn signal.
☐ **c.** Nora was speeding.
☐ **d.** Frank saw Nora's car too late.

B ▶ **LISTEN FOR DETAILS.** Listen again. Then answer the questions.

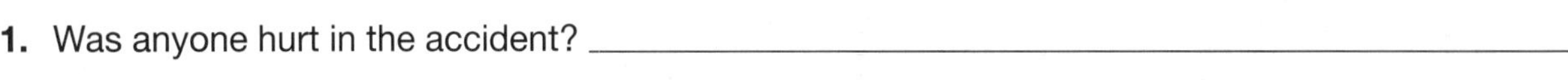

1. Was anyone hurt in the accident? ______
2. Why did Nora want to get her cell phone? ______
3. Does Frank have insurance? How do you know? ______
4. Why did Nora want to take pictures of the accident? ______

______

C **LIST.** Listen to the conversation again. What four things did Nora and Frank go back to get from their cars?

1. ______
2. ______
3. ______
4. ______

D **DECIDE.** What should Nora and Frank do next?

______

______

3 PRONUNCIATION

A ▶ **PRACTICE.** Listen. Then listen again and repeat.

'd = ***would***	I'**d** rather drive a small car. We'**d** prefer a safe car.
'd = ***had***	He'**d** started changing lanes. She'**d** already checked her car.

Pronouncing *had* and *would*

Had and *would* usually have a short, weak pronunciation when used with another verb. After a pronoun, use the contraction *'d* for either *had* or *would.*

B ▶ **APPLY.** Listen. Circle the words you hear. Then listen again to check your answers.

1. **She / She'd** slowed down because of the rain.
2. **He / He'd** already started moving into the right lane.
3. **He / He'd** left his cell phone in the car.
4. **We / We'd** prefer to buy from a dealer.
5. **They / They'd** like the red car.

4 CONVERSATION

Nora is talking to an officer at the police station.

A ▶ **LISTEN AND READ.** Then practice the conversation with a partner.

Officer: What can I do for you?
Nora: My name is Nora Peters. I was just involved in a car accident.
Officer: You'll have to fill out an accident report. Can I see your driver's license, vehicle registration, and insurance card?
Nora: Certainly. Here they are.
Officer: Thank you. Now, exactly where did the accident happen?
Nora: On Center Street, near Ashland Avenue.
Officer: Had anything unusual happened before the accident?
Nora: Not really. It was raining, and I had just slowed down. . . .

B **ROLE-PLAY.** Make a similar conversation. Then change roles.

Student A: You are talking to a police officer about a car accident. Tell the officer when, where, and how the accident happened. Describe the damage to your car.

Student B: You are a police officer at the Green Avenue Police Station. Get personal information and details about the accident that Student A was involved in.

I can describe a car accident. ☐ I need more practice. ☐

For more practice, go to MyEnglishLab.

Lesson 8

Grammar

Past perfect

Past perfect statements

Nora **had** just **started** to slow down when she saw Frank's car.

Frank **hadn't noticed** the car coming from the opposite direction when he started to make his turn.

Past perfect questions and answers

A: **Had** Nora **looked** at the damage to her car before she talked to Frank?
B: Yes, she **had**.

A: When Frank and Nora called the police station, **had** they already **taken** pictures?
B: No, they **hadn't**.

A: Where **had** Frank **left** his cell phone?
B: He'**d left** it in his car.

Grammar Watch

- Use the past perfect to describe an event that happened before another event in the past.

  *Frank **had started** moving into the left lane before he saw Nora.*

  or

  *Before he saw Nora, Frank **had started** moving into the left lane.*

Frank started moving.
Then Frank saw Nora.
Now

A **PUT IN ORDER. Read each sentence. Decide which action happened first and which one happened second. Number the earlier action *1* and the later action *2*.**

1. Sarah Miller had just gone into her office when she heard a loud crash.
2. She rushed out of the building. There had been a car accident at the corner.
3. Sarah had forgotten her phone at home, so she went back to the office to call 911.
4. One of the drivers was yelling that another driver hadn't used his turn signal.
5. When Sarah came back out, both of the drivers had gotten out of their cars.
6. One of the drivers was looking at the car's fender. The fender had been crushed.

Grammar

B MATCH. Match the beginning of each clause to its ending clause.

d 1.	It had rained,	a.	because she hadn't seen the red light.
____ 2.	It was dark,	b.	but he hadn't used his turn signal.
____ 3.	She had dropped her phone,	c.	right before she saw the car in front of her.
____ 4.	He moved into the left lane,	d.	and the roads were wet.
____ 5.	She had stepped on the gas	e.	but the streetlights hadn't come on yet.
____ 6.	She didn't stop at the intersection	f.	so she reached down to get it.

C COMPLETE. Use the past perfect.

1. **A:** What happened to your car?

   B: I had an accident last week. I had just pulled (pull) onto the highway when a truck ran into me.

   A: That's terrible! Did anyone get hurt?

   B: The truck driver had minor injuries because he ____________ (not remember) to put on his seatbelt.

   A: ____________ you ever ____________ (have) an accident before?

   B: Yes. I was in a fender bender last year.

2. **A:** Felix and I were in an accident yesterday.

   B: Oh, no! Is everyone all right?

   A: Fortunately, no one got hurt. But you know, Felix is a terrible driver.

   B: I agree. ____________ you ever ____________ (ride) with him before?

   A: No, I ____________ (not have). Yesterday was the first time—and the last!

Show what you know!

1. **MAKE CONNECTIONS.** Talk about a car accident that you have been involved in or seen.
2. **WRITE.** Write a report of that accident. Describe what happened. Remember to use the past perfect to show time order in the past.

   I was driving to school one day when suddenly a car pulled out in front of me. I hadn't slowed down, so I hit the car. The driver had been on his phone when the accident occurred.

I can use the past perfect. ☐ I need more practice. ☐

For more practice, go to MyEnglishLab.

Lesson 9

Writing

Write about how to make a major purchase

WRITING PROMPT: Think about a major purchase you made recently. What did you do before you decided what to buy? Write a paragraph to describe the steps you took during the shopping process.

1 STUDY THE MODEL

A **ANALYZE.** Read the model and Writing Skill. Then answer the questions.

How I Bought a Used Car

I recently bought a great used car. First, I researched different kinds of cars online. Based on what I learned, I decided I would prefer to buy a used hybrid. Next, I checked ads online to compare prices. Then, one week later, I saw an ad for the car I wanted. I went to see it, and I liked it. Next, I used the VIN (Vehicle Identification Number) to check online if the car had ever been in an accident. After that, I asked my brother's mechanic to inspect the car. Everything was OK, so, finally, I bought the car. I love it!

Writing Skill: Use time words to show sequence

Use time words and phrases, such as *first, next,* and *then,* to signal different steps in a process.

1. Underline the time words the writer used to signal the different steps.
2. What did the writer do after she saw an ad for the car she wanted?
3. What did the writer do right before she bought the car?

B **TAKE NOTES.** Complete the outline with information from the model.

How the writer bought a used car
First, she researched different kinds of cars online.
Next,
Then
Next,
After that,
Finally,

Writing

2 PLAN YOUR WRITING

A **BRAINSTORM.** Discuss your ideas for the Writing Prompt with a partner.

B **ORGANIZE.** Use this outline to organize your ideas before writing.

How I bought a ________________

First,

Next,

Then

After that,

Finally,

3 WRITE

DESCRIBE. Write about the steps you took when you made a major purchase. Remember to use time words and phrases to signal different steps in the process. Use the model, the Writing Skill, and your ideas from Exercise 2 to help you.

4 CHECK YOUR WRITING

A **REVISE.** Use the Writing Checklist to review your writing. Make revisions as necessary.

B **COLLABORATE.** Read your writing with a partner. Use the checklist again to improve your writing.

WRITING CHECKLIST

- ☐ Did you describe the process of how you made a major purchase?
- ☐ Did you include several different steps?
- ☐ Did you use time words to show the order of the steps?
- ☐ Did you use correct capitalization, punctuation, and spelling?

I can use time words to show sequence. ☐ I need more practice. ☐

For more practice, go to MyEnglishLab.

Soft Skills at Work

Lesson 10 Respond well to feedback

1 MEET IVAN

Read about one of his workplace skills.

I respond well to feedback. For example, when my manager gives me feedback, I try to learn what I can do better. Then I make sure to change my behavior in the future.

2 IVAN'S PROBLEM

A READ. Write *T* (true) or *F* (false).

Ivan has a new job as a salesperson at a car dealership. He loves the job because he gets to meet a lot of new people every day. However, some days are so busy that Ivan has a hard time keeping track of who he's talked to. Ivan is supposed to maintain a list of people's names and phone numbers, but he often forgets to update the list. At the end of the week, Ivan's manager is frustrated. He wants to know why there are so few people on Ivan's list.

_____ **1.** Ivan likes meeting new people in his job as a car salesperson.
_____ **2.** Ivan's supervisor wants him to keep track of the people he talks to.
_____ **3.** Ivan has a long list of the names and numbers of people he talks to.

B ANALYZE. What is Ivan's problem?

____

____

3 IVAN'S SOLUTION

A COLLABORATE. Ivan responds well to feedback. How does he answer his boss's question about the list? Explain your answer.

1. Ivan tells his manager that selling cars is important, but keeping the list isn't important.
2. Ivan thanks his manager for the comment and asks for advice on how to do his job better.
3. Ivan asks his customers to write down their names and phone numbers for him.
4. Ivan ____.

B ROLE-PLAY. Role-play Ivan's conversation with his manager.

Show what you know!

1. **REFLECT.** How do you respond well to feedback at school, at work, or at home? Give an example.
2. **WRITE.** Now write an example in your Skills Log.

   When my manager gives me feedback, I change my behavior. For example, my manager recently told me I needed to proofread my reports more carefully. I've started editing them several times before submitting them to her.
3. **PRESENT.** Give a short presentation describing how you respond well to feedback.

I can give an example of how I respond well to feedback. ☐

Unit Review: Go back to page 125. Which unit goals can you check off?

8 How Are You Feeling?

PREVIEW

Who are these people? What are they talking about?

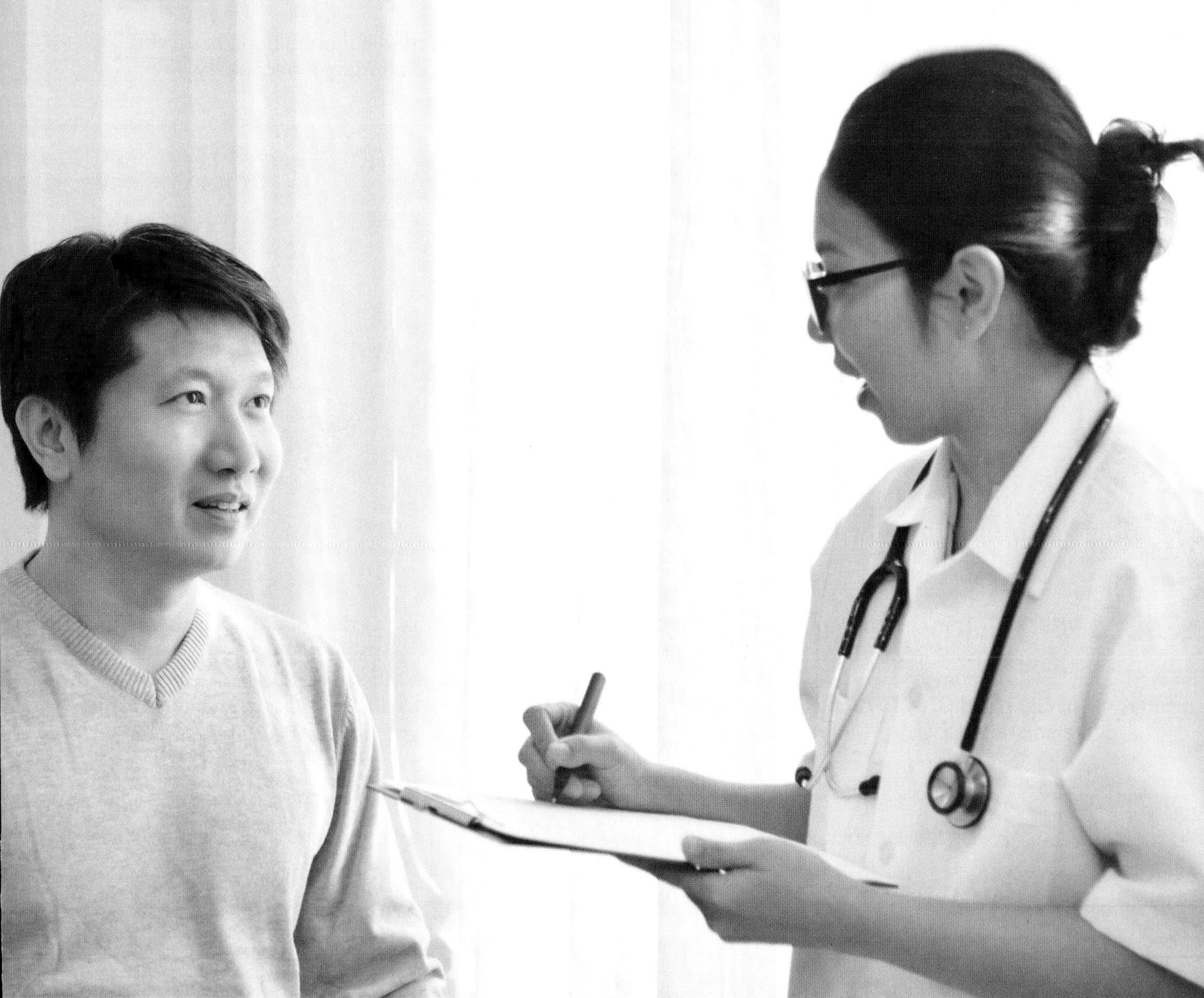

UNIT GOALS

- ☐ Communicate with medical personnel
- ☐ Interpret and complete a health insurance form
- ☐ Report a medical emergency
- ☐ Identify healthcare services within the community
- ☐ Write about a health problem
- ☐ **Academic skill:** Scan a list for details
- ☐ **Writing skill:** Include sensory details
- ☐ **Workplace soft skill:** Be professional

Lesson 1

Listening and Speaking

Communicate with medical personnel

1 BEFORE YOU LISTEN

A **EXPLAIN.** What are some reasons people go to see a doctor? What happens during a visit to the doctor?

B **INTERPRET.** Read the medical history form on page 147. Which medical conditions have you heard about before? Which symptoms can you describe? Use a dictionary if necessary.

2 LISTEN

Irma Garcia is talking to her doctor at the City Center Clinic.

A **LISTEN FOR MAIN IDEA.** Listen to the first part of the conversation. What four symptoms has Mrs. Garcia been experiencing?

1. ______________________
2. ______________________
3. ______________________
4. ______________________

B **PREDICT.** Think about Mrs. Garcia's symptoms. What do you think the doctor's diagnosis will be?

C **LISTEN FOR DETAILS.** Listen to the whole conversation. Write *T* (true) or *F* (false). Correct the false statements.

__F__ 1. Mrs. Garcia hasn't been feeling well for the past ~~six~~ two weeks.

_____ 2. Dr. Miller thinks that Mrs. Garcia has a bad cold.

_____ 3. Mrs. Garcia has been eating some new foods lately.

_____ 4. Mrs. Garcia's daughter just came home from college.

_____ 5. Mrs. Garcia may be allergic to something new in the house.

_____ 6. Dr. Miller wants Mrs. Garcia to get some testing done.

3 PRONUNCIATION

A **PRACTICE.** Listen. Then listen again and repeat.

sneezing	**st**omachache	**cl**inic	**dr**owsiness
sleepiness	**str**oke	**qu**estion	**pr**e**scr**iption

Consonant clusters

Many words and syllables begin with a group of consonant sounds. We say the consonants in a group closely together.

B **APPLY.** Listen. Circle the words you hear. Then listen again to check your answers.

1. sneeze / sees
2. spoke / stroke
3. queen / clean
4. describe / prescribe
5. grow / glow
6. dry / die

4 CONVERSATION

A **LISTEN AND READ.** Then practice the conversation with a partner.

Irma: Excuse me. My name is Irma Garcia. Is my prescription ready yet?
Pharmacist: Let me check. Have you been waiting long?
Irma: About half an hour, I guess.
Pharmacist: I'm sorry. I have the prescription right here. Did Dr. Miller talk to you about this medication?
Irma: She told me to take one tablet daily.
Pharmacist: Did she explain the possible side effects, such as sleepiness?
Irma: Yes, and she told me that the medicine could also cause dry mouth.
Pharmacist: OK. Be sure to read the information on the label and follow the directions. Please give your doctor a call if you have any problems.

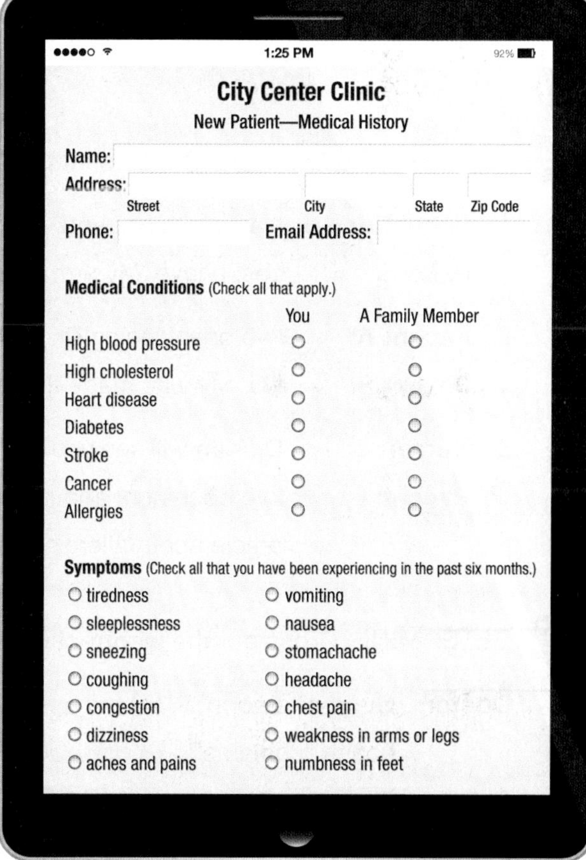

1:25 PM 92%

City Center Clinic
New Patient—Medical History

Name:
Address: Street City State Zip Code
Phone: Email Address:

Medical Conditions (Check all that apply.)

	You	A Family Member
High blood pressure	O	O
High cholesterol	O	O
Heart disease	O	O
Diabetes	O	O
Stroke	O	O
Cancer	O	O
Allergies	O	O

Symptoms (Check all that you have been experiencing in the past six months.)

O tiredness	O vomiting
O sleeplessness	O nausea
O sneezing	O stomachache
O coughing	O headache
O congestion	O chest pain
O dizziness	O weakness in arms or legs
O aches and pains	O numbness in feet

B **MAKE CONNECTIONS.** Keep track of your medical history.

1. Fill out a medical history form like the one shown. Then list other details of your medical history, such as immunizations, surgeries, and medications.
2. Discuss why it's important to know your medical history and the medical history of your family.

I can communicate with medical personnel. ☐ I need more practice. ☐

For more practice, go to MyEnglishLab.

Lesson 2

Grammar

Present perfect continuous

Present perfect continuous		
Statements		
I've **been sneezing** a lot lately.		
This **has been going on**	*for*	about two weeks.
My throat **has been hurting**	*since*	last Tuesday.
I **haven't been feeling** well	*since*	my daughter **came** home.

Questions	Short answers
Has Mrs. Garcia **been feeling** tired recently?	Yes, she **has**.
Have you **been eating** any new kinds of food?	No, I **haven't**.

Grammar Watch

- Use the present perfect continuous to show that an action started in the past and is still going on.
- To show how long an action has been going on, use the present perfect continuous with *for* + a length of time, or *since* + the time the action began.
- *Since* can also introduce a clause. The verb in the *since* clause is in the simple past.

A **INVESTIGATE.** Underline the present perfect continuous.

1. **Receptionist:** It's nice to see you. Have you been feeling better since your last visit?
   Patient: Yes, I have. My arm hasn't been hurting at all. I'm just here for a follow-up.
2. **Patient A:** I've been seeing Dr. Kim for two years. Have you been coming here long?
   Patient B: No. My wife made this appointment for me. I've been getting sleepy at work lately.
3. **Nurse:** Dr. Kim will see you now. I hope you haven't been waiting too long.
   Patient: I've been here about fifteen minutes, but that's OK. I've been reading an interesting article about allergies. Maybe I'll finish it after I see the doctor.

B **DETERMINE.** Cross out the incorrect words.

Doctor: Good afternoon. What brings you here today? **Has / Have** you been having some health problems?

Patient: I've been feeling very tired **for / since** the past few months.

Doctor: **You have / Have you** been experiencing any other symptoms?

Patient: Yes, I **am / have**. I'm a carpenter, and I sometimes get cuts on my hands at work. The cuts **been / have been** taking longer to heal.

Doctor: You wrote here that there's a history of diabetes in your family.

Patient: That's right. My grandmother was diabetic, and so is my mother. She **is taking / has been taking** insulin **for / since** 2005.

C COMPLETE. Use the present perfect continuous.

Dr. Kim: Good morning, Mrs. Garcia. How *have* you *been doing* (do) since I saw you last month?

Mrs. Garcia: Great! I ______ (sleep) much better. The congestion in my nose is gone, and I ______ (not / cough) at night.

Dr. Kim: ______ you ______ (take) your medicine regularly?

Mrs. Garcia: Yes. I ______ (follow) your instructions, Dr. Kim.

Dr. Kim: ______ the medication ______ (cause) any side effects?

Mrs. Garcia: No. Everything ______ (go) perfectly.

Dr. Kim: And your daughter?

Mrs. Garcia: Well, she ______ (work) in the garden lately. She gave all her houseplants away when she learned about my allergy!

Show what you know!

1. **RELATE.** Many students suffer from stress. Check (✓) any symptoms of stress that you have been experiencing.

- ☐ get headaches
- ☐ feel tired
- ☐ have stomachaches
- ☐ have difficulty sleeping
- ☐ get frequent colds
- ☐ other: ______

2. **LIST.** List five things that have been causing you stress. Use the present continuous.

I've been working extra hours at my job.
My car has been having problems . . .

I can use present perfect continuous. ☐ I need more practice. ☐

For more practice, go to MyEnglishLab.

Lesson 3 Workplace, Life, and Community Skills

Interpret a health insurance enrollment form

A **GIVE EXAMPLES.** When have you used your health insurance to help cover medical costs? What kind of insurance was it? What type of plan did you have?

B **SCAN. THEN READ.** What type of information does each of the five sections of the health insurance form ask for? After scanning, read the entire enrollment form.

https://www.ablephone.com/enrollmentform

ABLE Phone Company **Health Insurance Enrollment Form**

Open Enrollment Period: You must enroll in your health insurance plan within one month of your date of hire. After that, you can only make changes during the first two weeks of January or the last two weeks of October.

Section 1: Employee Information

Name (first, last) Patricia Noon
Address 112 East Street
City, State, Zip Middletown, CT 06457
Phone Number 860 - 555 - 3263
Starting Date January 5, 2019

Social Security Number 123 - 45 - 6789
○ Male ● Female Birthdate 11 / 20 / 1990
Marital Status ○ Single ● Married
Employment Status ● Full-Time ○ Part-Time

Section 2: Type of Enrollment - Select (●) one.

○ Waive (I do not wish to enroll in the company plan.)
● Enroll
○ Change (I want to change my information or plan choice.)

Section 3: Members Covered - Indicate who you wish to cover.

● Self ● Spouse ● Dependent(s)

Name (first, last) of all others to be covered		Birthdate
Spouse	John Noon	04 / 25 / 1989
Dependent	Maria Noon	12 / 03 / 2017
Dependent		
Dependent		

Section 4: Reason(s) for Changing Type of Plan - Mark all that apply.

● New Employee ○ Marriage ○ Divorce ○ Birth ○ Change of Spouse's Employment

Section 5: Type of Insurance Plan

HMO - Health Maintenance Organization - *You must pick a doctor from a given network.*
PPO - Preferred Provider Organization - *You can pick doctors outside of a network.*

○ HMO Network 1 ● HMO Network 2 ○ HMO Network 3 ○ PPO

Types of Insurance Plans: Monthly pay period cost

Plan Name	Employee only	Employee + 1 dependent	Employee + 2 or more dependents
HMO-NW 1	$254	$508	$719
HMO-NW 2	$323	$646	$914
HMO-NW 3	$410	$820	$1,161
PPO	$588	$1,174	$1,662

Effective 1/1/2018 – 12/31/2018

C DEFINE KEY WORDS. Find the words on the left in the health insurance form. Match the words with their definitions.

____ **1.** dependent	**a.** group of doctors and services
____ **2.** network	**b.** person for whom you provide food, clothing, housing; child
____ **3.** enroll in	**c.** officially join
____ **4.** spouse	**d.** choose not to have or do something
____ **5.** waive	**e.** husband or wife

D LOCATE DETAILS. Use the information from the form to complete the sentences.

1. The employees at ABLE Phone Company can change their health insurance plan during the months of ________________ and ________________.
2. Patricia's Social Security number is ________________.
3. Patricia was born on ________________.
4. Patricia has been working at the company since ________________.
5. Patricia's husband's name is ________________. ________________ is her daughter's name.
6. Patricia was 27 when her daughter was born. Her husband was ________________ years old.

E EVAULATE. Answer the questions.

1. What are the four types of insurance plans offered?
2. Which insurance plan is the most expensive?
3. Why do you think PPO's are more expensive than HMO's?
4. What are the advantages of HMO insurance?

F GO ONLINE.

1. **SEARCH.** If you work, find the health insurance plan for your company. If you don't work, find the health-plan website for a government employee, such as a city or county employee or a postal service worker. What website is it on? ________________________
2. **COMPARE.** How is the health insurance plan you found similar to the plan found by another classmate? How is it different?

G DECIDE. Would you be more likely to choose a plan for your family in which you had to choose a doctor from a given network (HMO) or a more expensive plan where you could choose any doctor (PPO)? Why?

I can interpret a health insurance enrollment form. ☐ I need more practice. ☐

For more practice, go to MyEnglishLab.

Lesson 4

Listening and Speaking

Report a medical emergency

1 BEFORE YOU LISTEN

A **EVALUATE.** Some medical conditions are serious or could become serious and require a 911 call for an ambulance. Check (✓) the situations that you think are medical emergencies.

- ☐ sneezing and coughing
- ☐ a stomachache
- ☑ a broken leg
- ☑ a stroke
- ☑ a heart attack
- ☐ congestion

B **DETERMINE.** What are some situations that would NOT require a 911 call?

2 LISTEN

A **LISTEN FOR MAIN IDEA.** Listen to the 911 call. What kind of medical emergency do you think the caller is describing?

a. broken arm **b.** heatstroke **c.** heart attack

B **LISTEN FOR DETAILS.** Listen again. Then circle the correct answers.

1. Which statement best describes the condition of the caller's husband?
   a. He is conscious and in no pain. **b.** He is conscious and sweating badly. **c.** He is unconscious.
2. What is the address of the emergency?
   a. 136 Main Street **b.** 136 Maple Street **c.** 136 Elm Street
3. How old is the caller's husband?
   a. 58 **b.** 85 **c.** 77
4. What ongoing condition is the caller's husband taking medication for?
   a. diabetes **b.** high blood pressure **c.** pain
5. Why is the caller's husband having difficulty breathing?
   a. He is overweight. **b.** He is diabetic. **c.** He is having chest pain.
6. Which statement best describes the caller?
   a. She is calm. **b.** She is frightened. **c.** She is angry.

C **STATE AN OPINION.** In your opinion, did the 911 dispatcher handle the call well? Why or why not?

____

____

3 CONVERSATION

A LISTEN AND READ. Then practice the conversation with a partner.

911 Dispatcher: 911. What's your emergency?
Caller: It's my wife. Her legs are so weak that she can't walk.
911 Dispatcher: Is your wife conscious, sir? Can she talk?
Caller: She's conscious, but she can't speak.
911 Dispatcher: Can I have your exact address, please?
Caller: 1175 West Hampton Street, Apartment 12-B.
911 Dispatcher: Thank you, sir. Now, can you tell me when the symptoms began?
Caller: Just a few minutes ago. At first, she had a bad headache. Then she couldn't stand up.
911 Dispatcher: Everything will be OK, sir. I know it's hard in a situation like this, but stay calm. The paramedics are on their way. Please stay on the line.

B INFER. Why did the 911 dispatcher continue talking to the caller until the paramedics arrived?

____

____

C ROLE-PLAY. Make a similar conversation about a medical emergency. Use one of the ideas below or your own idea. Then change roles.

- A family member may have food poisoning.
- A friend or family member is bleeding heavily.
- A co-worker may have broken an arm or a leg.
- A child has swallowed dish detergent or other cleaning fluid.

Student A: A family member, friend, or co-worker has just had a medical emergency, and you call 911. Tell the 911 dispatcher what has happened and describe the person's condition and symptoms. Follow the instructions of the 911 dispatcher.

Student B: You are a 911 dispatcher and Student A calls you about a medical emergency. Listen as Student A describes the condition of the person who needs medical attention. Ask questions to find out information you need to know. Give Student A instructions about how best to handle the situation.

D PRESENT. Describe a 911 call that you or someone you know made.

I can report a medical emergency. ☐ I need more practice. ☐

For more practice, go to MyEnglishLab.

Lesson **5**

Grammar

Such . . . that and *so . . . that*

Such + noun + *that*				
It was	**such**	a terrible situation	**that**	the caller couldn't remain calm.
The man had		serious symptoms		his wife called 911.

So + adjective or adverb + *that*				
His legs are	**so**	weak	**that**	he can't walk.
You got to the ER		quickly		we were able to give you excellent care.

So + *much* or *many* + noun + *that*					
He has	**so**	**many**	vague symptoms	**that**	it's difficult to say what the problem is.
I was in		**much**	pain		I couldn't move.

Grammar Watch

- Use *such* with nouns.
- Use *so* with adjectives or adverbs.
- Use *so many* with plural nouns. Use *so much* with non-count nouns.

(See page 264 for a list of non-count nouns.)

A **INVESTIGATE.** Circle the examples of *such* + noun phrase and *so* + adjective or adverb. Underline the clauses beginning with *that.*

Your Medical FAQs

Home | FAQs | About Us

Q: *When should you go to the emergency room?*

A: Most situations are not medical emergencies. However, here are five situations in which you should definitely go to the ER.

1. You have such a tight chest that you can't breathe.
2. You have such a bad headache that you can't walk or talk.
3. You become so dizzy that you can't sit or stand.
4. You are so weak that you faint.
5. You are bleeding so heavily that the bleeding can't be controlled.

B **PUT IN ORDER.** Write the sentences.

1. so / high / My blood sugar/ used to be / that it was dangerous.
   My blood sugar used to be so high that it was dangerous.
2. exercise / I / so / that I don't have much time to watch TV / frequently
3. these days / eating / healthy foods / I'm / such / that I feel like a new person.
4. weight / so / I've / much / lost / that people don't recognize me.

C **COMPLETE.** Use *so, such,* or *so many* to complete this letter from a doctor to the local newspaper.

Dear Editor,

Your recent article on healthy living raised ___such___ an important issue that I left copies in my waiting room for my patients. Many of them complain that they have __________ responsibilities at work that they have no time to eat healthy meals or get exercise. However, as your article points out, we can all make small changes __________ easily that there is no excuse not to.

Small changes can lead to big benefits. Let's take breakfast as an example. Medical experts say that breakfast is __________ an important meal that no one should skip it. But thousands of children start their school day on empty stomachs. This has become __________ a serious problem that many schools now serve breakfast. And what about adults? Why are __________ of us still skipping breakfast? We say we're __________ busy that we don't have time for breakfast. Well, it's time to find the time! This idea seems __________ simple that everyone should understand it.

D **APPLY.** Use *such . . . that, so . . . that, so much . . . that,* or *so many . . . that* to combine the sentences.

1. I'm busy. I don't have time to exercise.
   I'm so busy that I don't have time to exercise.
2. Gyms are expensive. I can't afford to go to one.
   ____
3. Exercising is boring. It's hard for me to keep doing it.
   ____
4. I'm tired when I come home from work. I just want to eat and go straight to bed.
   ____
5. I have chores on the weekend. I can't find the time to work out.
   ____
6. I haven't exercised in a long time. I'll never be able to get back into shape.
   ____
7. I was in pain the last time I worked out. I never want to do it again.
   ____

Show what you know!

1. **DISCUSS.** What two things must people do to stay healthy? What gets in your way of staying healthy?
2. **WRITE.** List five excuses people use for not exercising or eating a healthy diet. Use *such . . . that* and *so . . . that* where possible.
   I have such a busy schedule that I don't have time to work out.
   Fast food is so inexpensive that many people choose it instead of healthier options . . .

I can use *such . . . that* and *so . . . that.* ☐ I need more practice. ☐

For more practice, go to MyEnglishLab.

Lesson 6

Reading

Read about life expectancy

1 BEFORE YOU READ

A **DISCUSS.** Look at the graph in the article below. Discuss. What information does it show?

B **PREDICT.** Skim the article. What is it about?

2 READ

Listen and read.

Academic Skill: Scan information for details

Scan information quickly to look for specific details such as facts or numbers.

Be Healthy and Live Long

People in the U.S. have been living longer and longer. In 1900, the average American lived to the age of 47. In 1950, the average life span was 68. In 2017, mean life expectancy reached 78.6. So, what would it take for the average American to live to the age of 100? Some experts believe that we can increase longevity if we look at the leading causes of death.

What the Numbers Say

The chart below shows that heart disease and cancer are the top causes of death in the United States. For every 100,000 people, 166 people died from heart disease. 156 died from cancer. Fortunately, deaths from these causes have been going down recently. Chances are good that they will continue to decline. Why? Modern medicine is constantly improving. Doctors are getting better at diagnosing and curing diseases.

The Top Five Causes of Death in the United States in 2016 (Deaths per 100,000 people)

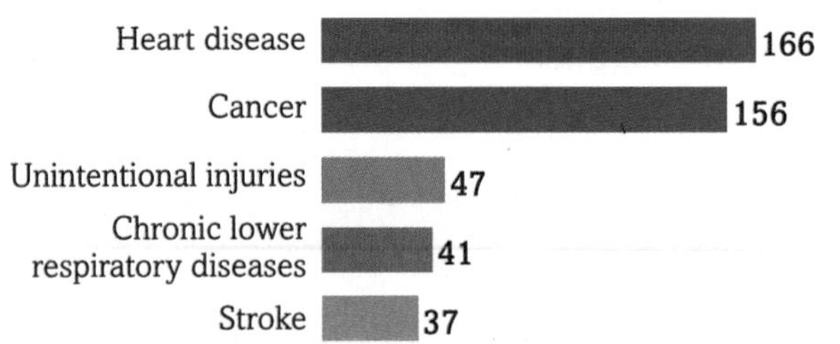

Source: NCHS, National Vital Statistics System, Mortality

What We Should Do

Doctors are also getting better at disease prevention. They know which conditions are responsible for deaths in the United States. They are working hard to stop these conditions from developing in their patients. For example, experts have concluded that smoking and obesity are risk factors that can lead to the two top causes of death, heart disease and cancer. Smoking rates have declined substantially in the United States in recent years. However, according to the Centers for Disease Control and Prevention, obesity rates still remain high. 36.5 percent of American adults are obese. Reducing the percentage of obese Americans could be one important way to help Americans live longer. Losing weight gives people a better chance of avoiding heart disease, cancer, and other potential causes of death.

A Weighty Issue

- Body Mass Index, or BMI, is used as a screening tool for determining healthy weights. A BMI of 25 to 30 means you are overweight. If your BMI is 30 or higher, you are obese.
- If you are overweight, losing a small amount of weight (even 10 percent of your weight) will help decrease your chances of having health problems.
- It is not just adults who have weight problems. One in three U.S. children are overweight or obese.

The research is clear. Life expectancy rates in the United States should continue to rise if we keep working to prevent the diseases that most often cause our deaths.

3 CLOSE READING

A **IDENTIFY.** What is the main idea?

a. Heart disease and cancer kill many people in the United States.
b. Experts think that smoking and obesity can lead to heart disease and cancer.
c. People will live longer in the United States if we can prevent the deadliest diseases.

B CITE EVIDENCE. **Complete the sentences. Where is the information located?**

Lines

1. The average life expectancy of Americans in 1950 was _____. _______
   a. 47 **b.** 68 **c.** 78.6
2. In recent years, _____ rates have fallen. _______
   a. smoking **b.** obesity **c.** accident
3. If your BMI is _____, you are obese. _______
   a. under 25 **b.** 25 to 30 **c.** over 30
4. _____ the children in the United States are overweight or obese. _______
   a. One third of **b.** Half of **c.** One quarter of

C INTERPRET GRAPHICS. **Complete the sentences about the bar graph.**

1. In 2016, for every 100,000 people, _____ people died from cancer.
   a. 166 **b.** 156 **c.** 47
2. In 2016, more people died from chronic lower respiratory diseases than from _____.
   a. stroke **b.** cancer **c.** unintentional injuries
3. The leading causes of death in the United States in 2016 were _____.
   a. injuries **b.** fatal accidents **c.** illnesses
4. For every 100,000 people, 37 died from stroke and 47 died from _____.
   a. tumor **b.** accidental harm **c.** cancer

D INTERPRET VOCABULARY. **Complete the sentences.**

1. In the context of line 2, the word *average* means _____.
   a. typical **b.** not too good or too bad
2. In the context of lines 3–4, the phrase *life expectancy* means _____.
   a. length of a person's life **b.** quality of a person's life
3. In the context of line 26, the word *substantially* means _____.
   a. in many ways **b.** a lot
4. In the context of line 20, the phrase *responsible for* means _____.
   a. the main cause of **b.** supposed to take care of
5. In the context of the infographic, the word *stroke* means _____.
   a. a type of brain illness **b.** a petting movement

E SUMMARIZE. **What are the most important ideas in the article?**

Show what you know!

1. **COLLABORATE.** What major factors that lead to disease are mentioned in the article? What other factors do you think contribute to disease in America?
2. **WRITE.** Describe four risk factors that cause diseases. Which factor do you think is the most dangerous? What should people do to try to reduce that factor?

Smoking, obesity, not exercising, and eating unhealthy foods cause diseases in the United States . . .

I can scan information for details. ☐ I need more practice. ☐

To read more, go to MyEnglishLab.

Lesson 7

Listening and Speaking

Identify healthcare services within the community

1 BEFORE YOU LISTEN

MAKE CONNECTIONS. Have you ever had the flu? When is flu season where you live? What can you do to prevent yourself from getting the flu?

2 LISTEN

In this podcast, the host is interviewing a Registered Nurse.

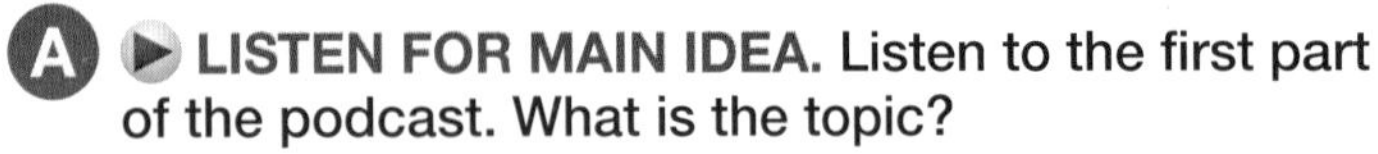

A ▶ **LISTEN FOR MAIN IDEA.** Listen to the first part of the podcast. What is the topic?

____

____

B ▶ **LISTEN FOR DETAILS.** Listen to the whole podcast. Write *T* (true) or *F* (false). Correct the false statements.

_____ **1.** The flu is not a serious illness.

_____ **2.** The flu is especially dangerous for small children, elderly people, and pregnant women.

_____ **3.** All infants can receive a flu vaccine.

_____ **4.** Pregnant women cannot get a vaccine.

_____ **5.** Flu strains are constantly changing.

_____ **6.** You must go to a doctor to get a flu vaccine.

C **INTERPRET.** Answer the questions.

1. What does the word *annual* mean? ______________________________
2. What does the word *strain* mean? ______________________________
3. What does the phrase *immune system* mean? ______________________________

D **DETERMINE.** Where in your community can you get a flu vaccine?

____

____

E **PRESENT.** Describe a recent visit to a healthcare professional. Why did you go? Where did you go? Who did you see? Were you satisfied or unsatisfied with the service?

Listening and Speaking

3 PRONUNCIATION

A ▶ **PRACTICE.** Listen. Then listen again and repeat.

medical o**be**sity immuni**za**tion **im**munize com**mu**nicate

B ▶ **APPLY.** Listen. Put a dot (•) over the stressed syllable in each word. Then listen again to check your answers.

1. examination
2. physical
3. community
4. specialize
5. participate

Stress patterns

In words that end in *-ical, -ity,* and *-tion,* stress the syllable just before the ending. In words that end in *-ize* and *-ate,* the stress is usually two syllables before the ending.

4 CONVERSATION

A mother has called the nurse at her daughter's school.

A ▶ **LISTEN AND READ.** Then practice the conversation with a partner.

Nurse: Good morning. This is Nurse Doyle speaking. How can I help you?
Mother: Good morning. I received a letter about my daughter. It says that she should get a medical check-up.
Nurse: What grade will your daughter be in when school starts?
Mother: Fifth grade.
Nurse: I see. Then your daughter must see a doctor. State law requires all fifth-grade students to have a physical examination. And your daughter's immunizations must be up to date, too.
Mother: OK. Then I guess I'd better make a doctor's appointment.
Nurse: Yes, and you'd better do it soon. We must receive the results of the medical exam and the list of immunizations no later than September 15th. That's the deadline.

B **ROLE-PLAY.** Make a similar conversation. Then change roles.

Student A: You are a parent. You don't have medical or dental insurance. You received a letter from your child's school. It says that your second grader cannot go to class until he or she has gone to a dentist. You think the requirement to have a dental exam is unfair because you can't pay for the exam.

Student B: You are a school nurse. You must talk to any parent who received a letter saying that his or her child needs to go to the dentist before that child can come back to school. The dental exam is a state requirement for all students in the second grade. Suggest some places that might provide dental treatment free of charge.

I can identify health-care services within the community. ☐ I need more practice. ☐

For more practice, go to MyEnglishLab.

Lesson 8

Grammar

Should, ought to, had better, and *must*

Should, ought to, had better, and *must*	
Everyone **should** get an annual flu vaccine.	
You **should not** wait until the last minute.	
Parents **ought to** have their children immunized before school begins.	
I'd better make a doctor's appointment soon.	
You**'d better not** forget. It's very important.	
Your daughter's immunizations **must** be up to date. It's a requirement.	
Where **should** I go for my flu vaccine?	
Should I make an appointment today?	Yes, you **should**. / No, you **shouldn't**.

Grammar Watch

- Use *should* or *ought to* for advice, suggestions, and opinions.
- Use *had better ('d better)* for strong advice or warnings.
- Use *must* when something is required or necessary.
- For negative meanings, use *should not (shouldn't), had better not ('d better not),* and *must not.*
- For questions, use *should.*

A INVESTIGATE. Underline the examples of *should, ought to, had better,* and *must.* Then number each example: *1* (advice, suggestion, opinion), *2* (strong advice or warning), or *3* (requirement).

Attention Employees!
Flu shots will be available for all MRC Tire Company employees at Smithson's drugstores during the month of September. Show your employee ID card to get the special price of $10.

A: I think that everyone should (1) get a flu shot.

B: I agree, but the company ought to give us the shots for free.

A: You'd better not say that too loudly. You should be grateful that we can get the vaccine for just $10.

B: You're right. It's a good deal. And it's very important, especially for someone like me.

A: Why especially for someone like you?

B: I'm over fifty, and I have heart disease. They say that anyone over the age of fifty or with medical conditions like heart disease or diabetes should get a flu shot every year. It's already September 24. I'd better go to Smithson's soon.

A: Don't forget to take your ID card. The announcement says that you must have an employee ID to get the $10 price.

Grammar

B **PUT IN ORDER.** Write the sentences.

1. annual / should / medical / Children / and / have / checkups / adults
   Children and adults should have annual medical checkups.
2. sleep / get / Everyone / seven to eight / ought to / of / hours
3. had better / their / stress / in / lives / Adults / reduce
4. people / should / active / give up / an / Older / lifestyle / not
5. must / We / to / health / take steps / protect / our

C **EVALUATE.** Find and correct six mistakes with *should, ought to, had better,* and *must.*

We all want our kids to learn the important things in life. So how do we teach them what they should to know about having a healthy lifestyle?

Encourage your child to be physically active. A child shouldn't sits in front of a TV or a computer for long periods of time. If children are doing homework, they should take a ten-minute exercise break every hour. Children also ought play games with other children—for example, in after-school sports programs. And remember that children learn by example, so the adults in your family had not better spend hours watching TV. Instead, children and adults can take walks or play sports together.

It's also important to eat healthfully. Few medical experts say that you must to eliminate pizza, French fries, or candy completely, but you ought not eat foods that are high in fat, sugar, and salt regularly. Show your children that fresh fruit and vegetables are delicious, too.

What our children learn now about healthy living can affect them for years to come.

Show what you know!

1. **BRAINSTORM.** Discuss advice, suggestions, recommendations, or requirements for good health.
2. **WRITE.** List five suggestions or recommendations for good health. Use *should, ought to, had better,* and *must.*
   You should get annual check-ups.
   You ought to get a dental exam every six months . . .

I can use *should, ought to, had better,* and *must.* ☐ I need more practice. ☐

For more practice, go to MyEnglishLab.

Lesson 9

Writing

Write about a health problem

WRITING PROMPT: Think of a health problem you have or have had. How do you feel when you have this problem? How do you look and sound? What can you taste or smell? Write a paragraph to describe the problem.

1 STUDY THE MODEL

A ANALYZE. Read the model and Writing Skill. Then answer the questions.

How do you know if you have the flu?

You may have the flu if you are suffering from any or all of these symptoms. You have a fever, so you feel very hot, and you look flushed. But sometimes you also get chills. You shiver and feel very cold. Your throat hurts. You have such a runny nose that it's hard to smell or taste anything. You may also have a cough that sounds dry instead of wet. Sometimes, you have a bad headache. Actually, your body aches all over. You look and feel very, very tired. You should rest!

Writing Skill: Include sensory details

When you describe something, use sensory details to help the readers see, hear, smell, taste, or touch what you are describing. These sensory details appeal to the reader's five senses and help a reader feel what you are feeling.

1. Underline the words the writer uses to describe how your body looks, sounds, and feels.
2. How do you sound when you have the flu?
3. How does having a runny nose affect how you feel about eating?

B TAKE NOTES. Complete the outline with information from the model.

Sensory Details: The Flu	
Sight	*You look flushed and tired.*
Hearing	
Touch	
Smell	
Taste	
Feelings	*Your throat hurts.*

Writing

2 PLAN YOUR WRITING

A **BRAINSTORM.** Discuss your ideas for the Writing Prompt with a partner.

B **ORGANIZE.** Use this outline to organize your ideas before writing.

Sensory Details: ____________	
Sight	
Hearing	
Touch	
Smell	
Taste	
Feelings	

3 WRITE

DESCRIBE. Write a paragraph about a health problem. Remember to include sensory details. Use the model, the Writing Skill, and your ideas from Exercise 2 to help you.

4 CHECK YOUR WRITING

A **REVISE.** Use the Writing Checklist to review your writing. Make revisions as necessary.

B **COLLABORATE.** Read your writing with a partner. Use the checklist again to improve your writing.

WRITING CHECKLIST

- ☐ Did you describe the symptoms of a health problem?
- ☐ Did you include sensory details to help the reader see, hear, feel, smell, or taste what you described?
- ☐ Did you use correct capitalization, punctuation, and spelling?

I can include sensory details. ☐ I need more practice. ☐

For more practice, go to MyEnglishLab.

Lesson **10** Soft Skills at Work

Be professional

1 MEET MAE

Read about one of her workplace skills.

I am professional. I stay calm in stressful situations. For example, when I'm overwhelmed, I communicate often with my supervisor and my co-workers.

2 MAE'S PROBLEM

A READ. Write *T* (true) or *F* (false).

Mae has been working as a nurse in the county hospital for two weeks. Mae is having a very busy night. The director asked her to help out in the emergency room. She has to take care of many patients and they are all having emergencies. One man broke his leg, another had a heart attack, and a baby just came in with a high fever. Mae is feeling overwhelmed.

_____ **1.** Mae is the director of a county hospital.

_____ **2.** Mae is trying to take care of many people at the same time.

_____ **3.** Mae is enjoying the challenges of helping people in the emergency room.

B ANALYZE. What is Mae's problem?

____

____

3 MAE'S SOLUTION

A COLLABORATE. Mae is professional. What does she do to feel less overwhelmed in her job?

1. Mae tells her co-workers that she doesn't want to work in the emergency room.
2. Mae asks her co-workers to call in another nurse for the night.
3. Mae talks with her co-workers to be sure there's a plan for each patient.
4. Mae ____.

B ROLE-PLAY. Role-play Mae's conversation with her co-workers.

Show what you know!

1. **REFLECT.** How are you professional at school, at work, or at home? Give an example.
2. **WRITE.** Now write your example in your Skills Log.

   I stay calm in a crisis by talking with my team. We make a plan together for how we will solve the problem.
3. **PRESENT.** Give a short presentation describing how you are professional.

I can give an example from my life of being professional. ☐

Unit Review: Go back to page 145. Which unit goals can you check off?

9 Partners in Education

PREVIEW

Why is it important for parents to be involved in their children's education?

UNIT GOALS

- ☐ Discuss a student's progress
- ☐ Interpret and respond to a report card
- ☐ Talk with school personnel
- ☐ Discuss school safety
- ☐ Write a letter to the editor
- ☐ **Academic skill:** Distinguish fact from opinion
- ☐ **Writing skill:** Use paragraph structure
- ☐ **Workplace soft skill:** Manage time well

Lesson 1

Listening and Speaking

Discuss a student's progress

1 BEFORE YOU LISTEN

A **INTERPRET.** The word *grade* has two meanings. What does it mean in each of these sentences?

1. My daughter is in the second **grade**.
2. Her **grade** on the spelling test was an A.

B **MAKE CONNECTIONS.** In many places in the U.S., the school system has three levels: elementary school, middle school, and high school. How are the schools organized where you live?

2 LISTEN

Mrs. Patel is talking to the guidance counselor at her children's school.

A ▶ **LISTEN FOR MAIN IDEA.** Listen to the first part of the conversation. What is the purpose of the appointment? Circle the answer.

The guidance counselor made the appointment with Mrs. Patel because ________________.

a. her son is having some problems with his grades
b. her son will start high school this fall
c. he wants her daughter to be a better student
d. he wants to help her daughter go to college

B **PREDICT.** Why does the guidance counselor think Monika should start thinking about college before starting high school?

C ▶ **LISTEN FOR DETAILS.** Listen to the whole conversation. Write *T* (true) or *F* (false). Correct the false statements.

__F__ 1. Monika is ~~already~~ not making plans to go to college.

_____ 2. Monika might be able to get a scholarship to go to college.

_____ 3. Mrs. Patel doesn't want her daughter to go to college.

_____ 4. There are special classes to help students prepare for college.

_____ 5. Mrs. Patel will bring her husband on her next visit to the guidance office.

D **ANALYZE.** Was your prediction about the guidance counselor's reason for starting to think about college correct? What did the counselor mean when he said, "Yes and no" to the statement that college was a long way off?

3 PRONUNCIATION

Highlighting information

Use stress to highlight information that is new or different. This information is often the last important word in a clause or sentence. To correct or disagree with something, highlight the information that is different.

A ▶ **PRACTICE.** Listen. Then listen again and repeat.

A: Her daughter has problems with her **grades**.
B: No, her son has problems with his grades.

A: Her daughter is sixteen years **old**.
B: No, her daughter is thirteen years old.

B ▶ **APPLY.** Listen. Put a dot (•) over the stressed words in each pair of sentences.

1. **A:** John's science teacher assigns too much homework.
   B: No, his math teacher assigns too much homework.
2. **A:** The elementary school is having an open house.
   B: No, the middle school is having an open house.
3. **A:** The school nurse left us a message.
   B: No, the school counselor left a message.

4 CONVERSATION

Mrs. Patel is now talking to one of her son's teachers.

A ▶ **LISTEN AND READ.** Then practice the conversation with a partner.

Teacher: I'm so glad you could come to talk about your son. I'm Mr. Manning, Robert's math teacher.
Mrs. Patel: It's nice to meet you. Robert says he's having some problems with math.
Teacher: Well, Robert is a great kid, and he seems to enjoy the class. But, yes, I think he needs a little help.
Mrs. Patel: I saw his last test. He got a 70. I think it was because he didn't study enough.
Teacher: That's possible. Since he's having some trouble, it would be good for Robert to have a tutor.
Mrs. Patel: That sounds like a good idea. Will it be expensive?
Teacher: No! We have a free after-school program. Students help each other. It's peer tutoring.

B **DEFINE.** What is a parent-teacher conference? What is Parent-Teacher Night?

____

____

C **PRESENT.** Describe an experience you have had talking to teachers or other school personnel—either for your child or for yourself.

I can discuss a student's progress. ☐ I need more practice. ☐

For more practice, go to MyEnglishLab.

Lesson 2

Grammar

Adverb clauses and infinitives to express reason and purpose

Adverb clauses of reason	
Main clause (result)	**Adverb clause (reason)**
I'd like Monika to start planning now	**because** she is one of our best students.
I want Robert to get some tutoring	**since** he is having some trouble in math.

Grammar Watch

- Use *because* and *since* to introduce adverb clauses that express reasons.
- Use a comma between the clauses only when the adverb clause comes first:
  Since he is having some trouble, I want Robert to get some tutoring. BUT:
  I want Robert to get some tutoring since he is having some trouble in math.

A INVESTIGATE. Draw one line under the reason. Draw two lines under the result.

1. I always go to Parent-Teacher Night because I like the personal contact with my child's teachers.
2. It's important to find out what the teachers are really like since my child spends so much time with these people every day.
3. Since there's a chance to talk one-on-one with the teachers, I can ask about ways for my daughter to improve.
4. Because our children's education is very important to us, my husband and I want to participate in school activities.
5. I enjoy Parent-Teacher Night because it gives me a chance to meet other parents.

B COMBINE. Use either *because* or *since* to combine the sentences. Keep the sentences in the same order.

1. I'm happy to see parents at Parent-Teacher Night. It means they care.
   I'm happy to see parents at Parent-Teacher Night because it means they care.
   OR I'm happy to see parents at Parent-Teacher Night since it means they care.
2. I want parents to help their children at home. I always explain my requirements.
   ____
3. The teachers feel proud. Most parents show a lot of respect for them.
   ____
4. Parents don't always know what's going on at school. Children don't tell them.
   ____
5. Communication between home and school is important. Parents and teachers should talk often.
   ____

Grammar

Infinitives and adverb clauses of purpose	
Main clause (result)	**Adverb clause or infinitive (purpose)**
You took off time from work	**to meet** with me.
I'll bring my husband	**so that** we can both talk to you.

Grammar Watch

- Use an infinitive or an adverb clause to express purpose.
- The *to* in an infinitive means *in order to.*
  You took off time from work to meet with me. = You took off time from work in order to meet with me.
- *So that* in an adverb clause is followed by a subject and a verb.

A INVESTIGATE. Underline the infinitives and adverb clauses that express purpose.

West Apollo Elementary School publishes this handbook to provide useful information for parents. It is especially important for you to look at the School Rules on page 8 so that you will understand West Apollo's policies and procedures. In addition, you should pay close attention to the calendar on page 11 so that you can make plans for days when school is closed. See the list of school personnel on page 10 to become familiar with our staff.

B COMPLETE. Use *to* or *so that* to complete each school rule.

1. You must provide the name and phone number of a family member ___so that___ the school can contact someone in case of an emergency.
2. West Apollo Elementary School doors will be locked at 7:45 A.M. ____________ protect the safety of our students.
3. If your child misses school, you must provide a written note ____________ explain the absence.
4. Cell phones must be silenced during class ____________ lessons are not disrupted.
5. Fire drills are conducted ____________ everyone is prepared if there is ever a real fire in school.

Show what you know!

1. **DISCUSS.** Do you think it is important for parents to be involved in their children's schooling? Why? In what ways can parents get involved?
2. **WRITE.** List five reasons why parents should be involved in their children's education. Use adverb clauses and infinitives to express the reason or purpose.

   Parents should attend school events so that they can get to know the other parents. Parents should meet with teachers in order to learn about their children's progress in school. Many parents volunteer at their children's school because they want to help improve the school . . .

I can use adverb clauses and infinitives to express reason and purpose. ☐ I need more practice. ☐

For more practice, go to MyEnglishLab.

Lesson 3

Workplace, Life, and Community Skills

Interpret and respond to a report card

1 INTERPRET A REPORT CARD

A **MAKE CONNECTIONS.** How often do children receive report cards? What kind of information normally appears on a report card? What type of grading systems can be used?

B **SCAN. THEN READ.** What information is in the *Academic Subjects* section of the report card? In the *Habits and Attitudes* section? In the *Social Habits section*? After scanning, read the entire report card.

http://www.westapollomiddleschool.org/reportcards

School Year:	2019–2020	Period:	1	Date:	11/15/19
Student Name:	Manuel Medina	Days Absent:	3		
Teacher Name:	Ms. Arlene Brown	Days Late:	1		

Academic Subjects	Grade and Comments
English Language Arts	**78** Needs to improve writing—Needs to read more
Mathematics	**98** Excels in all aspects of math
Science	**72** Has trouble with science vocabulary
Social Studies	**70** Difficulty with reading affects ability to perform well on tests
Computer Lab	**95** Has done an excellent job on all computer assignments

Habits and Attitudes		
Work Habits		
Follows directions		
Completes all class and homework assignments	X	Needs to turn in homework regularly and on time

Social Habits		
Works well in groups	X	Needs to participate in group activities
Shows respect for others	✓	Is very polite to all individuals
Is responsible and reliable		

Key

90–100 = A (Excellent)	60–69 = D (Poor)	X = Needs improvement
80–89 = B (Good)	Below 60 = F (Failing)	✓ = Exceptional
70–79 = C (Average)		

C **DEFINE KEY WORDS.** Find the words on the left in the report card. Match the words with their definitions.

____	**1.** academic	**a.** the highest score
____	**2.** grade	**b.** notes that a teacher writes about a student
____	**3.** A	**c.** relating to schoolwork
____	**4.** comments	**d.** an explanation of the grades and symbols on a report card
____	**5.** key	**e.** score given for an assignment or course
____	**6.** work habits	**f.** the typical way a student completes assignments

D LOCATE DETAILS. Write *T* (true) or *F* (false). Correct the false statements.

_T_ 1. Manuel was absent more often than he was late.

____ 2. The lowest grade on Manuel's report card is in social studies.

____ 3. Manuel has a C in two classes.

____ 4. Manuel has done well on all computer assignments.

____ 5. Manuel's grade in science is a 70.

E DISCUSS. What should a parent do if a child receives a low or failing grade on a report card?

2 RESPOND TO A REPORT CARD

Manuel's mother, Bertha Medina, has written to Ms. Brown, the teacher. And Ms. Brown has answered.

A EXPLAIN.

1. Why did Bertha Medina write the note?
2. How does Ms. Brown respond?

B DETERMINE.

1. What does Ms. Medina need to do now to arrange a meeting with Ms. Brown?
2. Are Ms. Medina and Ms. Brown going to meet in the morning, afternoon, or evening? Why?
3. What are Ms. Medina and Ms. Brown going to discuss?

C WRITE. Write a note to your child's teacher about something you would like to discuss. If you don't have children, write a note to your English teacher about your own learning. Use Ms. Medina's email as a model.

D GO ONLINE.

1. **SEARCH.** Find the website for a Parent-Teacher Association (PTA) for a neighborhood school. What is the website? ____________________
2. **LIST.** List some activities that the PTA has already completed. List the activities that the PTA is planning to do in the future.

E ANALYZE. Why are the activities planned by the PTA important for the students? for the teachers? for the community?

To: Ms. Brown
From: Bertha Medina
Subject: Manuel's report card

Dear Ms. Brown,

My husband and I looked at Manuel's report card yesterday. We are concerned about his grades in social studies, science, and English. We have been trying to get him to read more, but it is difficult.

Could we have a conference to talk about how to help him? I would prefer to meet in the early evening after work, but I can be available almost anytime.

Thank you for your help.

Sincerely,

Bertha Medina

To: Bertha Medina
From: Ms. Brown
Subject: Re: Manuel's report card

Dear Ms. Medina,

Thank you for contacting me about Manuel's grades.

I would be happy to meet to discuss ways to help Manuel read more. I can be at the school in the evening so you don't have to miss work. Please call me at 310-555-9904 to set up a day and time for our conference.

Sincerely,

Arlene Brown

I can interpret and respond to a report card. ☐ I need more practice. ☐

For more practice, go to MyEnglishLab.

Lesson 4

Listening and Speaking

Talk with school personnel

1 BEFORE YOU LISTEN

A **MAKE CONNECTIONS.** If you were enrolling a child in a new school, what would you want to find out about the school?

B **EXPLAIN.** In some school districts, parents have to prove that their family lives in that district. Why? What things can the parents use to show their home address?

2 LISTEN

Mr. López is taking his daughter to the West Apollo Elementary School. He is going to talk to the school secretary.

A ▶ **LISTEN FOR MAIN IDEA.** Listen to the first part of their conversation. Why is Mr. López at school?

____

B ▶ **LISTEN FOR DETAILS.** Listen to the first part of the conversation again. Answer the questions.

1. Why is Marta changing schools?
____
2. What grade is Marta in?
____

C ▶ **EXPAND.** Listen to the whole conversation. Circle the correct answers.

1. Where is Marta transferring from?
   a. School District 15 **b.** López School **c.** Newtown Elementary School
2. What does Mr. López use to prove his address?
   a. his lease **b.** a water bill **c.** an electric bill
3. What other information did Mr. López bring with him?
   a. Marta's health records **b.** Marta's schedule **c.** an emergency contact form
4. What type of form does the secretary give Mr. López?
   a. medical form **b.** emergency contact form **c.** application form
5. What information does the secretary give Mr. López?
   a. a list of school rules **b.** a list of school supplies **c.** a medical form
6. When will Marta begin school?
   a. today **b.** next week **c.** no information

3 CONVERSATION

A **LISTEN AND READ. Then practice the conversation with a partner.**

Mr. Lopez: I have a question.

Secretary: Certainly.

Mr. Lopez: I heard that there's a free lunch program. Is that true?

Secretary: Yes. We have a free lunch program for students who need financial assistance.

Mr. Lopez: That's great. What do I need to do?

Secretary: Here's an application. You'll need to fill it out, and you'll need to provide documents that show income.

Mr. Lopez: No problem. One more thing.

Secretary: Sure.

Mr. Lopez: I'd like to talk with my daughter's teacher. Would that be possible?

Secretary: Yes, but you'll need to make an appointment.

Mr. Lopez: OK. Wednesday is best for me.

Secretary: First, let me get your daughter's name again and the teacher's name.

B **ROLE-PLAY. Make a similar conversation. Then change roles.**

Student A: You are a parent. Call the school. Choose one of the reasons below for your call.

Reasons for the call

a. You want information about the breakfast program, and you want to speak to the principal.
b. You want information about after-school programs, and you want to speak to your child's teacher.
c. You want information about the school calendar, and you want to speak to the guidance counselor.

Student B: You are the school secretary. Answer the parent's questions. Also help the parent make an appointment.

C **MAKE CONNECTIONS. Schools have many different programs for students.**

1. What kinds of school programs do you know about? ______________________________

____

2. What other programs do you think schools ought to have? ___________________________

____

I can talk with school personnel. ☐ I need more practice. ☐

For more practice, go to MyEnglishLab.

Lesson 5

Grammar

Adjective clauses

Adjective clauses: Relative pronoun as subject of the clause		
Main clause	**Adjective clause**	
	Relative pronoun as subject	**Verb (+ Object)**
We have a free lunch program for students	**who/that**	need financial assistance.
I brought an electric bill,	**which/that**	has my name and address on it.

Grammar Watch

- Use *who* for people.
- Use *which* for things.
- Use *that* for either people or things.

A INVESTIGATE. Underline the adjective clauses. Circle the person or thing that the adjective clauses give information about.

The Parent-Teacher Association is an organization which works on both the national and local levels. At the local level, parents and other family members meet to share ideas that can improve student learning. The PTA members also work on special projects. For example, they sometimes sell candy, cookbooks, or tickets to a dance to earn money which can help the school buy new computers. In some cases, the money is used to pay guest speakers, who come to the school to teach students for a day. The local PTA does a lot of good, and it gives the people who participate in its activities a feeling of belonging to the community.

B APPLY. Cross out *that* and replace it with *who* or *which*.

1. Schools in the U.S. have programs ~~that~~ which help parents get involved in their children's education.
2. Parents that know what their children are doing in school can help them do better.
3. Parent-teacher conferences are important meetings that give parents one-on-one time with school personnel.
4. Parents can ask for a translator that speaks their language.
5. Guidance counselors that work at the school can request meetings with parents.

Grammar

Adjective clauses: Relative pronoun as object of the clause		
Main clause	**Adjective clause**	
	Relative pronoun as object	**Subject + Verb**
I need a phone number	**(which/that)** or **Ø**	we can call.
You're the person	**(who/that)** or **Ø**	I spoke with.

Grammar Watch

You can leave out the relative pronoun (*who, which,* or *that*) altogether when the pronoun is the object of a clause.

A **INVESTIGATE. Underline the relative pronoun in each line. Circle the person or thing the relative pronoun refers to. Double underline the subject and verb that follow the relative pronoun. Then cross out the relative pronoun to show it can be omitted.**

Dear Parents:

Please become involved in our schools! Here are examples of things that you can do.

1. Volunteer for one of the many field trips which our students go on.
2. Find time to coach a sports team. Think about the future athletes that you can help.
3. Help organize a multicultural night that students, parents, and teachers can attend.

Remember: Everything that you do helps all our children.

B **DECIDE. Circle the relative pronoun. Then cross out the relative pronoun if it can be omitted.**

1. Silvia is the kind of mother who likes to be involved in her children's education.
2. Are there things which I can do to help my son with his schoolwork?
3. The project that Mrs. Bentley assigned shouldn't take more than an hour.
4. Parents should talk to their children about the work that they're doing in class.
5. Charlie told his mother the name of the teacher who helped him.

Show what you know!

1. **EXPLAIN. How were your parents involved in your school? Think of children that you know now. How are the parents involved? How has the ways in which parents are involved in children's schools changed?**
2. **WRITE. List at least five things today's parents can do to help in their children's schools. Use adjective clauses.**

Parents can volunteer at fundraising events which support the school.
Parents who speak other languages can help interpret for newcomer families.
They can also chaperone field trips that the school organizes . . .

I can use adjective clauses. ☐ I need more practice. ☐

For more practice, go to MyEnglishLab.

Lesson 6

Reading

Read about after-school programs

1 BEFORE YOU READ

A **DISCUSS.** What did you do after school when you were a child? What do the children you know do after school?

B **PREDICT.** Skim the article. What is it about?

Academic Skill: Distinguish fact from opinion

When you read, be careful to distinguish between facts and opinions. A fact is something that can be proven, or is true. An opinion is what someone believes or thinks.

2 READ

Listen and read.

CENTRAL VALLEY BEACON: Commentary

Don't Cut Our After-School Programs

The Central Valley School Board just made an extreme proposal. They want to drastically reduce funding for after-school programs next year. They argue that these programs are a waste of money. The programs were supposed to improve students' academic and social skills. However, the programs haven't achieved these goals. Therefore, it's time to get rid of them. This proposal is upsetting to me, and I strongly disagree with it. In my view, after-school programs can be very valuable. They just need to be managed in the right way.

I can't deny that our local after-school programs have some problems. Some critics claim that the programs are little more than babysitting services. That's why they are so ineffective in improving student skills. But babysitting is an important function of the programs. The parents in our community work long hours. They need someone to take care of their kids until they get home. However, after-school programs shouldn't just keep kids out of trouble. They should try to do more. So yes, our local programs may need more structure and supervision. However, that doesn't mean that the after-school programs are a waste of money. Numerous studies show the opposite. According to these studies, many after-school programs really do benefit students, families, and communities. Students who frequently attend after-school programs benefit the most. They get higher test scores. They behave better in the classroom. They drop out of school less often. They engage in fewer risky behaviors. Finally, many programs encourage exercise and good eating habits. In this way, they help to reduce obesity.

Why are some after-school programs more effective than others? The Harvard Family Research Project summarized 10 years of research on this topic. The research established that successful programs have three important characteristics. First, students attend them regularly, over a long period of time. Second, they have high-quality programming and staffing.

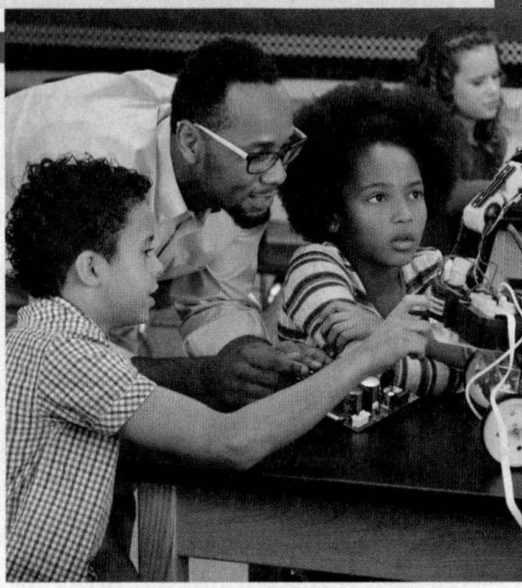

And third, they involve students and parents in planning. This makes students more enthusiastic.

It's not easy to develop truly effective after-school programs. However, I believe that we need to try. We shouldn't eliminate these programs. Instead, we should fund them more wisely. We should study successful programs and copy what they are doing. I think our after-school programs are capable of so much more. They can improve student outcomes in many different areas. And if they do that, they will pay for themselves.

3 CLOSE READING

A **IDENTIFY.** What is the main idea?

a. The Central Valley School Board wants to give much less money to after-school programs next year.
b. After-school programs can improve student outcomes significantly if they are managed effectively.
c. Students who frequently attend after-school programs usually stay in school until graduation.

B **CITE EVIDENCE.** Answer the questions. Where is the information located? **Lines**

1. Is the statement that the Central Valley School Board wants to cut funding for after-school programs a fact or an opinion? Why?

   ______________________________ ______

2. Is the statement that after-school programs are a waste of money a fact or an opinion? Why?

   ______________________________ ______

3. Is the statement: "In my view, after-school programs can be very valuable" a fact or an opinion? Why?

   ______________________________ ______

4. Is the statement that after-school programs are sometimes babysitting services a fact or an opinion? Why?

   ______________________________ ______

5. Is the statement that students who frequently attend after-school programs get higher test scores a fact or an opinion? Why?

   ______________________________ ______

6. Is the statement that successful after-school programs have three important characteristics a fact or an opinion? Why?

   ______________________________ ______

C **INTERPRET VOCABULARY.** Answer the questions.

1. In the context of line 2, what's another way to say *proposal*?
   a. suggestion **b.** marriage offer
2. In the context of line 3, what's another word for *funding*?
   a. students **b.** money
3. In the context of line 24, what's another way to say *ineffective*?
   a. uninterested **b.** unsuccessful
4. In the context of line 54, what's another word for *established*?
   a. built **b.** proved
5. In the context of line 66, what's another way to say *eliminate*?
   a. get rid of **b.** give away

D **SUMMARIZE.** What are the most important ideas in the article?

Show what you know!

1. **COLLABORATE.** Discuss an after-school program that you know about. In what ways is it similar to the programs described in the article? In what ways is the program successful? In what ways doesn't it work very well?
2. **WRITE.** Describe how to make after-school programs you know about more successful.
   My daughter's school can do a few things to improve its after-school programs. It can hire more staff and . . .

I can distinguish fact from opinion. ☐ I need more practice. ☐

To read more, go to MyEnglishLab.

Lesson 7

Listening and Speaking

Discuss school safety

1 BEFORE YOU LISTEN

DECIDE. What makes a school safe? What can school officials do to improve student safety?

2 LISTEN

The West Apollo Elementary School principal is talking to the safety advisory committee.

A ▶ **LISTEN FOR MAIN IDEA.** What does the principal want the advisory committee to do?

B ▶ **LISTEN FOR DETAILS.** Listen again. Then circle the correct answers.

1. Before today, how many times had the committee met?
   a. none **b.** one **c.** two
2. How many improvements does the mayor want each school to make?
   a. three **b.** four **c.** five
3. Who is on the safety advisory committee?
   a. parents, teachers, police officers **b.** parents, teachers, community leaders **c.** parents, teachers, people who live near the school
4. Which places are **NOT** mentioned?
   a. classrooms **b.** playgrounds **c.** parking lot

3 PRONUNCIATION

A ▶ **PRACTICE.** Listen. Then listen again and repeat.

The teachers **should have** ("should of") stopped the fight.

They **shouldn't have** ("shouldn't of") allowed it to start.

You **must have** ("must of") heard about the plan.

Past modals

When you say past modals such as *may have, must have, might have, should have, shouldn't have, could have,* and *couldn't have,* link the two words together and pronounce them as one word. *Have* usually sounds like *of* (or *a* in fast speech).

B ▶ **APPLY.** Listen. Circle the words you hear. Then listen again to check your answers.

1. I **should have / shouldn't have** told her about the problem.
2. The teachers **could have / couldn't have** stopped the fight.
3. They **should have / shouldn't have** talked to the parents.
4. My son **could have / couldn't have** been involved in the fight.
5. You **should have / shouldn't have** gone to the meeting.

4 CONVERSATION

A ▶ **LISTEN AND READ.** Then practice the conversation with a partner.

Parent A: I was disappointed in our meeting today. I think we should have talked much more about playground safety.
Parent B: I agree. Too many kids get hurt on the school playground.
Parent A: Right. We need good-quality equipment. I'm not sure the swings and slides we have now are good quality.
Parent B: And the children need better supervision. Who is watching them on the playground?
Parent A: I don't know. My son told me there was a fight last week. Nobody did anything about it. The teachers should have stopped it.
Parent B: Stopped it? The teachers shouldn't have allowed it to start!

B **RANK.** Imagine you are members of a school safety committee.

1. Decide which three things are the most important. Number them *1, 2,* and *3.*

_____	knowing what to do in case of fire	_____	knowing what to do in case of bad weather
_____	supervising students on the playground	_____	protecting students online
_____	preventing bullying	_____	other: ____________________

2. Explain the reasons for your rankings.

____

____

I can discuss school safety. ☐ I need more practice. ☐

For more practice, go to MyEnglishLab.

Lesson 8

Grammar

Past modals

Past modals: Expressing degrees of certainty about the past				
Subject	**Modal**		**Past participle**	
They	**may (not)** **might (not)** **must (not)** **can (not)** **could (not)**	**have**	noticed	the problems.

Grammar Watch

- Use *may (not) have, might (not) have,* or *could have* to show that you are not certain about something in the past.
- Use *must (not) have* to show that you are almost certain about something in the past.
- Use *cannot have, could not have (can't have, couldn't have)* to show disbelief about something in the past.

A **INVESTIGATE.** Underline the past modal phrases.

Student: Ms. Lee, I can't find my bike helmet. I might have left it here. Did you see it?

Teacher: No, I'm sorry. I didn't. Could you have left it at home?

Student: No, I was wearing it this morning.

Teacher: Well, that's good. You should wear it whenever you ride. You may have left it in the cafeteria.

Student: Oh, you're right! I got breakfast this morning. I must have forgotten it there.

B **COMPLETE.** Use *may have, may not have, must have,* or *couldn't have.*

1. **A:** Where is Mr. Chen?
   B: He was out yesterday, so he ____________________ heard about the safety meeting.
2. **A:** The superintendent of schools was here. She looked very pleased.
   B: She ____________________ noticed the safety signs.
3. **A:** I'm not sure the safety committee checked the equipment on the playground.
   B: They ____________________ checked it yet. There are still no seats on the swings!
4. **A:** Did you see Victor at the meeting?
   B: He ____________________ been there, but I didn't see him.

Grammar

Past modals: Expressing regrets or opinions about the past				
Subject	**Modal**		**Past participle**	
The teachers	**should**	**have**	**stopped**	the fight.
	shouldn't		**allowed**	it to start!

Grammar Watch

- Use *should have* to talk about actions that did not happen in the past, and now you regret it.
- Use *should not have* to talk about things that did happen, and now you regret it.

C **INVESTIGATE.** Underline the past modal phrases.

Nurse: Hello, Mrs. Silva. I'm calling to let you know that Ava fell off a playground structure. She was climbing on top of a slide.
Parent: What was she doing on top of the slide? She shouldn't have been there.
Nurse: That's right. The teacher warned the kids not to climb on the slides, but some of them did it anyway. They should've listened to the teacher.
Parent: Is Ava OK?
Nurse: Yes, she seems fine. She said her arm hurts a little. It doesn't appear to be broken. I put some ice on it, and I kept an eye on her for an hour. I sent her back to class a few minutes ago.
Parent: An hour! Someone should've called me sooner.
Nurse: We tried to call you immediately, but we got your voicemail.
Parent: Oh, I'm sorry. I turned my phone off while I was in a meeting. I should've kept it on. Well, thanks for calling me now. Do I need to pick Ava up early today?
Nurse: That's up to you.

D **APPLY.** Some children behaved in unsafe ways on the bus. Write sentences saying what they should have or shouldn't have done.

1. The children played loud music. *They shouldn't have played loud music.*
2. They didn't wear their seatbelts. ______
3. They ran up and down the aisle. ______
4. They put their heads out the windows. ______
5. They didn't show respect for the driver. ______
6. They got out of their seats. ______
7. They didn't listen to the bus driver. ______

Show what you know!

1. **DISCUSS.** Nine-year-old Van Le has back problems. His doctor said the problem was Van's backpack. What other possible causes can you think of?
2. **WRITE.** List another possible cause for Van's back problems. Use past modals. Then say what his parents should or should not have done.

Van could have hurt his back while playing a sport. Van's parents should have asked Van when his back started to hurt . . .

I can use past modals. ☐ I need more practice. ☐

For more practice, go to MyEnglishLab.

Lesson 9

Writing

Write a letter to the editor

WRITING PROMPT: Think about a recent decision in a school you are familiar with. Do you agree with it or disagree with it? Why? Write a letter to the editor to express your opinion about the decision.

1 STUDY THE MODEL

 **ANALYZE.** Read the model and Writing Skill. Then answer the questions.

Letter to the Editor

I recently learned that there will be seven teacher in-service (training) days in the West Apollo School District next year. When teachers have in-service days, the children are off from school.

I was upset about this news because it will have a negative impact on some families in our district. It's true that students benefit from the work their teachers do during training. However, some parents can't take time off from work or pay for extra childcare when schools are closed. How will these families cope with so many in-service days?

We need to speak up about this issue. I plan to talk to the principal of our children's school and the school board about it. I encourage other parents to do the same.

Writing Skill: Use paragraph structure

When a letter or an essay includes more than one paragraph, it's important to put similar information together.

1. Circle the paragraph that describes the writer's opinion. Underline the paragraph that describes what the writer thinks people should do next.
2. What kind of information did the writer put in the first paragraph?
3. What does the writer mean in the concluding sentence?

B **TAKE NOTES.** Complete the chart with information from the model.

Topic: Teacher in-service days		
Paragraph 1:	**Paragraph 2:**	**Paragraph 3:**
A description of the issue the letter is about		

Writing

2 PLAN YOUR WRITING

A **BRAINSTORM.** Discuss your ideas for the Writing Prompt with a partner.

B **ORGANIZE.** Use this chart to organize your ideas before writing.

Topic: ____________		
Paragraph 1:	**Paragraph 2:**	**Paragraph 3:**

3 WRITE

STATE AN OPINION. Write a letter to the editor about a school decision that you agree or disagree with. Remember to put similar information together in your paragraphs. Use the model, the Writing Skill, and your ideas from Exercise 2 to help you.

4 CHECK YOUR WRITING

A **REVISE.** Use the Writing Checklist to review your writing. Make revisions as necessary.

B **COLLABORATE.** Read your writing with a partner. Use the checklist again to improve your writing.

WRITING CHECKLIST

- ☐ Did you describe the issue you wrote about?
- ☐ Did you describe how you felt about the issue and why?
- ☐ Did you suggest next steps at the end of the letter?
- ☐ Did you put similar information together in your paragraphs?

I can use paragraph structure. ☐ I need more practice. ☐

For more practice, go to MyEnglishLab.

Lesson 10

Soft Skills at Work

Manage time well

1 MEET SALIM

Read about one of his workplace skills.

I manage time well. I respect company time. I understand I am on the company clock. I am punctual and take my responsibilities seriously.

2 SALIM'S PROBLEM

A READ. Write *T* (true) or *F* (false).

Salim is supervising the construction of a new building. He needs to leave work early this afternoon. Salim forgot that it is report card pick-up day at his son's school. Salim asks his co-worker, Sam, if they can switch shifts. Sam is annoyed. He says Salim should have asked him sooner.

_____ **1.** Salim is the supervisor at a construction site.

_____ **2.** Salim needs to leave work to pick-up his son's report card.

_____ **3.** Salim asks Sam to take his shift for him, and Sam happily agrees.

B ANALYZE. What is Salim's problem?

____

____

3 SALIM'S SOLUTION

A COLLABORATE. Salim manages time well. How does he handle needing to leave work early today? Explain your answer.

1. Salim tells Sam he will skip report card pick-up day and work his shift instead.
2. Salim tells Sam that he is sorry, and he will remember to take time off in advance next time if Sam helps him out today.
3. Salim decides that no one will notice if he just leaves work a bit early.
4. Salim ____.

B ROLE-PLAY. Role-play Salim's conversation with Sam.

Show what you know!

1. **REFLECT.** How do you manage time well at school, at work, or at home? Give an example.
2. **WRITE.** Write your example in your Skills Log.

   There are always so many things to do at home—grocery shopping, doing laundry, cleaning the house. Making and tracking a to-do list helps me manage my time.

3. **PRESENT.** Give a short presentation describing how you manage your time well.

I can give an example of how I manage my time well. ☐

Unit Review: Go back to page 165. Which unit goals can you check off?

10 Safety First

PREVIEW

What types of accidents can occur at work?

UNIT GOALS

- ☐ Give a progress report
- ☐ Talk about preventing accidents at work
- ☐ Interpret and complete an accident report
- ☐ Recognize requirements for promotions
- ☐ Write about ways to improve workplace safety
- ☐ **Academic skill:** Identify time words
- ☐ **Writing skill:** State problem, causes, and solutions
- ☐ **Workplace soft skill:** Take responsibility

Lesson 1

Listening and Speaking

Give a progress report

1 BEFORE YOU LISTEN

A **PRIORITZE.** Which factor is most important to an employer? Speed (how fast employees work) or quality (how good employees' work is)? Why? What other things does an employer want or expect from an employee?

B **DETERMINE.** When people or companies need to build something, they often hire a *contractor* to manage the project. The contractor often hires *subcontractors.* What tasks do you think each person does?

2 LISTEN

Sam is a contractor. He is talking to his subcontractor, Oleg. The subcontractor is building the kitchen cabinets.

A **LISTEN FOR MAIN IDEA.** What is the problem?

B **LISTEN FOR DETAILS.** Listen again. Write *T* (true) or *F* (false). Correct the false statements.

__F__ **1.** The wood arrived from the supplier ~~a week ago~~ yesterday.

____ **2.** The work on this project is one week late.

____ **3.** The subcontractor didn't call the contractor about the problem.

____ **4.** The contractor asks the subcontractor to hurry.

____ **5.** Finishing the project on time is more important than staying within the budget.

____ **6.** The contractor doesn't care about the quality of the work.

____ **7.** They need to finish the cabinets so that the counters can be installed.

C **PROBLEM SOLVE.** What could the subcontractor have done differently? What could the contractor have done differently?

____

____

3 CONVERSATION

A ▶ **LISTEN AND READ.** **Then practice the conversation with a partner.**

Sam: Jan? This is Sam Baker. I wanted to give you a progress report on the work we're doing on the kitchens at 215 River Road.

Building Manager: Oh, good. I was just going to call you.

Sam: Well, here's the thing. I just spoke to Kurt, my subcontractor, and he's running a little behind schedule—but we're doing everything we can.

Building Manager: How much behind schedule? What's the problem?

Sam: Five sinks are on backorder. We got the supplier to rush the order, but we won't get them until next Monday.

Building Manager: Can you find a different supplier?

Sam: I had Kurt check around, and it doesn't look like anyone else has what we need. I'll have him check some other places, and I'll get back to you.

Building Manager: Call me tomorrow.

B **ROLE-PLAY.** **Make a similar conversation. Then change roles.**

Student A: You are a contractor. A building manager has hired you to remodel twelve bathrooms in an apartment building. Your subcontractor is having problems. He is supposed to remodel one bathroom every two days, but he is behind schedule.

Student B: You are the building manager. Tenants are upset because the schedule for remodeling their bathrooms keeps changing. You want a progress report.

C **REFLECT.** **Talk about your own job or school experiences.**

1. How much pressure is there to work fast? Why? ____________________

2. How much pressure is there to do quality work? Why? ____________________

D **STATE AN OPINION.** **How easy or difficult is it to make employers or instructors happy? State support for your opinion.**

____

I can give a progress report. ☐ I need more practice. ☐

For more practice, go to MyEnglishLab.

Lesson 2

Grammar

Make/have/let/get + object + verb

Make/have/let/get + Object + Verb			
Why didn't you	**make**	them	**rush** the order?
I'll	**have**	him	**check** some other places.
Could you	**let**	him	**measure** the space?
We	**got**	the supplier	**to rush** the order.

Grammar Watch

- Use ***make* + object + base form** when someone requires another person to do something.
- Use ***have* + object + base form** when someone asks another person to do something.
- Use ***let* + object + base form** when someone allows another person to do something.
- Use ***get* + object + infinitive** when someone persuades another person to do something.

A INVESTIGATE. Underline *make/have/let* + object + base form and *get* + object + infinitive.

Instructions for new cashiers:

- If customers have a store card, have them scan their cards before checking out.
- If you need to check the price of an item, get your bagger to find the information, so you can continue helping the customer.
- Always let customers take their time getting their money out. Never make the customer rush.
- If customers are paying by credit card, don't forget to have them sign the receipt.

B DETERMINE. Cross out the incorrect noun or pronoun to make the second sentence true.

1. The manager had me drive the forklift.
   The manager / I drove the forklift.
2. Our boss let us go home early on July 3.
   We / Our boss went home early on July 3.
3. The supervisor made them work faster.
   The supervisor / They had to work faster.
4. Pam got Yuki to work the night shift.
   Yuki / Pam changed her shift.

Grammar

C **APPLY.** Use the verb given to restate what the person wanted or allowed. The restatement should be in the simple past.

1. **Supervisor:** All employees must turn off their machines at night.
   (*have*) The supervisor had the employees turn off their machines at night.
2. **Foreperson:** Harry, remember to clean off your shoes.
   (*make*) The foreperson ____________________
3. **Boss:** You can use the company van this weekend.
   (*let*) My boss ____________________
4. **Ray:** Ben, please work until the job is finished.
   (*get*) Ray ____________________
5. **Manager:** New workers, please don't ask questions until the training is over.
   (*not let*) The manager ____________________
6. **Jody:** Dan, I want you to meet all the people working on the site.
   (*have*) Jody ____________________

Show what you know!

1. **DISCUSS.** What things might an employer ask or allow you to do at work?
   - have you work late
   - have you work on weekends
   - make you wait for your paycheck
   - make you work in unsafe conditions
   - get you to do something you'd never done
   - let you take several breaks
   - let you leave early
   - let you try a new procedure
2. **WRITE.** What expectations should a good manager have for his or her employees? List five things. Use *make/have/let/get* + object + verb.
   1. A manager should have workers complete all their training on time.
   2. A manager shouldn't let workers play on their phones at work . . .

I can use *make/have/let/get* + object + verb. ☐ I need more practice. ☐

For more practice, go to MyEnglishLab.

Lesson 3

Reading

Read about workplace safety

1 BEFORE YOU READ

A **DISCUSS.** Look around your classroom. What kind of safety equipment do you see? What is it for?

B **PREDICT.** Skim the article. What is it about?

Academic Skill: Identify time words

When you read, look for dates and words such as *before, after, next,* and *finally* that show the sequence in which events occurred.

2 READ

Listen and read.

http://www.onthejobsafety.com

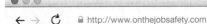

Triangle Shirtwaist Factory Fire

On March 25, 1911, fire broke out in the Triangle Shirtwaist Factory in New York City. Inside the factory, the workers were all women. Some of them were only 15 years old. Many of the workers escaped. But on the 9th floor, there were only two exit doors. One exit was filled with smoke. The other exit door was locked. The workers on that floor were trapped. One hundred and forty-eight workers were killed.

The Triangle Shirtwaist Factory fire made the newspaper headlines. People were outraged to learn of the working conditions there. Women and children of 12 or 13 years old worked fourteen-hour shifts. The factory was dangerous and unsanitary. Unfortunately, most workplaces at that time were both unsafe and unclean. In factories, mills, and mines, adults and children worked long hours. They used dangerous machines. They had no clean air to breathe. They were often injured. Sometimes, they were killed.

Before the fire, the public had been unaware of these conditions. But after the fire, many people wanted to make workplaces safer. They began to demand that the government do something about the problem. Workers also organized into powerful unions to protect the rights of the workers. The unions fought for safer conditions. Finally, in 1970, the government took action. It created the Occupational Safety and Health Administration (OSHA) to help ensure workplace safety.

The purpose of OSHA is to prevent injuries and deaths in the workplace. The agency enforces rules for safety. For example, each workplace has to have a sprinkler system, fire extinguishers, and exit doors. This equipment protects workers when there is a fire. OSHA also requires employers to identify workplace hazards that put employees at risk. Employers have to eliminate or reduce these hazards. For example, there might be a dangerous chemical in the workplace. The employer needs to replace it with a safer chemical.

The agency also publishes safety and health training materials. Supervisors are required to display OSHA posters in workplaces. These brochures and posters help employees learn the safe ways to do things. OSHA inspectors visit workplaces regularly. They make sure companies and their employees follow the rules. What happens if a company does not follow safety and health regulations? It has to pay a fine.

Some people feel that OSHA should be tougher on employers who disregard or ignore safety rules. But the agency has evidently made a big difference in working conditions. Workers in the United States are now much safer than they used to be.

3 CLOSE READING

A **IDENTIFY.** What is the main idea?

a. On March 25, 1911, the Triangle Shirtwaist Factory Fire killed 148 workers.
b. The Triangle Shirtwaist Factory Fire exposed unsafe working conditions, and this eventually led to the creation of OSHA.
c. Some people think OSHA doesn't punish unsafe employers enough, but the agency has improved working conditions in the United States.

B CITE EVIDENCE. Complete the sentences. Where is the information located? **Lines**

1. Before March 25, 1911, _____. _______
   a. many people were upset about unsafe working conditions in the United States
   b. many people didn't know about unsafe working conditions in the United States
   c. children did not work with adults in factories
2. 148 workers died in the Triangle Shirtwaist Factory Fire because _____. _______
   a. all the exit doors in the factory were locked
   b. the workers on the 9th floor of the factory couldn't escape
   c. workers couldn't breathe because the air was too smoky
3. The government created OSHA _____. _______
   a. right after the Triangle Shirtwaist Factory Fire
   b. almost 60 years after the Triangle Shirtwaist Factory Fire
   c. at the same time that workers organized into unions
4. Before 1970, _____. _______
   a. the government didn't enforce safety and health rules in workplaces
   b. all workplaces had sprinklers and fire extinguishers
   c. there were no unions in workplaces
5. An OSHA inspector's main job is to _______
   a. help workers form unions
   b. make sure workplaces are safe
   c. send employers to prison for not protecting workers

C INTERPRET VOCABULARY. Complete the sentences.

1. In the context of line 6, the word *outraged* means _____.
   a. insulted b. angry and shocked
2. In the context of line 14, the word *unions* means _____.
   a. organizations that join together b. organizations that fight for workers
3. In the context of line 16, the word *occupational* means _____.
   a. relating to physical activities b. relating to work
4. In the context of line 20, the word *hazards* means _____.
   a. dangers b. safety equipment
5. In the context of line 26, the word *disregard* means _____.
   a. don't know about b. don't pay attention to

D SUMMARIZE. What are the most important ideas in the article?

Show what you know!

1. **COLLABORATE.** Are working conditions safe for all workers today? What are some jobs that are still dangerous? Why?
2. **WRITE.** Name one dangerous job. Explain what employers, workers, and the government can do to make that job safer.

   I think construction workers have dangerous jobs. To make construction work safer, employers should . . .

I can identify time words. ☐ I need more practice. ☐

To read more, go to MyEnglishLab.

Lesson 4

Listening and Speaking

Talk about preventing accidents at work

1 BEFORE YOU LISTEN

IDENITFY. What is this machine? What are some of the safety hazards of working with a machine like this?

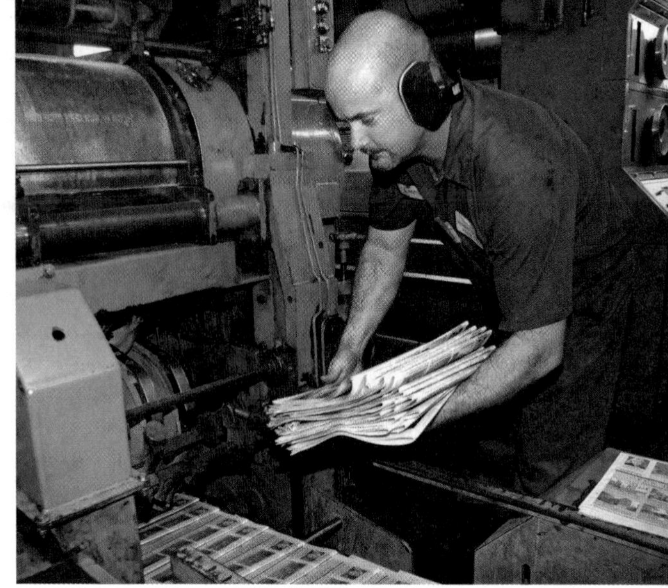

2 LISTEN

Asad works on a printing press. He has a new co-worker, Clara.

A **LISTEN FOR MAIN IDEA.** What is Asad worried about?

____

____

B **LISTEN FOR DETAILS.** Listen again. Write *T* (true) or *F* (false). Correct the false statements.

__T__ **1.** The workers are not supposed to wear loose-fitting clothes when they operate the press.

_____ **2.** Clara didn't go to the safety training.

_____ **3.** The company didn't give Clara a safety training manual.

_____ **4.** Clara didn't read the safety training manual.

_____ **5.** Clara read the safety training manual, but she didn't remember everything.

_____ **6.** Asad sometimes does a safety check of his equipment before he starts.

_____ **7.** Asad told Clara to keep her hands away from the machine.

C **DETERMINE.** Answer the questions.

1. Name at least one thing that Asad does as part of his safety check. ______________________

____

2. What are some other things you might want to check? ______________________

____

3 PRONUNCIATION

Sentence flow

The words in a sentence are usually pronounced together without stopping. Link a consonant sound at the end of one word to a vowel sound at the beginning of the next word without stopping.

A ▶ **PRACTICE.** **Listen. Then listen again and repeat.**

He was out of work for a month.

That's awful.

I'll go back and read it again.

Good idea.

Do you have any questions?

B ▶ **APPLY.** **Listen. Draw a line (◡) to show where a consonant sound is linked to a following vowel sound. Then listen again to check your answers.**

1. These machines are dangerous.
2. Don't wear a bracelet when you're operating the press.
3. I'll take it off right now.
4. Make sure the guards are all on the machine.

4 CONVERSATION

A ▶ **LISTEN AND READ.** **Then practice the conversation with a partner.**

A: You know, Luis cut himself badly last year and couldn't work for a month.

B: Oh! That's awful!

A: I know. So that's why I want to be sure everyone is taking safety precautions.

B: You're right. I think I'll go back and read the safety manual again. Maybe I'll make notes to myself to help me remember.

A: Good idea. There are some useful pointers in the manual. I don't want you to injure yourself.

B **MAKE CONNECTIONS.** **Have you or someone you know ever worked in a dangerous environment? Discuss the questions.**

1. What were the safety hazards?
2. What did you or that person do to keep safe?

C **PRESENT.** **Research a dangerous job. What makes the job dangerous? What safety measures do people take?**

I can talk about preventing accidents at work. ☐ I need more practice. ☐

For more practice, go to MyEnglishLab.

Lesson 5

Grammar

Reflexive pronouns

Reflexive pronouns			
Subject pronoun		**Reflexive pronoun**	
I		**myself**	
You (singular)		**yourself**	
You (plural)		**yourselves**	
He		**himself**	
	hurt		at work.
She		**herself**	
We		**ourselves**	
They		**themselves**	

Grammar Watch

- Use a reflexive pronoun when the subject and object of a sentence refer to the same people.
- Remember: If the subject and object are different, use an object pronoun: *The supervisor helped her at work.*
- You can also use a reflexive pronoun to emphasize that someone or some group did something alone. *By* is sometimes added: *I installed the safety equipment (by) myself.*

(See page 265 for a list of verbs that are often used with reflexive pronouns.)

A **SELECT.** A nurse's aide wrote a social media post about her first day at work. Circle the reflexive pronouns and underline the nouns they refer back to.

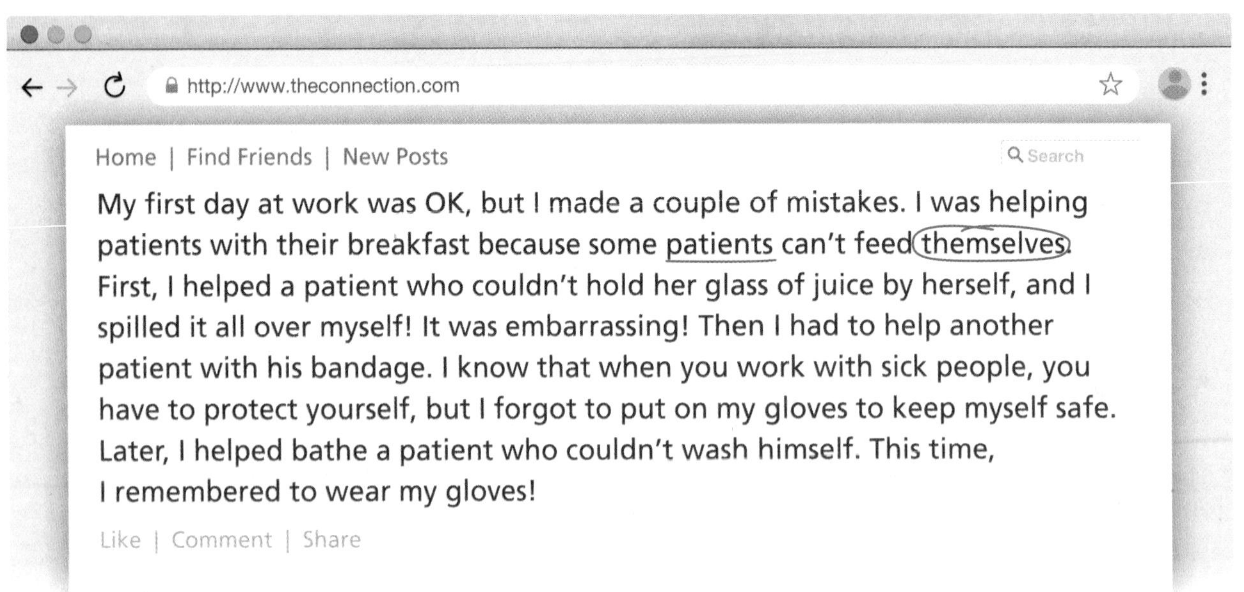

http://www.theconnection.com
Home | Find Friends | New Posts
Search
My first day at work was OK, but I made a couple of mistakes. I was helping patients with their breakfast because some patients can't feed themselves. First, I helped a patient who couldn't hold her glass of juice by herself, and I spilled it all over myself! It was embarrassing! Then I had to help another patient with his bandage. I know that when you work with sick people, you have to protect yourself, but I forgot to put on my gloves to keep myself safe. Later, I helped bathe a patient who couldn't wash himself. This time, I remembered to wear my gloves!
Like | Comment | Share

Grammar

B **DETERMINE.** Cross out the incorrect words.

1. **A:** Wang burned **him / himself** on the bread oven today. I feel bad. I should have warned **him / himself** that the oven was really hot.
   B: Don't blame **you / yourself**. It was an accident.
2. **A:** Can you move those wires out of the way? People might trip on **them / themselves** and hurt **them / themselves**.
   B: OK, I will.
3. **A:** Never operate this forklift by **you / yourself**. Someone else should always be nearby in case you have an accident.
   B: I know. The supervisor already told **me / myself** that.

C **COMPLETE.** Use the correct reflexive pronouns.

1. Salma is a deli worker. When she slices meat, she is careful not to cut ___herself___.
2. Ironworkers often work high up on bridges and tall buildings. They take special care to keep ________ safe on the construction site.
3. The scaffold rope broke, and Hakeem lost his balance, but he kept ________ from falling.
4. The company doesn't want us to injure ________ on the machines.
5. You shouldn't use a tall ladder by ________. You should have someone hold it.
6. I have to attend the course so I don't hurt ________ on the new equipment.

Show what you know!

1. **COLLABORATE.** Ask and answer the questions.
   1. Have you ever hurt yourself on the job? What happened?
   2. Do you know other people who have hurt themselves on the job? What happened?
   3. If you hurt yourself at work, do you tell your boss? Why?
   4. Do you do everything you can to keep yourself safe at work? Explain.
2. **WRITE.** Choose one of the questions above and write a paragraph about what happened. Use reflexive pronouns.

   When my sister worked for a cleaning company, she hurt herself when she fell off of a ladder. She fractured her ankle. She was not supposed to use the ladder by herself, but her co-worker was out that day. Her co-worker felt terrible about it and blamed himself, but my sister did not blame him.

I can use reflexive pronouns. ☐ I need more practice. ☐

For more practice, go to MyEnglishLab.

Workplace, Life, and Community Skills

Lesson 6

Interpret and complete an employee accident report

1 INTERPRET AN EMPLOYEE ACCIDENT REPORT

A **MAKE CONNECTIONS.** What kinds of injuries can happen at work? If someone is injured at work, who should they report the injury to?

B **SCAN. THEN READ.** What type of information is in each section. After scanning, read the report.

www.https://axelroofing.com

Employee's Accident Report

Section 1: Instructions

The Employee Accident Report MUST be completed for every work-related accident, preferably within 24 hours of the incident.

Employee Responsibilities

1. Seek emergency or other medical treatment as needed.
2. Notify the supervisor or other person in charge.
3. Fully complete the "Employee Information" and "Accident Information" sections. Sign and date the report.
4. Give the form to the supervisor or other person in charge for a signature.

(Please print neatly in ink or complete electronically.)

Section 2: Medical Treatment

For serious injuries that need emergency medical attention, please seek treatment at Mountain View Emergency Department or the nearest medical facility. For non-serious injuries, employees should seek treatment for work-related injuries at:

Mountain View Health Center
1601 Foster Drive
Mountain View, CA 94040
Phone: 650-555-9823

Section 3: Workers' Compensation Rights

Employees have the right to apply for Workers' Compensation benefits. They have one year from the date of injury to do so. For more information regarding Workers' Compensation, call 650-555-3339.

Section 4: Employee Authorization

I understand that it is my right to apply for Workers' Compensation benefits and that I have one year from the date of this accident to do so. I also authorize release of medical information regarding this accident.

Employee Signature: Charles Beaumont Date: 2/25/19

Section 5: Employee Information

Employee Name: Charles Beaumont ID Number: 5673472 Male ● Female ○ Date of Birth: 4/16/80

Home Address: 18 Center Street - Apt. 6B (Street) Mountain View (City) CA (State) 94040 (ZIP Code)

Home Phone No. 650-555-4827 Cell Phone No. 650-555-1029 Job Title: Roofer Employment Start Date: 5/1/2008

Section 6: Accident Information

Date of Accident: 2/24/19

Location of Accident: 200 Blossom Lane, Mountain View, CA

Describe in detail how the accident occurred:

I was repairing the roof of a barn. The ladder gave way because the ground was soft. I fell backwards approximately 35 feet to the ground.

Number of days missed from work: 3 Type of leave used: sick days Number of days worked with restrictions: 0

Name of witness (es): Mike Cabrera Phone No. 650-555-8304

Was safety equipment provided? Yes ● No ○ Was safety equipment used? Yes ● No ○

Section 7: Healthcare Provider Information

Part of body injured: lower back

Type of injury: sprain

Medical treatment sought: Dr. Lao, Mountain View Health, 1601 Foster Drive, Mountain View CA 94040 (Name and Address of Medical Provider) 650-555-1122 (Phone)

Return to work date (as stated by physician): 2/28/19

C DEFINE KEY WORDS. Find the words on the left in the accident report. Match the words with their definitions.

_____ 1. Workers' Compensation
_____ 2. treatment
_____ 3. authorization
_____ 4. incident
_____ 5. preferably
_____ 6. OSHA

a. medical attention for an illness or injury
b. signed form to give approval or permission
c. something that happens; a specific event
d. ideally
e. plan that provides wages and benefits to employees hurt on the job
f. the federal agency that regulates work safety

D LOCATE DETAILS. Circle the correct answers.

1. Who is Charles Beaumont?
   a. the doctor b. the supervisor c. the injured employee
2. What should an employee who is seriously injured do first?
   a. fill out the form b. get medical attention c. contact the supervisor
3. How much time does an employee have to file a Workers' Compensation claim after the injury?
   a. a month b. six months c. a year
4. Where should an employee go for treatment of a non-serious, work-related injury?
   a. Mountain View Health Center b. Mountain View Emergency Department c. any emergency room
5. Who was a witness to the accident?
   a. Dr. Lao b. Mike Cabrera c. Charles Beaumont
6. What date can Mr. Beaumont return to work?
   a. February 28, 2019 b. February 24, 2019 c. February 25, 2019

E DISCUSS. Answer the questions.

1. Why is it important to fill out an accident report form?
2. Why should you file a Workers' Compensation Claim if you are injured at the workplace?

2 COMPLETE AN EMPLOYEE ACCIDENT REPORT

A GO ONLINE.

1. **SEARCH.** Find an accident report form. What website is it on? ______________________________
2. **COMPARE.** How is the accident report you found similar to the accident report found by a classmate? How is it different?

B WRITE. What types of information does the accident report you found ask for? Imagine that you had an accident at a job. Provide the information needed on the accident report.

I can interpret and complete an employee accident report. ☐ I need more practice. ☐

For more practice, go to MyEnglishLab.

Lesson 7

Listening and Speaking

Recognize requirements for promotion

1 BEFORE YOU LISTEN

BRAINSTORM. What are some reasons that a manager gives an employee a raise (more money) or a promotion (higher-level job)? Make a list.

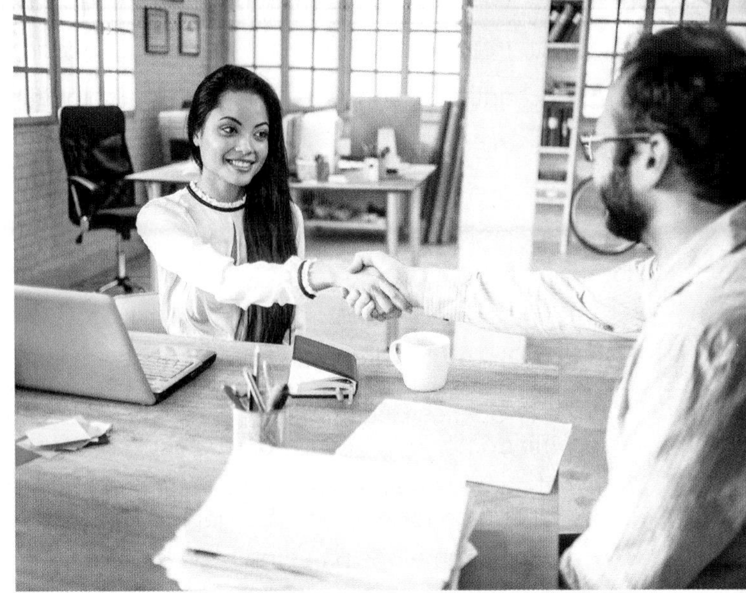

2 LISTEN

Lisa works at Dependable Delivery, a package-delivery service. She is talking to her manager, Don.

A ▶ **LISTEN FOR MAIN IDEA.** What good news does Don give her?

____

____

B ▶ **LISTEN FOR DETAILS.** Listen again. Then write the correct words to complete each sentence.

1. Lisa started working as a sorter ________________ ago.
2. Lisa can move ________________ packages in an hour.
3. Lisa has made mistakes with only ________________ packages in three months.
4. Her manager is promoting Lisa to the position of ________________ supervisor.
5. In her new position, Lisa will be responsible for ________________ people.
6. Lisa will start her new position ________________.
7. Lisa and her manager will meet again at ________________.

C **DECIDE.** Would you rather get a raise or a promotion? Why?

____

____

____

Listening and Speaking

3 PRONUNCIATION

A ▶ **PRACTICE.** Listen. Then listen again and repeat.

no	job	other
ago	not	done
promoted	operate	company

Vowel sound for *o*

The vowel *o* can spell several different sounds.

B ▶ **APPLY.** Listen. Write each word in the correct column of the chart in Exercise A. Then listen again to check your answers.

1. only
2. stop
3. don't
4. doesn't
5. come
6. problem

4 CONVERSATION

A ▶ **LISTEN AND READ.** Then practice the conversation with a partner.

A: You know, I've been working here for five years now, and they still haven't promoted me.

B: Wow, that's too bad. Do you have any idea why not?

A: Not really. I think I'm a good employee.

B: You don't come to work late, do you?

A: No, I come in on time every day. And I work hard. I don't think my manager likes me.

B: Why don't you ask for a transfer? You could come and work in our operations department. My manager is demanding but very supportive. And I think there's an opening.

A: I don't know. Maybe. Tell me more about the department. What's it like?

B **PROBLEM SOLVE.** The woman in Exercise A doesn't think her manager likes her. Discuss the questions.

1. What might be some other reasons that she didn't get a promotion?
2. What do you think she should do?

C **PRESENT.** Describe a time you received a positive review from a manager or an instructor. How did that review help you grow?

I can recognize requirements for promotion. ☐ I need more practice. ☐

For more practice, go to MyEnglishLab.

Lesson 8

Grammar

Could you/I . . . ? / Would you mind . . . ? / Why don't you/I . . . ? to make polite requests

Could you/I . . . ? / Why don't you/I . . . ? / Would you mind . . . ?					
Questions				**Affirmative answers**	**Negative answers**
Could	**I**	**talk**	to you?	Yes, of course.	Sorry, I'm busy.
Would you mind		**working**	on Saturday?	**Not at all.**	I'm sorry, but I can't. I'd rather not.
Why don't	**I**	**help**	you with that?	Thanks.	That's OK, I don't need any help.
	you	**ask**	the supervisor?	Good idea.	I don't think that's a good idea.
	you	**work**	overtime tonight?	Sure.	Sorry, I can't.

Grammar Watch

- Use *Could I/you* and *Would you mind* to make polite requests for permission or help.
- Use *Why don't I . . .* to make offers.
- Use *Why don't you . . .* to make suggestions.
- The answer to *Would you mind* is negative when you want to agree with the request.

A **INVESTIGATE.** Read this message from a manager to an employee. Underline the requests, suggestions, and offers.

Sorry you've been sick this week. Why don't you take the day off tomorrow? Why don't I help you catch up with the work then? Would you mind working on Friday instead? Could you please call me as soon as possible to let me know? I hope you feel better soon.

B **MATCH.** Match the requests or suggestions at the left with the correct responses.

____ **1.** Could I take a break now?
____ **2.** Could you show me how to use this ladder?
____ **3.** Why don't we clean up now?
____ **4.** Would you mind saying that again?
____ **5.** Why don't I help you with that box?
____ **6.** Why don't you finish it tomorrow?
____ **7.** Why don't I hold that for you?

a. Not at all. I said, put on your protective glasses.
b. No problem. You've been working a long time.
c. I can't. It's due today.
d. Thanks a lot. It's really heavy!
e. Good idea. We made a big mess.
f. It's OK. I can hold it.
g. Sure. You hold it this way.

Grammar

C **COMPLETE.** Use one of the expressions in the box. You will use some expressions more than once.

Could I	Could you	Why don't I	Why don't you	Would you mind

1. **A:** Why don't I get that down for you?
   B: Thanks. I'd appreciate that.
2. **A:** ________________ working on Sunday?
   B: I'm sorry, but I can't. I'm going to a wedding.
3. **A:** ________________ answer the phones for me for a couple of minutes?
   B: Sure. No problem.
4. **A:** ________________ borrow your copy of the safety manual?
   B: I'm sorry. I don't have it. I lent it to Sam.
5. **A:** ________________ tell your supervisor your idea?
   B: I'm already planning to. I'll talk to her tomorrow.
6. **A:** ________________ moving those boxes away from the exit?
   B: Not at all. They're a safety hazard where they are.
7. **A:** ________________ carry a bottle of water with you so you don't get thirsty?
   B: Good idea. It's really hot out here.

Show what you know!

1. **BRAINSTORM.** Discuss these situations. How would you offer or request help?
   - You work in a clothing factory. You see a co-worker using a sewing machine while wearing a long-sleeved sweater. Suggest that your co-worker take off her sweater.
   - You work in a warehouse. Your co-worker has had back problems, and she is unable to finish unpacking a shipment on time. You offer to help.
   - You are a construction worker. You forgot to bring your protective glasses to work. Ask your supervisor if you can borrow his extra pair of glasses.
   - You are a delivery driver. You don't feel well. Ask another driver to cover your shift for you.
2. **WRITE.** You have a problem at work. Write a message to your supervisor or co-worker asking for help. Use *could you* and *would you mind.*

   Hi Megan,

   My daughter is sick today, so I need to take off from work. Would you mind covering my shift for me?

I can use *could you, why don't you,* and *would you mind* to make polite requests. ☐ I need more practice. ☐

For more practice, go to MyEnglishLab.

Lesson 9

Writing

Write about ways to improve workplace safety

WRITING PROMPT: Think about potential safety-related problems at your workplace or school. What are some possible solutions to the problems? Write an email to a supervisor about a problem and suggest solutions.

1 STUDY THE MODEL

A ANALYZE. Read the model and Writing Skill. Then answer the questions.

To: trwilkins@dataaces.com
Subject: Suggestions to improve workplace safety

Hi Tracy,

I have identified a safety problem in our data-entry department. Many of our data-entry clerks have been injuring themselves on the job. They have developed carpal tunnel syndrome. This is happening because they type for seven-eight hours a day, which strains their wrists.

One solution to this problem is to replace all our keyboards with ergonomic keyboards (see below). These keyboards keep the typist's wrists and fingers in a more natural position. Another solution is to provide workshops on how to avoid carpal tunnel. These workshops would talk about the importance of stretching and taking frequent breaks.

These solutions may be expensive, but I think they could really improve workplace safety. Could we meet to discuss these ideas sometime soon?

Best,
Lola Herrera
Data-Entry Manager

Writing Skill: State problem, causes, and solutions

When you write about a problem, follow these steps:

1. identify the problem
2. explain the causes of the problem
3. suggest possible solutions

1. Underline the problem, circle the cause of the problem, and put a box around the solutions.
2. What is happening in the data-entry department, and why?
3. What two suggestions does the writer make to her supervisor?

B TAKE NOTES. Complete the outline with information from the model.

What is the problem?

Data-entry clerks are injuring themselves. They have developed ______

What is the cause of the problem?

______

What are two possible solutions to the problem?

1. Replace standard keyboards with ______
2. ______

2 PLAN YOUR WRITING

A **BRAINSTORM.** Discuss your ideas for the Writing Prompt with a partner.

B **ORGANIZE.** Use this outline to organize your ideas before writing.

What is the problem?

____

What is the cause of the problem?

____

____

What are two possible solutions to the problem?

1. ____

____

2. ____

____

3 WRITE

PROPOSE. Write an email to your supervisor describing a safety problem. Remember to identify the problem, explain its causes, and suggest at least two possible solutions. Use the model, the Writing Skill, and your ideas from Exercise 2 to help you.

4 CHECK YOUR WRITING

A **REVISE.** Use the Writing Checklist to review your writing. Make revisions as necessary.

B **COLLABORATE.** Read your writing with a partner. Use the checklist again to improve your writing.

WRITING CHECKLIST

- ☐ Did you identify a problem and explain its causes?
- ☐ Did you suggest two possible solutions to the problem?
- ☐ Did you use correct capitalization, punctuation, and spelling?

I can state problem, causes, and solutions. ☐ I need more practice. ☐

For more practice, go to MyEnglishLab.

Lesson 10

Soft Skills at Work

Take responsibility

1 MEET MARTA

Read about one of her workplace skills.

I take responsibility. For example, when I have a problem at work, I address it as quickly and completely as possible. I try to make sure that the issue is resolved.

2 MARTA'S PROBLEM

A **READ.** Write *T* (true) or *F* (false).

Marta was just hired as a manager at a shoe factory. During her first week, an employee fell off a tall ladder and hurt his back. Another employee got an electrical shock. Marta is worried that her workplace is unsafe. She gave a training to the employees on important OSHA policies and hung safety posters around the factory. However, Marta wants to do more. She wants to be sure her team is safe.

_____ **1.** Marta is worried because some employees have been hurt.

_____ **2.** Marta has given a safety training and hung OSHA safety posters.

_____ **3.** Marta knows that she has done all she can to protect her team.

B **ANALYZE.** What is Marta's problem?

____

____

3 MARTA'S SOLUTION

COLLABORATE. Marta takes responsibility. How does she improve safety at her factory? Explain your answer.

1. Marta hires a team to come check the factory's equipment and safety policies.
2. Marta tells her employees to let her know if they have problems with their equipment.
3. Marta gets rid of all the ladders at the factory.
4. Marta ____.

Show what you know!

1. **REFLECT.** How do you take responsibility at school, at work, or at home? Give an example.
2. **WRITE.** Write your example in your Skills Log.

   I take responsibility at work. For example, when we needed to update our safety policies, I reached out to OSHA to get a copy of their most recent inspection checklists.
3. **PRESENT.** Give a short presentation describing how you take responsibility.

I can give an example of how I take responsibility. ☐

Unit Review: Go back to page 185. Which unit goals can you check off?

11 Know the Law!

PREVIEW

Where are these people? What are they doing?

UNIT GOALS

- ☐ Identify misdemeanors
- ☐ Interpret Miranda rights and identify people in a courtroom
- ☐ Describe what happens in a courtroom
- ☐ Discuss traffic laws
- ☐ Write about different legal systems
- ☐ **Academic skill:** Break down long sentences
- ☐ **Writing skill:** Use signal words to compare and contrast
- ☐ **Workplace skill:** Be accountable

Lesson 1

Listening and Speaking

Identify misdemeanors

1 BEFORE YOU LISTEN

A **INTERPRET.** These signs warn against misdemeanors, or crimes that are not very serious. What does each sign mean?

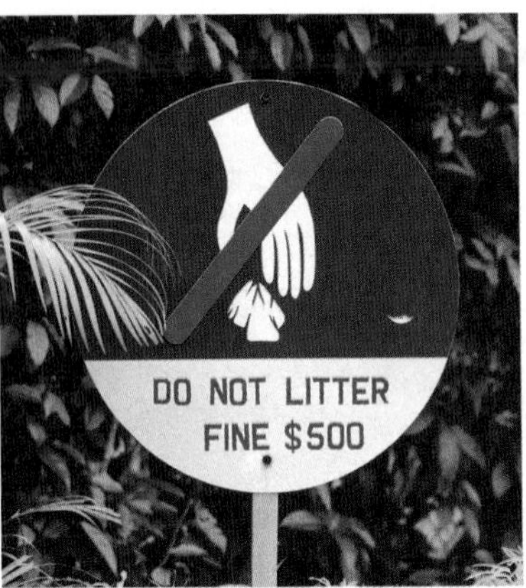

B **COMPARE.** Are the actions in the signs illegal in other countries? Give examples.

2 LISTEN

This podcast is from a series that gives career advice.

HAVE YOU EVER BEEN CONVICTED OF A CRIME?
○ No ○ Yes
If yes, explain number of conviction(s), nature of offense(s), and sentence(s) imposed.

A ▶ **LISTEN FOR MAIN IDEA.** What is the topic of the podcast?

B ▶ **LISTEN FOR DETAILS.** Listen again. Then write *T* (true) or *F* (false). Correct the false statements.

____ **1.** Making a late payment on a bill is a misdemeanor.

____ **2.** Writing a bad check is a misdemeanor.

____ **3.** Trespassing is an example of a felony.

____ **4.** Littering is an example of a misdemeanor.

____ **5.** Some applications ask about felonies only.

____ **6.** Most employers are concerned about parking tickets and speeding tickets.

____ **7.** The podcast guest tells the listeners to be truthful on job applications.

C **DISCUSS.** Why do you think employers ask about an applicant's criminal background? Do you think it's more important not to have a criminal record for some jobs than it is for others? Explain.

3 CONVERSATION

A **LISTEN AND READ. Then practice the conversation with a partner.**

A: What's wrong? You seem upset today.

B: It's my son. He rode the train without buying a ticket yesterday. The ticket was $2.00, but now we have to go to court and pay a $75 fine.

A: Oh, that's terrible! I'm sorry.

B: Paying the fine is bad enough, but I'm more worried about his criminal record. He's only seventeen. Getting a job will be difficult for him now, right?

A: No, I don't think so. Not paying a fare is a misdemeanor in some places, but in our city it's only an infraction.

B: What's an infraction?

A: It's a violation of a law, but it's not a serious crime. It's usually possible to pay a fine, and that's it. Infractions don't require jail time or community service, and they don't go on a criminal record.

B: Well, that's good news! Now I need to help him find a job so he can pay me back the $75!

B **ROLE-PLAY. Make a similar conversation. Then change roles.**

Student A: You are sitting on the front steps of your friend's apartment building, waiting for a taxi. Someone comes out of the building and asks you to leave. You refuse because you aren't doing anything wrong, and there is nowhere else to sit.

Student B: You own the building where Student A is sitting. You explain to Student A that it is illegal to trespass or loiter on private property. You tell him or her to leave.

C **EVALUATE. Which of the following misdemeanors do you think is most serious? Why?**

- Driving without a valid license or insurance
- Improper disposal of trash
- Disturbing the peace
- Deliberately damaging someone's property

____

____

____

I can identify misdemeanors. ☐ I need more practice. ☐

For more practice, go to MyEnglishLab.

Lesson 2

Grammar

Gerunds as subjects; *It* + infinitive

Gerunds as subjects	*It* + infinitive
Trespassing is a crime.	**It** is a crime **to trespass**.
Not lying on a job application is important.	**It** is important **not to lie** on a job application.
Getting a job will be difficult for my son.	**It** will be difficult for my son **to get** a job.

Grammar Watch

- A gerund can be the subject of a sentence. A gerund is singular and takes a singular verb.
- When a sentence has *it* as the subject and an infinitive later in the sentence, *it* has the same meaning as the infinitive. *It is a crime to trespass. (It = to trespass.)*
- Place *not* immediately in front of a gerund or infinitive to make it negative.

A **INVESTIGATE. Circle the gerunds used as subjects. Underline *it* used as the subject and double underline the infinitive that has the same meaning as *it.***

When Emma was 16 years old, she took a candy bar from a store without paying for it. Shoplifting is a misdemeanor. Now she is 22 and wants to apply for a job as a receptionist at an elementary school. It is hard to get a job at a school if you have a criminal record. Emma spoke to a lawyer about her problem. He told her that it's possible to expunge the misdemeanor from her record. Expunging a criminal record means the record is destroyed. Emma was young when she committed the crime, and it wasn't a very serious crime. Most importantly, she hasn't had any legal problems since then. For these reasons, her lawyer thinks it will not be difficult to get rid of her criminal record.

B **COMPLETE. Use the gerund or infinitive form of the verbs.**

A: I learned something new today. ___Not cleaning up___ **(not, clean up)** after your dog in the city is illegal. It was a difficult lesson for my friend ____________ **(learn)**. He was out walking his dog this morning. When he stopped to chat with a neighbor, his dog did what dogs do. When my friend started to walk away from the mess, a police officer gave him a ticket. The fine is $200!

B: It seems like a reasonable law to me. It's nice ____________ **(have)** clean streets. ____________ **(step)** in a dog's mess would be disgusting! It's not my job ____________ **(clean up)** after someone else's dog.

A: I agree with you, but it was still shocking ____________ **(hear)** how much the fine is.

Grammar

C **APPLY.** Write new sentences with the same meaning as the original sentence. Use a gerund as the subject.

1. It is illegal to write a bad check.
   Writing a bad check is illegal.
2. It is our civic duty to follow the laws of our society.
   ____
3. It is against the law in most states to text while driving.
   ____
4. It's illegal not to put your school-aged children in school.
   ____

D **APPLY.** Write new sentences with the same meaning as the original sentence. Use *it* plus an infinitive.

1. Learning about laws in different countries is interesting.
   It is interesting to learn about laws in different countries.
2. Taking a driving test for someone else is illegal.
   ____
3. Checking with your neighbors before you have a loud party is a good idea.
   ____
4. Not disposing of trash properly is a crime.
   ____

Show what you know!

1. **DISCUSS.** What are some laws that you think are surprising or unusual? What laws do you think are important? Why?
2. **WRITE.** List five or six laws that you think are important. Use a gerund or *it* plus an infinitive as subjects.

   1. Wearing a seatbelt is an important law. It can save lives.
   2. Keeping children secured in car safety seats is also important.
   3. It is our duty as parents to protect our children . . .

I can use gerunds as subjects and *it* + infinitive. ☐ I need more practice. ☐

For more practice, go to MyEnglishLab.

Workplace, Life, and Community Skills

Lesson 3 Understand the Miranda warning and know your rights

1 UNDERSTAND THE MIRANDA WARNING

Miranda Warning

Section 1
You have the right to remain silent.

Section 2
Anything you say can and will be used against you in a court of law.

Section 3
You have the right to an attorney.

Section 4
If you cannot afford an attorney, one will be provided for you.

Section 5
Do you understand the rights I have just read to you? With these rights in mind, do you wish to speak to me?

A **EXPLAIN.** In the U.S., every person has rights even if they are being arrested. If someone is being arrested, what rights does he or she have?

B **SCAN. THEN READ.** The Miranda warning is based on rights granted by the Constitution's Fifth Amendment. The Miranda warning is read to you by a police officer. In which section do the police ask questions for you to answer? After scanning, read the entire Miranda warning.

C **DEFINE KEY WORDS.** Find the words on the left in the Miranda warning. Match the words with their definitions.

_____ **1.** silent
_____ **2.** right
_____ **3.** attorney
_____ **4.** afford
_____ **5.** court
_____ **6.** Miranda warning

a. lawyer
b. not speaking, being quiet
c. a set of statements that must be read to a suspect before legal questioning
d. the place where legal matters are decided
e. have enough money to pay for
f. that which is due to everyone by the law

D **LOCATE DETAILS.** Circle the correct answers.

1. Who gives or reads the Miranda warning?
a. the suspect **b.** the police officer **c.** the victim

2. According to the Miranda warning, what is a suspect not required to do?
a. get arrested **b.** talk to a lawyer **c.** talk to the police

3. According to the Miranda warning, what will the government provide for free?
a. a phone call **b.** a lawyer **c.** transportation

4. How many questions do the police ask the suspect in Section 5 of the Miranda warning?
a. five **b.** three **c.** two

5. The Miranda warning is based on which amendment to the constitution?
a. First amendment **b.** Second amendment **c.** Fifth amendment

2 KNOW YOUR RIGHTS: HOME SEARCH

A Read the information about rights in the U.S.

B **SYNTHESIZE.** The article quotes several phrases to say in order to protect your rights. Underline those phrases and then write them out for yourself.

C **PROBLEM SOLVE.** Read the situation. Then discuss the question.

> Hassan lives in an apartment with his wife and children. His brother has recently come to visit from their country of origin. Two police officers are standing outside the door to the apartment and are asking to come in.

Hassan knows his rights. What does he do to protect these rights? Explain your answer.

a. Hassan opens the door. He immediately starts to record everything that he and the officers discuss.

b. Hassan knows that he shouldn't discuss anything about himself or his brother with law officials until he has talked to a lawyer. He tells the officers to wait while he calls his lawyer.

c. Hassan asks the officers for a search warrant. He states that he and his brother both have the right to remain silent and that they wish to speak to a lawyer.

d. Hassan ______________________________.

KNOW YOUR RIGHTS

The U.S. constitution protects the rights of individuals when interacting with officers of the law, such as police or immigration officers.

Officers may only enter your home or search your car with your permission or a valid search warrant. A valid warrant must be signed by a judge. It must describe in detail the area to be searched. Only if the officers have a valid warrant, do you have to allow them to enter.

You have the right to remain silent. Even when the official has a warrant to search your home, you do not have to answer any questions. It is important to exercise the right to silence because anything you say can be used against you. If you want to exercise your right to be silent, say, "I want to remain silent."

In any interaction with legal officials, it is important to remain calm. You can always first ask, "Am I free to go?" If the officials say 'yes,' leave calmly. If they say 'no,' ask, "Can you tell me why you are stopping me?"

If you are under arrest, you have the right to speak to a lawyer. Ask for one immediately by saying, "I want to talk to a lawyer."

Finally, record the details of any interaction with law officials as soon as possible. This will help you remember the interaction and help you protect your rights.

No matter your immigration or citizenship status, all individuals in the U.S. have certain rights under the Constitution. It is your duty to know and protect your rights.

D GO ONLINE.

1. **SEARCH.** Find information on what to do if you are stopped by the police in your car. Answer the questions.
   a. What is the name of the website? ______________________________
   b. What is one thing you should do? ______________________________
   c. What is one thing you should say? ______________________________
2. **COMPARE.** How is the information you found similar to the information found by another classmate? How is it different?

I understand the Miranda warning and know my rights. ☐ I need more practice. ☐

For more practice, go to MyEnglishLab.

Lesson 4

Listening and Speaking

Describe what happens in a courtroom

1 BEFORE YOU LISTEN

MAKE CONNECTIONS. Have you ever seen a TV courtroom show? Do you think these shows present courtrooms as they are in real life? Explain.

2 LISTEN

Lisa and Alex are watching TV.

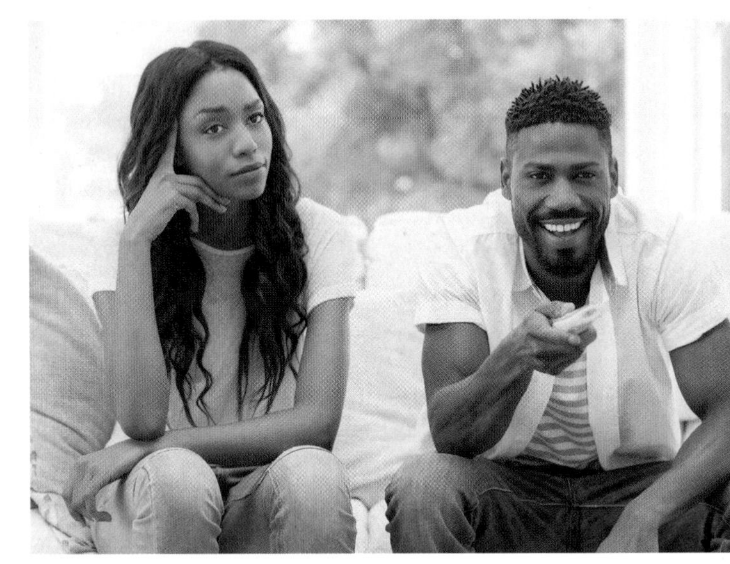

A ▶ **LISTEN FOR MAIN IDEA.** How does Lisa feel about TV courtroom shows?

B ▶ **LISTEN FOR DETAILS.** Listen again. Then circle the correct answers.

1. Alex thinks courtroom TV shows are about ____________.
   a. real law and justice
   b. bad relationships
   c. people complaining
2. Lisa thinks courtroom TV shows are about ____________.
   a. real cases
   b. made-up cases
   c. serious crimes
3. In the TV court case, the man borrowed money from his roommate to pay his ____________.
   a. rent
   b. car payment
   c. court fees
4. The man refused to pay his roommate back because ____________.
   a. he didn't have enough money
   b. he wanted to move
   c. they had a fight
5. The case reminded Lisa that ____________.
   a. she needs to make a car payment
   b. Alex owes her money
   c. she owes Alex money

C **REFLECT.** If you had to go to court, would you want the case to be shown on TV? Why or why not?

____

____

Listening and Speaking

3 PRONUNCIATION

A **PRACTICE.** Listen. Then listen again and repeat.

The program **is** watched by millions of people.

The cases **are** heard by judges.

The roof **was** damaged.

I heard you **were** involved in a court case.

Pronouncing *is, are, was, were*

The verbs *is, are, was,* and *were* are usually unstressed and have a weak pronunciation when another word comes after them. The verb is said quickly and quietly.

B **APPLY.** Listen. Circle the word you hear. Then listen again to check your answers.

1.	**a.** is	**b.** are	**c.** was	**d.** were
2.	**a.** is	**b.** are	**c.** was	**d.** were
3.	**a.** is	**b.** are	**c.** was	**d.** were
4.	**a.** is	**b.** are	**c.** was	**d.** were
5.	**a.** is	**b.** are	**c.** was	**d.** were

4 CONVERSATION

A **LISTEN AND READ.** Then practice the conversation with a partner.

A: I heard you were involved in a court case recently. What happened?

B: Well, I painted a woman's house last summer. While I was there, some landscapers were working in the neighbor's yard. They cut down a tree, and it fell on the woman's roof.

A: Uh-oh . . .

B: Uh-oh is right! The roof was damaged pretty badly. I saw the whole thing. The woman took the landscapers to small claims court. She wanted them to pay for the repairs to the roof.

A: So you were called as a witness during the trial?

B: Yes. I told the judge what happened, and the woman won the case.

A: It's a good thing you were there!

B **PRESENT.** Have you ever witnessed a crime or been involved in a legal dispute?

- If yes, were you called to court as a witness? What happened?
- If no, talk about a court case that you read or heard about. Who were the witnesses? What did they say?
- Did you agree or disagree with the outcome? Why?

I can describe what happens in a courtroom. ☐ I need more practice. ☐

For more practice, go to MyEnglishLab.

Lesson 5

Grammar

Passives: simple present and simple past

Passive: Simple present		
This show	**is watched**	all over the country.
These court cases	**are heard**	by judges on TV.

Passive: Simple past		
The case	**was decided**	by a judge.
	was heard	by a jury.
The roof	**was damaged**	pretty badly.

Grammar Watch

- You usually use the active voice in English:
  *The police **asked** Mr. Carlson to describe the crime scene.*
- Use the passive voice when you don't know who the agent (the person or thing that did the action) is, or when you don't want to emphasize the agent:
  *Mr. Carlson **was asked** to appear as a witness.*
- Use *by* with the passive if you mention the agent:
  *Curtis was questioned **by the lawyer** for the defense.*
- Do not mention the agent if the agent is obvious:
  A tree fell on the woman's roof. The roof was damaged pretty badly.

A **INVESTIGATE.** Is the sentence active or passive? Write *A* (active) or *P* (passive).

__P__ **1.** The defendant was arrested by the police chief.

____ **2.** The police told the defendant he had the right to remain silent.

____ **3.** The defendant was allowed to post bail.

____ **4.** The defendant was released by the judge.

____ **5.** The defendant entered a plea of "not guilty."

____ **6.** The case was dismissed because of lack of evidence.

Grammar

B **COMPLETE.** Use the simple present passive.

Criminal trials ___are heard___ (heard) by a jury of twelve people. The defendant ______________ (question) by the prosecutor and the defense attorney. Then the witnesses ______________ (question). Evidence, such as photos and documents, ______________ (show) to the jury. The case ______________ (discuss) by the jurors outside the courtroom. During the trial, jurors ______________ (not/allow) to read, watch, or listen to stories about the trial. The outcome ______________ (decide) by the jury.

C **COMPLETE.** Use the simple past passive.

Sorry I didn't call you yesterday. I ___was called___ (call) for jury duty. The case was unbelievable. A woman was suing the city because she broke her ankle when she tripped over a bump in the sidewalk. She wanted the city to pay for her medical expenses. But when she ______________ (question) in court, her story didn't make sense. When she ______________ (ask) where she was when she tripped, she couldn't remember. Then her doctor ______________ (call) to the stand. He said that she told him that she had fallen down the stairs in her house! The case ______________ (end) soon after, and all the jurors ______________ (dismiss).

Show what you know!

1. **DISCUSS.** Describe a court case you read or heard about. Use the active and passive voice. Ask and answer the questions.
   - Who was accused, and what was the person accused of?
   - Was the case decided by a jury or a judge?
   - What was the verdict? Was the defendant found guilty or not guilty?

2. **WRITE.** Summarize that court case. Use passives.

   I heard about an interesting court case. A restaurant was sued by a customer who spilled some hot coffee. Her hand was badly burned . . .

I can use passives in the simple present and simple past. ☐ I need more practice. ☐

For more practice, go to MyEnglishLab.

Lesson 6

Reading

Read about DNA evidence

1 BEFORE YOU READ

A **DISCUSS.** What kinds of evidence do police and lawyers use to prove that criminals are guilty of crimes?

B **PREDICT.** Skim the article. What is it about?

Academic Skill: Break down long sentences

Break long sentences into smaller "chunks" to make them easier to understand. One way to do this is to look for punctuation such as commas or connecting words like *when, before, after, although,* and *if.*

2 READ

LISTEN AND READ.

DNA and the Law

October 4th, 2011, was a happy day for Michael Morton. On that day, he was released from the prison where he had spent the last 25 years. He should never have been put there in the first place. Back in 1986, Morton had been convicted of murdering his wife. But new DNA evidence revealed that another man was guilty of the crime.

The Innocence Project was responsible for Morton's release. They requested additional DNA testing on evidence from the crime scene. They were confident that the evidence would exonerate Morton. They were correct.

Sadly, Michael Morton is not alone. Many prisoners are innocent of the crimes they have been sent to prison for. Why were these prisoners wrongfully convicted? Reasons can include eyewitness mistakes, false confessions, and poor legal defense. The Innocence Project has made it their mission to free these prisoners through DNA testing. To date, they have helped to exonerate 354 people.

How does DNA testing work? DNA is genetic material from the body. It is found in our blood, skin, and saliva. No two people have the exact same DNA. After a crime occurs, police collect DNA samples, such as blood, from the crime scene. Then they use a computer to compare this DNA to DNA samples from an FBI database. Sometimes the DNA in the evidence matches someone's DNA from the database. If that happens, that person is probably guilty of the crime.

Cases like Morton's have made DNA testing seem like a magical tool to identify guilty criminals. But the truth is more complicated than that. Police have limited time and money to solve cases. They see DNA evidence as a quick and easy way to prove guilt. However, it has recently become clear that DNA evidence can sometimes be misleading. When police find DNA evidence, they may not thoroughly investigate other aspects of the crime. Human errors of various kinds can also make DNA tests give inaccurate results. Even when tests identify a person's DNA correctly, that person may not be guilty of the crime. All this means that lawyers can now successfully call DNA evidence into question in court.

DNA testing is still the most accurate way we have to prove that someone is guilty or innocent of a crime. Nobody denies this. However, law enforcement officials are now making an effort to use this powerful tool more carefully.

3 CLOSE READING

A **IDENTIFY.** What is the main idea?

a. Michael Morton was freed from prison because DNA testing proved that he did not commit the crime he had been jailed for.
b. The Innocence Project has freed 354 wrongfully convicted people through DNA testing.
c. DNA testing is the best way to prove either guilt or innocence, but the police need to use it carefully.

B CITE EVIDENCE. Answer the questions. Where is the information located? **Lines**

1. What happened on October 4th, 2011, and why? ______
   a. Michael Morton was arrested.
   b. Michael Morton was released from the prison.
2. What is the Innocence Project trying to do? ______
   a. The Innocence Project is trying to use DNA evidence to get wrongfully convicted prisoners released.
   b. The Innocence Project is trying to help people realize that DNA testing can be inaccurate.
3. How do police test DNA after a crime occurs? ______
   a. They collect DNA samples at the crime and compare the DNA to a database.
   b. They collect DNA samples from all suspects.
4. Why is DNA evidence sometimes misleading? ______
   a. The DNA database was faulty.
   b. Human error is always possible.
5. Find this sentence in the article: *On that day, he was released from the prison where he had spent the last 25 years.* ______
   What is the correct way to break it into chunks?
   a. On that day, / he was released from the prison / where he had spent the last 25 years.
   b. On that day, he / was released / from the prison where he had spent / the last 25 years.
6. Find this sentence in the article: *Back in 1986, Morton had been convicted of murdering his wife.* ______
   What is the correct way to break it into chunks?
   a. Back / in 1986, Morton / had been convicted of murdering / his wife.
   b. Back in 1986, / Morton had been convicted / of murdering his wife.

C INTERPRET VOCABULARY. Complete the sentences.

1. In the context of line 5, the word *convicted* means _____.
   a. accused b. found guilty
2. In the context of line 11, the phrase *exonerate Morton* means _____.
   a. prove Morton innocent b. suggest that Morton is innocent
3. In the context of line 17, the word *confessions* means _____.
   a. statements in which a person admits that he or she has done something wrong
   b. statements in which a person accuses another person of doing something wrong
4. In the context of line 27, the word *database* means _____.
   a. DNA samples in a laboratory b. information in a computer system
5. In the context of line 49, the phrase *making an effort to* means _____.
   a. trying to b. able to

D SUMMARIZE. What are the most important ideas in the article?

Show what you know!

1. **COLLABORATE.** How do law enforcement officials use DNA testing to investigate crimes and convict criminals? What does the article say about the benefits and drawbacks of DNA testing? Do you agree?

2. **WRITE.** Do you think DNA testing has improved the fairness of our legal system or not? Give reasons for your opinion.

   I think DNA testing has improved the fairness of our legal system because it is more accurate than confessions and eyewitnesses. However, . . .

I can break down long sentences. ☐ I need more practice. ☐

To read more, go to MyEnglishLab.

Lesson 7

Listening and Speaking

Discuss traffic laws

1 BEFORE YOU LISTEN

A **LIST.** Make a list of all the traffic laws you can think of. What can happen if you break traffic laws?

B **RECALL.** Read the words and their definitions. Which words have you heard before?

contest (verb): to say formally that you do not think something is right or fair

fine (noun): money you have to pay as a punishment for breaking the law

be in the right (verb phrase): not to have broken the law or done something wrong

points on a license (noun phrase): penalties you receive for traffic violations; If you get too many points, you may lose your license.

run a stop sign (verb phrase): to drive past a stop sign without stopping (a traffic violation)

ticket (noun): a printed note saying that you must pay money because you have done something illegal while driving or parking your car

traffic school (noun): a course in traffic safety and safe driving practices

2 LISTEN

A ▶ **LISTEN FOR MAIN IDEA.** What topic is the former traffic-court judge answering questions about?

____

B ▶ **LISTEN FOR DETAILS.** Listen again. Write *T* (true) or *F* (false). Correct the false statements.

__T__ **1.** Caller 1 got a ticket because she didn't stop for a stop sign.

_____ **2.** A branch was covering the stop sign.

_____ **3.** The judge thinks that Caller 1 should contest the ticket.

_____ **4.** The judge thinks that if Caller 1 shows a picture of the sign, she won't have to pay the fine.

_____ **5.** It is impossible for the second caller to have the points on his license removed.

_____ **6.** The former judge says it is not difficult to sign up for traffic school.

C **STATE AN OPINION.** Should people be required to go to traffic school if they have committed traffic violations? Why or why not?

____

____

3 PRONUNCIATION

Short unstressed words

Words like *a, the, at, of, to,* and *for* are usually unstressed and have a weak pronunciation, unless they are at the end of the sentence. The vowel sound is quiet and short.

A ▶ **PRACTICE.** **Listen. Then listen again and repeat.**

Look **at** this.
Take **a** picture **of the** sign.
I got **a** ticket **for** running **a** stop sign.
BUT
How much is it **for**?

B ▶ **APPLY.** **Listen. Circle the word that is unstressed and pronounced quickly and weakly. Then listen again to check your answers.**

1. I got (a) ticket last night.
2. My ticket is for speeding.
3. I didn't see the speed limit sign.
4. I'll go to court next Monday.
5. I'll be there at 9:00 A.M.

4 CONVERSATION

A ▶ **LISTEN AND READ.** **Then practice the conversation with a partner.**

A: Look at this! I got a parking ticket!

B: Oh, no. How much is it for?

A: One hundred bucks! But why did they give me a ticket? I didn't get a ticket last night even though I parked in exactly the same spot!

B: Look! Your car is the only one on this side of the street.

A: You're right!

B: Let's see—look at this sign. It says that the city sweeps this side of the street every Tuesday morning. That's why everyone moved their cars to the other side of the street last night—except you!

A: That explains why I got the ticket! My car was blocking the street sweeping truck.

B **ROLE-PLAY.** **Make a similar conversation. Then change roles.**

Student A: You got a speeding ticket. A camera took a picture of you while you were speeding by a school. You don't understand why you got the ticket, because you never drive above the regular speed limit.

Student B: Tell Student A that he or she was in a school zone and got a ticket for driving too fast when children were in the area. Explain the posted speed limit shown at the right.

C **MAKE CONNECTIONS.** **Sometimes the signs stating traffic laws are hard to understand. Have you ever had trouble understanding a traffic sign? Describe the sign.**

I can discuss traffic laws. ☐ I need more practice. ☐

For more practice, go to MyEnglishLab.

Lesson **8**

Grammar

Adverb clauses of condition and contrast

Adverb clause (condition/contrast)	Main clause (result)
As long as you **have** a safe driving record,	you **can get** a good insurance rate.
Even if you **are** mad at another driver,	you **shouldn't honk** your horn.
Even though I **parked** in the same spot,	I **got** a ticket.

Grammar Watch

- Use *as long as* to show that the conditions in the clause are needed for something to happen.
- Use *even if* to show that the condition in the clause does not matter; the result does not change.
- Use *even though* when there is a surprising or unexpected contrast between the information in the two clauses.
- An adverb clause can start or end a sentence. Use a comma after the adverb clause only when it starts the sentence.

A INVESTIGATE. Underline the adverb clauses of condition or contrast.

In the United States, it is generally legal to make a right turn even if you are at a red light. You must make a complete stop first. As long as there are no pedestrians or cars coming, you can make a right turn. You can never make a left turn at a red light even if there are no other cars on the road. Even though right turns are generally legal, you should check for signs at the traffic light. You cannot make a right or left turn when there is a sign stating "No turn on red."

B DECIDE. Read the first statement. Write *T* (true) or *F* (false) for each of the following statements.

1. As long as you have a valid driver's license, you are allowed to drive anywhere in the country.

_____ **a.** You don't need a valid driver's license to drive anywhere in the country.

_____ **b.** You are allowed to drive anywhere in the country if you have a valid driver's license.

2. Even though she obeyed all the traffic laws, she had an accident.

_____ **a.** She obeyed all the traffic laws, but she had an accident anyway.

_____ **b.** She didn't obey all the traffic laws; that's why she had an accident.

3. Even if the speed limit is high, many drivers slow down in bad weather.

_____ **a.** Many drivers like to drive at a slower speed when the weather is bad.

_____ **b.** Many drivers like to drive at a higher speed when the weather is bad.

C **COMPLETE.** Use the phrases in the box. Use each phrase twice.

as long as   even if   even though

1. ________________ you obey the traffic laws in your state, you won't get a traffic ticket.
2. ________________ her headlights didn't work, she drove her car at night. But then she got a ticket.
3. The police officer gave the couple a ticket ________________ they said that they would buy a car seat for their baby as soon as possible.
4. You shouldn't honk your horn in a traffic jam ________________ you are really late for an appointment.
5. ________________ you have a valid driver's license, you can drive in any state.
6. ________________ you are a good driver, you should still take the defensive driving course.

D **APPLY.** Complete the sentences with your own ideas.

1. Even if everyone obeyed the traffic laws, ________________________________.
2. Even if an intersection doesn't have a traffic light, ________________________________.
3. As long as you drive carefully, ________________________________.
4. As long as you wear your seat belt, ________________________________.
5. Even though the light was red, ________________________________.
6. Even though she had never driven, ________________________________.

Show what you know!

1. **DECIDE.** Discuss the questions.
   1. Should drivers be required to drive at lower speeds if the weather is bad?
   2. Should people below the age of 16 be permitted to drive?
   3. Should older people be allowed to drive as long as they pass vision and driving tests?

2. **WRITE.** Choose one of the three topics. Write a short paragraph expressing your opinion. Use adverb clauses of condition and contrast.

   I think older people should be allowed to drive as long as they can pass a vision and driving test. Someone can still be a good driver even if he or she is 90 years old . . .

I can use adverb clauses of condition and contrast. ☐   I need more practice. ☐

For more practice, go to MyEnglishLab.

Lesson **9**

Writing

Write about different legal systems

WRITING PROMPT: Think about traffic laws or another type of law in two different countries. What are the similarities between the laws in these countries? What are the differences? Write a paragraph comparing the laws.

1 STUDY THE MODEL

A **ANALYZE.** Read the model and Writing Skill. Then answer the questions.

U.S. Freeways versus German Autobahns

How do major roads in the United States compare with those in Germany? The most famous difference between American freeways and German autobahns is that on freeways, there are speed limits that vary by state. In contrast, on the autobahn, there is no speed limit in certain sections.

On both freeways and autobahns, drivers are supposed to pass other cars in the left lane. Similarly, on both types of roads, tailgating (driving very close behind another vehicle) is against the law because this can cause accidents. However, in Germany, both these laws are much more strictly enforced than in the United States.

Writing Skill: Use signal words to compare and contrast

When comparing and contrasting two things, use words such as *similar, similarly, both,* and *like* to signal similarities and words such as *but, in contrast,* and *however* to signal differences.

1. Underline the words the writer uses to signal similarities and circle the words the writer uses to signal differences.
2. What are some similarities between freeways and autobahns?
3. What are some differences between freeways and autobahns?

B **TAKE NOTES.** Complete the chart with information from the model.

Freeway laws versus Autobahn laws	
Similarities	**Differences**
Drivers are supposed to pass ________________.	There are speed limits ________________, but there are no speed limits ________________.
________________ against the law.	Laws about passing on the left are ________________ on the autobahn.
	Laws against ________________.

2 PLAN YOUR WRITING

A **BRAINSTORM.** Discuss your ideas for the Writing Prompt with a partner.

B **ORGANIZE.** Use this chart to organize your ideas before writing.

Topic: ______________________________	
Similarities	Differences

3 WRITE

COMPARE. Write a paragraph about laws in two different countries. Remember to compare and contrast the laws using words to signal similarities and differences. Use the model, the Writing Skill, and your ideas from Exercise 2 to help you.

4 CHECK YOUR WRITING

A **REVISE.** Use the Writing Checklist to review your writing. Make revisions as necessary.

B **COLLABORATE.** Read your writing with a partner. Use the checklist again to improve your writing.

WRITING CHECKLIST

- ☐ Did you compare and contrast laws in two different countries?
- ☐ Did you describe similarities and differences between the laws?
- ☐ Did you use words to signal similarities and differences?
- ☐ Did you use correct capitalization, punctuation, and spelling?

I can use signal words to compare and contrast. ☐ I need more practice. ☐

For more practice, go to MyEnglishLab.

Lesson **10**

Soft Skills at Work

Be accountable

1 MEET TRUNG

Read about one of his workplace skills.

I am accountable. For example, I take ownership for my team's work, including their mistakes.

2 TRUNG'S PROBLEM

A READ. Write *T* (true) or *F* (false).

Trung is the head of the Human Resources department at his company. A former employee is filing a lawsuit against the company for breaking a law. Trung knows that one of his managers made a mistake in following the law. Trung is worried his managers do not understand employment laws and how to follow them.

_____ **1.** Trung is filing a lawsuit against his company for breaking a law.
_____ **2.** Trung believes that one of his managers broke the law.
_____ **3.** Trung is worried that his team doesn't know how to follow employment laws.

B ANALYZE. What is Trung's problem?

____

____

3 TRUNG'S SOLUTION

A COLLABORATE. Trung is accountable. What does he do about the lawsuit? Explain your answer.

1. Trung brings the managers together to tell them who made the mistake.
2. Trung brings the managers together to tell them they will get training so they better understand the employment laws better.
3. Trung convinces the former employee not to file a lawsuit.
4. Trung ____.

B ROLE-PLAY. Role-play Trung's conversation with his team of managers.

Show what you know!

1. **REFLECT.** How are you accountable at school, at work, or at home? Give an example.
2. **WRITE.** Write your example in your Skills Log.

   I am accountable at work. I take ownership for my mistakes. Then I can focus on preventing similar mistakes in the future.
3. **PRESENT.** Give a short presentation describing how you are accountable.

I can give an example from my life of being accountable. ☐

Unit Review: Go back to page 205. Which unit goals can you check off?

12 Saving and Spending

PREVIEW

Where are the people? What are they doing?

UNIT GOALS

- ☐ Describe banking services
- ☐ Prepare a monthly budget
- ☐ Learn about tax forms and interpret a W-2 form
- ☐ Talk about dreams for the future
- ☐ Write about a worthwhile charity
- ☐ **Academic skill:** Summarize
- ☐ **Writing skill:** State main idea and supporting details
- ☐ **Workplace skill:** Take initiative

Lesson **1**

Listening and Speaking

Describe banking services

1 BEFORE YOU LISTEN

A **MAKE CONNECTIONS.** Do you use an app for mobile banking? What banking services do you use online? What banking services do you go to the bank for?

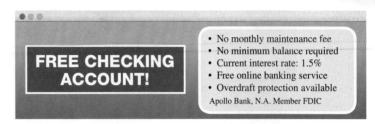

FREE CHECKING ACCOUNT!

- No monthly maintenance fee
- No minimum balance required
- Current interest rate: 1.5%
- Free online banking service
- Overdraft protection available

Apollo Bank, N.A. Member FDIC

B **EXPLAIN.** Discuss this online advertisement for a checking account. What does each line mean? Discuss any unfamiliar vocabulary.

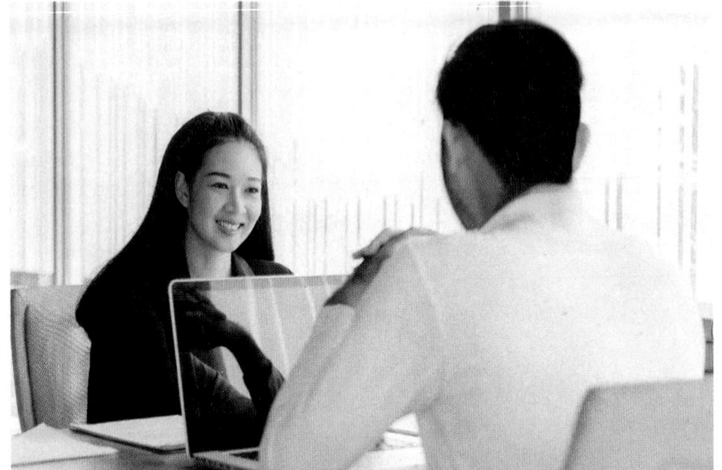

2 LISTEN

The customer service officer at Apollo Bank is talking to a customer.

A ▶ **LISTEN FOR MAIN IDEA.** What kind of account does the customer decide to open? Why?

B ▶ **LISTEN FOR DETAILS.** Listen again. Write *T* (true) or *F* (false). Correct the false statements.

_____ **1.** The MyMoney account has a good interest rate.

_____ **2.** A MyMoney account requires a minimum balance of $1,000.

_____ **3.** There is a free checking account, but it doesn't pay interest.

_____ **4.** The interest-free checking has a maintenance fee of $30 per month.

_____ **5.** If the customer gets overdraft protection, she will have to pay a fee if she uses the service.

_____ **6.** The customer thinks she will make a lot of overdrafts.

C **REFLECT.** Would you open an account at Apollo Bank? Which account would work best for you? Explain.

____

____

D **PRESENT.** Describe the banking services that you typically use. Which of those services are most important to you? Why?

3 PRONUNCIATION

A ▶ **PRACTICE.** **Listen. Then listen again and repeat.**

password **check**ing account **cred**it card **main**tenance fee

Compound words

When two words function together as one word, they form a compound word. You usually stress the first word in a compound word.

B ▶ **APPLY.** **Underline the compound noun in each sentence. Put a dot (•) over the stressed syllable. Then listen again to check your answers.**

1. I'm thinking about opening a savings account.
2. I looked at the website for my bank.
3. One of their accounts has an interest rate of 3%.
4. You have to pay a service fee if your balance is less than $1,000.

4 CONVERSATION

The customer service officer and the customer are finishing their conversation at the bank.

A ▶ **LISTEN AND READ.** **Then practice the conversation with a partner.**

A: OK, you're all set! Do you have any questions?

B: Actually, I do. Can I pay my bills online?

A: Definitely. You can even set up automatic payments for your bills. You can also check your account balance at any time.

B: Really? That sounds great. But is it safe?

A: Yes. Our website is secure, and you'll create your own password, so no one else can access your account.

B: Great. The online option really sounds like the best one for me.

B **ROLE-PLAY.** **Make a similar conversation. Then change roles.**

Student A: You want to open a savings account. Ask the customer service officer about the options for savings accounts.

Student B: You are a customer service officer. A customer wants to open a savings account. Tell the customer about two different options. The SaveMore account has a 2.25% interest rate. There is a minimum balance requirement of $500. The regular savings account offers a 1.2% interest rate. You can open an account with as little as $25. There is no minimum balance requirement.

I can describe banking services. ☐ I need more practice. ☐

For more practice, go to MyEnglishLab.

Lesson 2

Grammar

Articles: *a, an, the,* no article (Ø)

Not Specific	Indefinite article	Singular count nouns
I'd like to open	a	**checking account**.
Please talk to	an	**assistant**.
Not Specific	**No article**	**Plural count nouns / Non-count nouns**
I won't have a problem with	Ø	**overdrafts**.
You don't earn		**interest**.
Specific	**Definite article**	**Singular or plural count and non-count nouns**
The bank replaced	the	**debit card** I lost.
The assistant told me about		**accounts** this bank offers.
The assistant gave us		**information** we wanted.

Grammar Watch

- Use the indefinite article with singular count nouns that are not specific.
- Do not use any article with plural count nouns or non-count nouns that are not specific.
- Use the definite article with singular count, plural count, or non-count nouns that are specific for you and your audience.
- Also use the definite article when you mention a person, place, or thing for the second time:

  *Please talk to **an** assistant. **The** assistant at that desk will help you.*

A **INVESTIGATE.** If the noun phrase has an article, underline the article and the noun phrase. Circle the noun phrases without articles.

What's the difference between debit cards and credit cards?

- When you use a debit card, you take out money from your bank account when you buy something. When you use a credit card, you borrow the money you spend from a credit card company or bank.
- Debit cards are easier to get than credit cards. Nowadays, when you open an account, the credit card company gives you a debit card.
- Most credit cards have very high interest rates. The credit card company charges you a monthly fee, or finance charge, for any unpaid balance.

Money Tip: Use a debit card for smaller purchases, like at the supermarket. Use a credit card for bigger purchases. But whichever card you use, make sure you don't spend too much!

B DETERMINE. Complete this advertisement. Cross out the incorrect words. (Ø means no article is necessary.)

So you want start **a / the** business. Congratulations! But where are you going to get **the / Ø** money you need? At Monrovia Bank, we can help you.

- Do you want to buy **a / the** car or truck for your business? Ask about our vehicle loans.
- Do you need **the / Ø** equipment, such as **the / Ø** appliances, tools, or computers? Our equipment loan may be **the / Ø** loan for you.
- Do you need to buy **a / Ø** real estate? With our real estate loans, you can build **a / the** new building or remodel **an / the** old building.

Contact our loan officers at www.monroviabank.com or call 1-800-555-3000 today!

C COMPLETE. Use *a, an, the,* or Ø. More than one answer may be possible.

________ Houses are expensive. Most people have to borrow ________ money if they want to buy ________ house, but ________ banks don't give ________ home loans to everyone. To get approved for ________ home loan, you need to show ________ bank that you have ________ job. You have a better chance of getting ________ loan if you have had ________ job for at least two years. You also need to have enough ________ savings to pay for part of ________ house, and you need ________ good credit. To check people's credit, ________ banks look at things like ________ credit card payments and bill payments. If you have a lot of ________ debt and your credit is bad, you should spend less and pay your bills on time. Try to make your credit good before you fill out ________ application for a loan.

Show what you know!

1. **ANALYZE.** Discuss the bank services below. Which services are easy to get? Which ones are more difficult to get? Explain why.

   business loan   checking account   debit card   mortgage   savings account

2. **WRITE.** Write a paragraph explaining how to get one of the bank services in Exercise 1.

   Getting a debit card is easy. When you apply for a checking account, most banks will automatically give you a debit card.

I can use articles: *a, an, the,* no article (Ø). ☐   I need more practice. ☐

For more practice, go to MyEnglishLab.

Lesson 3

Reading

Read about financing a business

1 BEFORE YOU READ

A **DISCUSS.** If you were starting a business, what type of company or service would you choose? Where would you get the money to start your business?

B **PREDICT.** Skim the article. What is it about?

Academic Skill: Summarize

Write a summary to show that you understand what you've read. Include the main idea and the most important information that supports the main idea.

2 READ

Listen and read.

Financing a $mall Business

Too many small businesses crash and burn because they run out of money. So, if you are starting a small business, make sure that you finance it properly. You need to figure out not only how much money your business will need, but where to get that money.

To calculate how much your business will need, look at two kinds of costs. The first is one-time start-up costs. These are costs you pay once, such as fees for licenses and permits, equipment, and so on. The second is ongoing expenses. These include rent, utilities, and employee salaries. You will need enough money to cover these expenses every month until your business starts to make a profit.

Next, figure out where you will get the money to cover these costs. You can save some or all of the money yourself. You can also ask for money from friends and family. But keep in mind that your relationships with these people may suffer if your business fails.

Many small business owners choose to apply for a bank loan. When you borrow money from a bank, you have to pay it back in a certain time frame with interest added on. Go to different banks and compare the loans they offer. Check payment schedules and interest rates. Choose a trustworthy bank that won't ask you to pay back more than you can afford each month.

The bank you choose will also require certain things from you. You'll have to submit an application for a loan, along with a detailed business plan. The business plan should include financial statements, an analysis of the market, and proof of collateral. (Collateral is what you promise to give the bank if you can't pay back the loan.) Banks lend to businesses that they think will be able to pay them back. Your plan should show that your business will probably be successful and profitable because you have put a lot of thought into it.

These are just a few of the ways you can get funding for your small business. Whichever method you choose, make sure that you don't bite off more than you can chew. With good planning, you'll be able to cover all your costs and keep your business in the black. Good luck!

WHERE THE MONEY COMES FROM

- 77 percent of small businesses rely on personal savings in the beginning.
- 82 percent of start-up funds for small businesses come from the entrepreneur's personal savings, or from family and friends.

Source: Small Business Trends

3 CLOSE READING

A **IDENTIFY.** What is the main idea?

a. Small business owners need to figure out how much money they need and then finance their businesses carefully.
b. Many small business owners use their own money or borrow money from family or friends to run their businesses.
c. If you don't write a good business plan and submit it with your loan application, the bank probably won't approve your loan.

B **CITE EVIDENCE.** Complete the sentences. Where is the information located? **Lines**

1. A good summary of the second paragraph in the article is: _____. _______
   a. One-time start-up costs include fees for licenses and permits, and equipment
   b. It is important to calculate both one-time start-up costs and ongoing expenses
   c. Ongoing expenses include costs like rent, utilities, and employee salaries
2. One possible disadvantage of borrowing money from your family is _____. _______
   a. your family may ask you to pay back more money than you can afford every month
   b. your family will probably ask you to fill out a loan application and show them a business plan
   c. you may start fighting with your family if the business fails and they lose their money
3. Most small businesses rely on the owner's personal savings, but _____ of businesses are **not** funded by personal savings. _______
   a. 77% b. 82% c. 23%
4. You should check different banks before you apply for a loan because _____. _______
   a. different banks offer different payment schedules and interest rates
   b. most banks are not trustworthy and will try to cheat you
   c. you should apply for many loans so you will have lots of money for your business
5. A good summary of the fifth paragraph in the article is: _____. _______
   a. A good business plan tries to show reasons why the business will be successful and profitable
   b. If you want a loan, you have to prove that you have property that you can give the bank if you can't pay back the loan
   c. Before banks lend you money, they will ask you to submit a loan application and a good business plan

C **INTERPRET VOCABULARY.** Complete the sentences.

1. In the context of line 2, the phrase *run out of* means _____.
   a. use up all their b. escape from
2. In the context of line 5, the phrase *figure out* means _____.
   a. ask other people b. decide after you think about
3. In the context of line 38, the word *submit* means _____.
   a. hand in b. obey
4. In the context of line 41, the phrase *analysis of* means _____.
   a. careful study of b. list of questions about
5. In the context of line 48, the word *profitable* means _____.
   a. good at making a great product that people like b. good at making more money than you spend

D **SUMMARIZE.** What are the most important ideas in the article?

Show what you know!

1. **COLLABORATE.** Which ways to finance a small business does the article describe? What other ways can you think of? What do you think the best way to finance a small business is?
2. **WRITE.** Imagine that you are going to start a small business. Describe the steps you will take to finance it.

I am going to open a restaurant. First, I will borrow money from my parents and . . .

I can summarize. ☐ I need more practice. ☐

To read more, go to MyEnglishLab.

Lesson 4

Listening and Speaking

Prepare a monthly budget

1 BEFORE YOU LISTEN

A **MAKE CONNECTIONS.** How good are you at managing your money? How do you track how much money you earn and spend every month?

B **ANALYZE.** This budget worksheet shows a couple's income and their expenses. What is *income*? Which expenses are *fixed*? Which are *variable*? Explain how these two kinds of expenses are different.

INCOME		EXPENSES	
		FIXED EXPENSES	
Angela's job	$2200/month	Rent	$1400/month
		Bus fare	$120/month
Ricardo's job	$2000/month	VARIABLE EXPENSES	
		Food	$700/month
		Utilities	$300/month
		Clothing	$100/month

C **LIST.** What *fixed expenses* are in your budget? What *variable expenses* are in your budget? Make two lists.

2 LISTEN

A financial expert is giving advice to a listener on the show *MoneyWise.*

A ▶ **LISTEN FOR MAIN IDEA.** What is the caller's problem?

B ▶ **LISTEN FOR DETAILS.** Listen again. Write *T* (true) or *F* (false). Correct the false statements.

F 1. The caller wants to ~~take out a personal loan~~ pay off his debt.

____ 2. The caller owes a total of about $20,000.

____ 3. The interest rate on the caller's credit cards varies from just under 9 percent to 18 percent.

____ 4. Patricia tells the caller to ask the credit card company to reduce his interest rate.

____ 5. Patricia tells the caller to increase his monthly payment by fifty dollars.

____ 6. Patricia tells the caller to get another job in order to earn more money to pay off his debt.

3 CONVERSATION

A **LISTEN AND READ.** Then practice the conversation with a partner.

A: Pablo, do you want to go out this weekend?

B: I can't. I'm trying to cut expenses.

A: Seriously? But you have a good job.

B: True, but I have to watch my money because I have many bills to pay.

A: Don't you keep a budget?

B: No, not really. I just try to make sure I have enough to pay the bills.

A: Well, if you make a list of your regular expenses, you'll know exactly how much money you have for other things.

B: That makes sense. And if I know exactly how much money I have, I won't worry so much all the time.

B **ROLE-PLAY.** Make a similar conversation. Then change roles.

Student A: You want to buy a car, but you can't save up enough money to buy one. Talk to your friend about the situation.

Student B: You think your friend should make a budget. With a budget, he or she will find out where money is being spent, and it will be easier to cut back and save.

C **EVALUATE.** Look at the budget in Exercise 1B. Imagine that the couple wants to save money to buy a new car. How can they cut their expenses? What can they do to have more income? Make suggestions.

D **PRESENT.** Describe a time that you made a budget. Did it help you save money? Why or why not?

E **PRIORITIZE.** In a balanced budget, the income is greater than the expenses. Create your own balanced budget. Use the budget worksheet in Exercise 1B as a model.

I can prepare a monthly budget. ☐ I need more practice. ☐

For more practice, go to MyEnglishLab.

Lesson 5

Grammar

Future real conditionals

Future real conditionals	
***If* clause**	**Result clause**
If you **make** a list of your expenses,	you **will know** exactly how much you spend.
If you **increase** your monthly payment,	you**'ll finish** paying off the loan sooner.
If you **don't cut** your expenses,	you **won't save** enough money.

Grammar Watch

- Use future real conditional sentences to talk about what will happen if something else happens.
- Use the simple present in the *if* clause. Use the future in the result clause.
- The *if* clause can start or end a sentence. Use a comma after the *if* clause only when the clause starts the sentence.

A **INVESTIGATE.** Underline the *if* clauses. Circle the verbs in the result clauses.

Saving money is not as hard as you may think. If you figure out how much money you need to save each month, it will be easier to meet your goals. There are some simple things you can do. For example, if you turn down the heat in your apartment, your utility bills will go down. If you watch TV instead of going to the movies, you'll save money on entertainment. You'll save money on repairs if you learn how to fix your own car. Be sure to keep your receipts. You'll be able to track your expenses better if you save your receipts. Remember, every penny counts. Small change can make a big difference.

B **DETERMINE.** Cross out the incorrect words.

1. **A:** If I **don't / won't** go back to Colombia next summer, **I / I'll** miss my sister's wedding. But the airfare is so expensive.

   B: I know. But you can still go. If **you / you'll** save $100 every month, **you / you'll** have enough money to buy a ticket by next summer.

2. **A:** If **I / I'll** take some computer classes, **I get / I'll be able to get** a better job. But I don't have enough money to pay for the classes.

   B: Those classes are important. You should save up the money to pay for them. If **you / you'll** make a budget, **you / you'll** see how much you're spending, and you can save more.

Grammar

C **COMPLETE.** Use the correct form of the verb.

A: I don't know what to do. My family in Mexico needs help, but with my salary, I don't think I can help.

B: You know, I send money to my parents and sisters in Colombia. If I ______________ (not / help) them, my two sisters ______________ (not / be able to) go to school.

A: Really? Can you show me how you do it? That is, if you ______________ (not / mind).

B: No, not at all. Budgeting is a lot of *ifs.* If you ______________ (not / do) this, then you ______________ (be able to) do that. For example, right now, you're renting a one-bedroom apartment. Here's one *if.* If you ______________ (not / mind) living in a studio, then you ______________ (save) a couple of hundred dollars in rent, maybe more. That's $200 that you can send to your family. Let's see you try another *if.*

A: OK. I have cable, but I don't use it very much because I can stream shows and movies online. If I ______________ (cut) cable, then I ______________ (save) $150 a month!

B: Yep. Let's see. How about commuting costs? Do you drive to work?

A: Yeah. If I ______________ (take the bus), I ______________ (not / spend) so much on gas.

B: Exactly! See how your savings can mount up by cutting here and there?

A: I sure do! Thanks. I feel better now.

Show what you know!

1. **BRAINSTORM.** Look at the budget you created in the last lesson, using the budget worksheet on page 276. Think of how you can cut back on your monthly expenses. For example, "If I bring my lunch to work, I'll save seventy-five dollars a month."

2. **WRITE.** Write a paragraph to describe ways that you can spend less and save more.

   I spend a lot of money on lunch at restaurants. I go to the sandwich shop almost every day and spend $6-10. If I bring my own sandwich from home, it will cost about half that price. If I don't buy a drink when I go to restaurants, I'll save $2.

I can use future real conditionals. ☐ I need more practice. ☐

For more practice, go to MyEnglishLab.

Lesson 6

Workplace, Life, and Community Skills

Understand tax forms and interpret a W-2 form

1 UNDERSTAND TAX FORMS

A DEFINE KEY WORDS. Read the passage. What is a W-2, 1040, and 1040EZ?

When you work in the U.S., a portion of your salary or income is paid to the government for taxes. At the end of the year, your employer sends you a summary of your earnings and the amount of federal and state taxes that you paid. This summary is called a wage and tax statement or W-2 form. Taxpayers must use their W-2 forms to file income tax forms each year. The federal income tax form is called the 1040 ("ten forty"). The short version of the form is called the 1040EZ. Taxpayers send their forms to the Internal Revenue Service (IRS).

B DETERMINE. Does your state have a state income tax? What other forms of taxes does your state have?

2 INTERPRET A W-2 FORM

A SCAN. Who is the employer? Who is the employee? What is the year for the wages reported?

	a Employee's social security number 354-00-7777	OMB No. 1545-0008	Safe, accurate, FAST! Use IRS e-file	Visit the IRS website at www.irs.gov/efile
b Employer identification number (EIN) 22-9006542			1 Wages, tips, other compensation $45,470	2 Federal income tax withheld $8,541
c Employer's name, address, and ZIP code Office World 10765 SW 6th Street Miami, FL 33174			3 Social security wages $45,470	4 Social security tax withheld $1,943
			5 Medicare wages and tips $45,470	6 Medicare tax withheld $922
			7 Social security tips	8 Allocated tips
d Control number			9 Advance EIC payment	10 Dependent care benefits
e Employee's first name and initial Carla M.	Last name Guzman	Suff.	11 Nonqualified plans	12a See instructions for box 12 Code
			13 Statutory employee ☐ Retirement Plan ☐ Third-party sick pay ☐	12b Code
			14 Other	12c Code
32 NW 106th Ct. Miami, FL 3317 f Employee's address, and ZIP code				12d Code

15 State	Employer's state ID number	16 State wages, tips, etc.	17 State income tax	18 Local wages, tips, etc.	19 Local income tax	20 Locality name
	22-9006542	$45,470	$0			

Form **W-2** Wage and Tax Statement **2018** Department of the Treasury—Internal Revenue Service

Copy B—To Be Filed With Employee's FEDERAL Tax Return.
This information is being furnished to the Internal Revenue Service.

B LOCATE DETAILS. Complete with information from the W-2.

1. Name of employee: Carla Guzmán
2. The employee's total compensation in 2018: $45,470.
3. Name of the employer: Office World
4. Amount of federal income tax withheld from the employee's pay: $8541.00
5. Amount of social security tax withheld from the employee's pay: $1,943.00
6. Amount of Medicare tax withheld from the employee's pay: $922.00
7. Amount of state income tax withheld from the employee's pay: 0

C INTEGRATE. Look at these sections of the 1040EZ form. Use Carla's W-2 to complete the missing information.

Income	1	Wages, salaries, and tips. This should be shown in box 1 of your Form(s) W-2. Attach your Form(s) W-2.	1	$45,470
Attach Form(s) W-2 here.	2	Taxable interest. If the total is over $1,500, you cannot use Form 1040EZ.	2	0
Enclose, but do not attach, any payment.	3	Unemployment compensation and Alaska Permanent Fund dividends (see page 10).	3	0
	4	Add lines 1, 2 and 3. This is your **adjusted gross income.**	4	$45,470

Payments, Credits, and Tax	7	Federal income tax withheld from box 2 of your Form(s) W-2.	7	$8541.
	8a	**Earned income credit (EIC).**	8a	0
	b	Nontaxable combat pay election 8b		
	9	Add lines 7 and 8a. These are your total payments.	9	1248
	10	Tax. Use the amount on line **6 above** to find your tax in the tax table on pages 18–26 of the booklet. Then, enter the tax from the table on this line.	10	$7,293

D CALCULATE. A *tax refund* is money that the government gives back to you if you have paid too much in taxes. Look at the W-2 form and the 1040EZ form. Will Carla get a tax refund, or does she owe additional taxes? How much?

E GO ONLINE. Go to the federal Internal Revenue Service website: www.irs.gov. Search for information about free tax preparation services.

1. What is the name of the program that offers free tax preparation services? ______
2. Who qualifies for this program? ______
3. What is the name of a business that offers free tax preparation? ______

I understand tax forms and can interpret a W-2 form. ☐ I need more practice. ☐

For more practice, go to MyEnglishLab.

Listening and Speaking

Talk about dreams for the future

1 BEFORE YOU LISTEN

DISCUSS. What stories have you heard about people who suddenly come into a lot of money? What do the people usually do with the money?

2 LISTEN

Two friends, Edgar and Carla, are talking about what they would do if they suddenly got a lot of money.

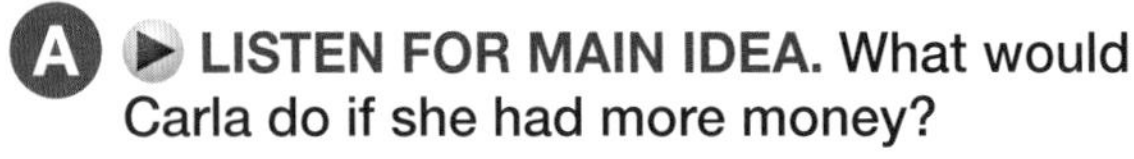

A ▶ **LISTEN FOR MAIN IDEA.** What would Carla do if she had more money?

____

____

B ▶ **LISTEN FOR DETAILS.** Listen again. Then answer the questions.

1. How much money did the person who works in Edgar's office get?

   ____

2. What did the person who works in Edgar's office do with the money?

   ____

3. Why does Carla want to go back to school?

   ____

4. What would Carla do for work if she went to medical school?

   ____

5. What would Edgar do differently in his life if he got a lot of money?

   ____

6. What would Edgar buy if he got a lot of money?

   ____

Listening and Speaking

3 PRONUNCIATION

A ▶ **PRACTICE.** Listen. Then listen again and repeat.

What **would you** do if you had a lot of money?

Would you quit your job?

Pronouncing *would you*

In conversation, *would you* is often pronounced "wouldja." The words are joined together and pronounced as one word.

B ▶ **APPLY.** Listen. Circle the words you hear. Then listen again to check your answers.

1. **Will / Would** you buy a house?
2. **Will / Would** you travel a lot?
3. Where **will / would** you go?
4. **Will / Would** you go to South America?
5. What **will / would** you do there?

4 CONVERSATION

A ▶ **LISTEN AND READ.** Then practice the conversation with a partner.

A: What would you do if you had a lot of money?
B: I would quit my job at this convenience store and start my own business. I've always wanted to be my own boss.
A: That sounds like a good idea.
B: Why? What would *you* do if you had a lot of money?
A: I think I would travel for a year or two.
B: Where would you go?
A: Australia. And South America. I've always wanted to go to Argentina and Brazil.
B: Hmm. . . . Maybe I'd join you. My business can wait a year or two.

B **REFLECT.** What would you do if you had a lot of money?

____

____

____

I can talk about dreams for the future. ☐ I need more practice. ☐

For more practice, go to MyEnglishLab.

Lesson 8

Grammar

Present and future unreal conditionals

If clause	Result clause
If you **had** a lot of money,	what **would** you **do**?
If I **had** a lot of money,	I **would buy** a house.
If that house **were** less expensive,	he **would** / **could / might** **buy** it.

Grammar Watch

- Use present and future unreal conditional sentences to talk about things that are untrue, imagined, or impossible.
- Use the simple past in the *if* clause. Use *would, could,* or *might* + the base form of the verb in the result clause.
- In the *if* clause, use *were,* not *was,* with all subjects when the verb is a form of *be.*
- In the result clause, *Would* expresses desired results. *Could* and *might* express possible options.

A **INVESTIGATE. Underline the *if* clauses. Circle the verbs in the result clauses.**

Let's face it, money is important. If I had more money, I would work less, and I would have more time to do the things I want to do. If I worked less, I would spend more time with my family. And if I had more time, I might take college classes. I could get a better job if I had a college degree. There's no doubt that my life would be very different if I had more money.

B **DETERMINE. Cross out the incorrect words. Then check (✓) the statements that are true for you.**

____ **1.** If someone **gives / gave** me a lot of money, **I / I would** start my own business.

____ **2.** If I **was / were** rich, **I'll / I'd** donate a lot of money to charity.

____ **3.** If I **had / would have** a lot of money, I **quit / might quit** my job.

____ **4.** If I **work / worked** part time, **I / I would** spend more time with my family.

____ **5.** If I **speak / spoke** better English, I **get / could get** a better job.

____ **6.** If I **have / had** health insurance, I would go the doctor more often.

Grammar

C **APPLY.** Under what conditions, if any, would you do these things? Write unreal conditional sentences. Use *would, could,* or *might* in the result clause.

1. cut back on your spending

   If I had a lot of expenses, I'd cut back on my spending.

2. loan money to a friend

   ______

3. ask a friend to loan you money

   ______

4. refuse to loan money to a family member

   ______

5. take out a loan for a large sum of money from a bank

   ______

6. quit your job

   ______

7. start your own business

   ______

Show what you know!

1. **DISCUSS.** What would you do if you had a lot of money, time, or power?
2. **WRITE.** Write a paragraph about the things you would do if you had a lot of money, time, or power. Discuss the impact on the groups of people named in the box. Use present/ future unreal conditionals.

my family	my friends	my school	my community	my country

If I had more money, I wouldn't work so much. If I didn't have to work all the time, I would spend more time with my friends and family . . .

I can use present and future unreal conditionals. ☐ I need more practice. ☐

For more practice, go to MyEnglishLab.

Lesson 9

Writing

Write about a worthwhile charity

WRITING PROMPT: Which charity or charitable organization do you think does good work? Write a paragraph about that charity and give details to show why people should contribute to it.

1 STUDY THE MODEL

A ANALYZE. Read the model and Writing Skill. Then answer the questions.

Doctors Without Borders

Doctors Without Borders is a very worthwhile charity. Each year, this organization sends volunteer doctors, nurses, and administrators to give free medical care to people in more than seventy countries. These volunteers provide all kinds of medical care, from surgery and nutrition programs to mental health care and doctor training. In 1999, Doctors Without Borders received the Nobel Peace Prize for its good works. It costs a lot to help victims of war, sickness, hunger, and natural disasters. If people didn't donate to the organization, it wouldn't be able to continue its important work. That's why I believe that everyone should give as much as they can to Doctors Without Borders.

Writing Skill: State main idea and supporting details

Every paragraph should have a clearly-stated main idea. Add details to support this idea, such as facts and examples.

1. Circle the main idea. Underline one detail that supports this idea.
2. Why is Doctors Without Borders a very worthwhile charity?
3. What types of medical care does Doctors Without Borders provide?

B TAKE NOTES. Complete the outline with information from the model.

MAIN IDEA

Doctors Without Borders is a very ____________________.

SUPPORTING DETAIL	SUPPORTING DETAIL	SUPPORTING DETAIL
It sends ________	________	________
________	________	________
________	________	________
________	________	________
________	________	________

2 PLAN YOUR WRITING

A **BRAINSTORM.** Discuss your ideas for the Writing Prompt with a partner.

B **ORGANIZE.** Use this outline to organize your ideas before writing.

MAIN IDEA

_______________ is a very worthwhile charity.

SUPPORTING DETAIL	SUPPORTING DETAIL	SUPPORTING DETAIL
________	________	________
________	________	________
________	________	________
________	________	________
________	________	________

3 WRITE

SUPPORT. Write a paragraph about a worthwhile charity and explain why people should contribute to it. Remember to add details to support your main idea. Use the model, the Writing Skill, and your ideas from Exercise 2 to help you.

4 CHECK YOUR WRITING

A **REVISE.** Use the Writing Checklist to review your writing. Make revisions as necessary.

B **COLLABORATE.** Read your writing with a partner. Use the checklist again to improve your writing.

WRITING CHECKLIST

- ☐ Did you clearly state a main idea about a worthwhile charity?
- ☐ Did you add details to support your main idea?
- ☐ Did you use correct capitalization, punctuation, and spelling?

I can state main idea and supporting details. ☐ I need more practice. ☐

For more practice, go to MyEnglishLab.

Lesson 10 Soft Skills at Work

Take initiative

1 MEET LAMISA

Read about one of her workplace skills.

I take initiative. When I learn what is needed, I follow through on those expectations. I can think of steps to take on my own.

2 LAMISA'S PROBLEM

A **READ.** Write *T* (true) or *F* (false).

Lamisa has worked as an accountant for years. She wants to start her own bookkeeping company. Lamisa has saved enough money to cover 75% of the start-up costs, but she needs to borrow the rest from the bank. Lamisa visits the bank, and the bank manager tells her that he needs to see a business plan. Lamisa has never created a business plan.

_____ **1.** Lamisa is an accountant who wants to set up her own company.

_____ **2.** Lamisa has saved up enough money to cover the start-up costs.

_____ **3.** As an accountant, Lamisa has lots of experience with business plans.

B **ANALYZE.** What is Lamisa's problem?

____

____

3 LAMISA'S SOLUTION

A **COLLABORATE.** Lamisa takes initiative. How does she get the money she needs to start her business? Explain your answer.

1. Lamisa tells the bank manager that she will borrow money from her friends and family.
2. Lamisa tells the bank manager that she will keep working until she saves more money.
3. Lamisa tells the bank manager that she will learn how to create a business plan.
4. Lamisa ____.

B **ROLE-PLAY.** Role-play Lamisa's conversation with the bank manager.

Show what you know!

1. **REFLECT.** How do you take initiative at school, at work, or at home? Give an example.
2. **WRITE.** Write your example in your Skills Log.

   I take initiative to earn extra money outside my regular job so I can buy a house. I searched for short-term work online. I save all the money I make in a separate account.
3. **PRESENT.** Give a short presentation describing how you take initiative.

I can give an example of how I take initiative. ☐

Unit Review: Go back to page 225. Which unit goals can you check off?

MY SOFT SKILLS LOG

This is a list of my soft skills. They are skills I use every day. They are important for work, school, and home. In a job interview, I can talk about my soft skills. I can give these examples from my life.

Unit 1: I take responsibility for my professional growth.

For example, ______________________________

____

____

____

Unit 2: I have integrity.

For example, ______________________________

____

____

____

Unit 3: I respect others.

For example, ______________________________

____

____

____

Unit 4: I'm adaptable.

For example, ______________________________

____

____

____

Unit 5: I locate information.

For example, ______________________________

____

____

____

Unit 6: I find creative solutions.

For example, ______________________________

____

____

____

MY SOFT SKILLS LOG

Unit 7: I respond well to feedback.

For example, ____

Unit 8: I'm professional.

For example, ____

Unit 9: I manage my time well.

For example, ____

Unit 10: I take responsibility.

For example, ____

Unit 11: I'm accountable.

For example, ____

Unit 12: I take initiative.

For example, ____

GRAMMAR REVIEW

UNIT 1

A Complete the conversation with the present continuous or the simple present. Cross out the incorrect verbs.

Patty: Hey, Chang. **Are you working / Do you work** again today?

Chang: Yes. Marty usually **is working / works** on Fridays, but today **I'm taking / I take** his shift.

Patty: Why? What **is he doing / does he do**?

Chang: **I'm not knowing / I don't know** for sure. I think his family **is visiting / visits**.

B Complete the conversation with the correct future form.

Alicia: Hey, Mom. I ________________ (**leave**) in a few minutes.

Mom: OK. What ________________ (**you / do**) tonight?

Alicia: Dania and I ________________ (**be going to / see**) a movie.

Mom: What time ________________ (**you / be going to / be**) home?

Alicia: I'm not sure. But don't worry. I ________________ (**will not / get**) home too late.

Mom: All right. Remember that you ________________ (**take**) me to work in the morning.

Alicia: Yep. I ________________ (**will be**) ready to leave at 7:00.

C Complete each conversation. Use the boldfaced verb or adjective in the question + *that*.

1. **A:** Why is Zac **upset**?
   B: He's ___upset that___ he didn't do well on his math test today.
2. **A:** What does Sofie **think** about this plan?
   B: She ________________ it's a good idea.
3. **A:** Why was Ray **surprised** this morning?
   B: He was ________________ he got a promotion at work.
4. **A:** What's wrong? Did you **forget** something?
   B: Yes. I ________________ I need to go to the bank this afternoon.
5. **A:** What did the police officer **say**?
   B: She ________________ I can get the accident report online.
6. **A:** Did you **know** about John's new restaurant?
   B: Yes. We ________________ he opened a restaurant last month.

GRAMMAR REVIEW

UNIT 2

A Complete the conversation. Use gerunds or infinitives. If possible, write two answers.

A: Ava doesn't like working OR to work (work) at the bank anymore. She wants ______ (find) a new job. Actually, she's thinking about ______ (make) a career change. She's interested in ______ (become) a nurse.

B: Really? Well, she'll probably need ______ (get) a college degree before she can get a nursing job. Is she planning on ______ (go) to school?

A: Actually, she started ______ (study) nursing at the community college a few years ago. Now she wants to continue ______ (work) towards her degree.

B: That's great. I think Ava will be very good at ______ (take) care of people. And I think she'll enjoy ______ (help) others.

B Complete the conversation. Use a preposition and a gerund.

A: Are you planning on working (work) at your aunt's restaurant this summer?

B: No, I'm not. I'm trying to choose ______ (go) back to school or applying for a job at the hospital.

A: That's exciting! What do you want to study?

B: I'm thinking ______ (study) nursing. I'm interested ______ (help) people.

A: I want to go back to school, too, but I'm nervous ______ (not have) enough money.

B: You can apply for financial aid. I'll text you the link to the application.

A: Okay. Thanks ______ (tell) me about it!

C Complete the conversations with the present perfect or the simple past. Cross out the incorrect verbs.

1. **A:** How long **have you worked / did you work** at your current job?

   B: Well, I **have started / started** last June, so **I've been / was** at this job for about six months.

2. **A:** **I've learned / learned** so much in my business class already, and the semester is only half over.

   B: Yeah, I **have taken / took** a business class last year, and I really **learned / have learned** a lot, too.

3. **A:** Adela **has been / was** a manager at Data Tech, Inc. for twelve months now. She **has accomplished / accomplished** a lot in a very short time.

   B: She sure has. It's hard to believe that she **has taken / took** that job only a year ago.

4. **A:** Gabe is a good employee. We **have hired / hired** him two years ago, and since then, he **has never missed / never missed** a day of work.

   B: Yeah, he **has had / had** a good reputation at his last job, too.

UNIT 3

A **Complete the paragraph. Cross out the incorrect participial adjectives.**

I used to be worri**ed / worrying** about crime in our town, and I was **frustrated / frustrating** by our litter problem. But things are changing. Community members are **interested / interesting** in making a difference. It's **satisfied / satisfying** to see people working to improve the community, and it's **encouraged / encouraging** to see them working together. The community is making some **excited / exciting** changes, and I'm **amazed / amazing** at our progress.

B **Read the first sentence in each item. Then complete the second sentence to express a wish for the opposite.**

1. There aren't a lot of restaurants in our neighborhood. We wish that ___*there were*___ more restaurants in our neighborhood.
2. Richard doesn't have time to go to the movies very often. He wishes that ________________ time to go to the movies more often.
3. Mrs. Salas worries a lot. Her children wish that she ________________ so much.
4. The school can't get a computer for every student. Everyone wishes that ________________ a computer for every student.
5. The bus is always late. I wish that ________________ always late.

C **Read the first sentence in each item. Then complete the second sentence. Use an object + infinitive.**

1. The residents of our community don't participate in community events. We should encourage ____________________ in community events.
2. I parked in my neighbor's parking spot last night. She reminded ____________________ there.
3. Several people in our neighborhood were robbed last week because they opened the door for strangers. The police warned ____________________ the door for strangers.
4. We are all invited to attend meetings of the City Council. The City Council president urges ____________________ its meetings.

UNIT 4

A **Complete the conversations. Put the words in parentheses in the correct order. If more than one answer is possible, write both answers.**

1. Would you please turn off the light OR turn the light off? **(turn / off / the light)**
2. Can you look at this with me? I'm having a problem, and I can't quite ____________________. **(figure / out / it)**
3. If you ever need help, you know you can always ____________________. **(count / on / me)**
4. Do you have a moment? I'd like to ____________________ with you. **(talk / over / these plans)**
5. She was really hurt by her co-worker's remark. It won't be easy for her to ____________________. **(get / over / it)**

B **Read Person B's response. Then write a negative question that Person A could have asked.**

1. **A:** Should I take my break soon?
   B: Yes, you should. You should take it when Dina finishes her break.
2. **A:** ____________________ about the schedule change?
   B: No, I didn't. I didn't hear anything about it.
3. **A:** ____________________ the equipment yet?
   B: No, they haven't. They haven't cleaned it because they've been doing other work.
4. **A:** ____________________ questions if she doesn't understand something?
   B: Yes, she should. She should ask questions any time she's not sure.
5. **A:** ____________________ the report tomorrow?
   B: No, we can't. We can't finish it tomorrow because Mr. Luna needs it today.

C **Read the first statement in each item. Then complete the second sentence to make an indirect instruction or request with the same meaning.**

1. My co-worker to me: "Wear comfortable shoes." My co-worker advised ____________________ comfortable shoes.
2. The supervisor to us: "Check the new schedule." The supervisor reminded ____________________ the new schedule.
3. Anita to Sarah: "Don't be late for work." Anita warned ____________________ late for work.
4. Shen to Franco: "Work carefully." Shen told ____________________ carefully.

UNIT 5

A **Combine the two clauses to make a conditional sentence. Keep the clauses in the same order and add *if* to one clause. Include a comma if necessary.**

1. a person is badly injured / don't move him or her
   If a person is badly injured, don't move him or her.
2. you don't have a smoke detector / you need to get one
   ____
3. get under a piece of furniture / there's an earthquake
   ____
4. you are prepared for a fire / you have a better chance of surviving it
   ____
5. call 911 / there's an emergency
   ____

B **Complete the sentences. Cross out the incorrect adverbs.**

1. You should check the weather frequently **until / when** there's a severe weather watch.
2. **Until / As soon as** we felt the earth shake, we got under the table.
3. They didn't know about the hurricane **as soon as / before** they saw the weather report.
4. **After / Before** the storm started, everyone stayed inside.
5. Stay on the phone with the 911 operator **until / after** he or she tells you to hang up.

C **Complete the sentences. Use the simple past or the past continuous.**

1. John ______________ **(chop)** vegetables when he cut his finger.
2. It was raining when Karen ______________ **(have)** the car accident.
3. The smoke detector went off while we ______________ **(sleep)**.
4. While I ______________ **(report)** the accident, the police arrived.
5. Mike ______________ **(break)** his leg while he was playing football.

UNIT 6

A **Complete the sentences with the correct form of the verb. Make the sentence negative if necessary.**

1. Tenants ______________ (allow) to have pets. It's against the rules.
2. Visitors ______________ (permit) to park in this lot. It's for tenants only.
3. Please don't throw away those soda cans. We ______________ (suppose) to recycle them.
4. The landlord must put a smoke alarm in your apartment. He ______________ (require) to do it.
5. The laundry room is open from 6:00 a.m. to 9:00 p.m. Tenants ______________ (allow) to use the laundry room during these hours only.

B **Complete the sentences with tag questions.**

1. You moved recently, ______________
2. We don't have to pay the rent yet, ______________
3. The tenants pay for electricity, ______________
4. The landlord didn't call back, ______________
5. The lock isn't broken, ______________
6. The windows are closed, ______________

C **Read the first statement in each item. Then complete the second sentence with reported speech. Use formal English.**

1. Tom told Beth, "I like my new neighbors."
   Tom told *Beth (that) he liked his new neighbors.*
2. The building manager said, "Your dogs are too noisy."
   The building manager said ______________
3. The tenant told his landlord, "I'll read the lease and return it to you on Friday."
   The tenant told ______________
4. Kim-Ly told the building manager, "Our lobby needs a new carpet."
   Kim-Ly told ______________
5. Lucy told Mike, "My neighbor plays his TV really loudly."
   Lucy told ______________

UNIT 7

A **Complete the conversations. Use the words in the box.**

get	than	rather	would you rather
to	buying	prefer	would you prefer

1. **A:** Would you ________________ take your car to a mechanic or do repairs yourself?
   B: I'd ________________ having a professional take care of any problems.
2. **A:** Would Theo prefer ________________ a new car ________________ a used car?
   B: Well, he would rather ________________ a new car ________________ a used one. But he doesn't want to spend a lot either.
3. **A:** ________________ a compact car or something larger?
   B: I'm not sure. What about you? ________________ drive a big car or a small one?

B **Complete the conversations. Change the direct questions to embedded questions.**

1. **A:** I wonder if you can take a look at my car's tires.
   (Can you take a look at my car's tires?)
   B: Sure. Can you tell me ________________________________.
   (What is the problem?)
   A: Well, the tread is really worn. I wonder ________________________________.
   (Do I need new tires?)
2. **A:** I just put new windshield wipers on my car, but they're not very good. I don't know
   ________________________________.
   (Why don't they work?)
   B: Hmmm. I wonder ________________________________.
   (Did you get the wrong size?)
   A: That might be it. I wasn't sure ________________________________.
   (What size should I get?)

C **Complete the conversations. Use the past perfect.**

1. **A:** My wife ________________ **(want)** a hybrid for a long time, so we finally bought one.
   B: I think you'll be happy with it. We ________________ **(decide)** to get a more fuel-efficient car a long time ago. So when the hybrid cars came out, we bought one right away.
2. **A:** After she ________________ **(save)** for about a year, Mary got a new car.
   B: Oh yeah? ________________ **(she / look)** at a lot of cars before she made her choice?
   A: Yes, she ________________ **(have)**. She ________________ **(go)** to several dealers.

GRAMMAR REVIEW

UNIT 8

A Complete the conversation. Use the present perfect continuous.

Dr. Pratt: Hello, Mrs. Lee. ________ you ________ (wait) long?

Mrs. Lee: No, I haven't, thank you.

Dr. Pratt: Good. So, how ________ you ________ (feel) since your last appointment?

Mrs. Lee: I ________ (get) better every day. I ________ (sleep) well at night, and I ________ (not take) naps during the day.

Dr. Pratt: That's great. And ________ you ________ (take) your medication?

Mrs. Lee: Yes, I have. My husband ________ (remind) me every night.

Dr. Pratt: Good. And ________ you ________ (exercise)?

Mrs. Lee: Well, my daughter and I ________ (walking) together every day.

Dr. Pratt: Very good. You ________ (do) everything right!

B Complete the conversations. Use *such* or *so*.

A: Why did Ken go home early?

B: He had a headache. He was in ________ much pain that he couldn't work.

A: What happened to Maggie's hand? Why is she wearing a bandage?

B: She burned it at work this morning. She remained ________ calm that no one knew she was hurt.

A: Can you recommend a good dentist?

B: Sure. Dr. Vu is wonderful, but she is ________ a popular dentist that it is difficult to get an appointment. She's booked for months.

A: Do you still go to the gym every weekend?

B: No, I don't. I have ________ a busy schedule that I can't work out as much as I'd like to.

A: What did Ben's doctor say about his condition?

B: She said that Ben's symptoms are ________ unusual that he needs to see a specialist.

C Complete the conversation. Cross out the incorrect words.

Malek: Hey, you look great! What have you been doing?

Susan: Nothing special—just following my doctor's warning. She said I **better / 'd better** make some lifestyle changes if I wanted to stay healthy.

Malek: Oh, yeah? What kinds of changes? Maybe I should make some changes, too.

Susan: Well, she said I **ought to / ought** get more exercise. She thinks I **should to / should** do some moderate exercise at least three times a week.

Malek: But I already have **so many / so much** things to do. I'm **so / such** busy that I don't have time!

Susan: Well, you can start by doing small things like taking the stairs instead of the elevator. It can make **so / such** a difference that you'll be amazed. Listen, we **had better / ought to** take a walk a few days a week at lunchtime. Do you want to go with me today?

Malek: Sure. Let's meet downstairs at 12:00, OK?

Susan: OK. And you **had better / have better** be there! Remember, your health is **such / so** important that you must **making / make** time to take care of yourself!

UNIT 9

A **Complete the sentences. Use *because / since, to,* or *so that.* Then state whether the adverb clause expresses Reason or Purpose.**

1. Because / Since Lin is having trouble with math, I want to talk to her teacher.

   Reason

2. Our son goes to after-school tutoring __________ he can get help with his math homework.

   ____

3. Parents and teachers should communicate __________ it helps students do better in school.

   ____

4. My daughter has to stay after school today __________ go to soccer practice.

   ____

5. I'm meeting with David's teacher tomorrow __________ we can talk about his progress so far this year.

   ____

6. Maddie didn't do very well on her exam __________ she was absent three days last week.

   ____

B **Circle the relative pronouns. Then replace each circled *that* with either *who* or *which.* Finally, cross out any circled *who* or *which* if it can be omitted.**

1. Students that have perfect attendance this year will receive a special award.
2. Janet is not very happy with the school which her son attends.
3. Parents that want to volunteer at the school need to fill out a special form.
4. The school is building a new playground that will include some exercise equipment.
5. I can't remember the name of the teacher who my daughter had for first grade.

(continued)

C Complete the conversations. Cross out the incorrect words.

1. **A:** I sent Manny's teacher a note, but she hasn't called or written me back.
   B: She **must not have / might have** gotten the note. She doesn't seem like the kind of person who ignores messages. When did you send it?
   A: Last week. I put it in Manny's backpack so that he could give it to her.
   B: You should check with Manny. He **could have / must not have** forgotten about it.
2. **A:** Did you go to the PTA meeting last night?
   B: No. I didn't go because I was really tired after work.
   A: I didn't go either, but we **should have / must have** gone. There's a new fundraiser this week, and we need information.
   B: Let's check the app. Someone **couldn't have / might have** posted the information there.
3. **A:** Ugh—that test was so hard! I **shouldn't have / can't have** done well on it.
   B: Me neither. I **should have / may have** studied more.

UNIT 10

A Complete the sentences. Use the words in the box.

have	makes	lets	get	made	had

1. They didn't want to work late, but the supervisor ________________ them stay until 9:00.
2. Please find Mr. Jones and ________________ him sign this. Then give it back to me.
3. The company ________________ employees leave early the day before some holidays.
4. Can you ________________ someone to take your shift? Ask your co-workers.
5. The store was so busy yesterday! My manager ________________ me work on the cash register, and I usually don't do that.
6. Our company ________________ us clock in and out for every shift.

B Complete the sentences with the correct reflexive pronouns.

1. Don't lift heavy objects by ________________. Get someone to help you.
2. I finished all the work ________________. No one helped me.
3. Mrs. Yang burned ________________ while cooking dinner.
4. Workers need to use caution with that machine. They could hurt ________________.
5. You and John can't do this project by ________________. You'll need some help.
6. We're really proud of ________________. We worked hard, and we got the job done.

C Complete the conversations. Use the words in the box.

Why don't you	Would you mind	Could I	Why don't I

1. **A:** ____________________ borrow your pen for a minute?
   B: Sure. Here you go.
2. **A:** I can't go to lunch with you today because I forgot my wallet.
   B: ____________________ lend you some money? You can pay me back tomorrow.
3. **A:** ____________________ driving me home after work today?
   B: No, it's no problem at all.
4. **A:** ____________________ talk to our supervisor about your problem?
   B: That's a good idea. I'll talk to her today after my shift ends.

UNIT 11

A Complete the sentences. Use the gerund or infinitive form of the verbs.

1. It's your responsibility ____________ **(understand)** the law where you live.
2. ____________ **(drive)** without a license is illegal.
3. It's a good idea ____________ **(pay)** fines as soon as possible.
4. ____________ **(not, follow)** the law can lead to serious legal problems.
5. It's important ____________ **(not, text)** and drive at the same time.

B Read the active sentence. Complete the passive sentence so it has the same meaning.

1. Attorneys on both sides of a case choose juries.
   Juries ____________ by attorneys on both sides of a case.
2. They sent the criminal to jail for ten years.
   The criminal ____________ to jail for ten years.
3. The government calls most U.S. citizens to jury duty sometime in their lives.
   Most U.S. citizens ____________ to jury duty sometime in their lives.
4. Lawyers explained the details of the case to the jury.
   The details of the case ____________ to the jury.
5. After hearing the facts, jurors discuss the case.
   After hearing the facts, the case ____________ by the jurors.

(continued)

C Complete the sentences. Use the subordinating conjunctions in the box. You may use each conjunction more than once.

even if	as long as	even though

1. Don't speed, ________________ you're in a hurry.
2. You won't get a ticket ________________ you follow the traffic laws.
3. ________________ I was really late for my appointment yesterday, I didn't speed.
4. ________________ there aren't other cars around you, you should still use your turn signals. It's a good habit to get into.
5. ________________ you study, you'll pass your driver's license test.
6. I always drive with my headlights on, ________________ it's not dark.

UNIT 12

A Complete the paragraph. Use *a, an, the,* or Ø.

With ________ credit card, you can buy things now and pay for them later. This can be useful, but it can also be expensive. That's because ________ credit card companies charge ________ interest on the amount you owe them. ________ debit card is different—it's linked to ________ bank account. When you pay for something with ________ debit card, the money comes out of ________ account it's linked to.

If you have ________ credit card, use it carefully. And make sure you always pay ________ full amount of the bill as soon as you can. Try not to have unpaid balance so you don't have to pay ________ interest charges.

B Complete the sentences so that they make future real conditional statements.

1. If I ________________ **(get)** a bank account, the bank ________________ **(give)** me a debit card.
2. We ________________ **(be able to)** go on vacation, if we ________________ **(save)** our money.
3. If she ________________ **(get)** a loan, she ________________ **(have to)** pay interest.
4. It ________________ **(be)** easier to save money, if you ________________ **(make)** a budget.

C Complete the sentences so that they make present unreal conditional statements.

1. They ________________ **(start)** their own business if they ________________ **(have)** enough money.
2. We ________________ **(save)** money if we ________________ **(take)** the bus instead of driving.

3. If I ______________ (not eat) out so much, I ______________ (spend) a lot less on food.

4. If you ______________ (open) a Mexican restaurant, people ______________ (come).

D **Complete the sentences with the correct form of the verb.**

1. If you suddenly ______________ (get) a lot of money, would you quit your job?

2. If she ______________ (need) money, I'll lend it to her.

3. I wouldn't do that if I ______________ (be) you.

4. If we stop buying coffee at the coffee shop, we ______________ (save) about $20 a week.

Unit 1, Lesson 2, page 8

Stative (non-action) verbs			
Emotions	**Mental states**	**Wants and preferences**	**Appearance and value**
admire	agree	hope	appear
adore	assume	need	be
appreciate	believe	prefer	cost
care	consider	want	equal
dislike	disagree	wish	look (seem)
doubt	expect		matter
fear	guess	**The senses**	represent
hate	hope	feel	resemble
like	imagine	hear	seem
love	know	notice	weigh
regret	mean	see	
respect	mind	smell	
trust	realize	sound	
	recognize	taste	
Possession and relationship	remember		
belong	see (understand)		
contain	suppose		
have	think (believe)		
own	understand		
possess	wonder		

Unit 1, Lesson 8, page 20

Common verbs that introduce noun clauses				
agree	doubt	guess	notice	remember
believe	dream	hope	predict	say
decide	feel	know	read	think
discover	forget	learn	realize	understand
Common adjectives that introduce noun clauses				
afraid	disappointed	pleased	sure	
angry	glad	sad	surprised	
certain	happy	shocked	upset	
convinced	lucky	sorry	worried	

Unit 2, Lesson 2, page 28

Infinitives and Gerunds					
Verbs + Infinitive (*to* + base form of verb)					
agree	can('t) wait	help	offer	refuse	wish
appear	choose	hope	pay	request	would like
arrange	decide	learn	plan	seem	
ask	deserve	manage	prepare	volunteer	
attempt	expect	mean	pretend	wait	
can('t) afford	fail	need	promise	want	
Verbs + Gerund (base form of verb + *-ing*)					
admit	delay	explain	keep (continue)	prohibit	suggest
advise	deny	feel like	mention	quit	tolerate
appreciate	discuss	finish	mind	recommend	understand
avoid	dislike	forgive	miss	regret	
can't help	enjoy	give up (stop)	postpone	report	
consider	escape	imagine	practice	risk	
Verbs + Gerund or Infinitive					
begin	continue	hate	love	remember	stop
can't stand	forget	like	prefer	start	try

Unit 2, Lesson 5, page 34

Gerunds as Objects of Prepositions			
Verb + Preposition			
admit to	complain about	insist on	rely on
advise against	count on	keep on	resort to
apologize for	deal with	look forward to	succeed in
approve of	dream about/of	object to	talk about
believe in	feel like/about	pay for	think about
choose between/among	go along with	plan on	wonder about
Adjective + Preposition			
afraid of	careful of	good at	satisfied with
amazed at/by	concerned about	happy about	shocked at/by
angry at	curious about	interested in	sick of
ashamed of	different from	nervous about	sorry for/about
aware of	excited about	opposed to	surprised at/about/by
awful at	famous for	ready for	terrible at
bad at	fed up with	responsible for	tired of
bored with/by	fond of	sad about	used to
capable of	glad about	safe from	worried about

Unit 3, Lesson 2, page 48

Participial Adjectives					
-ing	*-ed*	*-ing*	*-ed*	*-ing*	*-ed*
alarming	alarmed	embarrassing	embarrassed	overwhelming	overwhelmed
amazing	amazed	encouraging	encouraged	pleasing	pleased
amusing	amused	exciting	excited	relaxing	relaxed
annoying	annoyed	exhausting	exhausted	satisfying	satisfied
boring	bored	fascinating	fascinated	shocking	shocked
confusing	confused	frightening	frightened	surprising	surprised
depressing	depressed	horrifying	horrified	terrifying	terrified
disappointing	disappointed	humiliating	humiliated	thrilling	thrilled
disgusting	disgusted	interesting	interested	tiring	tired
disturbing	disturbed	irritating	irritated	touching	touched

-ed Adjective + Preposition			
alarmed at/by	disgusted with/by/at	frightened of/by	surprised at/about/by
amazed at/by	disturbed by	horrified at/by	terrified at/by
amused at/by	embarrassed about/by	interested in	thrilled at/with/by
bored with/by	encouraged by	irritated with/by	tired of
confused about/by	excited about	pleased with	touched at/by
depressed about	exhausted by	satisfied with	worried about
disappointed in/with	fascinated with/by	shocked at/by	

Unit 3, Lesson 8, page 60

Verbs + Object + Infinitive					
advise	cause	expect	invite	prepare	teach
allow	choose	force	need	promise	tell
ask	convince	hire	permit	remind	urge
beg	encourage	instruct	persuade	require	want
					would like

Unit 4, Lesson 2, page 68

Phrasal Verbs: Separable			
Phrasal Verb	**Meaning**	**Phrasal Verb**	**Meaning**
bring . . . up	*raise (children)*	look . . . up	*try to find (in a book, etc.)*
bring . . . up	*call attention to*	make . . . up	*invent*
call . . . back	*return a phone call*	pass . . . up	*decide not to use*
call . . . off	*cancel*	pay . . . back	*repay*
check . . . out	*examine*	pick . . . out	*choose*
cheer . . . up	*cause to feel happier*	pick . . . up	*lift; stop to get*
clean . . . up	*clean completely*	point . . . out	*indicate*
clear . . . up	*explain*	put . . . away	*put in an appropriate place*
close . . . down	*close by force*	put . . . back	*return to its original place*
cover . . . up	*cover completely*	put . . . off	*delay*
cross . . . out	*draw a line through*	put . . . together	*assemble*
cut . . . up	*cut into small pieces*	set . . . up	*prepare for use*
do . . . over	*do again*	shut . . . down	*stop (a machine, etc.)*
figure . . . out	*understand*	sign . . . up	*register*
fill . . . in	*complete with information*	start . . . over	*start again*
fill . . . out	*complete (a form)*	take . . . back	*return*
fill . . . up	*fill completely*	talk . . . into	*persuade*
find . . . out	*learn information*	talk . . . over	*discuss*
give . . . back	*return*	tear . . . down	*destroy*
give . . . up	*quit, abandon*	think . . . over	*consider*
hand . . . in	*submit*	throw . . . away	*put in the trash*
hand . . . out	*distribute*	turn . . . down	*lower the volume; reject*
help . . . out	*assist*	turn . . . off	*stop (a machine, etc.)*
leave . . . out	*omit*	turn . . . on	*start (a machine, etc.)*
let . . . down	*disappoint*	turn . . . up	*make louder*
look . . . over	*examine*	write . . . down	*write on paper*

Phrasal Verbs: Inseparable			
Phrasal Verb	**Meaning**	**Phrasal Verb**	**Meaning**
count on	*depend on*	get over	*feel better after something bad*
fall for	*feel romantic love for*	look after	*take care of*
get along with	*have a good relationship*	look forward to	*feel excited about*
get off	*leave (a bus, train, etc.)*	look into	*investigate*
get on	*board (a bus, train, etc.)*	run into	*meet accidentally*
get through	*finish*	stick with	*not quit, not leave*

GRAMMAR REFERENCE

Unit 6, Lesson 8, page 120

Reported Speech: Changes to preserve meaning		
Direct Speech		**Reported Speech**
Ellen said, "My apartment **is** near the stairs."	→	Ellen said (that) her apartment **was** near the stairs.
The landlord told us, "They **didn't pay** last month's rent.	→	The landlord told us (that) they **hadn't paid** last month's rent.
The building manager said, "**I've called** the plumber about the leak in your bathroom."	→	The building manager said (that) he **had called** the plumber about the leak in my bathroom.
The building manager told me, "the plumber **is fixing** the leak."	→	The building manager told me (that) the plumber **was fixing** the leak.
He explained, "My neighbor's dog **was barking** all night."	→	He explained (that) his neighbor's dog **had been barking** all night.
The tenants said, "We**'ve called** the landlord about that problem."	→	The tenants said (that) they ***had called*** the landlord about that problem.
The landlord replied, "**I'll call** your neighbor about the situation."	→	The landlord replied (that) he ***would call*** our neighbor about the situation.
My neighbor told me, "You **should send** a letter of complaint to the landlord!"	→	My neighbor told me (that) I **should send** a letter of complaint to the landlord.*

* Note: Do not change the modals *should, could, might,* and *ought to* when changing direct to reported speech.

Unit 8, Lesson 5, page 154

Non-count nouns					
Drinks	**Food**		**Abstract ideas**	**School subjects**	**Other**
coffee	beef	pasta	advice	art	furniture
juice	bread	pepper	beauty	ESL	homework
milk	broccoli	pie	fear	geography	information
soda	butter	rice	happiness	history	jewelry
tea	cereal	salad	help	language arts	mail
water	cheese	salt	love	math	medicine
	chicken	soup	luck	music	money
Community problems	chocolate	spinach	time	physical education	paper
crime	fish	sugar		science	
garbage	fruit	yogurt		social studies	
graffiti	ice cream			technology	
noise	jam/jelly			world languages	
traffic	lettuce				
trash	mayonnaise				
	meat				

Unit 10, Lesson 5, page 194

Verbs and expressions used reflexively			
allow oneself	be proud of oneself	help oneself	see oneself
amuse oneself	behave oneself	hurt oneself	take care of oneself
ask oneself	believe in oneself	introduce oneself	talk to oneself
be angry at oneself	cut oneself	keep oneself (busy)	teach oneself
be hard on oneself	dry oneself	look at oneself	tell oneself
be oneself	enjoy oneself	prepare oneself	treat oneself
be pleased with oneself	feel sorry for oneself	remind oneself	

UNIT 1 – CATCHING UP

Page 6, Listen, Exercises 2A and 2B

Brenda: I need a burger, fries, and a garden salad.
Victor: At 10:00 in the morning? I'm just making breakfast now. It's too early for lunch.
Brenda: Look, I agree, but that's what the customer wants. Can you do it?
Victor: What the customer wants, the customer gets. Hey, I know you. You're Brenda. Brenda Kraig, right?
Brenda: Yes.
Victor: I'm Victor Pérez. My family lived next door to you on Juniper Street. Do you remember me?
Brenda: Victor, hi. How are you? When did you start working at the Royale?
Victor: About a year ago, but I usually work later. I'm a line cook six nights a week.
Brenda: So what are you doing here now? Where's Manny?
Victor: Manny isn't working today. He's taking the day off to take care of some personal things.
Brenda: I hope nothing's wrong. But, hey, we can talk more during our break. Right now, my customer is waiting. I need the burger, fries, and salad.
Victor: Coming right up.

Page 12, Listen, Exercises 2A and 2B

Brenda: Hi Victor, what are you looking at?
Victor: A list of job openings at the new Palm Café.
Brenda: Why are you looking at job listings? Don't you like your job here?
Victor: Yes, I like it, but I want to get ahead. I don't want to be a line cook forever. I'm planning to become a sous-chef, like Dina is here. She oversees just about everything that goes on in the kitchen and supervises the staff.
Brenda: Do you need special training to be a sous-chef?
Victor: Yes. That's why I'm starting cooking classes at Helman Culinary School next month.
Brenda: That's great! How long will it take to finish the culinary program?
Victor: Two years. I'll take daytime classes and work in the evening. Ten years from now, I'd like to have my own restaurant.
Brenda: Wow! That's really ambitious. You're going to be busy, but I know you can do it!
Victor: Thanks, Brenda. So, how about you? What's your long-term goal?
Brenda: I'm taking classes at the community college now. I'll get an Associate's degree in Hospitality Management next year. I want to be a manager at a hotel or restaurant. I'm very happy here at Café Royale. Maybe I'll stay here and manage the restaurant.

Page 18, Listen, Exercises 2A and 2B

Jackie: Hello, everyone. Welcome to "Real-Life Entrepreneurs." I'm your host, Jackie Adams. Today's episode is about opening a new restaurant. Our guest is Susie Costa. Susie has worked in the restaurant business for over fifteen years. This year, she decided that it's time to open her own restaurant. Her new restaurant, Asian Cottage, is opening in two weeks. Thanks for joining us, Susie.
Susie: Thanks for having me. I'm excited to be here.
Jackie: Tell us about Asian Cottage.
Susie: Well, like you said, it's opening in two weeks. We're going to offer popular dishes from China, Japan, Thailand, and Vietnam.
Jackie: Why did you choose Asian food?
Susie: I guess I chose Asian because it's my personal favorite. And I discovered that our city has plenty of good Chinese, Japanese, and Vietnamese restaurants, but none of them combines the various cuisines of different Asian countries. I think that my future customers will love my restaurant because they'll be able to try the various cuisines in one place. I think they'll also like the prices. I've noticed Asian restaurants are often very expensive. I'm going to offer affordable prices in a casual setting. I'm lucky that I found the perfect location. Asian Cottage is downtown, right across from the bus stop on Main and Holman.
Jackie: It sounds like you've got a great business plan. Are you excited about your grand opening?
Susie: Yes, of course, but I'm also nervous.
Jackie: What are you nervous about?
Susie: I'm worried that my restaurant won't be successful. I've planned carefully, but I know that even the best plans sometimes fail. In fact, I read that fifty percent of small businesses fail in the first five years. I had to borrow a lot of money from the bank to open my restaurant. It's a big risk.
Jackie: Yes, it *is* risky, but that's what being an entrepreneur is about. I'm sure your restaurant will do great. I can't wait to go try it!
Susie: Thanks, Jackie.

UNIT 2 – TELL ME ABOUT YOURSELF

Page 26, Listen, Exercises 2A and 2B

Catherine: Good afternoon. I'm Catherine Tote. I'm an employment specialist here at Sun County Career Center.
Nedim: Hello. I'm Nedim Buric. It's nice to meet you.
Catherine: People in Sun County come to our Career Center for many reasons—to learn English, to take training classes, to use our computer center. What brings you here today?
Nedim: I want to find a job as soon as possible.
Catherine: We can help you with that, Mr. Buric. But before we can start looking at available positions, there are several things we need to talk about.
Nedim: I'm sure you'd like to know about my work experience. I'm not employed at the moment. I came to the U.S. just last month. Before that, I was a university student in my home country, Bosnia.
Catherine: Do you have any job experience?
Nedim: Yes. My uncle is a lawyer. I worked in his office part time while I was in school.
Catherine: Do you have good computer skills?
Nedim: Yes. I've always been a fast learner when it comes to computers. I'm also a very organized person. I'm very careful with details, and I'm an excellent problem solver.

Catherine: I see. Did you finish school?
Nedim: Not yet. I studied for two years in Bosnia. But then I decided to come to the U.S. with my family. I expect to complete my degree in a year or so, in night school.

Page 32, Listen, Exercises 2A and 2B

Lisa: When I moved to the U.S. from Hong Kong twenty years ago, I didn't know anyone, and it was difficult for me to find a job. I tried looking in the newspaper, but there weren't a lot of things that I was capable of doing. I was really worried about not having enough money to live on when I finally saw a "Help Wanted" sign in the window of a flower shop. I went in and talked to the store manager, filled out an application, and started working the next day. I was lucky to get hired. It was difficult at that time to find out where the job openings were.
Lisa: Today, you have more ways to find a job. Just think about it . . . You can go online to look for work, and there are several job placement agencies in our neighborhood. But in my opinion, networking is the best thing you can do. You have family, and we have friends and neighbors who might be able to help you. You should think about talking to everyone you know to get information about possible jobs.

Page 38, Listen, Exercises 2A and 2B

Interviwer: Tell me a little about yourself, Mr. Santos. How long have you been a driver?
Steve: Ten years. I've worked for Trends Supermarkets since 2016. Before that, I was with Grand Supermarkets.
Interviwer: OK. I see from your application that you have a commercial driver's license and you've driven a number of different kinds of trucks.
Steve: That's right. And I've never had an accident.
Interviwer: That's excellent. So, if you don't mind my asking, why are you thinking about leaving your current employer—Trends?
Steve: A couple of reasons. First of all, I want to work days. Most of the driving I do now is at night. Also, I think there will be more opportunities for me in a company like yours. I'm interested in working as a dispatcher someday.
Interviwer: So, in other words, you'd like to work in the office some day?
Steve: Yes. I think it would present a new and different kind of challenge. I think I'd be good as a dispatcher because I've had so much experience as a driver and I would understand the big picture. Plus, I'm good with technology and I like to problem-solve.

UNIT 3 - COMMUNITY LIFE

Page 46, Listen, Exercises 2A and 2B

Mali: Hi, Eric. I'm going to the Thai Festival this weekend. Do you want to come? My friends and I go every year.
Eric: The Thai Festival? What's that, Mali?
Mali: It's a celebration of the Thai New Year. It's on the first Sunday in April. Come on. You'll have fun.
Eric: Do you think so?
Mali: Definitely. It's really fun. There's traditional dancing and music. They have kick boxing demonstrations. There are stands with traditional Thai crafts.
Eric: Well, it sounds interesting . . .
Mali: Oh, and the food! The food is amazing! All the restaurants are open, but there are also stands with food.
Eric: Hmm. I love Thai food. It's really hot!
Mali: Oh, one thing. Kids might throw water at you. Don't be surprised.
Eric: You're kidding, right?
Mali: No! It's part of the tradition. People have water guns or containers of water and throw it at each other.
Eric: Wow. OK. So what time do you want to go?

Page 51, Interpret GPS Directions, Exercise 1E

F1: Head west on W. Berks St. toward N. Howard St.
F1: Turn right onto N. Howard St.
F1: Turn left onto W. Diamond St.
F1: Turn right onto N. Hancock St.
F1: Turn left onto W. Susquehanna Ave.
F1: Turn right onto N. Palethorp St.
F1: Destination will be on the left.

Page 51, Follow GPS Directions, Exercise 2A

F1: Proceed to the route and the map guidance will start.
F1: Turn right on Vine St.
F1: Turn right on Main St.
F1: Continue to follow the road for one mile.
F1: In a quarter mile, turn left on Hanson Park Dr.
F1: Turn left on Hanson Park Dr.
F1: Your destination will be on the right.
F1: You have arrived.

Page 52, Listen, Exercises 2A and 2B

Chen: I wish the city would do something about cleaning up the park in our neighborhood. There's trash everywhere, and there's graffiti on all the benches.
Ting: You know, when I go downtown, everything is nice and clean. I wish the Streets and Sanitation Department didn't spend all of their time downtown. I wish they would come to our neighborhood once in a while.
Chen: They want things to look good downtown for the businesses and tourists, but you have a point. What about us? We pay taxes, too.
Ting: And it's not just the streets and parks. I wish we had better garbage pick-up at our house. I'm never sure which day of the week the garbage truck is going to come, and last week they never came at all.
Chen: Did you complain?
Ting: Yes. But there was still no garbage pick-up until yesterday.
Chen: We have to keep calling to complain about it and about the vacant lot on the corner of Lawrence Avenue and River Street.
Ting: The amount of trash in that vacant lot is horrible. It's a health hazard. Where does it all come from?
Chen: Hmm, I think a lot of it is from the fast food restaurants on Lawrence. The teenagers who go there eat their burgers and fries and throw the empty containers in the vacant lot.
Ting: What are they doing hanging out by the vacant lot? They should be in school.
Chen: And after school, they should be going to the community center. I just wish there were more after-school programs in the community.

Page 58, Listen, Exercises 2A and 2B

Resident: Most of us in the neighborhood want to have better services. We don't want the city to take away services that we already have.

Clara: Exactly what services are you talking about, sir?

Resident: The last time we met with you, we asked you to increase the number of police officers at the Southland District Police Station. Instead, the station is closing. Do you expect us to be happy with that decision?

Clara: Please, sir. I urge you not to believe everything you hear. The police station isn't closing. I spoke with the mayor and the chief of police. I couldn't convince them to provide more patrol officers, but don't worry. We have a plan.

Resident: Let's hear it. We'd like you to explain how we can reduce the crime in this area.

Clara: The idea is to expand our community-policing program in the Southland District.

Resident: Do you mean that we do the work instead of the police?

Clara: No, of course not. The program encourages neighborhood residents to work *with* the police to identify problems and find solutions. The police will still investigate specific incidents, but with community policing, they expect to see fewer crimes.

Resident: I see. Because we can help the police identify problems before the crimes occur?

Clara: Exactly. The first meeting of the Southland Community-Policing Program will take place next week. How many people in this room plan to attend?

UNIT 4 – ON THE JOB

Page 66, Listen, Exercises 2A and 2B

Robert: Welcome to People's Bank. I'm sure you'll like working here. Are you ready to get started training to be a teller?

Sandra: Yes. I'll just observe you today, right?

Robert: That's right. You'll observe a manager for the first week. By the end of the week, you'll be ready to take care of customers on your own. Of course, I'll still help you out whenever you need.

Sandra: Great. It'll be helpful to see the bank's procedures firsthand.

Robert: That's the idea. OK, let's start out with deposits. I'll walk you through the process of depositing checks.

Sandra: Do customers still make deposits in person? I always make deposits by using an ATM or taking a picture of the check and uploading it to the banking app.

Robert: That's a good question! A lot of people deposit checks electronically like you do, but other customers still prefer to deposit their checks in person. Some of our customers still aren't familiar with mobile banking. They might ask you to help them set up the app on their phones. Are you comfortable with that?

Sandra: Yes, definitely.

Robert: OK, great. Now, for customers making deposits here at the bank, they'll need to endorse the back of the check and fill out a deposit slip. Pay special attention to the dollar amount on the deposit slip. Make sure it's the same as the amount on the check. Next, look up the customer's account and key in the deposit.

Sandra: Then do I print a receipt for the customer?

Robert: No, the teller doesn't always print a receipt. The customer has a choice. Find out if the customer would like you to print out a receipt or send a text or email copy of the receipt. Is everything clear so far?

Sandra: Yes, but it's a lot of information to take in. I need to write some of this down.

Robert: Sure, but it's already one o'clock. Why don't we get something to eat now? I'll go over the procedures again after lunch. How does everything sound to you so far?

Sandra: OK . . . I'm a little nervous, but I'll get over it.

Page 72, Listen, Exercises 2A and 2B

Resident: Mr. Peng seems to be doing well today, but I'd like to take a look at his records. Nina, could you show me Mr. Peng's records?

Nina: Of course . . . Hmm. I don't see any recent vital signs.

Resident: Didn't someone take Mr. Peng's vital signs this morning?

Nina: Misha was the nursing assistant on duty this morning. I thought she did it, but you're right. They're not here. Maybe she forgot to record them. I'll take his vitals right now.

Resident: Thanks, Nina.

Page 72, Listen, Exercise 2C

Resident: How is Mrs. Worth doing today, Nina?

Nina: She's doing quite well.

Resident: How many times has Mrs. Worth been out of bed since her gall bladder operation?

Nina: She got up once and sat in the chair for an hour.

Resident: She had the procedure yesterday. She needs to start walking. Haven't any of the nurses tried to take her down the hall?

Nina: There aren't a lot of nurses on the floor right now, but I'll walk with her down the hall as soon as I finish my rounds.

Resident: OK, good. Thank you.

Page 78, Listen, Exercises 2A and 2B

Dennis: Hi, Helena. How are you today?

Helena: Just fine, thanks. I'm a little nervous, though.

Dennis: Oh, you don't need to be nervous. The performance review is a conversation, really.

Helena: OK.

Dennis: First of all, I want you to know that we're happy in general with your work.

Helena: Oh, thank you!

Dennis: Yes, the quality of your work is very good. You're meeting your quotas, which is really important. I gave you a "3" in both categories.

Helena: Thank you. I understand how important it is to get all the packages out on time.

Dennis: Exactly. And you're good at following instructions. I gave you a "3" there, too.

Helena: Sometimes I have to ask for clarification . . .

Dennis: That's great. You should always ask if you're not sure. It's better to ask than to do the wrong thing.

Helena: OK. Good.
Dennis: I know you also have a positive attitude. That's really important.
Helena: Thanks. I agree. It makes things more pleasant when people are positive.
Dennis: I really appreciate that you work well with your co-workers. I've noticed that you often volunteer to help them if you finish your work early. You deserve the "4" I gave you for teamwork.
Helena: I enjoy working with everyone. I like being part of a team.
Dennis: Well, it shows. So I think the only thing that we need to talk about is the issue of clothing, well, jewelry and shoes, really. I had to give you a "2" in safety procedures. Employees are supposed to leave earrings and rings at home and not wear jewelry on the job. Yesterday, you were wearing a long necklace that could have gotten caught in the machinery. And the other day, you were wearing sandals. You know that company policy requires all employees to wear shoes that will protect their feet and prevent them from slipping and falling if the floors are wet.
Helena: I'm so sorry. I stopped wearing my earrings and rings, but I didn't realize that I couldn't wear a necklace. It won't happen again. And I know about the shoes. I just forgot. I understand. Safety is very important.

UNIT 5 – SAFE AND SOUND

Page 86, Listen, Exercises 2A and 2B

Thank you all for being here this evening. I'm happy to see that so many people are concerned about fire safety. Tonight's class will focus on what you can do to prevent a fire in your home. Let's begin with a room that's very important in many homes—the kitchen.

Cooking is the number-one cause of house fires in the U.S. When you're in the kitchen, pay attention to what you're doing. Keep hair and clothing away from fire, and keep your cooking areas clean. If a pan of food catches fire, immediately put a lid over it and turn the stove off. Also remember to turn off the stove and oven when you finish preparing your food. And never leave the kitchen while food is still cooking on the stove. Remember that it takes only a few seconds for a fire to start.

If you have children, you should be extra careful. They're curious, so they'll want to know what's going on in the kitchen. Teach children not to touch anything on the stove.

Now, are there any questions before I go on?

Page 92, Listen, Exercises 2A and 2B

Host: Today we're discussing hurricanes with meteorologist Dr. Kay Wilkins. Dr. Wilkins, welcome.
Dr. Wilkins: Thank you. It's a pleasure to be here.
Host: Let's begin with the basics. What are hurricanes and how are they different from other storms?
Dr. Wilkins: Hurricanes are giant tropical storms that bring heavy rainfall and *very* strong winds. The wind speed is what makes them different from other tropical storms. When a tropical storm's wind speed reaches 74 miles per hour, it's classified as a hurricane.
Host: What causes hurricanes? How do they form?
Dr. Wilkins: Hurricanes form over warm ocean water. When warm, moist air rises above the ocean surface, it pulls in the surrounding, cooler air. This cycle causes clouds to form and these clouds start rotating with the spin of the earth. When there's enough warm water spinning, a hurricane forms.
Host: You said hurricanes need warm water in order to form. Does that mean we need to worry about hurricanes only in the summer months?
Dr. Wilkins: Not exactly. Officially, hurricane season in the Atlantic Ocean is from June 1 through November 30. Most hurricanes will occur during these six months, but there have also been bad storms in May and December.
Host: Are all hurricanes dangerous?
Dr. Wilkens: Hurricanes often occur out at sea and cause no harm, but when they move towards land, they can be extremely dangerous and cause major damage. After a hurricane reaches land, it often produces a storm surge.
Host: What is a storm surge?
Dr. Wilkens: That's when the high winds push the water toward the shore. This causes water levels to rise up to twenty feet, or even more. This can cause major flooding in coastal regions.
Host: What about people who live inland? Do they have to worry about hurricanes?
Dr. Wilkins: Since hurricanes get their power over water, coastal areas are usually the hardest hit. But inland areas can also experience flooding. Even a category 1 storm can cause severe flooding.
Host: What do the different categories mean?
Dr. Wilkens: The categories are based on the storm's wind strength. A Category 1 hurricane is the weakest, with wind speeds from 74 to 95 miles per hour. A Category 2 storm has wind speeds of 96 to 110 miles per hour. The strongest storm is a Category 5, with wind speeds starting at 157 miles per hour.
Host: And can you explain the difference between a hurricane watch and a hurricane warning for our listeners?
Dr. Wilkins: Of course. The National Weather Service issues a hurricane watch when there is the possibility of a hurricane within the next 36 hours. A hurricane warning means that you can expect a hurricane to arrive in your area within 24 hours. As soon as you hear the warning, make sure that your emergency preparations are complete.
Host: Tell me, Dr. Wilkins. What's the most important thing that everyone should know about hurricanes?
Dr. Wilkins: To take them seriously. Always follow the evacuation order and go to a safe location.

Page 98, Listen, Exercises 2A and 2B

Host: Hello, and welcome to *Community Matters.* Today, we're going to talk about a very important group of people, 911 dispatchers. In the event of an emergency, the first person you speak to will likely be a 911 dispatcher. They are responsible for taking your call, getting you help as quickly as possible, and informing the police officers, firefighters, or paramedics of the situation. To tell us more about it, we're going to talk to Mark Jones, a 911 dispatcher. Welcome to *Community Matters,* Mark.

Mark: Thanks. It's great to be here.

Host: Tell us a little about your career.

Mark: This is my fifth year working as a 911 dispatcher. I'm responsible for taking 911 calls. I dispatch the emergency responders to the emergency, keep the callers calm, and keep the emergency responders informed about what is going on.

Host: How did you choose this career?

Mark: Well, I always knew I wanted to help people. My parents were both nurses when I was growing up. I thought about being a nurse too. But one day, I met a 911 dispatcher. As she was telling me about her career, I knew that it was the right job for me.

Host: What kind of training or experience do you need to be a dispatcher?

Mark: Many dispatchers have degrees in law enforcement, emergency management, public safety, or psychology, but it's also possible to start out with only a high school diploma. The emergency call center where I work provided me with the necessary training. I had to complete a 12-week certification program, which included CPR and first aid certification.

Host: So, what is a typical day like?

Mark: Some days I have back-to-back calls the entire shift. Other days I might have a whole hour with no calls. I never know what to expect. Many of the calls I take do not require emergency assistance at all. For example, I can't respond to a call about a power outage. I would tell that caller to contact the utilities company. And if I get a call about a crime that occurred a couple of days ago, I would tell the caller to contact the police department directly, not 911.

Host: OK, last question: What is the most important information you gather?

Mark: That's easy: location. The first question I ask any caller is: "Where are you?" If I don't have the location, there's nothing I can do to help.

UNIT 6 – MOVING IN

Page 106, Listen, Exercises 2A and 2B

Jenn: Hi, I'm calling about the apartment ad online.

Susan: Yes, we have several units available. What are you looking for?

Jenn: I'm looking for an apartment for me, my husband, and our one-year-old daughter. I prefer three bedrooms, but two bedrooms would also be OK.

Susan: We have an unfurnished three-bedroom apartment for $2,000 a month.

Jenn: That's pretty expensive. Does it include utilities?

Susan: Yes, it includes water, electricity, and gas.

Jenn: How about cable and Internet?

Susan: No, I'm sorry. You're required to pay for your own cable and Internet.

Jenn: What amenities does the apartment complex offer?

Susan: We have a gym, an outdoor swimming pool, a basketball court, two tennis courts, a playground, and a picnic area.

Jenn: Oh, that's really nice! Is parking included?

Susan: Yes, you are allowed one parking permit for the open, uncovered parking lot. If you would like a covered parking spot, it's $50 a month.

Jenn: Are visitors allowed to allowed to park in the lot?

Susan: Yes, visitors are permitted to park here, but you're required to come to the office and get a visitor's parking tag for your guests.

Jenn: How soon could I move in?

Susan: We have a unit available now. You can move in as soon as you pay the first month's rent and the $800 security deposit.

Jenn: What's the security deposit for?

Susan: You're required to pay the security deposit in case you damage anything in your apartment. If there is no damage, you'll get the deposit back when you move out. It's $800, but if you have pets, it's $1,000.

Jenn: OK. Can I come look at the apartment today?

Susan: Sure. Just come to the main office at the entrance on South Street. We're open until six this evening.

Page 112, Listen, Exercises 2A and 2B

Henry: Welcome to *This Week.* I'm your host Henry Scott. Our guest today is Manny Lopez, a tenant rights lawyer. Today, Manny is going to answer questions on tenant law in Texas. Manny, it's nice to have you back on our show.

Manny: Thanks, Henry. Glad to be here.

Henry: Last week, we asked our guests to send in their questions and complaints about their landlords. Our first question is from Chris in Dallas. Chris writes: "The smoke alarms in my apartment don't work anymore. I called the landlord several times, but he never called me back. He has to replace the smoke detectors, doesn't he?" OK, Manny. Can you help Chris with this question?

Manny: Yes. In Texas, the landlord is required to put a working smoke detector outside each bedroom. But if the smoke detectors stop working, you have to notify the landlord in writing. Send your landlord a message explaining the problem. Make sure to keep a copy of the email.

Page 112, Listen, Exercise 2C

Henry: Now for our next question. Eva in San Antonio writes: "My landlord is going to raise my rent to $1,700 a month. He isn't allowed to do that, is he? I still have six months left on my lease. It doesn't end until September 1st. I'm a good tenant. I always pay my rent on time." Hmmm. What do you think, Manny? If her lease isn't up, her landlord can't raise the rent, can he?

Manny: That's right. It sounds like Eva's lease is still in effect. That means the landlord is not allowed to raise her rent until after September 1st. But after that date, she'll have to sign a new lease, and then the landlord can raise the rent.

Page 118, Listen, Exercises 2A and 2B

Oscar: What's that noise? It's so loud.

Marta: The neighbors are watching TV.

Oscar: Which neighbors? The ones in 2A?

Marta: No, 2C.
Oscar: What's their name?
Marta: I don't remember. I've only seen them in the hallway.
Oscar: Well, I'm going over there and telling them they have to turn down the TV. We just got the baby to sleep.
Marta: I already went over there.
Oscar: You did?
Marta: Yes, I told them the baby was sleeping, and I asked them if they could be quieter.
Oscar: What did they say?
Marta: They didn't say anything. They slammed the door in my face.
Oscar: What! I'm going over there right now!
Marta: Oscar, don't lose your temper. Yelling at them won't do any good. Let me call the building manager.
Oscar: What can he do?
Marta: He can call them and remind them about the building rules—no loud TV or music after 10 p.m. They might listen to him. He also said we could call the police if there's noise after 10 p.m.
Oscar: I'm not calling the police about noise. I'll go over there and settle it myself.
Marta: OK, fine, but let me call the building manager first. It's better if we let him handle it.

UNIT 7 – BEHIND THE WHEEL

Page 126, Listen, Exercises 2A and 2B

Eva: Mark, look at this app. It has car listings from different dealerships in our area.
Mark: Dealers are pretty expensive. I don't think we can afford a new car.
Eva: Oh, I'm looking at listings for used cars. The dealers have both new and pre-owned cars. Or would you prefer to buy a car from a private owner?
Mark: No, I guess I'd prefer to buy from a dealer. We can get a warranty from a dealership but not from an individual seller.
Eva: Exactly. Look. Here's a compact car with good gas mileage. It looks nice! It has an entertainment system and a sunroof.
Mark: It's nice, but we can live without those optional features. Wouldn't you rather get a four-door car?
Eva: Yes, I would. I didn't even notice it was a two-door. We also need to think about safety features. We need airbags and antilock brakes.
Mark: I think those are standard features these days. We should look for a rearview camera.
Eva: Right. So we're looking for a four-door sedan, three or four years old, with a rearview camera.
Mark: That's right. Hey, I just realized that we've never talked about color. Would you rather have a light color or a dark color—like black, maybe?
Eva: Hmm . . . Well, now that I think about it, I've always wanted to drive a *red* car.
Mark: Red, huh? I heard somewhere that red cars get more speeding tickets.
Eva: Really? Hmm. Then I won't speed. I can't get a ticket if I'm not speeding, right?
Mark: Right. How about this . . . Let's look at these listings and see what's out there and what kind of deal we can get. Then we'll worry about the color.

Page 131, Talk about Buying Car Insurance, Exercises 2C and 2D

Amy: I'm ready to call and get a quote for car insurance.
Tom: Good. Are you ready for all the questions they'll ask?
Amy: I thought I would be asking most of the questions.
Tom: Actually, your premium will depend on how you answer some of their questions.
Amy: Really? What kinds of things will they ask?
Tom: They'll want to know what kind of car you drive. If you own a sports car, for example, the premium is usually higher.
Amy: OK. What else will they ask? How about safety features? A salesperson at the used-car lot told me that having lots of safety features would probably help keep my premium low.
Tom: Yes. That's true. And they'll want to know how many miles you expect to drive each year.
Amy: How can I predict how many miles I'll drive?
Tom: It's just a guess. Premiums are usually higher for people who drive a lot.
Amy: OK. Is there anything else I should know?
Tom: They'll probably ask you if you're single or married and also your age.
Amy: Why do my marital status and my age make a difference?
Tom: I think there are statistics that show that older, married people have fewer accidents.

Page 132, Listen, Exercises 2A and 2B

Jake: This is Jake Alexander, and you're listening to *All Things Auto.* It's time for our Car Care Question of the Week. I have an email here from Nicole. Nicole writes, "Can you tell me what your number-one car-care tip is?" Well, listeners, when it comes to car maintenance, there's one thing you should always remember, and that is "Don't delay. Do it today." Of course, you should change the oil regularly. For most cars, that's every three months or every 3,000 miles. But there are other things that you should do regularly, too. Your car's tires are very important for your safety, so inspect them once a month. Check the tread, and check the air pressure. If you don't know how much air your tires should have, look in your owner's manual. Finally, check for leaks once a week. Look under the hood and under your car. And look for color. For example, transmission fluid is red. Engine coolant is bright green or yellow, and oil is light brown. If you see a problem, take your car to a good mechanic right away. Fix small problems before they become serious. It's impossible to say exactly how many years this will add to the life of your car, but you'll definitely save money, and you'll have a vehicle that's safer and easier to drive. Remember, listeners—"Don't delay. Do it today!"

Page 138, Listen, Exercises 2A and 2B

Nora: Are you OK? You aren't hurt, are you?
Frank: No, I'm fine. How about you? Are you all right?
Nora: Yes, but I can't say the same for my car. The right headlight is out, and there are big dents in the hood and fender.
Frank: I don't know what happened. I'd already started moving into the right lane when I saw you. By that time, there was nothing I could do. I remember

putting on my turn signal and looking for cars coming from the opposite direction, but I didn't see any cars.

Nora: I didn't see you either—until the very last minute. I had just slowed down because of the rain, but there still wasn't enough time for me to stop. You know, we should pull the cars to the side of the road. I'll grab my phone.

Frank: Are you going to call the police? I think we should do that.

Nora: Yes. We have to report the accident. It's the law. Besides, our insurance companies will definitely want a police report.

Frank: My insurance card and my driver's license and vehicle registration are in the car. I'll get them.

Nora: I'll get mine, too. And we're supposed to take pictures.

Frank: I wonder why we're supposed to do that.

Nora: The insurance companies will need pictures of the damage.

Frank: Oh, of course. That makes sense.

UNIT 8 – HOW ARE YOU FEELING?

Page 146, Listen, Exercises 2A and 2C

Dr. Miller: Good morning, Mrs. Garcia. What brings you here today?

Irma Garcia: To tell you the truth, Doctor, I haven't been feeling well for the past couple of weeks.

Dr. Miller: What seems to be the problem?

Irma Garcia: For one thing, I can't sleep at night. I have a lot of congestion, so I can't breathe.

Dr. Miller: Anything else?

Irma Garcia: Yes. I feel achy. My whole body hurts! Oh, and I've been sneezing a lot lately.

Dr. Miller: Hmm . . . And you say this has been going on for about two weeks?

Irma Garcia: Right. At first, I thought I had a cold, but now I'm worried that it's something more serious.

Dr. Miller: I think you might have an allergy. The question is what's causing it. Is there anything different about where you live or work?

Irma Garcia: No, my husband and I live in the same house, and I still work in our family business.

Dr. Miller: OK. What about your diet? Have you been eating any new kinds of food?

Irma Garcia: Well, I eat the same food as always, but I've been cooking a lot more since my daughter came home from college a few weeks ago.

Dr. Miller: Aha! That could be the answer.

Irma Garcia: What? You think I'm allergic to my daughter?

Dr. Miller: No, Mrs. Garcia. Not your daughter, but maybe something your daughter brought into the house, such as perfume or a houseplant. We'll do a few tests to find out for sure.

Page 152, Listen, Exercises 2A and 2B

Dispatcher: 911, what is your emergency?

Caller: I need an ambulance here.

Dispatcher: OK. Where are you located?

Caller: 136 Elm Street.

Dispatcher: OK. Can you tell me what's going on?

Caller: It's my husband and he's . . . I don't know, he's having chest pain. And he's sweating, really badly.

Dispatcher: Is he conscious or unconscious?

Caller: He's conscious . . . but he's having so much chest pain it's hard for him to breathe.

Dispatcher: Try to stay calm. You need to help him until the paramedics get there. How old is your husband?

Caller: 58.

Dispatcher: Does he have any ongoing medical problems?

Caller: Yes, he has diabetes.

Dispatcher: Is he taking medication for that?

Caller: Yes.

Dispatcher: Is he on any other medication?

Caller: No, I don't think so. Are the paramedics almost here?

Dispatcher: Yes, help is on the way. You're doing great.

Page 158, Listen, Exercises 2A and 2B

Host: Hello, listeners! And welcome to our podcast, *Community Matters.* Well, it's that time of year again. Flu season is here, so you'd better get your annual flu shot soon. To tell us more about why it's so important to get a flu shot, we've invited Wendy Cole, a registered nurse, to our program today. Thanks for joining us, Wendy.

Wendy: Thanks for inviting me. I'm happy to spread the word about how important it is to get an annual flu vaccine. You may not think of the flu as a serious disease, but complications can lead to illness, hospitalization, and even death.

Host: Who is at the greatest risk?

Wendy: Children under the age of five, adults 65 years of age and older, and pregnant women have the greatest risk of developing complications from the flu, but it's important to understand that anyone can get the flu, and more importantly, anyone can *give* the flu to someone else. Even if you are not in a high-risk group, you could get the flu without even knowing it, and then pass it on to someone with a weaker immune system. That's why everyone should get the flu vaccine. It's the best way to protect you and your loved ones.

Host: Is the vaccine available to everyone, even newborn babies and pregnant women?

Wendy: No, infants must be at least six months old before they can get the vaccine. It's available to everyone else, though, including pregnant women.

Host: What if I got the vaccine last year? Will that be enough to protect me this flu season?

Wendy: Unfortunately, no. You must get a new vaccine every year for two reasons. First, the body's immune response from a vaccination declines over time. And second, flu viruses are constantly changing. New flu strains may arise every year or old strains may change. With all the different strains, old vaccines can become useless.

Host: Do you have to see a doctor to get the flu vaccine?

Wendy: No, you don't. You can call your doctor's office and make an appointment to see the nurse if you're only getting the flu vaccine. You can also go to a walk-in clinic or community health fair.

Most pharmacies and even grocery stores also offer the vaccine. Some employers offer free vaccines to their workers. You should ask your employer if they have this service.

Host: This is great information! Thanks again for being here today. Listeners, stay healthy this flu season. Get your flu shot today!

UNIT 9 – PARTNERS IN EDUCATION

Page 166, Listen, Exercises 2A and 2C

Mr. Bowman: Thanks for coming to my office today. I know you took time off from work to meet with me. I want to talk to you about your daughter.

Mrs. Patel: Monika? Oh, Monika is a good student. My son has some problems with his grades, but not Monika.

Mr. Bowman: Oh, yes. Your daughter is an excellent student! And that's exactly why I want to talk with you. Since Monika will start high school next fall, it's time to start thinking about college.

Mrs. Patel: College? Uh, Monika is only 13 years old. College is a long way off.

Mr. Bowman: Well, yes and no.

Mrs. Patel: What do you mean, "Yes and no"?

Mr. Bowman: It's never too early to start thinking about college. I'd like Monika to have as many opportunities as possible, because she is one of our best students.

Mrs. Patel: Thank you.

Mr. Bowman: But when I talk to Monika about college, she isn't interested, because she thinks she can't afford it.

Mrs. Patel: Well, my husband and I can take care of our family, but we don't make a lot of money.

Mr.Bowman: Many schools offer scholarships and financial aid to help students pay for their education.

Mrs. Patel: Oh, really? How can we make sure Monika gets a scholarship?

Mr. Bowman: Well, there are no guarantees. But the first thing to do is talk to Monika about classes that will prepare her for college.

Mrs. Patel: OK, and I'd like to make another appointment with you. Next time, I'll bring my husband so that we can both talk to you about scholarships and financial aid.

Page 172, Listen, Exercises 2A, 2B, and 2C

Secretary: Good morning. How can I help you?

Mr. López: Hello. I'm Pablo Lopez, and this is my daughter, Marta. I need to enroll Marta in school. We just moved here.

Secretary: Oh, yes. You're the one I spoke with on the phone last week. Marta finished first grade at Newtown Elementary, right?

Mr. López: Yes, that's right. She's ready for second grade.

Secretary: OK, I can help you get her enrolled. Do you have proof that you live in School District 15? For example, can you show me the lease for your new apartment?

Mr. López: I don't have a lease, but I brought an electric bill that has my name and address on it.

Secretary: Perfect. Now, I'll need a few other things from you. Do you have Marta's school records from Newtown?

Mr. López: Yes. I also brought her birth certificate and her medical and dental records.

Secretary: Excellent. I'll also need a phone number that we can call if there's an emergency. Here's a form you can fill out with that information.

Mr. López: OK.

Secretary: And here's a list of school supplies—pencils, notebooks, and folders—which your daughter has to bring with her to class.

Mr. López: Thank you.

Secretary: You're welcome. Let me know if you have any questions.

Page 178, Listen, Exercises 2A and 2B

I want to welcome you to the first meeting of this advisory committee. Before we do anything else, I'd like to explain the purpose of the committee.

Because he has talked about it so many times, you must have heard about the mayor's plan to improve school safety. He could not have come up with this plan without the support of parents' advisory committees all over the city. The plan requires all schools to identify five improvements to keep students safe and to create a better atmosphere for learning. I am asking you as advisory committee members to assist me in preparing a school safety plan for West Apollo Elementary School.

Every person in this room has something to contribute to our plan. Some of you are parents, and your children might have talked to you about problems at school. Some of you live near here, so you are familiar with problems in the neighborhood. The teachers in this group are familiar with how students behave in classrooms, in the cafeteria, and on the playground. Any one of you may have thought about changes that we should make in our procedures and school buildings. I hope all of you will contribute your ideas to our safety plan.

UNIT 10 – SAFETY FIRST

Page 186, Listen, Exercises 2A and 2B

Sam: Oleg, what's going on with the cabinets? They should be almost finished by now.

Oleg: I'm sorry, Sam. The wood was out of stock. It didn't arrive until yesterday.

Sam: Then we're a whole week behind schedule! Why didn't you make the supplier send a special order?

Oleg: The wood wasn't available. I couldn't make the supplier send something they didn't have. I had them rush the order as soon as the product was available.

Sam: This is really bad news. Why didn't you let me know there was a problem with the order?

Oleg: I did. I texted you last week.

Sam: I didn't see your text. Why didn't you call?

Oleg: I called twice and left voicemail messages both times. I also let your office assistant know about the problem. She said I should text you.

Sam: Oh. Well, never mind . . . But listen. I need you to finish those cabinets right away. How soon do you think you can get the job done?

Oleg: Two weeks is the best I can do.

Sam: Come on. Can't you do it in a week and a half? Maybe you can get someone to help you finish the job sooner.
Oleg: Sure, but it will cost more. I'll have to pay another worker. Which is more important: time or money?
Sam: We have to stay within the budget, so I guess money. You really can't finish it sooner on your own?
Oleg: Sorry, but I need two weeks to make quality cabinets. You want me to do a good job, don't you?
Sam: OK, you're right. Two weeks. In the meantime, can you let the counter guy measure space for the counter? He needs to install the counters as soon as the cabinets are ready.
Oleg: Oh, sure. No problem.

Page 192, Listen, Exercises 2A and 2B

Asad: Wait! Don't turn on the press yet!
Clara: What's the matter?
Asad: You can't wear a bracelet when you're operating the press . . . See those moving rollers? Your bracelet could get caught in the roller. You could hurt yourself very badly.
Clara: Oh. I'll take it off right now.
Asad: Didn't you go to the safety training?
Clara: I did. But I thought they just said no loose clothing.
Asad: Or jewelry, like bracelets and necklaces. These machines are dangerous. Did you read the safety manual yet?
Clara: Yes, of course, but I don't remember everything it said.
Asad: I see. OK. Let's do a safety check. I always do a safety check before I start. First, make sure the guards are all on the machine. Make sure you're not wearing long sleeves or jewelry. Keep your hands a safe distance from the rollers. OK, now it looks like you're ready to start. I'm going to watch you work for a while to make sure you're working safely.
Clara: Thanks so much, Asad!
Asad: You're welcome.

Page 198, Listen, Exercises 2A and 2B

Don: Hi, Lisa. Could I talk to you for a minute?
Lisa: Oh, sure. Umm, is everything OK?
Don: Yes! Here, have a seat. I want to talk to you about your future with Dependable Delivery.
Lisa: Oh, thanks! That's great.
Don: You've been doing an excellent job. Let's see. You started out with us six months ago as a sorter . . . You're very efficient. I can see you're moving 400 packages in an hour.
Lisa: Thank you.
Don: And you're accurate. I see you've made mistakes with only three packages in three months.
Lisa: I try my best.
Don: Also, when your co-workers need help, you try to help them.
Lisa: Well, thanks. I guess we're all part of a team.
Don: The other thing that's important is safety practices. You follow the safety practices you learned in the safety-training course.
Lisa: Well, safety is important. I don't want to get hurt!
Don: Right, everyone wants to be safe. But you're especially conscientious. Vikram told me that you saw him lifting the wrong way and warned him . . . that's the kind of thing we like to see in a supervisor. So . . . I'm promoting you to the position of training supervisor.
Lisa: Oh, wow! That's great . . .
Don: You'll be responsible for seven employees, starting on the 12th. Why don't you come to my office tomorrow morning—let's say at 10:15?—and I'll give you more details.
Lisa: Thank you, Don. I'm really excited to have this opportunity.
Don: You're welcome. You earned it.

UNIT 11 – KNOW THE LAW

Page 206, Listen, Exercises 2A and 2B

Host: Good afternoon, listeners. This week we're talking about job applications. I asked you to send in your questions about filling out applications. One question that came up again and again was what to include when an application asks if you've ever been convicted of a crime. Several of you wanted to know if it is necessary to include that parking ticket you got ten years ago, or the collection fee you paid for a past due hospital bill. We have attorney David Ross here today to answer those questions. David, thanks for joining us.
David: It's my pleasure.
Host: In regards to criminal background, can you explain what we must include on a job application?
David: Sure. I'll start with the example you gave earlier. Paying a bill late is not a crime. It's important to pay your bills on time so you don't get late fees and damage your credit score, but making late payments won't go on a criminal record. Writing a bad check, on the other hand, is a crime. It's important to make sure you have enough money in your bank account before you write a check. It could be a misdemeanor or even a felony in some states.
Host: Could you briefly explain the difference between a misdemeanor and a felony?
David: Of course. A felony is a serious crime, such as kidnapping, arson, fraud, burglary and murder. Felonies are punishable by long prison sentences. Misdemeanors are much less serious. Trespassing, loitering, littering, vandalizing property, and disturbing the peace are some examples of misdemeanors. Misdemeanors are usually punished by a fine and sometimes a short jail sentence of less than one year.
Host: So in terms of job applications, do we have to include both misdemeanors and felonies?
David: Most of the time, yes. It's important to read the question carefully. If the application specifically asks about felonies, then you do not have to include misdemeanors. But most applications say: "Have you ever been convicted of a crime other than a traffic violation?" Misdemeanors are less serious than felonies, but they are still crimes. But that parking ticket you mentioned earlier? That's a minor traffic violation. You don't need to include it or small speeding tickets. But you *are* required to include serious violations like reckless driving or driving while intoxicated.
Host: What should our listeners do if they are not sure what to include?

David: If they're applying for a position with a company that has a Human Resources department, they can call and ask to speak with HR. They don't have to give their names. They can say something like, "Hi, I'm applying for a job with your company. I got a ticket for littering last year. Do I need to include that on my application?"
Host: What is the most important advice for our listeners?
David: Honesty is the best policy. It might be embarrassing to tell employers about your criminal background, but lying about it will only make matters worse.

Page 212, Listen, Exercises 2A and 2B

Lisa: Alex! Don't tell me you're watching that program again.
Alex: What do you mean? What's wrong with this program?
Lisa: It's garbage.
Alex: How can you call it garbage? This program is watched by millions of people all over the country. It shows how the law works.
Lisa: Oh, do you really believe that? There's no real law on that show, just people complaining about their relationships.
Alex: Oh, come on, Lisa.
Lisa: Those aren't real cases at all—those stories are all made up. And they certainly aren't heard by real judges. They're all actors . . .
Alex: Ah, ah, ah, not true—some of the shows are real cases. Or they're based on real ones.
Lisa: Oh, brother.
Alex: Listen to this case that was just on. It's really interesting. There were two roommates. One roommate was behind on his car payments, and the bank was going to repossess his car. So he got his roommate to lend him $2,000 for the car payment.
Lisa: Uh—not a good idea.
Alex: Uh, yeah! You're right about that! The roommates got into a big fight and moved out. And the guy with the car didn't pay back the $2,000 he owed his roommate. So they went to court, and the case was decided by a judge. He said to the guy who loaned his friend the money, "Well, your friend has to pay you the money back, but here's some advice. Never lend money to your friends."
Lisa: Hmm. That reminds me . . .
Alex: What?
Lisa: You owe me 50 bucks.

Page 218, Listen, Exercises 2A and 2B

Host: Welcome back to *Car Chat!* I'm your host Frank Evans, and I'm here with former traffic-court judge, Carl Mansfield. He's here to answer your questions about traffic violations. Caller 1, you're on the air.
Caller 1: Hi, Carl. A police officer recently gave me a ticket for running a stop sign. But I couldn't see the sign because a tree branch was hanging over it. Do I really have to pay the fine?
Carl: It sounds like you're in the right. I advise you to ask for a trial to contest the ticket. But, first go back to the stop sign and take a picture of it. Then you can show the picture to a judge in traffic court. He or she will probably dismiss the ticket.
Caller 1: Thanks, Carl.
Carl: You're welcome. Caller 2? How can I help you?
Caller 2: I've gotten a few traffic tickets, so I have some points on my license. I heard that if I go to traffic school, I can get the points on my license erased. Is that true?
Carl: Well, that depends on the state where you live. In this state, as long as your traffic violations aren't too serious, you can go to traffic school to get the points erased from your license. What kind of tickets are they?
Caller 2: Oh, they're mostly parking tickets. But I did get one ticket for speeding. How do I sign up for traffic school?
Carl: Well, it's easy. You can sign up online. After you complete the course, they'll give you a certificate. As soon as you show the certificate, your driving record will be clean again.
Caller 2: Great! Thanks for the information!

UNIT 12 – SAVING AND SPENDING

Page 226, Listen, Exercises 2A and 2B

John: Hello. What can I do for you?
Ling: Hi. I'd like to open a checking account.
John: OK. We have several options. Our MyMoney account is very popular. There's no monthly maintenance fee, and it has a pretty good interest rate.
Ling: That sounds good.
John: It requires a minimum balance of $1,500, though.
Ling: Uh . . . What happens if I go below fifteen hundred?
John: Well, you'll be charged a monthly maintenance fee.
Ling: I see. You know, a lot of banks offer free checking. Don't you have something like that?
John: Sure we do. You want an interest-free checking account then. There's no minimum balance requirement.
Ling: Yeah, interest-free checking—that's what I want. Are there any fees I should know about?
John: Well, the usual—you pay an overdraft fee if you write a check or make an automatic bill payment for more than the amount in your checking account. If you're interested, the bank offers overdraft protection for a monthly flat fee.
Ling: And how much is that?
John: $30.
Ling: No, thanks. I'll just have to keep an eye on my account balance.
John: OK . . . Interest-free checking then. Let me get your information . . .

Page 232, Listen, Exercises 2A and 2B

Host: Welcome back to *MoneyWise.* I'm Helen Duncan. We're here today with financial expert Patricia Wong. Patricia is taking questions from our listeners now. Here's our first caller.
Rafael: Hi, Patricia, I'm Rafael. Thanks for taking my call.
Patricia: No problem. I'm here to help you with your money questions. Go ahead.
Rafael: I have a lot of debt, and I'm having a hard time paying all my bills each month.
Patricia: What kind of debt, Rafael?
Rafael: Credit card and some personal loans.

Patricia: How much in personal loans and credit card debt are we talking about?
Rafael: Uh, I borrowed $5,000 from my credit union and I have about $20,000 in credit card debt.
Patricia: I see. That's $25,000 more or less. How old are you and what do you do?
Rafael: 27. I work in a hospital—I'm a technician.
Patricia: And what's the interest rate on your credit cards?
Rafael: They vary—from 9.99% to 18%.
Patricia: Whoa! What happened? Why 18%?
Rafael: Well, I missed a payment on one of my credit card bills.
Patricia: That's what usually happens. Well, your situation isn't hopeless, Rafael. The first thing that you should do is talk to the credit card companies. Try to get the rate lowered on the card with the 18% interest rate. If they lower the rate by just a point or two, it will make a big difference in your monthly payment.
Rafael: OK. I'll try.
Patricia: Next, if you can, pay off the cards with the highest interest rate by increasing your monthly payment. Let's say you're paying $50 a month now on a balance of $1,000. If you increase your monthly payment to $75, you'll finish paying the loan seven months sooner.
Rafael: That sounds like something I can do. It's just $25 a month more than I'm paying now.
Patricia: Here's one more idea for you: try to get a second job and use your second income to pay off your debt. If you follow just one or two of those suggestions, you'll start reducing your debt in no time. Good luck.
Rafael: Thanks so much, Patricia. Those are all good suggestions.

Page 238, Listen, Exercises 2A and 2B

Edgar: Hey, what would you do if you suddenly inherited a lot of money?
Carla: I'd be quiet about it, and I'd keep working for a while. Why?
Edgar: This guy in my office—turns out he had a rich uncle. Well, the uncle died and left him half a million!
Carla: Really? What's he going to do with the money?
Edgar: He already spent it! He bought a really expensive sports car and a motorcycle! Then he quit his job. And now he's traveling around the world.
Carla: That's crazy. That money will disappear quickly. If I came into a lot of money, I would do something more useful with it.
Edgar: Like what?
Carla: I'd go to medical school. I've always dreamed of becoming a doctor.
Edgar: You don't like being a nurse?
Carla: I do, but I'd rather be a doctor.
Edgar: Then you'd still work here?
Carla: No, I'd go back home—to Haiti. I'd build a clinic in my village, and I'd give the people in my village free medical care.
Edgar: You have such a good heart! As for me, if I found myself with a lot of money, I'd probably spend it on myself!
Carla: What would you do?
Edgar: I'd quit my job for sure. I don't like my job. Then I'd pay off all my debts. Finally, I'd buy a big house on the beach.
Carla: But wouldn't you get lonely in that big house all by yourself?
Edgar: Oh, no! I wouldn't live there by myself. I'd invite my parents, my brothers and sisters, cousins, even my closest friends to live with me.
Carla: Whoa! That would be an entire village!
Edgar: Exactly. Imagine what fun that would be. Of course, I'd invite you to come and visit me.
Carla: It's a deal!

MAP OF THE UNITED STATES AND CANADA

INDEX

ACADEMIC SKILLS

CIVICS

GRAMMAR

INDEX

LISTENING

SPEAKING

WORK SKILLS

CREDITS

Photos:

Front Cover: Pixelfit/E+/Getty Images; Asiseeit/E+/Getty Images; Photographer/Moment/Getty Images; Kiyoshi Hijiki/Moment/ Getty Images.

To the Teacher:
Page vi (cellphone): Tele52/Shutterstock; vi (front cover): Pixelfit/ E+/Getty Images; vi (front cover): Asiseeit/E+/Getty Images; vi (front cover): Photographer/Moment/Getty Images; vi (front cover): Kiyoshi Hijiki/Moment/Getty Images; vi (MyEnglishLab screenshot): Pearson Education, Inc; vi (ActiveTeach screenshot): Pearson Education, Inc; vi (CCRS page, bottom, left): Wavebreakmedia/Shutterstock; vi (CCRS page, top, right): Illustration Forest/Shutterstock.

Unit Tour:
Page vii: Martinedoucet/E+/Getty Images; viii (left): Ariel Skelley/ DigitalVision/Getty Images; ix (right): Tele52/Shutterstock; xxii (top): Courtesy of Sarah Lynn; xxii (center): Courtesy of Ronna Magy; xxii (bottom): Courtesy of Federico Salas Isnardi.

Pre-Unit: Getting Started
Page 2 (left): Ocskay Mark/Shutterstock; 2 (right): ESB Basic/ Shutterstock

Unit 1
Page 5: Rawpixel.com/Shutterstock; 6: Steve Debenport/E+/ Getty Images; 10: Syda Productions/Shutterstock; 12: Steve Debenport/E+/Getty Images; 12 (cell phone): Tele52/Shutterstock 13: Tetra Images/Getty Images; 18: Asiseeit/E+/Getty Images; 20: JGI/Jamie Grill/Blend Images/Getty Images.

Unit 2
Page 25: RubberBall Productions/Brand X Pictures/Getty Images; 26: Steve Debenport/E+/Getty Images; 32: Horizon Images/Motion/Alamy Stock Photo; 33: Chainarong06/ Shutterstock; 36: IQoncept/Shutterstock; 38: Africa Studio/ Shutterstock.

Unit 3
Page 45: Patrick Poendl/Shutterstock; 46: Peter Treanor/Alamy Stock Photo; 47: Stuart Jenner/Shutterstock; 52: BJI/Blue Jean Images/Getty Images; 56: Yellow Dog Productions/DigitalVision/ Getty Images; 58: Juice Images/Cultura/Getty Images; 59: Viktor Holm/Folio Images/Alamy Stock Photo.

Unit 4
Page 65: Jacob Lund/Shutterstock; 66: Mavoimage/123RF; 70: Filadendron/E+/Getty Images; 72: Hero Images/DigitalVision/ Getty Images; 76 (top): Prasit Rodphan/123RF; 76 (center): Laflor/E+/Getty Images; 76 (bottom): Amelie Benoist/BSIP SA/ Alamy Stock Photo; 79: Tempura/E+/Getty Images.

Unit 5
Page 85: Trappe/Agencja Fotograficzna Caro/Alamy Stock Photo; 86: PJF Military Collection/Alamy Stock Photo; 87 (top, left): Maksim Shebeko/123RF; 87 (top, right) Johan Lenell/123RF; 87 (bottom, left): Weerapat Kiatdumrong/123RF; 87 (bottom, right): Markik/Shutterstock; 92: John T Takai/Shutterstock; 93: PARINYA ART/Shutterstock; 98: Paul Burns/Tetra Images, LLC/ Alamy Stock Photo.

Unit 6
Page 105: Ariel Skelley/DigitalVision/Getty Images; 106 (left): Gmast3r/123RF; 106 (right): Wavebreak Media Ltd/123RF; 112: Georgejmclittle/123RF; 118: Lakov Filimonov/123RF.

Unit 7
Page 125: Don Mason/Corbis/Getty Images; 126: Ronnachai Palas/123RF; 129 (cell phone): Tele52/Shutterstock; 130 (cell phone): Tele52/Shutterstock; 132 (old tire): Roman Silantev/123RF; 132 (stack tires): Maksim Vivtsaruk/Shutterstock; 133: William Casey/Shutterstock.

Unit 8
Page 145: Aekkarak Thongjiew/123RF; 146: Wavebreakmedia/ Shutterstock; 147 (cell phone): Tele52/Shutterstock; 152: Galina Barskaya/Shutterstock; 158: Pat Canova/Alamy Stock Photo.

Unit 9
Page 165: Martinedoucet/E+/Getty Images; 166: Ariel Skelley/ DigitalVision/Getty Images; 172: Monkey Business Images/ Shutterstock; 176: Ariel Skelley/DigitalVision/Getty Images; 178: Monkey Business Images/Shutterstock.

Unit 10
Page 185: Elena Elisseeva/Shutterstock; 188: Wavebreak Media Ltd/123RF; 190: George Rinhart/Corbis Historical/Getty Images; 192: David R. Frazier Photolibrary, Inc./Alamy Stock Photo; 198: Portishead1/E+/Getty Images; 202: Webphotographeer/E+/ Getty Images.

Unit 11
Page 205: RichLegg/E+/Getty Images; 206 (left): Jeffrey Coolidge/Photodisc/Getty Images; 206 (center): Jonathan G/ Shutterstock; 206 (right): Rob Walls/Alamy Stock Photo; 212: Wavebreakmedia/Shutterstock; 215 (cell phone): Tele52/ Shutterstock; 216: Laura Doss/Corbis/Getty Images; 219: Baoyan Zeng/Shutterstock.

Unit 12
Page 225: Jack Hollingsworth/Photodisc/Getty Images; 226: Prasit Rodphan/Alamy Stock Photo; 238: Heide Benser/Corbis/ Getty Images.

Illustrations: Luis Briseño, pp. 127; ElectraGraphics, pp. 12, 15, 17, 24, 42, 44, 50, 51, 64, 76, 78, 84, 97, 104, 111, 116, 124, 129, 130, 144, 147, 150, 164, 170, 184, 196, 204, 215, 224, 236, 237, 244, 281-282; Luis Montiel, pp. 138; Fred Willingham, pp. 128